Shaping Policy in India

Shaping Policy in India

Alliance, Advocacy, Activism

Rajesh Chakrabarti
Kaushiki Sanyal

OXFORD
UNIVERSITY PRESS

OXFORD
UNIVERSITY PRESS

Oxford University Press is a department of the University of Oxford.
It furthers the University's objective of excellence in research, scholarship,
and education by publishing worldwide. Oxford is a registered trademark of
Oxford University Press in the UK and in certain other countries.

Published in India by
Oxford University Press
2/11 Ground Floor, Ansari Road, Daryaganj, New Delhi 110 002, India

ISBN-13: 978-0-19-947553-7
ISBN-10: 0-19-947553-9

Typeset in Adobe Garamond Pro 11/13
by The Graphics Solution, New Delhi 110 092
Printed in India by Rakmo Press, New Delhi 110 020

Contents

Tables, Figures, and Boxes

Tables

Figures

Boxes

Foreword

Public policy is both ubiquitous and often opaque. The complex regulatory role of the modern institutions, its vast ambitions in terms of social engineering, its economic responsibilities, and the demands of legitimacy, make the state constantly act on our lives in every way imaginable. Our public discussions, our politics, even often our sense of self and identity, constantly engage with questions of public policy. Yet the processes by which policy is made, the complex distributional questions that go into the making of sustainable policy, the ways in which knowledge is incorporated into the process and in equal terms stymied by vested interests, remain opaque to most citizens. In recent years, there has been a growing demand to unpack the domain of public policy. Interest in public policy courses has increased, institutions and think tanks dedicated to the study of public policy are proliferating fast, and the general level of public awareness and contestation of policy has increased.

A proper analysis of public policy raises a number of questions. The first set of questions is what might be called epistemological. What are the cognitive maps of policymaking actors and citizens? In advancing policy proposals, all of us, from specialists to citizens, operate with a *causal picture* of the world; we make some assumptions about the likely consequences of a particular action or proposal. These apply to large-scale structural choices (for example, is integration into the global economy good or bad? Is public versus private provision in health or education likely to lead to better consequences?). But it also applies to smaller regulatory changes. How do we understand the way in which we acquire knowledge and beliefs on these matters? What shapes these cognitive maps? We hope that these cognitive maps, particularly of policymaking elites, are constituted by a careful sifting of arguments and evidence. But this turns out not to be quite as simple a matter. The production of these causal pictures of the world is a complicated process. In an open society, where ideas are subject to public debate, one hopes that these cognitive maps are themselves subject to contestation and reflexive correction. But this process is often more complicated than we recognize. Often, there will be good faith disagreement over these causal processes for a variety of reasons: indeterminate evidence, different diagnostics, and so forth.

Second, there is political economy and the paradox of policy formulation. Policies are easier to enact when they are consistent with an underlying distribution of power. But surely the purpose of a lot of policies is to reconfigure the existing distribution of power. How does one resolve this paradox? Almost all policies have distributive consequences. How do we understand social coalitions that sustain support for policies? How does the political settlement drive policy? Third, there is the challenge of institutional setting. What assumptions do we make about state capacity in policy formulation? What is the role of institutional design in facilitating or subverting policy? Fourth, what is the broader international context that makes a policy outcome more or less likely? One of the remarkable things in the history of policy is the range of international influences that frame policy debates. Fifth, there are long-term enabling dynamics of policymaking. Do the broad social or economic preconditions for making a policy successful exist?

The authors of this extremely useful book have their own distinctive take on the policy process in India. But one of the things that make this book beneficial is that it asks almost all the questions raised above. It shows that policymaking involves a complex dynamic. This book thus provides a clear and accessible guide to the thicket of policymaking. It embodies several virtues that anyone interested in public policy should bring to bear on the subject. It is methodologically pluralistic, in that it recognizes that the kind of knowledge required for public policy will necessarily draw on a range of disciplines and methods. This text is quite sensitive to the idea that the kind of knowledge that is useful for public policy depends on the questions being asked. The book overwhelmingly emphasizes the fact that public policy is not an entirely autonomous domain of activity: it is embedded in a variety of knowledge practices, social norms, political processes, institutional cultures. A proper study of public policy therefore requires a broad understanding of society in general. The book deploys a variety of case studies to understand policy processes in different domains. One of the singular advantages of this book is that it deploys judiciously chosen case studies across a range of policy domains: it draws examples from social policy, economic policy, institutional change, and regulatory interventions. It draws on examples where there are deep distributive conflicts; yet it also looks at domains of policymaking where, in principle, it is easier to craft win-win situations. It looks at policies that have gestation periods of decades, and policies that were enacted quickly. It looks at policies that come against the backdrop of social movements and policies that are largely a result of behind-the-scenes discussions within institutions. In short, the authors do an admirable job of conveying the variety of contexts, settings, and considerations that shape public policy. It also does an admirable job of giving the reader a sense of the debates on the subject. There is simply no other guide of its sort available.

PRATAP BHANU MEHTA
Vice Chancellor, Ashoka University
Formerly President and Chief Executive
Centre for Policy Research, New Delhi

Preface

This book is an attempt to better understand the emerging market reality of policymaking in India. Much has been written on the subject, particularly about specific laws and schemes in India. And yet a broad understanding of how the system works in reality, beyond the institutional outlines eked in the Constitution, remains sketchy at best. The interface of the legislative bodies and civil society, increasingly vocal in recent years, remain relatively less explored. The role of judiciary and media in policymaking could benefit from greater analysis.

The central questions that the book seeks to shed light on include these. How are policies and laws made in India? How do various stakeholders—political players, civil society, judiciary, media, corporates, and multilateral agencies—contribute to this multidimensional, time-consuming, and complicated process? What is the ground-level grammar of their engagement? Where are the boundaries for each kind of participant? How much and how often are the envelopes pushed?

It was fairly clear, even before embarking on this inquiry, that universal answers to these queries would be elusive. The dynamics of the movements were likely to be extremely context-specific, differing from policy to policy, and across legislations. It, therefore, seemed that it would be futile to look for answers only in codified documents. Rather, there was a need to get at least glimpses of how the multi-stakeholder process worked in reality. That led us to our choice of the method of enquiry: case studies. We document nine detailed case studies of activism or campaigns leading to legislation or at least introduction of bills in Parliament during the period 1999–2014.

A few of these case studies, like the Right to Education, Land Acquisition, and Right to Food Security were widely discussed in media. Others were less clearly documented. We have developed these nine cases from detailed first-hand interviews of individuals involved in the process together with extensive secondary research. The result is a set of cases that we believe are valuable in themselves as stand-alone, brief histories of the emergence of specific laws. It is also important to note here, however, what these case studies are *not* meant to be. This is not an exercise in passing judgment on specific laws or the struggle to get there or to glorify or denigrate the individuals and institutions involved. The purpose and intent of recording these cases studies are to simply provide an objective description of the events. Of course, objectivity in recording political processes is always a challenge but we made every effort possible to verify facts and 'balance out' inputs by consulting competing parties to ensure that the 'facts' alone are presented.

It is also important to realize that as a method of inquiry, case studies fall somewhere between pure theory and hard empirics of statistical data. But going by the famous quote ascribed to Einstein, 'All that counts cannot be counted', we believe that an attempt to reduce the complex political process purely to statistical figures would miss out on the complexities and variety of ground reality that case studies can capture. But this richness comes at a price—that is, lack of universal conclusions. We do not make any claim that the entire range of political processes has been spanned by the nine case studies documented here. In fact, the processes can be as varied as the instances and contexts themselves. The case studies can only be indicative, never exhaustive.

Our exercise is not theory agnostic either. We carry out a thorough review of the literature to identify potentially relevant theories and present them upfront before delving into the case studies. Theories of political processes, sparse to begin with, are almost without exception developed in the context of mature Western democracies. Their applicability to the chaotic Indian reality, therefore, remains suspect. With that caveat, we delve into the case studies equipped with the prism of extant theories.

It is, perhaps, important to reiterate here that our purpose in writing this volume is not simply to document nine landmark political processes, interesting as they may be in their own right. Our goal is to detect patterns, if any, among these evolutions. The accounts of these very different struggles are, therefore, structured and presented in as similar a manner as possible, so that parallels, if any, emerge out of them to the interested reader.

We carry out the exercise of analysing the commonalities of these diverse case studies and their 'fit' with extant theories in our final chapter. Unsurprisingly perhaps, we find limited explanatory power of the existing theories on these case studies. Clearly, the literature has a gaping lacuna when it comes to understanding the drivers of the dynamics of multi-stakeholder political processes. We take a few baby steps in the much harder task (and we must thank one of the anonymous referees of this book for pushing us in that direction) of filling the gap by building such a theory. Our scanning of frameworks that might provide the scaffolding for a new theory in this area led us to the emerging area of complexity theory in political processes that appear to be the only one broad enough to address the varied characteristics of the analysed case studies. We conclude in the fervent hope that better minds than ours will be prompted by our rather introductory effort in this field to build a full-fledged theory of such complex processes.

We also recognize that theories notwithstanding, emergent patterns themselves often lie in the eyes of the beholder and we hope the enthusiastic readers with fresh perspectives will be able to generate new hypotheses from comparing and contrasting the case studies here that may well have escaped us.

We are also cognizant of the fact that this book deals only with the pre-legislation journey and not with arguably the more challenging post-legislative implementation. In that sense, this volume deals with only the first half of policymaking. Indeed, monitoring of implementation is also a critical political process, and one that is becoming increasingly and deservedly multi-stakeholder with inputs from civil society, media, and judiciary. We leave that subject for, hopefully, a future volume.

Our hope in presenting this book to the interested reader is to stimulate interest in contemporary policy reality in India and foster systematic thinking about public policy. The extent to which it helps improve the focus of public policy research and answer questions for the curious reader and informs the practitioner—in government, civil society, or any other constituency—would be the litmus test of the value of our efforts.

Acknowledgements

A very large number of people contributed in myriad ways to the project that finally resulted in the present book. We apologize in advance to those whom we would doubtless fail to mention despite our best efforts.

The preliminary case study drafts were prepared by a group of very enthusiastic Indian School of Business (ISB) students across both campuses of ISB who took the case studies up as their Faculty Initiated Research Projects (FIRPs). Amit Manchanda, Anand Agarwal, Chayan Dhir, Gautham Muthukumar, Niyati Srivastava, Yateen Suman, Ashwarya Prasad, Vidhi Nayar, and Setal Patel worked on building the first structures of the narratives of six of the nine cases covered here.

Much of our research for the case studies was primary in nature and we spoke to a wide cross-section of people who played major roles in the respective movements. The list of people we talked to is provided in Table 1.1. These extremely busy people readily took out time to meet us or talk to us over the phone despite their busy schedules. In many cases, they also suggested other sources. Without their inputs, this book would simply have not been possible. We are deeply grateful to them for their time and inputs.

We gratefully acknowledge the research support and, at times, administrative assistance provided by Abhishek Das, analyst at the Bharti Institute of Public Policy, Indian School of Business. He acted as the lynchpin of the entire project, providing background research, coordinating interviews, and other related activities. Kushal Sagar Prakash of the Wadhwani Foundation provided critical support by actually providing excellent second drafts of select chapters and in compiling the chapters.

The entire team at the Bharti Institute and Sakshi Chawla at the Wadhwani Foundation pitched in wholeheartedly when we most required their assistance. We are particularly grateful to the Learning Resource Centre (LRC) at ISB that provided admirable support by promptly acquiring our endless list of book requests and addressing, within hours and sometime even minutes, our reference requests. We were particularly fortunate to have had encouragement and overall guidance from several senior scholars that gave us the confidence to proceed with the project and the enthusiasm to complete it. Barbara and Deepak Lal were the most valuable source of encouragement and advice from early on. Laurent Jacque of The Fletcher School, United States of America and Prajapati Trivedi of ISB encouraged us to push forward in the endeavour. Amit Nandkeolyar of ISB provided much-needed advice. Ajay Kela, CEO and President, Wadhwani Foundation, most generously allowed Rajesh to devote time to the project. Amir Ullah Khan was someone whose moral support, views, and advice we freely availed of throughout the project. The team at Oxford University Press provided excellent feedback and kept the project admirably on time. We are particularly grateful to the two anonymous referees from the Press who made us do a thorough and extremely useful revision of the manuscript.

The O.P. Jindal Global University in Haryana provided part of the home for the final stage of this project. Special thanks to the vice chancellor, Raj Kumar, and the dean of Jindal Global Business School, Tapan Panda, for their support.

Finally, Manisha Mishra of United Nations Children's Fund (UNICEF) saw merit in our book idea very early on and provided funding for the project as well as critical inputs to the idea itself at its germinating stage. Her vote of confidence was a huge morale booster for us. The UNICEF funding also set a much-needed time frame for the project.

We alone remain responsible for the errors and shortcomings that we are sure have crept into and remained in the book despite our best efforts. We can only appeal to the reader's indulgence and kind feedback here.

Abbreviations

AAP	Aam Aadmi Party
ABVP	Akhil Bharatiya Vidyarthi Parishad
ACB	Anti-Corruption Bureau
ACF	Advocacy Coalition Framework
AFSPA	Armed Forces Special Protection Act
AIDS	Acquired Immune Deficiency Syndrome
AIDWA	All India Democratic Women's Association
AIPWA	All India Progressive Women's Association
AISA	All India Students Association
AISF	All India Students Federation
ANSAC	American Natural Soda Ash Corporation
AP	Andhra Pradesh
APL	Above Poverty Line
ARC	Administrative Reforms Commission
ARDC	Agricultural Refinance and Development Corporation
ASER	Annual Status of Education Report
ASSOCHAM	Associated Chambers of Commerce and Industry of India
AWAG	Ahmedabad Women's Action Group
BASIX	Bhartiya Samruddhi Investments and Consulting Services
BBA	Bachpan Bachao Andolan
BCCI	Board of Control for Cricket in India
BEAG	Bombay Environmental Action Group
BGVS	Bharatiya Gyan Vigyan Samiti

BHU	Banaras Hindu University
BJP	Bharatiya Janata Party
BMM	Bandhua Mukti Morcha
BPL	Below Poverty Line
BPNI	Breastfeeding Promotion Network of India
BSP	Bahujan Samaj Party
BUPC	Bhumi Uchhed Pratirodh Committee
CA	Chartered Accountant
CABE	Central Advisory Board of Education
CACL	Campaign Against Child Labour
CACP	Commission for Agricultural Costs and Prices
CAG	Comptroller and Auditor General
CARE	Cooperative for Assistance and Relief Everywhere
CBI	Central Bureau of investigation
CCC	Consumer Coordination Council
CCI	Competition Commission of India
CCS	Centre for Civil Society
CEO	Chief Executive Officer
CERC	Consumer Education Research Council
CHRI	Commonwealth Human Rights Initiative
CIC	Central Information Commission
CII	Confederation of Indian Industry
CIL	Coal India Limited
CJI	Chief Justice of India
CM	Chief Minister
CMP	Common Minimum Program
CNG	Compressed Natural Gas
COPRA	Consumer Protection Act
CPI(ML)	Communist Party of India (Marxist-Leninist)
CPI(M)	Communist Party of India (Marxist)
CRY	Child Rights and You
CSR	Centre for Social Research
CUTS	Consumer Unity and Trust Society
CVC	Central Vigilance Committee
CVO	Central Vigilance Officer
CWG	Commonwealth Games
DFID	Department for International Development
DG	Director General

DGP	Director General of Police
DHAN	Development of Humane Action
DLF	Delhi Land & Finance
DRSC	Department Related Standing Committee
ECCE	Early Childhood Care and Education
EGA	Employment Guarantee Act
EGS	Employment Guarantee Scheme
FAA	First Appellate Authority
FAOW	Forum Against Oppression of Women
FAR	Forum Against Rape
FCI	Food Corporation of India
FICCI	The Federation of Indian Chambers of Commerce and Industry
FIR	First Information Report
FIRP	Faculty Initiated Research Project
FISME	The Federation of Indian Small and Medium Enterprises
FOI	Freedom of Information
FORCES	Forum for Creche and Child Care Service
FPS	Fair Price Shops
FY	Financial Year
GM	Genetically Modified
GPS	Global Positioning System
GSP	Generalised System of Preferences
HC	High Court
HPC	High Powered Committee
HRLN	Human Rights Legal Network
IA	Interim Application
IAC	India Against Corruption
IAD	Institutional Analysis and Development
IAS	Indian Administrative Services
IBA	Indian Banks Association
ICAI	The Institute of Chartered Accountants of India
ICMR	Indian Council of Medical Research
IFMR	Institute for Financial Management and Research
IIC	India International Centre
ILO	International Labour Organization
IMF	International Monetary Fund

INC	Indian National Congress
INDUS	Indo-US Child Labour Project
INGO	International Non-governmental Organization
IPO	Initial Public Offering
IPR	Intellectual Property Rights
IRC	Institutional Rational Choice
IRDA	Insurance Regulatory and Development Authority
IRS	Indian Revenue Services
ISB	Indian School of Business
JAM	Jan Adhikar Manch
JLG	Joint Liability Group
JNU	Jawaharlal Nehru University
JNUSU	Jawaharlal Nehru University Student Union
JPC	Joint Parliamentary Committee
JSA	Jan Swasthya Abhiyan
JVKS	Jagtikiran Virodhi Kruti Samiti
LA	Legislative Assembly
LAA	Land Acquisition Act
LARR	Land Acquisition, Rehabilitation and Resettlement Act, 2013
LGBTQ	Lesbian, Gay, Bisexual, Transgender, and Queer
LRC	Learning Resource Centre
MBBS	Bachelor of Medicine and Bachelor of Surgery
MCA	Ministry of Company Affairs
MDM	Mid Day Meal
MFDC	Microfinance Development Corporation
MFI	Micro Finance Institutions
MFO	Microfinance Organisation
MHRD	Ministry of Human Resource Development
MKSS	Mazdoor Kisan Shakti Sangathan
MP	Member of Parliament
MRTP	Monopolies and Restrictive Trade Policies
MRTPA	Monopolies and Restrictive Trade Policies Act
MRTPC	Monopolies and Restrictive Trade Policies Commission
MSP	Minimum Support Price
MUDRA	Micro Units Development and Refinance Agency
MVF	Mamidipudi Venkatarangaiya Foundation

MYRADA	Mysore Resettlement and Development Agency
NABARD	National Bank for Agriculture and Rural Development
NAC	National Advisory Committee
NACDOR	National Confederation of Dalit Organisations
NAFRE	National Alliance for the Fundamental Right to Education
NAPM	National Alliance of People's Movement
NBA	Narmada Bachao Andolan
NBFC	Non-Banking Financial Companies
NCAER	National Council of Applied Economic Research
NCC-USW	National Campaign Committee for Unorganised Sector Workers
NCDHR	National Campaign for Dailt Human Rights
NCE	National Coalition for Education
NCLP	National Child Labour Project
NCP	National Competition Policy
NCPCR	National Commission for the Protection of Child Rights
NCPRI	National Campaign for Peoples' Right to Information
NCW	National Commission for Women
NDA	National Democratic Alliance
NFIW	National Federation of Indian Women
NFSA	National Food Security Act
NGO	Non-governmental Organization
NITI	National Institution for Transforming India
NOF	Net Owned Fund
NPE	National Policy on Education
NPR	National Policy on R&R
NREGA	National Rural Employment Guarantee Act
NSSO	National Sample Survey Organisation
NSUI	National Students' Union of India
NTPC	National Thermal Power Corporation
NTUI	New Trade Union Initiative
OECD	Organisation for Economic Co-operation and Development
OSS	Operational Self-Sufficiency

PDS	Public Distribution System
PIL	Public Interest Litigation
PIO	Public Information Officers
PM	Prime Minister
PPP	Public Private Partnership
PSU	Public Sector Undertaking
PTR	Pupil/Teacher Ratio
PUCL	People's Union for Civil Liberties
RMK	Rashtriya Mahila Kosh
RS	Rajya Sabha
RTE	Right to Education
RTF	Right to Food
RTI	Right to Information
SACCS	South Asian Coalition on Child Servitude
SBLP	SHG-Bank Linkage Program
SDM	Sub-Divisional Magistrate
SEBI	The Securities and Exchange Board of India
SEWA	Self Employed Women's Association
SEZ	Special Economic Zone
SFI	Students' Federation of India
SHG	Self-Help Group
SIA	Social Impact Assessment
SIDBI	Small Industries Development Bank of India
SKS	Swayam Krishi Sangam
SMS	Short Message Service
SRO	Self-Regulating Organization
SSA	Sarva Shiksha Abhiyan
SUCI	Socialist Unity Centre of India
TDP	Telugu Desam Party
TMC	Trinamool Congress
TOMCO	Tata Oil Mills Company
TPDS	Targeted Public Distribution System
TRAI	Telecom Regulatory Authority of India
UEE	Universal Elementary Education
UN	United Nations
UNDP	United Nations Development Programme
UNICEF	United Nations Children's Fund
UP	Uttar Pradesh

UPA	United Progressive Alliance
USDOL	US Department of Labour
VIP	Very Important Person
WTO	World Trade Organization
WWF	Working Women's Forum

1

The Policymaking Process

Overview and Theoretical Frameworks

Policy is a truce between competing claimants; it is always uneasy.
—Bayley (2015)

Analytic case studies can provide a wealth of information and detail about a particular policy or process, even if they are ad hoc in the sense that they have no grand conceptual framework proposing causal links to empirically verify.
—Smith and Larimer (2013)

About the Book

The Context

On 16 December 2012, a young woman was brutally raped, tortured, and left bleeding on a deserted road in New Delhi. On 2 April 2012, exactly 3 months and 17 days later, India enacted a law that revised the penalty for sexual offence, broadened the scope of sex crimes, and brought about other far-reaching changes in its criminal codes. In those 3 months and 17 days, the country had experienced widespread protests, had constituted a committee headed by a retired judge to discuss the matter, drafted legislation, introduced the bill, passed it through both houses of Parliament, and got it signed into a law.

Contrast this with the case of the Lokpal and Lokayuktas Act, where the bill was first introduced in Parliament in 1968 but the law finally got enacted in 2013, more than half a century later.

How effective is the Indian polity in making laws and policies to address changing ground realities? How do its gears work? Which stakeholder groups are more successful in bringing about policy change, through what methods, and in what contexts?

These are the questions that this book seeks to investigate. Clearly, there are no universal answers to these broad questions, but it is likely that a close look at a small set of major laws and policies, and even failed attempts at legislation, will give us a better appreciation of the complex sociopolitical process of policy formulation in the world's largest democracy.

The query is hardly untimely. India has one of the highest number of laws on its statute books—there are over 3,000 laws at the central level only—with some of them dating back to the British era. Each of these laws carries a larger back story about the competition, coalition building, lobbying, and compromises carried out by various actors, government and non-government, to give shape to the final piece of legislation enacted by Parliament. Somewhat surprisingly, however, there is scant documentation of how these laws evolved from being an idea to being enacted.

One may ask what purpose such an exercise would serve. Arguably, the best way to measure the effectiveness and understand the mechanics of a democratic polity is to put under the lens the extent and channels of influence that the average citizen has on the law or policymaking process. Democracy is neither limited to, nor guaranteed by, the ability of the citizens of a nation to periodically elect their rulers. In fact, as the Lokpal agitation in India suggests, there are times when large sections of the population may feel completely disenfranchised despite well-functioning legislatures with duly elected members at federal and state levels. The ballot, the symbol of democracy, therefore, is also not the final guarantee of the citizens' influence over policies and political priorities. Equally importantly, the political system is but only one channel of giving voice to the population. Access to judicial sanctions, a vocal civil society, and a vigilant media, all complement and circumscribe the extent of influence of one another and that of the elected representatives of the people in being the vehicle of voices of citizens or citizen and interest groups in the policymaking process.

The way these various stakeholder groups engage and debate with one another, as well as with the interest groups they represent, can be highly complex and context-specific. The context itself will be determined by the culture and political climate of the country in question, and, of course, the nature of the political issue. The search for a universal formula, therefore, will be predictably futile. Our investigation is still not bereft of value, however. The exercise would help us answer, if only in part, the following questions, among others: What interplay of forces shapes India's public policy? How representative is India's policymaking apparatus? Which institutions, allies, ideas and motivations form the policy narrative? Through what channels do the opinions and aspirations of the common man influence, if at all, the policy of the day? What key circumstances, contexts, personal influences, or networks have been influential? What strategies and mechanisms of advocacy have worked, what have not? Has the resilience of Indian democracy impacted how policies are formulated?

These are not easy questions to address in virtually any political context, but it is particularly difficult in the context of India, given the diversity of political, economic, and social institutions and stakeholders. However, the difficulty in answering or addressing this question can only be matched or exceeded by the importance of a better understanding of these critical questions for scholars, policymakers, analysts, and activists alike, from the political science and public policy point of view.

This introductory chapter is a scene setter rather than a systematic overview of the whole field of study. It includes a brief outline of the existing literature on external influences on the policy process; key theoretical models for understanding the policy process; a summary of the policymaking process in India; and a brief description of the book and its relevance for public policy scholars and practitioners alike.

Outline of the Scope of the Book

Rigorous studies on the connection between policy, protests, and democracy are limited within and outside India, primarily because the 'one size fits all' approach of theoretical studies does not translate well in the tumultuous and complex world of policymaking. Most existing studies are country and context specific. For example, Gamson's (1975) seminal work *The Strategy of Social Protest* studied the outcomes of social movements in the US. Other works such as Meyer et al. (2005) use a range of movements in the US, from anti-war campaigns to organic agriculture movement, to examine how changing historical, political, and organizational contexts matter in setting the stage for collective action that results in issue creation and newfound social policies and vice versa. Some of the key researches in comparative public policy attempt to explain how policies come about (Castles 1998, 2002; Crepaz 1996; Huber et al. 1993; Schmidt 1997; Scruggs 1999, 2003), but are organized along policy areas.

In India too, while some areas of public policy are studied in depth (such as measuring policy effects), others are not. For instance, questions related to why policies are formulated and designed in particular ways, and the political shaping of policies 'on the ground', do not receive much attention. Thus, the literature on the interplay of non-state actors and policy is sparse. This is not surprising, given that public policy as a field has started developing in the country only recently. Public policy is a separate discipline in many universities in the US, including ivy leagues such as Harvard, Princeton, and Columbia. In contrast, most universities in India do not offer a degree in public policy (Chaudhuri 2015). Most of the literature on policymaking is found in the discipline of public administration, which focuses on the formal institutional process. Recent literature (Ayyar 2009; Mathur 2009; 2013) has started acknowledging the complexity of the policy process and the role played by non-state actors, but no systematic study of their specific influence has been carried out. There are many individual accounts of key movements and campaigns (Rao 2002; Ray 1999) for specific policy changes, but we did not come across any study that attempted a comparative analysis of the policies.

Since most of the policy process theories have been developed outside India, it is possible that their relevance to our specific context may be limited. Therefore, it is important to undertake a study which is specific to India in order to understand how well these theories fit our reality. But before we come to any conclusion about theoretical frameworks, we need to gain insights into the policy process, not through anecdotal evidence but a systematic study of the evolution of certain laws in the country.

This book is a step in that direction. By observing the evolution of nine major laws using a consistent lens, we provide preliminary evidence about the suitability of existing political theories to explain the policy development process in an emerging market. Further, using the learning from the nine in-depth case studies in this volume, we suggest a new framework of connecting the effectiveness of campaigns to the level of aggression of the champions.

It is also important to point out what this book omits. The focus of the book is on formulation of laws while completely accepting the fact that laws constitute only one form of policy measure. Also, and perhaps in a more glaring manner, the book deals exclusively with the formulation of laws and neither attempts to describe their implementation issues nor seeks to evaluate their effectiveness in actually achieving their objectives. Many great laws are known to have been rendered ineffective through poor implementation, particularly in developing countries. Hence, this is clearly an important omission. However, studying the implementation challenges of the laws or evaluating their effectiveness are ambitious exercises in themselves and beyond the scope of this volume. The current volume zeroes in exclusively on the (relatively) narrow topic of evolution of laws.

Methodology: Taking a Qualitative Approach

Understanding the interactions of policy actors is key to gaining insights into the policy process. While similarities exist between the policy processes of the developed and developing world, there are many important differences. This book attempts to understand the external influences on the policy process in India, not through general theories and broad processes of policy change, but by surveying and narrating the journey of a range of laws/bills and raising interesting questions about the changing nature of the relationship of the state with the civil society. The choice of laws/bills were limited to the last 15 years (1999–2014) in order to balance political change—both the United Progressive Alliance (UPA) and National Democratic Alliance (NDA) periods are covered—and availability of documentations, key informants, and stakeholders. Each of the laws/

bills chosen for the book are what can be called landmark (defined for our purpose to mean those which were attempting to bring about significant change in the existing policy landscape) in their specific field, covering social, political, economic, and environmental issues. These laws do not cover all landmark laws passed in these 15 years, but are a representative sample.

Borrowing tools and concepts used in management, political science, and sociology, the book plans to bring a new understanding to the process of influencing policy in India. The case study method, which is ideal for a holistic, in-depth investigation of a particular event, has been used to study the journey of a selection of laws/bills, which came about due to activism from various non-state actors. Some of the questions the case studies address are: Who are the key players in the policy process and what is their relative importance? What strategies do activists use to influence the policy process and how have those strategies changed over time? How have the political institutions and actors responded to the changing policy process?

For each case study, a large cross-section of stakeholders and key informants were interviewed in addition to secondary research about the facts and figures. This empirically informed evidence about advocacy in India is useful to explore how India's policymaking process fits in with different theoretical frameworks used to understand policymaking in other countries. Also, we hope it would stimulate research by more scholars in diverse fields, which would add to the ongoing policy debates about strategic choices and options, opportunities and incentives, the necessity of coalition building, and possible ways of doing it.

Case studies inevitably have very heavy and detailed information requirements. The sources of information for the case studies of our book include published material—books, articles, and newspaper reports—and, far more importantly, first-person narratives of several of the key players and ring-side observers. Table 1.1 presents the list of individuals interviewed for the case studies, either directly by the authors or by students of ISB who worked on creating the preliminary drafts of several of the case studies. While the individuals have been categorized according to the primary case they were interviewed about, sometimes their views, suggestions, and accounts

Table 1.1 List of Key Respondents for Case Studies

Case Study	Individuals Interviewed
Competition Act	Pradeep Mehta, Vinod Dhall, Suhaan Mukherjee, S. Chakravarthy
Right to Information Act	Shailesh Gandhi, Nikhil Dey, Komal Ganotra
Right to Education Act	Ambarish Rai, Parth Shah, Anil Sadgopal, C.V. Madhukar, Ravi Prakash Verma
Child Labour Bill	R. Venkat Reddy, Bhuwan Ribhu
Microfinance Bill	Vijay Mahajan, Alok Prasad, Matthew Titus, Vipin Sharma, Prabhu Ghate
Criminal Law Amendment Act	Shruti Kohli, Flavia Agnes, Rajesh Talwar, Ashima Kaul, Karuna Nundy, Julie Thekkudan, Abhishek Arya, Shivani Agarwal, Amitabh Kumar, Suneeta Dhar, Pervin Verma, Pallavi Kaushal, Shwetasree Majumdar
Right to Food Security Act	N.C. Saxena, Harsh Mander, Biraj Patnaik
Lokpal Act	Swami Agnivesh, Anna Hazare, Kumar Vishwas, Ashwin Mahesh, Vinod Dua, Abhishek Gupta, J.M. Lyngdoh, Venkatesh Nayak, Kiran Bedi
Land Acquisition Act	Jairam Ramesh, Debabrata Bandyopadhayay, Abhirup Sarkar, Subhomoy Bhattacharya, K.P. Krishnan, Namita Wahi, Muhammad Ali Khan

also informed other cases in the book. The final view or opinion presented in the case studies is, of course, that of the authors.

Roadmap for the Book

The literature on public policy in India is rich in valuable empirical work on accounts of individual social movements. The legislative process is also being increasingly well documented in recent years (Dua et al. 2014; Kashyap 2011; Pai and Kumar 2014). However, there is relatively less work in developing a coherent overview of policy process and a link of the ground-level policy experience with the extant theoretical framework. This book attempts to make a small contribution in that area.

What does this book plan to offer the reader? The following section in this chapter, 'An Essential Background', attempts to set the scene by providing a quick survey of the existing literature. The next chapter delves deeper, by exploring the nature of interaction between various groups in a democracy, with particular attention to the Indian situation. It then looks, in greater depth, at the major existing theories of policymaking and how well they apply to the Indian reality. Finally, it provides a synopsis and preview of the major takeaways from the case studies that follow, in light of these existing theoretical frameworks.

The rest of the book focuses on the case studies of the selected laws. Chapters 3 to 11 take each selected law/bill and narrate the story of the journey of each of them from ideation to enactment. The selected cases studies are: the Competition Act, 2002; the Right to Information Movement; the Right of Children to Free and Compulsory Education Act, 2009 (Right to Education Act or RTE); the Child Labour Bill (which became an Act in 2016); the Microfinance Bill, 2012; the Criminal Law (Amendment) Act (Rape Laws), 2013; the National Food Security Act, 2013 (also Right to Food Act); the Lokpal and Lokayuktas Act, 2013; and the Land Acquisition, Rehabilitation and Resettlement Act, 2013 (also Land Acquisition Act). Each case study focuses on the external actors that influenced the process, the strategies adopted by them to influence the process, the role of the bureaucracy and the legislature in shepherding the law through legislative process, and the current debates related to the law.

At the end of each of the case studies, we connect the particular trajectory of that law-making process with one or more existing theories of policymaking (a summary is shown in Table 2.3).

We also take a step towards formulating our own framework of how laws get made in India. The framework, which we call the 'legislative strategy framework', tries to answer the following question:

What strategies and conditions in the policy subsystem work best in having a higher impact on the legislative agenda of the government (represented as enactment of a law). For this purpose, we study the style of activism (ranging from confrontational to collaborative) and the willingness of the elected stakeholders (government) to engage with the demands of the non-elected stakeholders (ranging from conflictual to cooperative) and measure the time taken to influence the legislative agenda of the government (categorized as long, short, and medium). This will broadly indicate what factors influence the legislative agenda of the government. Admittedly, this would be a subjective assessment on all counts.

The concluding chapter attempts to sketch a broad outline of the proposed 'legislative strategy framework' that the 'reality check' of the nine case studies suggest may be a theoretical structure more suited to law-making in India. In the chapter, we compare the nine case studies through the lens of the proposed framework and draw certain conclusions about the nature of the law-making process in India. We end the book with some other possible frameworks through which the Indian law-making process can be studied by future scholars.

A word of caution is probably appropriate here to avoid future disappointment for the reader. The present volume has no pretensions of saying the final word on the policy process in India and only attempts a preliminary theorization. The nine very unique journeys will not, unfortunately, unanimously point to an obvious list of factors, agents, and methods that predictably determine law making. A fully fleshed out theory—if it is at all possible to create one such—will require much more research and data points. For many readers, therefore, the book will raise more questions than it answers. The authors will consider their efforts well rewarded if those questions are just a little deeper and better informed that the initial ones.

An Essential Background

Social Movement and Policymaking: A Dipstick
Literature Review

Worldwide, the connection between social movements and policy changes is under-theorized and under-studied (Meyer et al. 2005).

Social movement scholars tend to treat the policy process as a black box within the state, which movements may occasionally shake into action. On the other hand, policy scholars treat movements as undifferentiated and unitary actors who may or may not respond to disruption. Most of the literature on social movements view change in policy as 'direct, short term' institution-based impact, and of relatively lesser importance than the larger social change that a movement may bring about (Giugni et al. 1999). Therefore, most of the literature is related to movement origins and their trajectories and the larger societal outcomes of social movements (see, for example, Benford and Snow 2000; Deng 1997; Gusfield 1981; McAdam et al. 1996; McCarthy and Zald 1977; Oliver 1989). But there are a few studies that have examined the strategies used to make an impact on the policymaking process (McAdam and Snow 2009; Meyer 2014; Smithey 2009b).

Students of public policy, on the other hand, acknowledge a place for social movements in the policymaking process, but assign it a relatively small place. There is a generic pattern in which social movements are recognized as exogenous political factors that could affect some part of the policy process, most notably agenda setting or the construction of social problems, 'target constituencies', and policy alternatives.

In India too, much of the policy studies research focused on the policy objectives and the impact assessment aspect and less on the policymaking process. Studies on policymaking process have been largely confined to examining the role of the state apparatus involved in policymaking—legislature, executive, political parties, bureaucracy, and to some extent, the judiciary—broadly in the area of public administration (Kapur and Mehta 2007; Mathur 2013; Mathur and Bjorkman 1994; Mathur and Jayal 1992; Rai and Johnson 2014; Sapru 2012). The role of non-state actors in bringing about societal change or reforms—campaigns, social movements, and protest movements—has remained the subject of study in disciplines such as social history, sociology, and anthropology, rather than public policy.

The literature on social movements is comparatively larger than studies on the policy process, but has followed similar trajectories as that outside the country (Kohli 2001; Shah 2004). It includes chronicles of major movements—theoretical frameworks to study social movements and the role of civil society in reforming the state. There have been a few scholarly works on the methods used to influence policymaking by business groups, but much less work has been done on other strategies such as advocacy, petitioning, public interest litigations (PILs), and media management (Jha 2004; Joshi 1999; Khan 1997; Kochanek 1974; Vyasulu and Vyasulu 2000). Another set of literature is related to the use of non-institutionalized legal or extra-legal collective political action which strives to influence civil and political society for social and political change.

Since this book is taking a relatively new approach to studying the process of policymaking, most of the literature from both the disciplines of social movement and policy studies do not directly address the questions that this book intends to cover. We provide a carefully chosen, select review of books that have relevance to our interest areas—how do policies come about, who are the external forces that influence the policy process, and what strategies/tactics for influencing policy change do they use—drawing from the literature in India and in some western democracies.

How Do Policies Come About?

Public policy is a relatively new subfield of political science, which emerged out of a recognition that traditional analyses of government decisions were incomplete descriptions of government activities (Anderson 1997; Cochran and Malone 2005; Gerston 2010). As the complexity of the relationship between society and its various public institutions increased, the need for more comprehensive assessments about the activities of the government has developed.

The importance of the public-policy process has become more relevant with the emergence of modern society, technological innovation, and burgeoning international transactions (Weible et al. 2011). With increased political participation by larger portions of the public, government decisions assumed greater importance and legitimacy (Fischer et al. 2007). Political scientists, in the first half of the twentieth century, analysed government in the context of its three major branches—the executive, the legislature, and the judiciary (Wilson 1908). They started expanding their perspectives of government activities from the second half onwards. Some examined the informal relationship between interest group and government (Truman 1951), other focused on the interdependence between government activities and diverse forces such as political parties or public opinion (Key 1965). More recent studies contend that government is not designed to be merely responsive nor is it neutral or benign (Huntington 1996; Zakaria 2008).

The discipline has seen the development of multiple frameworks for understanding the policy process—from the first-generation rationalism and incrementalism to second-generation Garbage Can, Multiple Streams, and Advocacy Coalition Framework. Until the mid-1980s, the most influential framework for understanding the policy process—particularly among American scholars—was the 'stages heuristic model'. As developed by Lasswell (1956b), Jones (1970), Anderson (1975), and Brewer and DeLeon (1983), it divided the policy process into a series of stages—usually agenda setting, policy formulation and legitimation, implementation, and evaluation—and discussed some of the factors affecting the process in each stage. This theory also stimulated research within the specific stages—most notably, agenda-setting (Baumgartner and Jones 1993; Cobb and Elder 1997; Cobb et al. 1976; Cohen et al. 1972; Edelman 1964; Kingdon 1984, 1995; Hargrove and Nelson 1984; Schattschneider 1960) and policy implementation. Originally developed by Lippman, the literature on agenda setting is quite vast in the US context, with scholars McCombs and Shaw (1972) developing it into a concrete concept.

In the late 1980s, this model was widely criticized (Nakamura 1987; Sabatier 1991; Sabatier and Jenkins-Smith 1993). Since then, a number of new theoretical frameworks of policy process have been developed. These include the following:

- Institutional rational choice model (Dowding 1995; Moe 1984; Ostrom 1986, 1990; Ostrom et al. 1993; Scharpf 1997; and Shepsle 1989) focuses on how institutional rules alter the behaviour of intended rational individuals motivated by material self-interest.
- Multiple streams framework (Kingdon 1984; Zahariadis 1992, 1995, 2003) views the policy process as composed of three streams: a problem stream consisting of data about various problems and

the proponents defining various problems; a policy stream involving the proponents of solutions to policy problems; and a politics stream consisting of elections and elected officials. In Kingdon's view, the streams normally operate independently of each other, except when a 'window of opportunity' permits policy entrepreneurs to couple the various streams resulting in a major policy change.

- Advocacy-coalition framework (Sabatier and Jenkins-Smith 1988, 1993) focuses on the interactions of advocacy coalitions—each consisting of actors from a variety of institutions who share a set of policy beliefs—within a policy subsystem.
- Punctuated equilibrium theory (Baumgartner and Jones 1993) argues that policymaking in the US is characterized by long periods of incremental change punctuated by brief periods of major policy change. The latter comes about when opponents manage to fashion new 'policy images' and there are large shifts in society or government, such as public opinion or election.
- Structural choice theory (Moe 1990) involves political and bureaucratic actors and interest groups. Describing the bureaucracy in terms of a two-tier hierarchy, Moe argues that the problem of information leads to interest group importance (based on reputation). But at the same time, the problems of political uncertainty and compromise are always present. This shapes interest group interaction with the president, bureaucracy, and legislature, and ultimately constricts and structures bureaucracy.
- Policy diffusion framework (Berry and Berry 1990, 1992) was developed to explain variation in the adoption of a specific policy innovation across a large number of states. It argues that adoption is a function of both the characteristics of the specific political systems and a variety of diffusion processes. Mintrom and Vergari (1998) integrated this framework with the literature on policy networks.

These theories are discussed in greater detail in Chapters 2 and 12, where we analyse the applicability of these theories and frameworks to Indian policymaking processes.

How distinctive is the policymaking process in developing countries of Asia, Latin America, and Africa from that of the developed world? Parliamentary institutions, bureaucracies, political parties, and interest groups in the developing nations often had quite a different significance than they had in Western nations, particularly the US. Scholars such as Easton (1953), Apter (1955), Pye (1958), Almond and Coleman (1960), Weiner and Wolman (1962), Sartori (1976), Horowitz (1989), Atkinson and Coleman (1992), Howlett and Ramesh (1998), Howlett et al. (2003), Corkery et al. (1995), Hai Do (2010), and Kesselman et al. (2012) have highlighted both the differences and similarities in terms of institutions, participants, resources, state capacity, relative importance of the state, the constraints, the window of opportunity, and many other parameters. However, the comparisons are based on broad parameters which may not capture many of the country-specific nuances of the policymaking process (Osman 2002).

The Indian Context: Public policy is still a nascent field in India (and most of the developing world) and the studies on the policymaking process are limited to a number of case studies which interpret specific policy processes and connect them to specific theoretical frameworks (Ayyar 2009; Currie 2000; Echeverri-Gent 1993; Harris 1988; Kohli 1987; Manor 1993; Mooij 1999; Varshney 1995). Velath P. Mathur (2009) and H.M. Mathur (2013) have taken a step towards understanding India's policymaking process by identifying the key actors and their roles in the process.

What Are the External Forces Influencing the Policy Process?

Policies are shaped through the interplay of a variety of actors and institutions. Actors include individual citizens, interest groups, pressure groups, and advocacy groups. Individual citizens can influence policy through collective action/advocacy by forming civil society organization (Cohen and Arato 1992; Sapru 2011). These can be categorized as civic institutions, interest and pressure groups, and social movements. The study of interest and pressure groups understood variously as issue networks, policy subsystems-, and advocacy coalitions is a subfield of studies in policy network (Berry 1997; Baumgartner and Leech 1998; Godwin et al. 2012). Knoke et al.'s study of an 'organizational state' approach argues that 'modern state–society relationships have increasingly become blurred, merging into a melange of inter-organizational influences and power relations'. These inter-organizational networks 'enable us to describe and analyze interactions among all significant policy actors, from legislative parties and government ministries to business associations, labor unions, professional societies, and public interest groups' (Knoke et al. 1996; Moran et al. 2008). Advocacy groups are more broad-based and profess to speak 'in the public interest', unlike interest groups, which focus on narrow sectoral interest (Moran et al. 2008).

Social movements are advocacy coalitions writ large, mobilizing the masses through campaigns and protests. Movements are generally much more than merely enacting a law; they are about altering the societal discourse. The literature on social movements took off at an unprecedented pace into a major area of research by the mid-1970s, examining questions of definition, theoretical frameworks, typologies, strategies, and impact. The reason was that many of the Western democracies were in turmoil in the 1960s—American civil rights and anti-war movements, the Mai 1968 revolt in France, students' protests in Germany, Britain, or Mexico, the worker–student coalitions of the 1969 'Hot Autumn' in Italy, the pro-democracy mobilizations in Madrid and Prague, and the early signs of women's and environmental movements. Till then, social movements had focused mainly on issues of labour and nation (Della Porta and Diani 2006). Although the study of social change focused relatively less on social movements before the mid-1960s, scholars who did attempt a systematic study include Strauss (1947), Herberle (1951), Blumer (1957), Cohn (1957), Hobsbawm (1959), Lang and Lang (1961), Smelser (1962), and Turner and Killian (1964). These scholars attempted to understand why people got caught up in collective action or what conditions were necessary to foment social movements.

As research in social movements picked up pace, it focused on the 'policy payoff' of social protest mobilization. For example, Lipsky's (1970) work showed that protest as a political strategy worked for those who were not well-positioned to represent their interests by conventional means. Piven and Cloward (1971) argued that welfare spending was essentially a policy intervention by the government to prevent protests and maintain social peace. Looking at the issue from the opposite end, Piven and Cloward (1977) used four historical cases to show that disruptive protest was the best means available to poor people to influence government policy on their behalf. Gamson's (1975) seminal work on outcomes of social movements identified 53 'challenging groups' that attempted to exercise influence in the US between 1800 and 1945, then assessed their political fate, that is, whether each group had received formal recognition as a legitimate actor in American politics and whether it had won some portion of its claims on policy. Predictably, Gamson's methodology raised many critical questions about how to define and measure success— and to his credit, Gamson reprinted some of the ensuing debates in the second edition of his book (1990). Over the years, scholars have studied the consequences of social movements in several Western countries (Giugni et al. 1999). Policy, institutional, cultural, short and long-term, and intended and unintended outcomes are among the types of consequences that have been studied in depth. Scholars of social movements addressed the context and outcomes of political mobilization, but public policy was treated as a relatively minor part of the structure of political opportunities that might spur social movements. Indeed, in his important book on the influence of social movements, Thomas Rochon (1998) contends that a focus on policy explores only one arena of social movement influence (the other is cultural change), one that is generally less permeable to movement influence.

In public policy literature, the place of social movements in the policy process is recognized but it occupies a relatively small place. Social movements were recognized as exogenous political factors that could affect some part of the policy process, most notably agenda setting (Baumgartner and Jones 1993; Kingdon 1984) or the construction of social problems, 'target constituencies', and policy alternatives (Schneider and Ingram 1997). Rarely, however, did the analyses go beyond this or address the mechanisms by which movements affect the policy process (Meyer et al. 2005). Thus, scholars of policy or social movement generally never went beyond acknowledging the importance of the other phenomenon in their subject of interest.

The Indian Context: The economic reforms introduced in India post 1991 changed the country decisively not only on the economic front, but socially and politically as well. This change was also reflected in policymaking, which was largely confined to the state apparatus till then. Increasingly, it started moving from a largely government activity to being a more inclusive, complex, and dynamic process involving not only the state apparatus but civil society organizations, non-governmental organizations (NGOs), corporates, 24×7 news channels, think tanks, and multilateral agencies such as the United Nations (UN), World Bank, and the International Monetary Fund (IMF). What were previously indisputably roles of government were now increasingly seen as more common, generic, societal problems, which could be resolved not only by political institutions but also by other actors.

A few scholars have taken notice of this phenomenon and tried to analyse it, the most prominent among them being Mathur and Björkman (2009) and Mathur (2013). These scholars studied the different sources of policymaking such as Parliament, bureaucracy, planning commission, research institutes, and in more recent years, NGOs. They concluded that in recent times there is greater acceptability of policy advice from diverse sources. R.V. Vaidyanatha Ayyar's book *Public Policymaking in India* (2009) complements the policy analysis literature with 'political' analysis that assesses the policy environment and provides a guide on how to proceed in order to further one's policy preference. This book uses principles of management to throw light on how ministers and civil servants can become better policy navigators by gaining a better understanding of the policy process and politics.

Other scholars and practitioners have attempted to understand the policymaking process—not always in full-length books but through articles and book chapters. Some have focused on the collective action of businesses in influencing policymaking. Key among them are Kochanek (1996), Sinha (2005), Yadav (2008), Baru (2009), Madan (2009), and Saha (2015). These studies have analysed the influence of industry bodies on trade policy and the strategies used by them. Some of them have also debated whether lobbying should be legally 'regulated' and attempted to throw light on how lobbying by businesses houses have changed over the years. Others have documented the journey of a particular law or the role of a particular group in bringing about policy change. For example, Bose (2010) has described the intense conflicts and contestations that led to the emergence of the Scheduled Tribes and Other Traditional Forest Dwellers

(Recognition of Forest Rights) Act in 2006, a landmark legislation on rights of forest dwellers. The role of the National Coalition for Education (NCE) in influencing the Right to Education Act has been documented in a case study by Grant (2010). Campaigns related to the Right to Information, the right to food, and India against Corruption, have been documented in detail by activists and scholars of the field. Ramesh and Khan (2015) gives a detailed description of the experience of Jairam Ramesh, the then Minister for Rural Development, in navigating the Land Acquisition Bill in Parliament. It also attempts to explain the rationale behind key provisions of the recently legislated Land Acquisition Act. The Nirbhaya case has been documented by Talwar (2013) in the larger context of how justice is meted out to ordinary victims of sex-related crimes whenever they approach the courts. Justice Seth (2014) chronicles her experiences as one of the three members of the Justice Verma Committee, formed in the aftermath of the Nirbhaya rape case. Ramesh (2015) tells the story of how, for the first time, the doors of the environment ministry were opened to welcome voices, hitherto unheard, into the policy-making process. It details efforts to change the way environment is viewed both by proponents of environmental security and those who value economic growth.

Shah's (2004) study reviewing the literature on social movements is a good starting point for getting a sense of the direction in which research on social movements progressed in India. In the 1960s, the academic writings related to social movements and policy change focused on the forms of protests and their legitimacy in a parliamentary democracy. Scholars such as Kothari (1960), David H. Bayley (1962, 1963), N. Bayley (1969), and Desai (1965) grappled with the continued phenomenon of public protests and agitations even after India gained Independence and established a parliamentary democracy. Their works probed the question of legitimacy or otherwise of such protests. From 1970s onwards, scholars started studying different types of movements, including peasant, grassroots (Gadgil and Guha 1998; Sheth 1984), and middle-class movements (Das 1982; Gupta 1982; Reddy and Sharma 1979). Some dealt with the political decision-making process and the factors responsible for the movement, others with the organizational structure of these movements. A select few studies which touched upon the impact on the political process are discussed in this chapter. M.S.A. Rao's (1978, 2000) volumes on 'Social Movements in India' studied diverse social movements in different parts of the country, such as the peasant movement, the Naxalite movement which aims at capturing state power, and the backward caste movement for asserting a higher status.[1] Mitra (1992), in his study of local elites and the politics of rural development, explored the attitudes of rural leaders in India, drawn from Panchayat members, cooperative societies, and community leaders, and their attitudes towards participation in the process of development and protest against what they considered iniquitous. Shah (2001) examined non- or extra-constitutional collective actions as agents of political and social changes, and social movements as a defining force in the political process. Tandon and Mohanty (2003) studied a set of movements of marginalized people and concluded that the state needed to be reformed so that it performed its task of responsible governance. They stated that this can be achieved if civil society plays a vigilant role in checking the corrupt and arbitrary exercise of the state. Deo and McDuie-Ra (2011) studied the gap between the theoretical understanding of collective action and the way it plays out in reality at the ground level in India. Kumar and Savyasaachi's (2013) edited volume defined the contours of 'transformative action' in social movements across South Asia (including India), arguing that these contours have been shaped by contestations over questions of equity, justice, and well-being on the one hand, and the nature and scope of new and classical social movements on the other. Gudavarthy (2013) attempted to map the discourse and politics of contemporary political movements in India by tracing the history of five most significant political movements—the civil rights, the Dalit and Naxalite struggles, the feminist politics, and the movements to arrest degradation of the environment—which have generated new political practices, actors, and a new expanded agency.

What Are the Strategies/Tactics Used for Influencing Policy Change?

To make an impact, external actors must be able to influence the institutional political actors. It is obvious that different political circumstances would require a range of strategies to win collective benefits. Different groups within similar movements often employ diverse strategies (Dalton 1995; Tarrow 1996). Values also influence how actors define specific goals and identify strategies which are both efficient and morally acceptable (Della Porta and Diani 2006).

Some of the collective action strategies are discussed by Goldstone (1980), Kitschelt (1986), Gamson (1990), Chong (1991), McAdam (1996), Cress and Snow (2000), Meyer et al. (2005), and McCarthy and Zald (2001). Some challengers may choose strategies as matters of moral commitment or taste (Jasper 1997) or identity (Polletta 2002). Others may employ strategies that match the political situation of the time of their founding, but find themselves unable to change with political circumstances (Cohn 1993; Valocchi 1990).

The Indian Context: In India, several case studies about the evolution of a specific policy or law illustrate the importance or power of protest or campaign in the political process. They also highlight the strategy of forming effective coalitions to influence the course of a legislation. In scholarly literature, Grover (1997) and Deo and Duncan McDuie-Ra (2011) identified some of the tools and strategies used by social activists and organizations to achieve positive social change, while Kumar and Savyasaachi (2013) examined the role of the internet in grassroots mobilizations and that of civil society networks in the making of participatory democracy.

The existing literature, as shown in the preceding paragraphs, does not include any scholarly work that seeks to systematically study the policy process in India. This book aims to fill this gap by studying a set of landmark laws to understand how policies are shaped. Here the emphasis is on analysing the policy process, the politics of the process, and not necessarily on how these policies impact society. The approach of the book is novel not only in the Indian context, but also globally, although a few others have used case studies to analyse social movements and policymaking processes in different country contexts.

Stages in the Law-making Process: Persuasion, not Coercion

Public policy has variously been defined as 'the sum total of government activities that have an influence on the lives of citizens' (Peters

1999); as a study of 'who gets what, when, and how' (Lasswell 1958); and as a study of 'public solutions which are implemented in an effort to solve public problems' (Cahn 2013). Politics and policymaking are mostly a matter of persuasion (Etzioni 1965; Neustadt 1960). On the one hand, policymakers must carry the electorate with them if their visions are to be translated into policy; on the other, policy influencers or entrepreneurs have to persuade the policymakers about the 'rightness' of their agendas before they get on to the ruling party's to-do list.

Before we describe India's policy process, we lay down some key principles that need to be kept in mind. First, the policy process is not linear, as often described in textbooks. Rather, it is best described as a set of actors competing to please distinct constituencies. Policy disputes can be about many things: the relative influence of the range of interested parties, the definition of particular conditions as problematic—which can be addressed by government intervention—the range of tools legitimately used by the government, and the ultimate objectives of any policy intervention (Stone 2002).

Second, existing policies are maintained by 'policy monopolies', a network of groups and individuals (both within and without government) who recognize each other as legitimate actors concerned with a particular set of policies. Members of this monopoly include elected officials, administrators in the bureaucracy, and activists in established interest organizations. Conflict among these actors plays out, generally, in a stalemate that allows only incremental reforms in the policy area. Efforts at reform launched from outside these networks take time to be recognized as legitimate actors (Baumgartner and Jones 1993).

Third, opportunities for policy reform, or 'open windows' in Kingdon's (1984) terms, come from a change in the balance of political power within that policy monopoly. Changes in politics, policy, or problems, as Kingdon notes, can create an open window, but the key element to focus on is the possible reconfiguration of a policy monopoly (Baumgartner and Jones 1993).

Fourth, policies reflect, and then shape, dominant social constructions of problems and of persons associated with those problems (Ingram and Smith 1993; Schneider and Ingram 1997). By demarcating certain actors as worthy, governments legitimize political and social action on their behalf and enable those actors to mobilize on their own behalf. Of course, the reverse is also true: by identifying certain people as authors of their own misfortunes, governments not only justify official inaction (or punitive or paternalistic action); they also create social, political, and psychological obstacles for their own mobilization.

Depending on the interplay of these forces, activists need to pursue their causes over a long or short period of time. We study India's policymaking process from this perspective.

Identifying Stage

Policies get made when an issue is put on the agenda—a notional list of topics that people involved in policymaking are interested in, and which they seek to address through developing, or exploring the possibility of developing, policies. Kingdon's (1995) approach to understanding the development of agendas and approaches associated with it (Baumgartner and Jones 1993; Cobb and Elder 1977; Cohen et al. 1972) has served to shape thinking about the origin of a policy idea. However, such theoretical models were developed primarily to apply to the US, which may not translate well in a parliamentary democracy because of the level of hierarchy found in executive-dominated systems with party governments (Richardson and Jordan 1979; Richardson et al. 1982). Some scholars like Wildavsky (1980) and Hogwood and Peters (1983) argue that true innovation in policy development is rare and that 'most policy making is actually policy succession: the replacement of an existing policy, programme or organization by another'.

How is this agenda set? Who influences the agenda? How do they influence it? Numerous players jostle for the space to influence the policy agenda—advocacy groups (NGOs, civil society organizations) (Baumgartner and Jones 1993; Birkland 2001; Kingdon 1995, 1995), interest and pressure groups (business lobbies, farmer lobbies, workers unions) (Kochanek 1996), think tanks and experts, and multilateral agencies. The media (Lippmann 1946; McCombs and Shaw 1972) and the judiciary also play a crucial role in the process because they are oftentimes the means through which some of these players work to influence the policy space. Within the institutional framework, bureaucrats, and political parties (Hopmann et al. 2012; Shroff et al. 2015) play a crucial role in setting the agenda.

In India's parliamentary democracy, law making is the domain of the legislature but the formal agenda is determined by the ruling party. Advocacy, interest, and pressure groups use a range of strategies to influence the policy agenda. Interest or pressure groups primarily use one-to-one lobbying with policymakers. Many business conglomerates fund national and state-level election campaigns. Big farmers also exert influence on the policy agenda through lobbying. Less powerful groups such as Dalit groups, women's rights groups, or environmental activists use collective advocacy and mass mobilization (the power of numbers) to influence policy agendas. Generally, tactics such as protest marches, sit-ins, strikes, fasting, innovative campaigns, and media publicity are used by these groups. Some of the tactics have been successful; some have had limited or no success. For example, the Mazdoor Kisan Shakti Sangathan, a farmers' and workers' group, ran a successful campaign for a Right to Information law, which was finally enacted in 2005. The campaign used the innovative tactic of *jan sunwai*s (public hearings) to expose the corruption in different government schemes. The Anna Hazare-led movement for the Jan Lokpal Bill successfully used fasting as a pressure tactic. However, many of the anti-big dam movements, most notably the Narmada Bachao Andolan (NBA), have had limited success in getting their agendas implemented. The success or lack thereof of many of these campaigns/movements cannot completely be attributed to strategies.

The media plays a very important role in shaping public opinion on these issues. In his groundbreaking study of the origins and diffusion of sexual psychopath laws, Sutherland (1950) argued that public policy is largely a result of two things: the manipulation of public opinion by the press and the influence of experts on the legislative process. Since then, sociologists, political scientists, and socio-legal and policy scholars have affirmed the crucial role the media and experts play in shaping the development, content, and institutionalization of various forms of public policy. Social media platforms such as Facebook, Twitter, YouTube, and blogs are the new-age tools for shaping public opinion and mobilizing people. These platforms have given voice to the hitherto apathetic middle-class Indians.

Also, champions within the legislature and bureaucracy are critical for taking the issue forward. Especially in times of electoral uncertainty, politicians could respond to disruption through policy concessions to groups represented in some fashion by the protestors. India's policy process also includes constitutional watchdogs such as the Comptroller and Auditor General of India (CAG) and the Election Commission, independent regulators, and statutory bodies like the Central Information Commission (CIC) and the Central Vigilance Commission (CVC).

A peculiar Indian innovation, the PIL[2] allows India's judiciary to set the agenda in many instances. Many public campaigns have been initiated based on a judicial order through a PIL. For example, the Supreme Court had provided guidelines for protecting women against sexual harassment at the work place (Vishaka guidelines); the right to food campaign was conceived after the 2001 interim order of the Supreme Court in a PIL filed by the People's Union for Civil Liberties (PUCL); the introduction of compressed natural gas (CNG) in public transport in Delhi was based on orders of the Supreme Court.

At times, India's international commitments through treaties or signing of UN Conventions may require a statutory change. For example, India had to modify its law on money laundering after signing various related UN Conventions.[3] International NGOs such as Greenpeace, Amnesty International, World Wildlife Fund, and Oxfam, and multilateral agencies such as UN, IMF, and the World Bank also exert some influence on the policy process through financial and technical aid.

The government can also decide suo moto that a law is required in a particular sector. It may get inputs from specialized bodies such as the National Human Rights Commission and the Law Commission of India, or appoint a group to study a sector and draft a law. These groups or bodies may hold consultations with independent experts and stakeholders. Furthermore, an individual Member of Parliament (MP) can also introduce a bill in either House. This is known as a Private Member's Bill (for example, Lok Sabha MP Kalikesh Singh Deo introduced the Disclosure of Lobbying Activities Bill in 2013 to regulate lobbying activities). Although these are generally never passed, they act as signalling devices to the government, which may introduce its own legislation on the subject.

Drafting Stage

Government bills are drafted by the concerned ministries, which are then vetted by other ministries. The process usually has the following stages. The domain department starts with what is known as a Legislative Intent. This is shared with the Law Department, which gives its inputs and comments mostly on the constitutional validity and permissibility of the various things desired or proposed in the legislation. Armed with this, the domain department then prepares the first draft of the law. If the department is a law-enforcing department, it is likely to have a litigation cell whose input is also taken. Then the draft goes to the legislative department which works on it, using its experience with similar and related laws to come up with a second draft, usually a significant improvement over the first one. This can take six to ten months. Then this draft goes to the internal committee of the department of legislative affairs, which, after revising it, will pass it on to the department of legal affairs which now examines, clause by clause, its constitutional validity. After this, it goes to the cabinet secretariat, which, after initial examination, will declare it fit for the cabinet. Major laws would then typically be referred to a Group of Ministers.

There are also times when the government approaches an independent expert to draft a law. It appointed the Financial Sector Legislative Reforms Commission, under the chairmanship of Justice B.N. Srikrishna, to reform the financial sector laws. In the aftermath of the Nirbhaya rape case, a three-member commission headed by Justice Verma was constituted to suggest amendments to the laws related to protecting women from rape and sexual violence.

The government may publish the draft legislation in the public domain for feedback (usually on the ministry's website). Drafts of the Electronic Service Delivery Bill, the National Sports Bill, and the Land Acquisition and Resettlement Bill were published for a specified time period (generally 20 to 30 days). It may also circulate the draft among a select set of stakeholders for comments. Following this, the draft is revised to incorporate such inputs and is vetted by the Law Ministry. It is then presented to the cabinet for approval.

An individual MP may solicit public feedback on his private member legislation. For example, Biju Janata Dal MP Baijayant Panda uses his personal website and social media tools such as Facebook to publicize the draft of his private member bills.

Legislative Stage

After the Cabinet approves the bill, it is introduced in Parliament. Under the Indian political system, Parliament is the central legislative (or law-making) body. Every bill goes through three Readings in both Houses before it becomes an act.

- During the *First Reading*, the bill is introduced in Parliament. The introduction of a bill may be opposed and the matter may be put to a vote in the House. In August 2009, the law minister withdrew the motion to introduce the Judges (Disclosure of Assets and Liabilities) Bill as many MPs were opposed to the Bill, on grounds that it violated the constitution.
- After a bill has been introduced, the presiding officer of the concerned House (speaker in case of Lok Sabha, chairman in case of Rajya Sabha) may refer it to the concerned Department Related Standing Committee[4] (DRSC) for examination. Generally, most bills are referred to these DRSCs; however, the presiding officer of the House has the discretion not to do so. For instance, key bills such as the Special Economic Zones Bill, 2005 and the National Investigation Agency Bill, 2008 were not referred to a DRSC. In contrast, the Lokpal Bill passed by the Lok Sabha was sent to a Select Committee by the Rajya Sabha although it had been examined by the DRSC. These DRSCs may solicit feedback from the public by issuing notices in key newspapers and the Gazette of India. The public comments are also tabled in the form of a report.
- The Standing Committee considers the broad objectives and the specific clauses of the bill referred to it and may invite public comments on a bill.
- Bills which come under the ambit of a number of different ministries may be referred to a Joint Committee.
- The Committee then submits its recommendations in the form of a report to Parliament. The government is, however, not bound to accept the recommendations of the DRSC.

- In the *Second Reading* (*Consideration*), the bill is scrutinized thoroughly. Each clause of the bill is discussed on the floor of the House and may be accepted, amended, or rejected.
- During the *Third Reading* (*Passing*), the House votes on the redrafted bill.
- If the bill is passed in one House, it is then sent to the other House, where it goes through second and third readings.
- During the second reading, the government, or any MP, may introduce amendments to the bill, some of which may be based on recommendations of the Standing Committee.
- After both Houses of Parliament pass a Bill, it is presented to the President for assent. The President has the right to seek information and clarification about the bill, and may return it to Parliament for reconsideration. (This may be done only once. If both Houses pass the bill again, the President has to assent.)
- After the President gives assent, the bill is notified as an act and brought into force.

Post-legislative Stage

Once bills are enacted, ministries draft and notify Rules (also known as subordinate legislation) to enable their implementation. These Rules are laid in Parliament and may be scrutinized by the Subordinate Legislation Committee, which is empowered to seek public feedback.

Post-legislative scrutiny of laws is not mandatory in India. It may, however, be undertaken by bodies such as the Law Commission of India, the DRSCs, or a specific commission appointed for the purpose, who may hold public consultations. Recently, rape laws were reviewed by the Justice Verma Committee before an ordinance was promulgated on the matter.

With this brief background to a vexingly complex law-making process, we delve into the relevant theories of policymaking and a synopsis of the findings from our case studies in the next chapter.

Notes

1. See http://www.epw.in/system/files/pdf/1979_14/44/special_articles_sociology_in_the_1980s.pdf (last accessed on 5 April 2016).

2. PIL in Indian law means litigation for the protection of public interest. It is litigation introduced in a court of law, not by the aggrieved party but by the court itself, or by any other private party. It is not necessary, for the exercise of the court's jurisdiction, that the person who is the victim of the violation of his or her right should personally approach the court. However, the person filing the petition must prove to the satisfaction of the court that the petition is being filed for public interest and not just as a frivolous litigation by a busy body.

3. Various UN Conventions such as the 1988 UN Convention against Illicit Traffic in Narcotic Drugs and Psychotropic Substances, the 1990 Political Declaration and Global Programme of Action, and the 1998 UN General Assembly Political Declaration on Global Drug Control called for member states to put mechanisms in place to combat drug-trafficking and money laundering.

4. Since 1993, 24 DRSCs were formed to scrutinize bills and other policies of the government (before 1993, bills were sometimes referred to ad-hoc committees for scrutiny).

2

Activism and Law Making

Extant Theories, Their Applicability, and New Findings

There is no such thing as a fixed policy, because policy like all organic entities is always in the making.

—Lord Salisbury

As outlined in the previous chapter, policymaking in any country is the result of a complex interplay between various stakeholder groups in the polity. The general direction and evolution of the policy process are also broader than the mechanics of individual legislations and the campaigns leading up to them. The grammar of the interaction is set by institutions, the relative power of the various groups, and, not to an insignificant degree, the political traditions of the society. As a result, before we dive into the specific case studies of the laws, we outline the nature and extent of the elbow room Indian democracy provides to various players, and analyse to what extent the extant theories explain the Indian reality.

Democracy and Its Dilemmas

The year 2011 was a watershed in the history of civil society activism, both globally and in India. Globally, the Occupy Wall Street movement saw a groundswell of support among ordinary American citizens as well as inhabitants of other countries. In India, the unprecedented popularity of the anti-corruption movement caught the state and civil society observers by surprise. The Jan Lokpal movement was unlike any other in recent history both in the audacity of its demands and the modalities of protest. Anna Hazare, the leader and symbol of the movement, went on an indefinite fast twice to bring the government to heel—first by insisting that civil society members be included in the committee to draft the Lokpal Bill and second by pushing for the enactment of the Jan Lokpal Bill in Parliament within a specified time frame.

Yet, doubts have been raised about both movements for different reasons. The Occupy Wall Street movement was criticized for its lack of leadership, dependence on the Internet, and inefficient protest methods. In the case of Jan Lokpal movement, doubts were raised not only about the proposed solution to corruption but also about the methods employed. Led by Arvind Kejriwal under the banner of India Against Corruption (IAC), the movement, many feared, set some possibly dangerous precedents by demanding that its version of the bill be passed, and in a specified time frame. It challenged the validity of established parliamentary procedures, if not the right of elected representatives to independently decide on policy matters.

Most democracies have to grapple with the question of legitimacy of civil society engaging with the policymaking process. The questions are endless. Are elected members the only legitimate representatives of the citizens of a country? Do citizens have a role in a representative democracy except voting periodically in elections? Can they organize and protest policies of the government? Can a group of citizens impose its will on a constitutionally mandated representative institution?

The idea of democracy emerged through many stages, from the signing of the Magna Carta in 1215, to the French and the American revolutions in the eighteenth century, to the widening of the franchise in Europe and North America in the nineteenth century. Its establishment as the gold standard for any country to aspire to— whether in Europe, America, Asia, or Africa—happened only in the twentieth century (Sen 1999).

Democracy, in its purest form, means that the people hold political power. The term 'democracy' is derived from two Greek words: *demos*, referring to the people, and *kratos*, referring to political power. Citizens, by majority vote, decide the public policies that will govern their behaviour. Each has one and only one vote and all votes are counted equally. Historically, this type of direct democracy was prevalent in the Athenian city state and in some of the Swiss states. But it is not characteristic of the politics of any modern nation state. Rather, today's democratic nations are republics, where the people do not govern directly. They affect political decisions indirectly by electing and influencing the behaviour of representatives who make public policy and control its implementation. Proponents of representative democracy argue that true government of the people is practically impossible in modern nation states.

There are differences within representative democracies too, in the arrangement of political power and checks and balances. Parliamentary and presidential systems are the two most prevalent forms. Most democratic nations follow a variation of either of the two systems. In a presidential system, the central principle is that the legislative and executive branches of government are separate. An executive branch is led by an elected president who serves as both head of state and head of government. In such a system, this branch exists separately from the legislature, to which it is not responsible and which it cannot, in normal circumstances, dismiss. Countries such as the US, Argentina, Brazil, Mexico, and the Philippines follow this system. In a parliamentary system, the political party that wins the most seats in the legislature during an election forms the government. The majority party chooses a leader to be the prime minister and the minority parties form the opposition. The prime minister and his cabinet are collectively responsible for all decisions taken by the government. Countries such as the UK, Australia, Greece, Hungary, Italy, Poland, and Germany have the parliamentary forms of government.

But there is an inherent contradiction between a representative's role as a policymaker and as a representative of a constituency. As a policymaker, his role is to legislate for the whole country, keeping in mind the national interest. In his representative role, he has to be responsive to the views of his constituents. For example, a policymaker may be a representative of a constituency of mostly farmers but he may have to balance farmers' interest in subsidized resources such as water and fertilizer with that of the environment. Also, a representative may be more responsive to the views of his constituents on some issues than on others. He may be quite responsive to citizens' demands for government funding for new roads but quite unresponsive to their demand for taking action against absentee primary school teachers (Mezey 2008).

Thus, in every representative system, citizens have a right to vote for candidates they feel will represent their interests the best. But once elected, representatives have the 'undemocratic' prerogative to act contrary to the views of their constituents if they feel it is in the national interest. In fact, Edmund Burke and James Madison—two legislators who were also political theorists—were clear that in such a situation, the representative's first obligation is to the nation as a whole (Mezey 2008: 34). Citizen activism is part and parcel of representative democracies since political institutions can work only through consent (Hansen 1993: 78). Therefore, the resistance to authority that is built into the system encourages a citizen activism that 'while frequently mundane in its direction, sets limit to the pursuit of the unlawful and unconscionable' (Hansen 1993: 78).

The Indian Context

India inherited the parliamentary form of democracy as a colonial legacy but its experiment was bold and unique because of the prevailing economic and social conditions at the time of Independence. As Pratap Bhanu Mehta puts it in his *The Burden of Democracy* (2003), it was a 'leap of faith for which there was no precedent in human history'.

The role of democracy remains a contested option for most developing countries although this question is well-settled for the developed world. According to Sen (1999), 'while no one really questions the role of democracy in, say, the United States or Britain or France, it is still a matter of dispute for many of the poorer countries in the world. India, of course, was one of the major battlegrounds of this debate.'

In its seventh decade since Independence, India has survived as a democracy taking the rough with the smooth. Representatives are elected by and are accountable to the people; all citizens hold equal political power summarized as 'one person, one vote'; the three organs of the state (legislature, executive, and judiciary) have separate powers with some checks and balances; and these three organs act as representatives of their constituencies. Political differences have been largely tackled within the constitutional guidelines. Power has changed hands from one party to another according to electoral and parliamentary rules. An unlikely and somewhat inelegant combination of differences, India still survives and functions remarkably well as a democratic system.

There is much to be celebrated about India's democracy, especially its resilience where many similarly placed nations have failed; but, on a democratic continuum, it is still somewhat closer to the starting line rather than the end. In terms of economic inclusion and equality, despite its democratic credentials, India's track record in improving the living conditions of many of its citizens, remains lackadaisical.[1] Especially if we compare India to many developing countries (South Korea, Singapore, or China) which were at India's level of development in the 1950s, it is evident that they have successfully pulled a much larger proportion of their population out of poverty, admittedly without necessarily having functioning democracies.[2]

In spite of having the basic building blocks of democracy, there are key areas where India has failed to reform. Its multi-party system boasts of 6 national parties and over 25 regional parties. However, most of them have not observed the basic norms of inner-party democracy. Leaders are chosen based on family connections, loyalty to the party bosses, and ability to attract funds during elections. In a bid to win elections at any cost, parties started giving tickets to local goons and criminals. This has led to criminalization of politics, massive corruption, and a complete lack of transparency in the financial dealings of the parties. Other problems include the politicization of the police and a rigid and inefficient bureaucracy. Within Parliament, voices of individual Members of Parliament (MPs) have got increasingly marginalized and subordinated since they are forced to vote along party lines on all issues, otherwise they can be expelled on grounds of defection. There are, of course, problems of bad policy design (top-down, based on good intent but not empirical evidence, lack of technical expertise) and poor implementation, which have exacerbated the situation. All of these factors impact the policy process in ways that is difficult to comprehend fully.

The dichotomy of resilient and relatively robust political institutions on the one hand and the persistent poverty and exploitation of weaker sections of society on the other have made space for a vocal and active civil society. Some point out the deficiencies of the state and give voice to the less powerful groups in society, while others seek to provide alternative solutions to address state failures in critical areas such as education, health, and employment.

India has a rich history of organized and spontaneous social activism from across the political-ideological spectrum, castes, and classes. Recorded broad-based people's movements date back to the nineteenth century and have been led for the rights of various marginalized groups—peasants, tribals, industrial workers, Dalits, and backward castes—throughout the decades, whether it is the Tebhaga movement of Bengal or the movement by mill workers of Mumbai.

Despite a democratic government or maybe because of it, movements, protests, and campaigns became a part and parcel of independent India. As research shows, the years immediately after Independence saw a rise in agitational politics. What is clear from the sheer variety of movements is the sense of collective identity that many of the hitherto oppressed groups developed, in spite of the deep social inequalities that plague our society. It is possible that the political equality these groups gained through universal adult franchise gave them a sense of their own latent power.

These movements often arose with the aim of bringing about changes in the living and working conditions, of access to benefits, affirmative action, and of protecting the environment. While social movements sought to bring in social change, counter movements sometimes arose in defence of status quo. Many of these movements had ended up with the formation of political parties. However, the reality of the large majority of the oppressed groups did not change drastically. While it is relatively easier to break into the political system through movements, it is far harder to bring about real change to the lives of the poor and oppressed. Some of these movements are almost counter-productive. For example, the labour movement that mostly caters to the organized sector. It leaves out of its purview the working conditions of almost 90 per cent of the workers who are in the unorganized sector. Some of the environmental movements have also been viewed as counter-productive to the overall development of the country, such as campaigns against mining, genetically modified (GM) crops, and dams. An interesting aspect of these movements is the use of agitational politics such as street campaigns, strikes and rallies as a tactic much more than movements in recent times, which use the media far more extensively due to the technological advances in recent times.

The decline of the mainstream institutions of representative democracy—the legislature, elections, political parties, and trade unions—in the run-up to the Emergency period (1975–7) allowed non-state groups to emerge and make a space for themselves. According to D.L. Sheth, failure in converting the economic demands of the poor into effective political demands led political parties to take recourse of ethnicizing and communalizing economic issues for electoral gains. This resulted in halting the political process, which in the 1950s and 1960s had worked for inclusion of ever new groups in electoral and party politics. By the mid-1970s, large sections of ex-untouchables, the tribal population, the occupationally marginalized groups from among the ritually low-ranking Hindu castes, and the other poor and landless among the minorities remained on the periphery of the mainstream of Indian politics. Of course, this did not affect their electoral participation, but it did reduce their political sense of citizenship as their struggle did not find articulation in the representational arena of politics (Sheth 1983).

The decline of institutional politics led to revitalization of the old social movements and between the mid-1970s and 1980s, it gave rise to thousands of new micro-movements (also known as grassroots movements) in the country. These movements were led by young people, many of whom left professional careers and took up issues and constituencies abandoned by political parties and trade unions, and those ill-served by the bureaucracy. The organizational form they evolved for themselves was not of a political party or a pressure group. It was that of a civil associational group, leading political struggles on issues articulated by the affected people (Sheth 1983).

Next, we discuss the major theories of policymaking, compare our nine case studies, and link them with one or more of the theories, where applicable. This gives us some insight about the applicability of these theories to the Indian context.

A Quick Review of Major Theories of Law-making in a Democracy

The existing theories of the policymaking process have been developed based on evidence from western democracies, primarily the US. There are limitations we need to keep in mind while extrapolating them to Indian circumstances. It may also be worth emphasizing that theories can only be constructed through a large collection of data points and observations. Few studies have been attempted to (a) link these theories with the realities of developing countries, particularly India (for detailed bibliography on policy process see bibliography by Mooij and de Vos 2003); and (b) develop new theories to explain the policymaking process in India.

Does this mean that these theories are totally inadequate in explaining the policymaking process in developing countries like India? Conclusively testing the relevance of these theories to Indian policymaking process requires a far larger research project than what has been attempted here. Rather, we have taken a first step towards analysing the policy process by gathering evidence about timeline, actors, influences, triggers, strategies, and role of the media for each of the laws. Therefore, the case studies in this book act as indicators of how certain policies came about and to what extent they follow the pattern of any of the processes hypothesized in the existing theories. Reality, particularly in the political sphere, rarely provides a 'yes-no' verdict on broad theories but appears to follow the theorized pattern to varying degrees. Our approach here has largely been to lay down the theories as well as chronicle the journeys of the laws for the reader to arrive at his own conclusion about how well the individual journeys align with the theories and whether the extant theories cover the critical aspects of these real life journeys.

It is quite possible that such a reading may lead to further theorization to address a void left unaddressed by existing theories. To aid the reader, we have matched the theories that we thought best described certain journeys, but we readily admit to the possibility of alternative mappings. There is also no attempt at carrying out a horse race between the various theories using the nine case studies, for the simple reason that more often than not, the theories focus on different aspects of the policy process and do not directly 'compete' with one another.

Key Theories of the Law-making Process

In Chapter 1, we had provided a highly stylized survey of the existing theories of policymaking processes. In this section, we examine these theories in greater detail to understand their relevance to the case studies chronicled in the later chapters.

Before we discuss the key theories, a few caveats are in order. It is fair to say that there is no general theoretical framework tying the study of public policy together. Theory-building in public policy have used two basic approaches to make sense of the complex world of public policy. The first is to simplify and make sense of that complexity ad hoc by simply using what works in a given situation (Sabatier 1999: 5). The second is through a scientific approach of cause and effects. Specifically, it means that underlying the highly complex world of public policymaking is a set of causal relationships, much like the assumptions about utility maximization and laws of demand and supply in economics. If these causal relationships can be identified, presumably, they can be linked together logically to build overarching explanations of how the field of public policy works. Thus far, generalizability has proved to be elusive, given the diffuse nature of public policy.

The ad hoc approach works better since it allows scholars to borrow from a full range of conceptual frameworks developed across the social sciences. It also lets scholars focus on the reality, as messy as it may be, rather than trying to shoehorn conceptual frameworks on to the reality. 'Analytic case studies can provide a wealth of information about a particular policy or process even if they are ad hoc in the sense that they have no grand conceptual framework proposing causal links to empirically verify', observed Smith and Larimer (2013: 16). This, however, makes it difficult to build cumulative and generalizable knowledge from what are essentially descriptive studies. Some argue that the attempt to produce generalizable theories of public policy is not only pointless, but hopeless. As Deborah Stone puts it, the scientific approach to public policy that has occupied the attention of many social scientists is, in effect, a mission to rescue 'public policy from the irrationalities and indignities of politics' (Stone 2002: 7). Smith and Larimer (2013), however, argue that this is a failing not only of policy studies but of many other disciplines including public administration and political science. They contend that policy scholars may not have produced a unifying theory but have done a commendable job of producing functional theories within a wide-ranging set of policy orientations such as policy process, policy evaluation, policy analysis, and policy design. Each of these orientations are disciplines in themselves, with a set of core research questions and conceptual frameworks.

Since this book focuses on the law-making process, some of the research questions include the following: (a) why do governments pay attention to some problem and not others? (b) how are policy options formulated? and (c) why does policy change? Based on these questions, some conceptual frameworks, such as bounded rationality, punctuated equilibrium, and advocacy coalition were developed. The theories themselves fall into three broad categories. The first might be called the *rational approach* (Rogow and Lasswell 1963), the second is the *incremental approach* (Lindblom 1959), and the third is the *pluralist* or *participatory approach*, a compromise model that combines the two. A brief overview of these frameworks is provided in the following paragraphs.

Stages Heuristic Model

The initial focus of the policy sciences was on developing theoretical frameworks to explain the policy process. But it was unclear what the process looked like or what was the starting point. A number of scholars developed the 'stages' model of the policy process, key among them being Lasswell (1956b), Easton (1965), Jones (1970), Mack (1971), Rose (1973), Jenkins (1978), Hogwood and Gunn (1984), and Dror (1989). The Stages Model, as developed by Lasswell (1956) and later Jones (1970), follows a linear pattern of decision-making, reflecting a rationalist perspective. First a problem must come to the attention of the government. Policymakers then develop solutions to the problem, ultimately choosing the one they perceive as most appropriate. They then evaluate whether it served the purpose or not. Both attempted to model the process of policymaking. Although Lasswell identified what could be considered stages of the decision process, it is with Jones that the first attempt was made to model the process of public policy decisions. He identified elements of the policy process such as perception, definition, aggregation, representation, formulation, legitimation, application, and evaluation. Later, James Anderson (1974), Brewer and DeLeon (1983), and Ripley (1985) refined the model in various ways, but fundamentally, it remained a rationalistic, problem-oriented, linear process on a continual loop. Based on Systems Theory, Easton (1965) developed an input-output model where inputs were various issues, pressures, information, and the like to which actors in the system reacted. The outputs were public policy decisions to do or not to do something.

Critiques, however, point out that (a) this is at best a descriptive classification of the policy process, not a theory of public policy since a hypothesis cannot be tested against this model; (b) this model divides rather than unites the scholars, as some focus on the agenda-setting aspect while others pay attention to implementation and analysis; and (c) this model assumes a linear trajectory of policymaking, discounting the idea of feedback loops between stages or different starting points for the entire process (DeLeon 1999: 23; Sabatier 2007). Its utility remains in the fact that it continues to provide a major conceptualization of the scope of public policy studies and a handy means of organizing and dividing labour in the field.

'Arenas of power' Approach/Typology Framework

The Stages Model describes the policy process but does not say anything about the type of policy produced and what their difference might mean for politics. This question was asked by Theodore Lowi, a political scientist, who wanted to determine if the process changed for different types of policy (Lowi and Olson 1970). Since public policy is an attempt to influence individual behaviour, the government uses different types of coercion based on its target. Lowi divided all policies into four categories: distributive policy, redistributive policy, regulatory policy, and constituent policy. The government uses coercion in each case either to change individual behaviour or the environment which leads to different types of politics. Each policy category amounted to an 'arena of power', and he saw policies as a predictable outcome of a regular subsystem of actors. Thus, if one knows the policy type, it is possible to determine the political interactions between actors in the subsystem.

Table 2.1   Lowi's Policy Typologies and Resulting Politics

Policy Type	Applicability of Coercion	Type of Politics	Congress	President
Distributive	Remote/ individual	Consensual, stable, logrolling	Strong, little floor activity	Weak
Redistributive	Immediate/ environment	Stable, bargaining	Moderate, moderate floor activity	Strong
Regulatory	Immediate/ individual	Conflictual, unstable, bargaining	Strong, high floor activity	Moderate
Constituent	Remote/ environment	Consensual, stable, logrolling	N/A	N/A

Source: Smith and Larimer (2013).

Following Lowi, James Q. Wilson constructed his own typology framework using similar assumptions. The political atmosphere is defined by people's expectations about the costs and benefits of a policy. According to him, politics is defined by whether cost and benefits are broadly or narrowly distributed. The four categories of politics are: majoritarian, entrepreneurial, client, and interest group. Where benefits were concentrated, there was stronger incentive for groups to form and cohere than public goods, which usually fell victim to the 'free rider' problem.

Table 2.2   Wilson's Policy Typologies

	Distributed Costs	Concentrated Costs
Distributed benefits	Majoritarian (broad public debates in legislatures and elections)	Entrepreneurial (strong political actor required to achieve policy passage)
Concentrated benefits	Client (behind the scene politics, success depends on the legitimacy which public opinion attributes to the interest being benefited)	Interest group (high level of conflict and bargaining)

Sources: Smith and Larimer (2013); authors.

Critics, however, observe that most policies do not fit neatly within a single category. Therefore, without a clear set of criteria for identifying policies, the typology framework is of little use (Greenberg et al. 1977; Kjellberg 1977; Steinberger 1980). The models were refined by Spitzer (1987) and Kellow (1988).

Bounded Rationality and Incrementalism: Decision-making is the core of public policy—who makes these decisions and why—that is, the reasons behind those decisions—are key questions for policy scholars. Broadly, scholars have used the rational choice theory to explain decision-making. The sheer complexity of most policy issues and the limited cognitive capacity of humans make fully rational decision-making virtually impossible. The basic tenet of bounded rationality, as propounded by Herbert Simon (1947, 1955), is that humans intend to be rational but are prevented from behaving in a fully rational manner by cognitive limitations. Factors such as memory, attention span, information processing capabilities, all limit a person's ability to achieve complete rationality. Instead, people choose from options that are not completely optimal but are good enough for the situation. Simon labelled such behaviour as 'satisficing', which allowed policymakers to make decisions that may not be perfect but can solve the issue at hand. Charles Lindblom (1959) applied these concepts to the study of public policymaking and found that policymakers 'muddle through' by making small changes from existing policies. According to him, the process is best characterized by small, incremental adjustments where policy decisions are a process of 'successive limited comparisons', with each decision building off previous decisions. This model became known as 'incrementalism'. Davis et al. (1966) first systematically tested Lindblom's notion of incrementalism by studying the public budgetary processes in the US. Some scholars have argued that incrementalism offers little in the way of testable predictions and its tenets are little more than a descriptive model of policymaking (Jones et al. 1998; Wanat 1974).

Public Choice and Tiebout Theory: Essentially a neoclassical economic idea, public choice, when applied to the public sector, means that governments should supply public programmes and services in a similar manner as the private sector businesses; that is, citizens, like customers, should be given choices in the programmes and services they consume and the associated costs of providing them. Driven by these quasi-market forces, governments will supply the demanded services efficiently. Charles Tiebout (1956) proposed one of the earliest public choice frameworks. Local jurisdictions, like centralized bureaucracies, are prevented from distributing public goods but they can offer services (quality of water, garbage removal, education, and taxation) that are comparatively superior to that of the surrounding localities. Citizens expressing preference for certain localities over others change the monopolistic relationship prevalent in centralized jurisdictions. Thus, for Tiebout, citizen choice is the key to improving organizational efficiency, and this choice manifests itself in the form of fragmented local governments. Critics have stated that this model equates democracy with free markets, but they are not synonymous. Further, it was not clear that public choice worked as well in practice as it did in theory. Empirical support for the model was mixed at best (Lyons et al. 1992). However, the model was later tested and refined by Schneider and Teske (1993), who propound that local governments can be competitive and efficient simply by responding to a small group of citizen-consumers who have high incomes and tend to be well-informed about services in communities.

Institutional Rational Choice (IRC): Some scholars argue that rules or institutions can be employed to improve the rationality of individual decision-making, thereby improving the quality of policymaking. Labelled Institutional Rational Choice, this approach to policymaking was advanced by Elinor Ostrom (1998, 2007). The belief is that institutions can be designed to solve collective-action problems. Policymakers, citizens, and other stakeholders make decisions in the context of institutional rules. These rules, in turn, shape individual preferences. A good example of this theory applied to a practical policy problem is John Chubb and Terry Moe's work on school choice (1988, 1990). Out of the IRC perspective, Ostrom and others developed an entire research agenda known as 'institutional analysis and development (IAD)', which used institutionalist theory to solve common-pool resource dilemmas (Ostrom 2011).

Subsystems Theory: Where does policy come from and how and why it changes are critical questions for understanding the policy process. The pluralist theoretical tradition in political science suggest that the policy process is mainly a competition among organized groups, each vying to get the government pay attention to its problems and take a particular action (Truman 1951). Early on, iron triangle theorists argued that the US Congress, the bureaucracy, and special interest groups formed an unbreakable triad, offering ideas and policy solutions with narrow benefits accrued to themselves at the expense of the public interest. But this was challenged in the 1970s and 1980s by scholars who claimed the process was more open, emphasizing the role of public and private organizations including think tanks, research institutes, interest groups, and ordinary citizens. In what came to be known as the Subsystems Theory, the policy process was seen as increasingly decentralized, fragmented, and characterized by informal and shifting alliances. Freeman (1965) and Heclo (1977, 1978) developed this conceptual framework to explain agenda-setting and policy-change. Heclo's research coined two terms—'issue networks' and 'technopols'. Issue networks tend to include politically active individuals with specialized policy knowledge who are drawn to the group for non-economic benefits. Within issue networks, those with specialized, technical knowledge of the policy at hand, or 'technopols', tend to wield more power. This theory was applied by Keith Hamm (1983) to the study of federal policymaking, revealing the close-knit nature of policy subsystems. Yet, these frameworks do not support a pluralist model since elites and well-funded groups exercise disproportionate indirect power.

Advocacy Coalition Framework (ACF): One of the best theories of the policy process, ACF was developed to address the questions raised by the Subsystems Theory. Its main proponent was Paul Sabatier (1988), who, following Heclo, argued that iron triangles are in reality highly permeable and often unpredictable. Sabatier and Jenkins-Smith (1999: 118) contended that there were five 'premises' to this framework, the basic premise being that the policy process is dynamic. Advocacy coalitions represented groups with shared beliefs (technical expertise and ideology) that coordinated activity following the emergence of a particular policy on the government agenda. These coalitions consisted of legislators, interest groups, public agencies, policy researchers, journalists, and other subnational actors. The ACF helped explain change in the policy process by arguing that advocacy coalitions engage in 'policy-oriented learning'. These groups continually adapt to changes in the political and socio-economic environment. They also revise their preferences in policy designs and goals based on new information. They coordinate with each other and develop long-term stable alliances. New coalitions are likely when there is severe dissatisfaction with existing policies. The ACF is constrained by its lack of standardized methodology and some of the practical issues of data collection, but remains a useful framework for understanding the policy process and generating empirically testable hypothesis (Weible et al. 2009: 127).

Punctuated Equilibrium Framework: The ACF gives some sense of where policy proposals originate, but how and why policies change remains a question. Baumgartner and Jones (1993) and Baumgartner et al. (2009) drew attention to the fact that the pace of change is not always constant or linear; in fact, there were periods of rapid and significant change, which they termed 'punctuated equilibria'. Significant change to a policy subsystem is likely to result in radical shift in policy and a new point of equilibrium. But what punctuates the equilibria? According to Baumgartner and Jones, the driving force for change is the issue definition—changes to the tone of an issue can lead to changes in the attention it receives. They gave examples of the nuclear power and the tobacco industry to illustrate their point. As issues emerge on the formal agenda, they leave an 'institutional legacy' resulting in a positive feedback system. Positive feedback is the process by which a change in policy-image based on criticism results in a new point of stability. Recent empirical studies continue to refine and expand this framework (Breunig and Koski 2012; John and Bevan 2012). However, it has some limitations—it is descriptive rather than predictive; policy change is not always in one direction, it can go both ways; and the psychological element of the framework is imperfectly understood.

Multiple-streams Approach: John Kingdon (1995) also argued that the best way to understand the policy process is by examining policy image. He stated that the agenda-setting process and alternative selection were best understood through the 'garbage can model', as theorized by Cohen et al. (1972). In this model, ideas were jumbled together and both problems and solutions were dumped in the proverbial policymaking 'garbage can'. Policy entrepreneurs then learnt to select alternatives by trial and error. Kingdon revised the garbage can model to include three separate streams: problems, policies, and politics. Each stream contributed to understanding why the government paid attention to some problems and not to others. This came to be known as the multiple-streams approach. The problem stream means that policy actors must first recognize that there is an existing problem. The most obvious way it happens is through a 'focusing event' such as the Nirbhaya rape case or the Bhopal gas tragedy. In the policy stream, alternative solutions are generated to address the emerging problem. Participants in the policy stream include both 'visible' and 'hidden' clusters of actors (Kingdon 1995). Alternatives move from being in the primordial soup to being a viable option through 'softening up' and through 'coupling' (Kingdon 1995: 200–1). Policy specialists, academicians, and interest groups can soften up the agenda to ensure favourable political receptivity. Coupling is the ability to link alternatives with problems. The political stream is characterized by bargaining among elected officials, constituents, and organized political forces. Events such as elections results and change in the national mood can determine whether a problem will find a receptive venue. The convergence of the three streams creates what Kingdon calls a 'policy window' or the opportunity for rapid change. The problem and political stream open the window; the political entrepreneur has to recognize the window and grab the opportunity of placing policy alternatives or 'couple' the three streams before the window closes. Some empirical work has been conducted on this framework, with mixed results (Robinson and Eller 2010; Liu et al. 2010). Zahariadis (2007) identifies weaknesses in the framework, such as a lack of use in the models of change, an inability to distinguish clear lines of separation between streams, and an absence of empirically falsifiable hypotheses.

How Well Do These Theories Apply to Non-Western Systems of Policymaking?

The literature on non-Western policy processes is broad-based rather than specific to India. Also, there are divergent views about the applicability of Western policy-process theories to non-Western processes. Pye (1958) argued that non-Western political systems were distinctive because the political sphere was not sharply differentiated from the spheres of social and personal relations, political parties tended

to represent a way of life, and that the political process was characterized with prevalence of cliques and political loyalty. But his view
was contested by Diamant (1959) and Horowitz (1989). Horowitz
(1989) argued,

> On the one hand, it is clear that the systemic frameworks of policy—
> the institutions, participants, resources, the weight of the state relative
> to the society, and the capacity of the state to work its will—all vary as
> between developing and Western countries. The same is true for the
> scope of policy activity, the configuration of issues, and the actual con-
> tent of policy. On the other hand, the policy process—the constraints,
> the ripe moments that produce innovation, the tendency for policy to
> have unanticipated consequences, and so on—appears to display regu-
> larities that transcend the categories of Western or Third World state.

Interestingly, Thomas and Grindle (1990) have pointed out that
contestations are more common in the policy-formulation stage in
developed countries, while for developing nations, the main area of
policy contestation is the process of policy implementation.

However, while many scholars acknowledge the differences that
exist between various countries' policy processes, there is a strong
sense that the insights from conceptual frameworks of policy process
that have been developed can transcend the boundaries of specific
cases, contributing significantly to the study of policy processes in
non-US settings.

Synopsis of the Case Studies: A Preview of the Learnings

There is no doubt that the policy-process literature, even if not particular to India, provides several insights regarding the nature of our
policy processes. However, it stands to reason that the policy process
is likely to be context-specific and informed by a country's history,
culture, institutions, social cleavages, and economic capabilities. Do
they significantly alter the nature of the policy process? It is not clear,
given the paucity of corroborating evidence so far.

To somewhat fill this knowledge gap, we have analysed the information gathered regarding the journey of the specified nine laws and
now seek to match these policy process theories to the processes followed in the evolution of the selected laws (see Table 2.3).

As Table 2.3 shows, there is wide variation in the policy processes in India. Some laws have come about after years of advocacy, some due to a triggering event, and some through bureaucratic pressures. Thus, the theories that seem to fit a case study vary. There are also cases where one theory does not explain the whole journey; multiple theories seem applicable, and in some cases, none seem to be applicable. However, there are common patterns that are observable in cases.

Some Key Observations

Almost none of the laws and bills were written on a tabula rasa or blank slate (except perhaps microfinance); each came into being as a replacement of an existing law or policy. Thus, most policymaking is actually policy succession, as observed by Hogwood and Peters (1982).

The reasons for this are many. In India, and increasingly in contemporary Western political systems, the government is present in virtually every policy space so that there are relatively few completely new activities in which the government could become involved. Existing laws may themselves create conditions requiring amendments. Thus, the problem to be tackled may not be a result of no policy but problems resulting from existing policy or law. Hogwood and Peters (1982) observe that policy succession could be a 'consequence of the relationship between the rate of sustainable economic growth and the financial implications of the existing policy commitments'. However, two of the proposed laws—child labour and microfinance— could not get enacted. These bills could not be passed due to a mix of legislative inertia and some push-back from groups opposed to the proposal.

Each of these laws or bills proposes significant innovation in the system. Therefore, each had to overcome certain initial hurdles: (a) legitimacy; (b) lack of champions within the bureaucracy or the political elites; and (c) lack of information on its effectiveness. A consensus about the need for policy change had to be built from ground up before there was acceptance at the political level, requiring significant amount of advocacy by CSOs, advocacy groups, and lobbies. Thus, each of the laws and bills (except the Competition Act,

Table 2.3 A Comparison of the Nine Policy Movement Case Studies along Multiple Parameters

Cases	Timeline		Key Actors	Influences/ Triggers
	Pre-legislative	Legislative		
Competition Act, 2002	1990–2001	6 August 2001: 2001 Bill introduced; August 2002: Standing Committee Report; December 2002: 2001 Bill passed; 2007 and 2009: Act amended twice.	Raghavan Committee, CUTS, law firms like Amarchand Mangaldas, Finance Minister Shri Yashwant Sinha, Vinod Dhall	India's liberalization of the economy in 1991; WTO; Chakravarthy Committee; Supreme Court
Right to Information Act, 2005	First phase: 1975–90; Second phase: 1990–2002; Third phase: 2003–10	July 2000: Introduction of FOI Bill; July 2001: Standing Committee Report; December 2002: Passing of Bill by both Houses of Parliament; December 2004: Introduction of RTI Bill; Standing	MKSS, NCPRI, CHRI, Parivartan, Consumer Education and Research Council, Bhrashtachar Virodhi Andolan; NAC judiciary	Corruption at local levels on government sponsored drought relief work in Rajasthan

Strategies	Geographical Spread	Role of Media		Probable Theoretical Framework
		Print/ Television	Social Media	
lobbying, advocacy	Delhi, Jaipur	Not used very strongly as a campaign tool. Op/eds have appeared about the issue regularly, however	Not used.	Incremental model of policymaking. The push came from the bureaucracy mostly, with some inputs from civil society.
Jan sunwais, public marches, rallies, sit-ins, mass meetings and hunger strikes. Slogans like 'Our money, our accounts' and 'The right to know, the right to live' used. Using membership	Rajasthan, Maharashtra, Gujarat, Himachal Pradesh, Delhi	Initially reported in local papers, it gathered momentum in mid-1990s as more corruption cases got exposed through Jan Sunwais	Not used till 2008. After 2008, it has been used to mould public opinion against the proposed amendments by some activists.	Advocacy coalition framework. The sustained advocacy campaigns organized by MKSS and later the national coalition on RTI— NCPRI—led to the enactment of the law. Also, key leaders

(Cont'd)

Table 2.3   (*Cont'd*)

Cases	Timeline		Key Actors	Influences/
	Pre-legislative	Legislative		Triggers
		Committee Report; May 2005: Bill passed by both Houses of Parliament		
Right to Education Act, 2009	First phase: 1950–90; Second Phase: 1990–2001; Third Phase: 2002–8	2001: 93rd Constitutional Amendment Bill introduced; 2002: CA Bill passed and Article 21A inserted in Constitution; 2005: Draft Bill circulated but not introduced; December 2008: RTE Bill introduced; February 2009: Standing Committee Report tabled; August 2009: RTE Bill passed in both Houses	NAFRE, CACL, SACCS, FORCES, CRY, Pratham, MV Foundation, Eklavya, Bachpan Bachao Andolan, Vidhayak Sansad, Shramjeevi Sangathan, etc.	

Strategies	Geographical Spread	Role of Media		Probable Theoretical Framework
		Print/ Television	Social Media	
in NAC to push the agenda. Lobbying with government		Some coverage of the campaigns and marches.		like Aruna Roy were part of the NAC.
Formation of coalitions such as NAFRE, CACL. Global campaign on Education. Shiksha Yatras to mobilize people at all levels. Conventions held at all levels. Post-card campaign. State level campaigns such as Bheek Morcha, Kori Pati Morcha,	Campaigns were held all over India; especially active in Mumbai and Delhi	Press conferences and press releases were held in the 1990s but reporting on RTE started after the 2002 constitutional amendment	Social media used only from 2007–8	Incremental model of policymaking till 1990s. Each Five Year Plan from 1950 onwards continued with the same idea with some tweaking. Committees and commissions were set up to recommend strategies some of which were implemented. Advocacy coalition framework from 1995 to 2009. The Unnikrishnan

(*Contd*)

Table 2.3   (Cont'd)

Cases	Timeline		Key Actors	Influences/ Triggers
	Pre-legislative	Legislative		
				Unnikrishnan judgment in 1992 on right to education being part of right to life
Child Labour (Prohibition and Regulation) Amendment Bill, 2012	1950–86: First Phase 1987–2012: Second Phase	December 1986: Act passed; 4 December 2012: Bill to amend Act introduced; December 2013: Standing Committee Report	Bachpan Bachao Andolan, MV Foundation, Swami Agnivesh, CACL, NCPCR	Sarva Shiksha Abhiyan; Right to Education
Microfinance Institutions (Development and Regulation) Bill, 2012	1998–2007: First Phase 2010–12: Second Phase	20 March 2007: Bill introduced but lapsed due to dissolution of Lok Sabha; October	BASIX, SKS, Sadhan, Spandana, Bandhan etc.	AP Ordinance was promulgated as a reaction to alleged coercive debt recovery practices of

Strategies	Geographical Spread	Role of Media		Probable Theoretical Framework
		Print/ Television	Social Media	
Voice of India campaign, media advocacy, lobbying with policymakers.				judgment of 1992 accelerated the involvement of CSOs.
Lobbying, marches, media glare on abuses, rescuing of children workers.	All over India	Used to some extent to spread awareness.	Used for some campaigns in latter part of the movement.	Advocacy coalition framework. Groups who believed in the eradication of child labour came together to form coalitions and pressurize the government for policy change.
SHGs and JLGs to lend money to poor women	Spread out in many parts of India but mostly concentrated in South India,	Insignificant	Insignificant	None of the theories fit this Bill except very broadly the advocacy coalition framework.

(Cont'd)

Table 2.3 (*Cont'd*)

Cases	Timeline		Key Actors	Influences/ Triggers
	Pre-legislative	Legislative		
		2010: Andhra Pradesh Ordinance; March 2011: Ministry of Finance forms committee to draft Bill; 22 May 2012: Bill introduced; February 2014: Standing Committee Report		MFIs leading to suicides. 2007 and 2012 Bills were drafted to regulate the MFI sector
National Food Security Act, 2013	1990–2011	22 December 2011: Bill introduced; January 2013: Standing Committee Report; July 2013: Ordinance promulgated; September 2013: Bill passed by both Houses of Parliament	PUCL, Human Rights Law Network, NGOs involved in the Right to food campaign (National Federation of Indian Women, National Alliance of People's Movement, Jan Swasthya Abhiyan,	Starvation deaths while foodgrains rotted in FCI godowns in Rajasthan

Strategies	Geographical Spread	Role of Media		Probable Theoretical Framework
		Print/ Television	Social Media	
	especially Andhra Pradesh			The push for the Bill came from a small group of MFIs but was opposed by the larger coalition.
Peaceful means like PIL, coalition formation, data collection, surveys, academic research, signature campaigns, conventions, use of RTI to expose	Started in Rajasthan and Orissa then spread in other parts of the country, especially Jharkhand, Chhattisgarh, Madhya Pradesh, Bihar, and Maharashtra	Media highlighted starvation deaths in Orissa, Jharkhand etc., reported views of academics and experts (proponents and opponents), highlighted campaigns	Used from 2008–9 but not extensively	A combination of Punctuated Equilibrium Framework and Advocacy Coalition Framework. The PIL filed by PUCL in a reaction to the rotting foodgrains in godowns while people were starving was

(*Cont'd*)

Table 2.3 (Cont'd)

Cases	Timeline		Key Actors	Influences/ Triggers
	Pre-legislative	Legislative		
			Rashtriya Viklang Manch, Bharatiya Gyan Vigyan Samiti etc.), academicians like Amartya Sen, Jean Dreze, and Ritika Khera, journalists like P. Sainath and Neelabh Mishra, NAC, judiciary, Supreme Court Commissioner's office, international NGOs (INGOs) such as Oxfam India and UNICEF	
Lokpal and Lokayuktas Act, 2013	2010–13	1963–2002: Eight Bills introduced (but not passed);	IAC, headed by Arvind Kejriwal and Anna Hazare; Baba Ramdev's	Corruption scandals, some of which were revealed through CAG report.

Strategies	Geographical Spread	Role of Media		Probable Theoretical Framework
		Print/ Television	Social Media	
corruption, Jan Sunwais, media advocacy, conferences, and seminars. Disruptive means like collective action, sit-ins, dharnas, rallies, and hunger strikes.		against Planning Commission's poverty line and cash transfer		the starting point. The court verdict in favour of food security led to the formation of coalitions all over the country who then campaigned for the law.
Fast unto death, mass mobilization through social	Mostly focused in Delhi's Ramlila Grounds and	Carefully crafted media strategy by IAC led to extensive	Platforms like Facebook, Twitter, and YouTube	Punctuated equilibrium framework and multiple stream theory.

(*Cont'd*)

Table 2.3   *(Cont'd)*

Cases	Timeline		Key Actors	Influences/ Triggers
	Pre-legislative	Legislative		
		August 2011: Lokpal Bill introduced; 9 December 2011: Standing Committee Report; 27 December 2011: Passed in Lok Sabha; 29 December 2011: Debated in RS but not passed; 21 May 2012: Bill referred to RS Select Committee; 23 November 2012: Select Committee Report tabled; December 2013: Bill passed in both Houses	group; NCPRI, celebrities such as Anupam Kher, Swami Agnivesh, Amir Khan	2G scam, Commonwealth Games scam, coal scam, Adarsh Housing Society scam; issue of black money

Strategies	Geographical Spread	Role of Media		Probable Theoretical Framework
		Print/ Television	Social Media	
media and traditional media, SMS and missed call campaigns, use of RTIs to get information on large-scale corruption, filing FIRs in police stations, undertaking rallies, and calling press conferences	Jantar Mantar with sporadic campaigns in Bengaluru, Mumbai, and other cities. Outside India there were protests in New Jersey, New York, and London	reporting on TV channels and newspapers. April: 5,576 news clips (prime time coverage 1,224 clips). August: Aaj Tak and Star News devoted 97 per cent of total news time on Anna's fast, corresponding figure for English channels, CNN-IBN, and NDTV was 87 Per cent.	were used extensively to mobilize people (150 Facebook pages related to the movement). SMS and missed call campaigns and online signature campaigns were used	The immediate trigger was the series of big ticket scams that came into the media glare in 2009–10. The IAC cashed in on the public mood of suppressed anger against the political class and used the Gandhian method of fasting to mobilize people. Here the problem was identified, the solution was proposed and politics used to push for policy change.

(*Cont'd*)

Table 2.3 (Cont'd)

Cases	Timeline		Key Actors	Influences/ Triggers
	Pre-legislative	Legislative		
Land Acquistion and Rehabilitation and Resettlement Act, 2013	1947–84: First Phase; 1984–2007: Second Phase 2009–11: Third Phase	1984: 1894 Act amended; 6 December 2007: Two Bills introduced (Land Acq and R&R); October 2008: Standing Committee Reports; 2009: LA Bill passed in Lok Sabha; pending in RS; Both Bills lapsed with dissolution of Lok Sabha; 7 September 2011: LARR Bill introduced; May 2012: Standing Committee Report; September 2013: Passed by both Houses	Narmada Bachao Andolan, Bhumi Uchhed Pratirodh Comiitee, Nandigram, POSCO Pratirodh Sangram Samity, and similar organizations	NBA, Nandigram, Singur, anti-Maha SEZ, and anti-POSCO movements, Bhatta Parsaul

Strategies	Geographical Spread	Role of Media		Probable Theoretical Framework
		Print/ Television	Social Media	
Grass root agitation, protest, political alignment	MP, West Bengal, Maharashtra, Odisha, UP (among many others)	Not used so much as a strategy but received wide and sustained coverage owing to sustained political agitation	Not used	A mix of advocacy coalition framework and Punctuated Equilibrium Theory. Issue networks such as Narmada Bachao Andolan, tribal rights groups were keys for agenda setting but the trigger for policy change came from incidents like Singur, Nandigram, and Bhatta Parsaul.

(Cont'd)

Table 2.3 (*Cont'd*)

Cases	Timeline		Key Actors	Influences/ Triggers
	Pre-legislative	Legislative		
Criminal Laws (Amendment) Act, 2013	First phase: 1975–84; Second phase: 1984–2000; Third phase: December 2012– March 2013	December 2012: Bill Introduced; 3 February 2013: Ordinance promulgated; 1 March 2013: Standing Committee Report; 19 March 2013: Revised Bill introduced; 1 March 2013: Passed in both Houses	Women's organizations such as Jagori, Nirantar, Manushi, Centre for Social Research, Saheli, Majlis; university students, students unions, political parties, professionals, lawyers, physiotherapy students	1970s: Supreme Court judgment after Mathura rape case; 2012: Brutal rape of Jyoti Singh, a 23-year-old student in Delhi

Strategies	Geographical Spread	Role of Media		Probable Theoretical Framework
		Print/ Television	Social Media	
Disruptive tactics such as protests, and rallies and peaceful tactics such as silent marches, candle-light vigils, protests in black, flash and freeze mobs. Also, gender sensitization workshops; innovative research, campaigns in the media, lobbying with policymakers	Nation-wide but more focused in Delhi	Spike in reportage of rapes after the Nirbhaya case and panel discussions on television channels	Extensive use of Twitter and Facebook to mobilize protestors after the Nirbhaya rape incident	Punctuated equilibrium framework and multiple stream theory. The 2013 Act was passed in the aftermath of the severe protests after a young student was brutally raped and thrown from a moving bus.

2002, to some extent) had significant involvement of CSOs and key champions within the ruling parties.

The speed with which the policy process works can be an indicator of efficiency of the system as well as quality of the law. If policy change comes through incremental steps, some serious, lasting mistakes may be avoided. However, it may also mean that the system is not efficient enough to deal with a perceived problem in a time-bound manner. As Table 2.4 indicates, the government has been responsive in some cases, especially where an external event has provided a trigger for change, as in the case of the Lokpal and Lokayuktas Act (although the pace slowed once the momentum of the IAC movement died down) and the Criminal Laws (Amendment) Act.

The enactment of the RTI Act is the only exception since there was no triggering event. However, the Common Minimum Programme of UPA in 2004 promised that 'the Right to Information Act will be made more progressive participatory and meaningful'. Also, the formation of the National Advisory Council (NAC), a quasi-government group headed by Sonia Gandhi, gave the impetus to the process since stalwarts of the RTI movement, Aruna Roy and

Table 2.4 Timelines of the Selected Laws and Bills

Act/Bill	Pre-legislative	Legislative
Competition Act	11 years	1.4 years
Right to Information (RTI) Act	15 years	5 months
Right to Education (RTE) Act	16 years	1 year—CA Act 8 months—RTE Act
Child Labour Bill	25 years	not passed;introduction to Standing Committee Report: 1 year
Microfinance Bill	14 years	not passed; introduction to Standing Committee Report: 1.9 year
Food Security Act	21 years	1.9 years
Lokpal Act	3 years	2.4 years
Land Acquisition Act	17 years	2 years
Criminal Laws Act	3 months	1 month

Source: Based on authors' own research and Lok Sabha and Rajya Sabha websites.

Jean Dreze, were members of the NAC. In other cases, the legislative process, on average, takes about a year and a half to complete but the pre-legislative process can vary widely. Bills such as those on Food Security and Land Acquisition, which were also pushed by the NAC members, got passed in roughly the same timelines.

Each of the laws has multiple actors influencing the policy process. These include both institutional and non-institutional actors. Institutional actors include the legislators, the political parties, the judiciary, the Comptroller and Auditor General of India (CAG), the NAC, the Planning Commission (now NITI Aayog), the Cabinet, Group of Ministers, the Law Commission, parliamentary standing committees, independent regulatory bodies, the bureaucracy, and politicians. Non-institutional actors include advocacy groups, non-governmental organizations (NGOs), policy entrepreneurs, multi-lateral agencies (the World Bank, the International Monetary Fund [IMF], UN agencies), business lobbies (the Federation of Indian Chambers of Commerce and Industry [FICCI], the Confederation of Indian Industries [CII], Associated Chambers of Commerce and Industry of India [ASSOCHAM]), interest groups, media, think tanks, and research institutes. The goals of non-institutional actors generally include changing policy, gaining access to the policy process, and changing social values. As the cases demonstrate, gaining access to the policy process requires different tactics but the system is open and porous enough to allow diverse sets of actors to gain legitimacy. For example, there were entirely different groups of non-state actors who advocated for the RTI Act as opposed to the microfinance or the child labour bill. However, there are also many overlaps, say among RTI, food security, and land acquisition, or among the RTE and the child labour bill, or the Criminal Laws Act and the Lokpal Act. But more probably, the overlap was issue-based rather than owing to a lack of plurality in the groups. The key role of civil society groups is to provide inputs to agenda-setting and policy-development processes. Policy entrepreneurs are innovators who actively seek dynamic changes in policy or politics. In the Indian context, people like Arvind Kejriwal (before he joined politics), Aruna Roy, and Kailash Satyarthi may be called 'policy entrepreneurs' since they were able to create new opportunities and mobilize citizen demand to support a fresh vision of the future.

Among the institutional actors, the CAG and the NAC have played an innovative role in the policy process. The CAG, by publicizing its findings in the 2G spectrum and other cases, created an atmosphere ripe for an anti-corruption movement. As a constitutional body, it had legitimacy with the citizens and its findings were credible evidence of corruption in the government. The NAC was set up by an executive order for the specific function—to 'oversee the implementation of the National Common Minimum Programme' of the government. Additionally, it was to 'provide inputs for formulation of policy by government and to provide support to government in its legislative business'. Although the members were carefully chosen, they came from diverse fields. The NAC gave space to a diverse set of civil society actors to participate formally in the political process. However, the members were a carefully chosen mix of civil society actors, technocrats, bureaucrats, and academicians broadly aligned with the UPA's policy agenda.

Clearly, India's policy process is reactive rather than proactive. Most of the time, the pace of the policy process got accelerated or was triggered by an external incident. The trigger for the Competition Act, 2002 was the economic liberalization that the country embarked on in the 1990s due to the balance of payment crisis. The impetus for the campaigns for the RTE Act and the Food Security Act came through judicial orders. Other examples include the Lokpal Act, the Criminal Laws (Amendment) Act, and the Land Acquisition Act. In cases where there has been no impetus or trigger, such as the Microfinance Bill or the Child Labour Bill, it did not result in policy change (although it should be noted that the Child Labour Bill got enacted in 2016).

In terms of geographical spread, Delhi and Rajasthan seem to be the hotbed of activity in the decade and half under study. It may be premature to make any definitive pronouncements, given that the sample size is small, but it is possible that proximity to Delhi is a factor for successful activism in Rajasthan. Land acquisition and microfinance stand apart in this respect because their spread includes West Bengal, Madhya Pradesh, Orissa, Andhra Pradesh, Chhattisgarh, and Jharkhand.

Strategies used by non-institutional actors to influence the policy process in India include those which are disruptive as well as peaceful/non-violent. Some of the movements such as the RTI used public hearings or *jan sunwai*s to expose corrupt officials publicly. In recent times, the tactics used by the IAC movement stand out as extremely effective. The use of Gandhian symbols (through the persona of Anna Hazare) and methods (fasting), combined with relentless media coverage at a time when big-ticket corruption cases were being reported in alarming frequency, ignited the middle-class public to join the protests in large numbers. The campaigns after the Delhi gang rape case also had a mainly middle-class following, but it was a more spontaneous protest against the lack of safety for women. But these two movements got the generally apathetic middle class on to the streets of Delhi.

The other campaigns included activists who belonged to the middle class as leaders or facilitators of the campaigns, but the mass mobilization were targeted at the poor. Demonstrations, processions, mass meetings, rallies, dharna, and sit-ins were preferred methods of protests in India right from the time of Independence (and before). In fact, these civil resistances increased after Independence since the state was unable to fulfil many of the demands of its citizens. Public agitations and protests were looked upon as instrumentalities supplementing law courts and parliamentary elections (Bayley 1963). These tactics were used by the women's movements as well as anti-dam activists quite extensively. As interest and advocacy groups got more organized and formalized, the government also started opening up avenues for consulting with outside groups—through informal consultations, seminars, conferences, and standing committee depositions (1992 onwards). The activists also started taking advantage of this window and along with their public campaigns, intensified their one-on-one advocacy with political parties and individual legislators.

The introduction of the concept of public interest litigations (PILs) was a great innovation that allowed activists to take the judicial route to get their agendas heard. Formation of networks, alliances, and coalitions with many groups working in similar areas in different parts of the country became a common strategy for many of the campaigns. As mobile phones and the internet became popular, new campaigns based on them were developed. They were also successfully used to mobilize people at a short notice, most notably during the agitations and protests after the Delhi gang rape.

The media, and in recent years, social media have played a very active role in the agenda-setting process in India. Newspaper articles, and more importantly, television debates now help form public opinion in the country. The extensive spread of mobile phones and the popularity of social media platforms such as Facebook, Twitter, and YouTube have helped people network and communicate at an unprecedented level. It has increased the level of transparency in the country, but also has some negative fallouts.

The most common framework that seems to fit India's policy process is a combination of punctuated equilibrium theory, multiple streams theory, and the advocacy coalition framework—the Lokpal Act, the Criminal Laws (Amendment) Act, the RTI Act, the Land Acquisition Act, the Child Labour Bill, and the Food Security Act. The incremental theory also works in some of the cases such as the Competition Act, 2002, and the first phase of the RTE Act. However, the Microfinance Bill does not fit well with any of these theories since the advocacy for the Bill has been muted and confined to a relatively small group. (This should become clearer to the reader once he/she goes through the case studies.) The Andhra Pradesh Ordinance, on the other hand, was a case of regulation by the bureaucracy to address a perceived problem. While there were media reports of farmer suicides due to coercive loan recovery practices, there were no groups actively demanding a law to govern the microfinance institutions (MFIs) in Andhra Pradesh.

What can we conclude from this about India's policy process? First, the relevance of these theories to the real world of bare-knuckle political arena with its pushes and pulls, bargains, and quid pro quos is somewhat suspect. Decisions in the political arena are influenced far more by the perception of a situation than by any rational concept of objective reality. It is far more than the difference between a pessimist seeing a glass half empty while an optimist sees the same glass as half full. One actor in the decisional drama may view a programme as essential for the national interest while another actor may be equally certain that it is nothing more than an example of petty bureaucrats wasting taxpayers' money. Add to this mix personal egos, party dynamics, and corruption. It becomes apparent how difficult it is not only to theorize but for any existing theory to be completely relevant to the realities of policymaking.

Second, most of the time, change happens slowly. The pace can sometimes be accelerated due to an unpremeditated incident, but there is merit in taking time to decide on a far-reaching policy change, otherwise the law would not require repeated amendments before it can actually become functional.

Third, the government is not a monolith. There are many components to it that have some say in the policy process.

Fourth, political parties are more powerful than individual MPs in a parliamentary democracy and especially in India, given the constraints placed on MPs due to the Anti-Defection Law.

Fifth, the power of non-violent resistance has been amply demonstrated in each of these case studies and would add to the list of strategies listed in the Global Non-Violent Action Database.

Sixth, the activism that preceded the enactment of many of these laws were predominantly campaigns, which had more specific goals and concentrated periods of activity. However, some of these campaigns were part of a larger movement, such as the women's movement or the environment movement in India.

Concluding Observations

In this book, we have attempted to use case studies of recent campaigns and movements to shed light on the mechanics of law-making in India and then view them through the prism of existing theories in political science and public policy. Real life policymaking processes are hairy, complex, and idiosyncratic. Also, the theorization that has taken place in this area—scanty as it may be—has occurred based on movements observed in developed societies. To what extent such theories may find relevance to developing-country reality, to what extent a democracy in a far poorer, significantly more heterogeneous, and culturally diverse former colony finds expression and uses methods and processes that bear resemblance to those of the affluent and developed West, has been another subject of investigation. Expectedly, our exercise has perhaps thrown up more questions than it has answered.

Institutions, Legitimacy, and Representation

The legislatures and the elected representatives are the central pieces of any democracy. However, as most of the case studies amply demonstrate, the policy process is scarcely driven by the elected representatives or by political parties themselves. These appear to arrive last on the scene, like the proverbial cops in Bollywood movies, and quickly jostle for credits. Civil society organizations and the judiciary appear to play far more prominent roles in many of the processes. The Lokpal movement and the subsequent emergence of the Aam Aadmi Party (AAP) as a prominent political formation bear ample evidence to the fissure between the elected and the electorate. The real policy drama seems to get enacted out in the streets till the government of the day seems to have no option but to embrace it as a legislative matter. Is this a trend only of our chosen cases or is this the general pattern? If the latter, is it evidence of a failed electoral system or of an open society allowing for multiple venues of public demands? What does it portend for the nature of politics going forward?

Class Affiliations

How far is political opinion coloured by memberships of classes and groups? Is there greater homogeneity in thinking among various groups like CSOs, bureaucracy, politicians, and the judiciary, than across these groups? Our cases seem to broadly suggest certain representative views among the different groups, albeit with dissenting voices. Is that an apt characterization in general? If yes, do people self-select into these groups or do their peers shape their views after their joining these groups? Are some groups more homogenous than others?

Policy Processes

What are the points of entry and influence in a policy process? It appears, from case studies as well as from general observation, that the policy process has become more open and participative over time, with standing committees seeking depositions across the spectrum and draft committee reports often made publicly available for comment. But how open is open enough? How does India's policy process compare to those in other countries with respect to openness? How do networks matter and operate in this place? Does membership of influential groups like the law fraternity, for instance, bestow individuals and groups with greater influence over the policy process?

Technology and Evolution of Methods of Communication

In recent years, particularly after the Arab Spring, the role of social media in organizing social movements and flash rallies has gained worldwide attention. Among the cases covered in this volume, at least two of the more recent ones—lokpal and criminal law amendment—seem to have used social media in a significant manner. But both of these, far more than others, were city-based, youth-and-middle-class-oriented movements. Is the reach of the social media in policy space still restricted to this demography or is it spreading beyond fast to help organize national, or at least, regional protests? How effectively is social media being used in peace time—that is, not for protests, but to communicate with lawmakers or civil society groups to give voice to the citizens' concern to be translated to policy?

Effectiveness of Policies

Finally, this volume has stopped short of looking at the impact of the policies since the subject of query has been the policy-forming process. What real impact have these policies had on the basic policy need of the citizens' groups? This is, of course, a difficult question to answer, but an extremely important one as well. A corollary to this is the question of what determines the effectiveness of policies.

This and many other questions constitute what promises to be an exciting and to the best of our knowledge presently unexplored research area in public policy in the Indian context, where we hope to see advances made in the near future. The nature, speed, and method of policy formation are both diverse across policies and fast-evolving over time. But a clearer understanding of how policies are shaped is as important for the public policy researcher as it is for the lawmaker, bureaucrat, jurist, and the activist.

Notes

1. Almost 30 per cent of Indians live below the poverty line, a quarter of its population is illiterate, and over 30 per cent of its children below 5 years are underweight.
2. Comparative figures with other countries on poverty and literacy.

3

The Road to the Competition Act, 2001

The Monopolies and Restrictive Trade Practices Act has become obsolete in certain areas in the light of international economic developments relating to competition laws. We need to shift our focus from curbing monopolies to promoting competition.
— Finance Minister Yashwant Sinha, Budget Speech 1999

...even in the Act, there is no precise definition of 'competition'.... (W)e have accepted 'competition' in the sense we understand—competition between two economic enterprises to draw customers towards their products. And, it has invariably been found that in large number of cases, the competition kills the competitor, and, ultimately, it degenerates into monopoly. To prevent that kind of a situation, the concept of a Competition Bill and Competition Commission has been brought.
— Shri Pranab Mukherjee, debating the Bill in Rajya Sabha

Background

The world of soaps and detergents hardly look like a key area of public policy concern. And yet, one could argue that the movement towards the Competition Act, 2002 really gathered momentum from a corporate merger in this part of the economy.

As India embarked on its still continuing journey of liberalization in 1991, its device to regulate competition had remained an old-style one—the Monopolies and Restrictive Trade Policies (MRTP) Act, 1969, amended in 1984. Conscious of the needs of what the future may be holding for the economy, the government amended the MRTP Act once more in 1991.

Three corporate mergers made headlines in the early years of the still uncertain liberalization—the entry of Coca Cola by acquiring several of Parle's brands, that of Gillette taking over Harbans Lal Malhotra & Sons, and the acquisition of the Tata Oil Mills Company (TOMCO) by Hindustan Lever Limited (HLL). While all three had implications for competition, the last one was perceived as the most competition-reducing by consumer activist groups in India. The takeover of ailing TOMCO, owner of strong brands like Hamam, 501, and OK, comprising about a fifth of HLL by sales volume in soaps and detergents, certainly augmented HLL's powers in the segment. Between the years 1992–3 (the year before the merger) and 1997–8, HLL's market share in soaps increased from about 20 per cent to 26 per cent, and in detergents, from 33 per cent to 47 per cent (Agarwal 2002).

Several consumer rights groups jointly challenged the proposed HLL–TOMCO merger before the MRTP Commission but failed as the MRTP Act did not have jurisdiction over this issue. They then approached the company bench of the Bombay High Court, challenging the merger on grounds of public interest, but lost there as well. The case reached the Supreme Court but the judgment there was no more sympathetic. The court opined that public interest could not be held against the stated law and the issue of reduced competition would only come up if after the merger, the new entity behaved in an anti-competitive manner.

The consumer movement in India had acquired a strong voice in policy circles. Deriving their strength from the Consumer Protection Act, 1986 (COPRA), the number of consumer groups had swelled from about 35 in 1986 to over 3,000 half a decade later, of which about 30 commanded substantial resources to be fairly effective. One of these consumer rights organizations, which was a strong voice in the HLL–TOMCO case, was Jaipur-based Consumer Unity and Trust Society (CUTS). Established in 1983–4 in the wake of the amendment in MRTP bringing in consumer protection provisions on unfair trade practices, (that is misleading advertising and deceptive claims), CUTS had been in the forefront of consumer rights action and had mounted successful campaigns including those against cigarette-maker Godfrey Philips, as well as matchbox makers. The loss of the appeal made the lacuna of MRTP—that post-1991 amendment, it did not cover 'combinations' (mergers and acquisitions)—clear to consumer groups. CUTS took on the relentless championing of a new Competition Act that would finally replace the MRTP Act.

MRTP and Competition Act Compared

Given the somewhat technical nature of the subject, it is perhaps useful to have a brief discussion about the MRTP Act and the Competition Act. While at first glance, both aim to protect and promote competition, the two laws had vastly different policy philosophy underpinnings.

The MRTP Act and the associated MRTP Commission were among the defining features of India's socialist era economic policies. It is safe to argue that it had its origins in the socialistic fear of large businesses and the political unacceptability of large income-inequality.

The Competition Act, on the other hand, was being demanded to inter alia protect consumers from exploitative pricing powers of players with dominant market shares. It stemmed from a world-view that while free enterprise should be welcomed and promoted, it is important to ensure that a reasonable level of competition prevailed in the marketplace that would prevent one or more players exploiting consumers individually, or in collusion. These differences become abundantly clear if the two Acts are compared side-by-side along several key dimensions. Table 3.1 provides this comparison.

How the Competition Act 2002 Came About

The Early Steps

While the implications of the exclusion of mergers and acquisitions 'combinations') from the MRTP Act in its 1991 amendment were now making consumer rights groups nervous at home, India's membership of the World Trade Organization (WTO) also pushed the nation towards an introspection of its competition policy. On 13 December 1996, the WTO's Singapore Ministerial Declaration 'agree(d) to ... establish a working group to study issues raised by Members relating to the interaction between trade and competition policy, including anti-competitive practices, in order to identify any areas that may merit further consideration in the WTO framework'.

Table 3.1   Differences between MRTP Act and Competition Act

Serial No.	MRTP Act, 1969	Competition Act, 2002
1	Based on the pre-reforms command and control regime	Based on the post-reforms liberalized regime
2	Based on size/structure as a factor	Based on conduct as a factor
3	Competition offences implicit and not defined	Competition offences explicit and defined
4	Complex in arrangement and language	Simple in arrangement and language and easily comprehensible
5	Frowns upon dominance	Acts upon abuse of dominance
6	Registration of business agreements, such as marketing, etc. compulsory	No requirement of registration of agreements
7	No combinations regulation (post-1991 amendment)	Combinations regulated beyond a high threshold limit
8	No competition advocacy role for the MRTPC	Competition Commission of India (CCI) has competition advocacy role
9	No penalties for offences	Penalties for offences
10	Reactive and rigid	Proactive and flexible
11	Unfair trade practices covered	Unfair trade practices omitted (Consumer Protection Act, 1986 will deal with them)
12	Rule of law approach	Rule of reason approach
13	Blanket exclusion of intellectual property rights	Exclusion of intellectual property rights, but unreasonable restrictions covered

Source: Chakravarthy 2006.

This pushed the matter to the Ministry of Commerce, which accordingly set up an expert group headed by S. Chakravarthy, former member, MRTP Commission, to study the interaction between trade and competition policy. The Group presented its report in 1999 and suggested establishment of a dedicated agency to regulate anti-competitive practices arising out of international trade agreements. It also recommended a new Competition Law.[1]

By 1999 however, several sectors had started a clamour for a new Competition Law. It seemed like an idea whose time had come. The CII declared its plan to draft a competition law almost immediately after the Chakravarthy committee's report. But the wheels of the government machinery had already started moving in this direction.

It is customary for the Union Finance Minister to invite various interest groups to present their views before the budget. Participants cannot but raise important economic policy issues in such meetings, often far beyond matters relating to budgetary allocation. It was at such a pre-budget meet before the 1999 budget with the newly appointed Finance Minister, Yashwant Sinha, that Pradeep S. Mehta, Secretary General of CUTS, made a strong case for a Competition Act. Minister Sinha had been sympathetic to the idea and the seed fell on fertile soil. Weeks later, in his budget speech on 27 February 1999, Sinha announced the government decision to appoint a committee to examine the issues involved in bringing about a 'modern Competition Law' to replace the MRTP Act.

The Raghavan Committee and Its Aftermath

Accordingly a nine-member, star-studded, high-level committee under the chairmanship of Shri S.V.S. Raghavan, a well-known public sector business leader and former chairman of Metals and Minerals Trading Corporation of India (MMTC), was established to examine provisions of the MRTP Act and make recommendations for a modern law in light of the liberalized economy. The other members were K.B. Dadiseth of Unilever, Rakesh Mohan, then head of the National Council of Applied Economic Research (NCAER), H.D. Shourie, consumer activist, S. Chakravarthy, former member of MRTP Commission, Sudhir Mulji, noted businessman, economist, and former chairman of the State Trading Corporation, P.M. Narielwala, former President, the Institute of Chartered Accountants of India (ICAI), and Pallavi Shroff, noted lawyer, besides the member secretary G.P. Prabhu.

The Raghavan Committee heard various interest groups including professional associations like the Institute of Company Secretaries of India, the Institute of Chartered Accountants of India, and the MRTP Bar Association. No one really opposed the law but debated it to get better clarifications. The strongest proponents were, probably expectedly, the consumer groups. The proposal to enact a new competition law met with resistance from the Federation of Small Industries Associations of India, which asked that the government continue its protectionist policies when it came to small industries. The move to enact a new competition law received support from an unlikely quarter—the trade unions and the Left. These groups believed that the provisions relating to combinations proposed in the Competition Act would protect interests of the workers and also that the MRTPC had proved to be ineffectual in this respect.

The strongest debate was around provisions related to combinations. Opponents questioned the need for such a provision after the 1991 amendments to the MRTPA had actually deleted restrictions on expansion and merger. The opposition was assuaged by fixing high thresholds beyond which the provisions would kick in.

The Raghavan Committee presented its report to the Government in May 2000. Perhaps unsurprisingly, it recommended a new competition law for the country, saying that the MRTPA had a limited scope in the evolving competition scenario. It also presented a draft Bill of the new law to the government.

Important points related to the Raghavan Committee's work have been summarized below (the following is an extract from *Competition Law and Policy in India: The Journey in a Decade* written by Vijay Kumar Singh, 2011).

1. The basic philosophy of the Act, being based on a post-reform scenario, is different. It seeks to replace the rigidity under the MRTP Act with pro-activeness and flexibility. The new law is simply arranged and easily comprehensible, categorizing the areas of concern into three—prohibition of anti-competitive agreements, prohibition of abuse of dominance, and regulation of combinations.
2. The control of the government over the regulatory body, the CCI, is minimal as compared to the MRTP Commission, as is evident from the provisions regarding selection of members and the chairman of the CCI and further autonomy granted under the Act.

3. Holding of dominant position is no longer a concern so long as it is not abused under the new law.

4. Concepts like cartels, collusion and price fixing, bid rigging, boycotts and refusal to deal, and predatory pricing have been introduced which were not present in the MRTP Act.

5. Provisions relating to mergers were repealed from the MRTP Act in 1991, thus leading many cases of mergers to escape from the clutches of the law. The new law provides for regulation of combinations beyond a particular threshold.

6. Competition advocacy has been introduced for creating awareness and imparting training about competition issues. This is with the aim to introduce a competition culture in the country.

7. The new law has moved from the earlier 'cease and desist' regime to stricter penalties and even jail terms for non-compliance of the orders of the Commission.

8. The Act has an extra-territorial reach based on the 'effects doctrine'.

The Raghavan Committee report, however, was far from unanimous. Four members, including Raghavan himself, appended dissent/supplementary notes to the Committee's report, recommending enactment of a new law. The most strident of the dissenting voices was that of Sudhir Mulji's, who argued from a liberal viewpoint that the proposed Concept Bill was too restrictive of competition. Chakravarthy, on the other hand, thought the bill was overly permissive and advocated stronger controls and slower liberalization in his supplementary note. Rakesh Mohan argued for a more gradual switch to the new regime with a three-to-five year 'advocacy' period, as opposed to one-year advocacy envisaged in the bill.

The Concept Bill was put on the government website in November 2000 and sparked heated debates in business circles. The bone of contention was the re-entry of preview of mergers that had been taken out in the 1991 amendment of the MRTPA. The industry feared that the authority would be manned by former bureaucrats of the socialist, command-and-control mindset who would be using their powers in the most disabling manner for industry. The government dealt with this by fixing a high threshold for mergers, that is merging companies with assets of Rs 100 million and turnover of Rs 300 million only would be scrutinized and only if there was a voluntary notification. However, the law as it stands today, does provide *suo moto* powers to the authority to examine any merger.

The debates caused a split within the government as well. The Ministry of Commerce and Industry opposed the bill, fearing, like industry, a return to the old 'inspector raj' days, and also thought this meant giving in too much to the demands of the WTO. It was also dead against the idea of offering national treatment to foreign companies.

On the other hand, the Ministry of Company Affairs (MCA), where the law would be housed, welcomed the law, pointing out its necessity in light of globalization through the WTO. The MCA itself, originally a part of the the Commerce and Industry ministry, had become part of the Ministry of Finance and Ministry of Law and had just recently emerged as a separate ministry. It is somewhat insulated from direct influence by the Industry on a regular basis because its main purpose is to administer the Companies Act. Here too, its interaction is more with the professional body of company secretaries.

The small-scale business association also had a strong view in the matter and here too, two organizations took up almost opposing views. The Federation of Small Industries Associations of India, Chennai made a fervent plea for reservation to the Raghavan Committee, citing the problems of small industries, for example in getting credit, the unfair trade practices of large businesses, and the competition from foreign competitors stemming from globalization. Reservation, however, was an anachronism given the spirit of the time. A demand for an exception from the full application of a competition law as prevailing in many countries, including industrialized ones, could have proved more effective. The Federation of Indian Small and Medium Enterprises (FISME), New Delhi, on the other hand, while echoing the unfair trade practices of large firms, argued that a healthy competition regime will be advantageous to them.

Media, too, was split on the issue—with some advocating the law, while others arguing that the law would stunt the growth of Indian industry.

Following time-honoured practices of most government committees, and possibly because of time and resource constraints, the Raghavan Committee did its job relying mainly on submissions made by various interest groups and the expert opinions of its members rather than any independent research. Some rigour came in, however, in that the committee had access to a senior economist of NCAER drafting a few chapters, and the consumer rights group CUTS providing some of the research, apart from the vast knowledge and experience of the members.

The Concept Bill went through several changes before becoming a draft Competition Bill that was introduced in Parliament in 2001. One important area was that of the coverage of Intellectual Property Rights (IPRs). The Committee had recognized the need to cover IPRs explicitly under the law, but when the bill was drafted at the Ministry of Law and Justice, it covered only unreasonable restrictions. Whether this was the legacy of the lacuna in the MRTPA or the effect of some corporate lobbying remains unclear. However, in most competition law jurisdictions, IPR abuses come under the 'abuse of dominance' provision, and so are indirectly covered, though with the risk of very imperfect understanding of such a provision and the possibility of smart lawyering getting to create poor case laws in the absence of explicit statute coverage.

Another important change was in the politically sensitive coverage on extra-territorial jurisdiction ('effects doctrine'), which would allow the authority to check abuses happening abroad but with an effect in India. In an important ruling in the *Haridas Exports* v. *All India Float Glass Manufacturers' Association case*,[2] the Supreme Court of India overruled the MRTPC on two complaints related to imports of soda ash and float glass, respectively. The court ruled that the Commission lacked jurisdiction in preventing imports of goods into India and also clarified the test of public interest upon which provisions of the MRTPA would kick in (the Commission had equated interest of Indian companies and their employees' with public interest and ruled that consumers should pay higher prices if this meant upholding public interest). The ruling highlighted problems with the MRTPC's jurisdiction when it came to extra-territorial aspects of monopolistic practices and also highlighted its flawed functioning.

However, the political lobbying and US retaliatory measures changed the thinking here. During his visit to India, US President Bill Clinton had it on his agenda for discussions with Prime Minister Atal Bihari Vajpayee. Later, the US International Trade Commission recommended withdrawal of GSP privileges against export of engineering goods as a cross retaliatory measure for the MRTPC's action against the American Natural Soda Ash Corporation (ANSAC), the soda ash cartel (which eventually got struck down by the Supreme Court), exposing the sectarian power in US policy.

The other major change in the draft Competition Bill from the Concept Bill was in the process of selection of chairman and members of the CCI. This proved to be a major issue a few years down the road and held back the implementation of the CCI itself. The Concept Bill had recommended that the selection process would be through a permanent collegium comprising the Chief Justice of India, Speaker of the Lok Sabha (lower house of the parliament), Governor of Reserve Bank of India, Finance Minister, and the minister in charge of company affairs. It had also proposed that the chairman need not be from the judiciary but should be an expert. The draft bill proposed in Parliament did not carry this provision, and instead provided for a summary selection process to be decided by the government.

Journey of the Bill in the Legislative Process

The Draft Competition Bill, 2001, based on the Raghavan Committee's report, was introduced in the Lok Sabha on 6 August 2001. On 21 August, the Bill was referred to the Department-related Parliamentary Standing Committee on Home Affairs by the Chairman of the Rajya Sabha, in pursuance of the Rules relating to the Department-related Parliamentary Standing Committees, in consultation with the Speaker of the Lok Sabha.

Proceedings at the Parliamentary Standing Committee

The Standing Committee examined the Bill in 12 sittings spread over almost one year and submitted its report on 21 November 2002 and heard representations from the following:[3]

- Secretary, Department of Company Affairs, Government of India;
- Secretary, Department of Consumer Affairs, Government of India;
- Dr S. Chakravarthy, Consultant, Department of Company Affairs, Government of India;

- Representatives of industry associations, consumer rights organizations, and associations of professionals as mentioned in Table 3.3;
- The Committee also invited comments from individuals/institutions/organizations interested in the subject by publishing advertisements in leading newspapers on 10 September 2001.

The Chairman and some members of the Committee also held informal interactions with Evan R. Cox, partner, Covington & Burling, a leading Washington based Law Firm, on the Bill on 15 February 2002.

The Committee also referred to the following documents in its deliberations over the Bill:

- A background note prepared for the Committee by the Department of Company Affairs (Ministry of Law, Justice and Company Affairs);

Table 3.2   Comparison of Bill and Proposed Changes by Ministry based on Standing Committee Recommendations

Post in Selection Committee	Original Provision in the Bill	Proposed Changes
Chairperson	Chief Justice of India or his nominee	No change
Member	Union Minister-in-charge of the Ministry of Finance	Secretary, Ministry of Finance
Member	Union Minister-in-charge of the Department Dealing with the Act	Secretary, Department of Company Affairs
Member	The Governor, Reserve Bank of India	Secretary, Ministry of Labour
Member	The Cabinet Secretary	Secretary, Department of Legal Affairs/Legislative Department

Source: Competition (Amendment) Bill, 2012; Standing Committee Report on the Competition (Amendment) Bill, 2012; and authors' own analysis.

- Responses of the Department of Company Affairs to the queries raised by the Committee and to comments received from individuals/organizations;
- The Monopolies and Restrictive Trade Practices Act, 1969;
- The Consumer Protection Act, 1986;
- Report of the High Level Committee on Competition Policy and Law (2002) (Volume I);
- New Indian Competition Law on the Anvil by S. Chakravarthy;
- Extract from Organisation for Economic Co-operation and Development (OECD), Journal of Competition Law and Policy on Leniency Programme to Fight Hard core Cartels.

Opening discussions on the Bill in the Rajya Sabha later, Shri Pranab Mukherjee, Chairman of the Standing Committee, called the Bill a 'major improvement in our corporate governance' and outlined the broad-based discussions that the Committee had held with stakeholders such as 'bodies representing trade, commerce and industry', 'but also a large number of professional bodies', and 'institutions associated with the stock market'.

It is perhaps instructive to see the recommendations made to the Standing Committee to get a glance of how various stakeholders can/do influence policymaking using the Standing Committee process. Major Chambers such as Associated Chambers of Commerce and Industry of India (ASSOCHAM) and Board of Control for Cricket in India (BCCI) stressed the need for the cooling period of at least fifteen to eighteen months after the enactment of new law. But the corporate sector was not united in its views. For instance, the Federation of Indian Chambers of Commerce and Industry (FICCI), Bajaj Auto Ltd., and Mahindra & Mahindra Ltd. opposed the enactment of the new law and suggested amendments to the MRTPA, 1969. Reliance Industries Limited was of the view that a simple Competition Law should be introduced at this stage. A stricter competition and merger control law, as proposed, may be adopted much later after the economy and companies have reached a position where it could sustain such restrictions imposed by the Competition Law. The BCCI, Tata Sons Ltd., Indian Merchants Chamber (IMC), Consumer Coordination Council (CCC), and CUTS welcomed the introduction of new law.

On conclusion of its examination of the Bill, the Committee made the following observations/recommendations:

1. The Bill has a contradiction, where the Statement of Objects and Reasons describes CCI as a quasi-judicial body; the Department of Company Affairs, in its representation to the Committee, said that CCI would be a judicial body, and also that it could sue and be sued (like a body corporate). The Committee pointed out that a judicial body never needs to sue anybody but it can issue orders for compliance. Similarly, a judicial body cannot be sued.

2. The Committee recommended different qualifications for the Chairman and Members of the CCI. The Draft Bill had laid down same set of qualifications for the Chairperson and Members.

3. The Committee also recommended that CCI, being a judicial body, should be headed by a Judicial Member, and the Chairperson of the CCI should be from amongst the serving or retired Judges of the High Courts.

4. The Committee was against the provision of having the Selection Committee (which would finalize a panel of names from which the Chairman and Members would be appointed) headed by the Minister-in-charge of Ministries in the Selection Committee as this may lead to executive interference in the functioning of the CCI. The Department proposed to change the original structure of the selection committee and this was accepted by the Committee.

The Committee said that members had two points of view regarding the proposal to enact a new law on competition in the country. One group believed that by enacting the Bill at this stage, India would lose its bargaining power at the WTO negotiations and the Bill ought to be delayed to 1 January 2005, by which time decisions on issues like competition policy, trade and investment, and related matters would be decided. Another point of view against the Bill was that Indian industry, both private and public sectors, needs certain safeguards and protection for a certain period. The present Bill takes away all such safeguards and protection. This Bill would allow multinational corporations (MNCs) to capture Indian industry and services sectors. This group wanted the MRTPA to be amended and the idea of a new law to be discarded.

The other group favoured passage of the Bill as it saw the MRTPA as an anachronism based on old economic theory. This group also felt that India needed to modernize its anti-trust framework to check the onslaught of foreign companies and to keep pace with the changing global economic environment. This group also wanted the public sector companies to be exposed to competition in the larger interest of the consumers. It also felt protectionist policies had stifled growth of the small sector which also ought to be exposed to competition.

Out of 64 clauses, the Committee recommended amendments in 19 clauses and adopted the remaining 45 clauses without any change, indicating that the second group prevailed.

Journey in the Lok Sabha

After receiving the Committee's report, the government moved quickly to have the Bill passed by Parliament. The government had accepted all but three recommendations of the Standing Committee. These three were as follows:

1. The Committee had observed that the CCI would be a judicial body, incapable of suing anyone. The government, unsure of the implications of this status, chose not to accept the position.
2. The Committee had also recommended that the Chairperson of the CCI should be a person from the judiciary. The government disagreed with that view, keeping judiciary as a body eligible but not mandatory for the chairperson to come from.
3. Finally, the government did not want to spell out the composition of the selection committee or the selection procedure of the CCI members, on the argument that the CCI was more like a regulatory body like the Securities and Exchange Board of India (SEBI), the Insurance Regulatory and Development Authority (IRDA), or the Telecom Regulatory Authority of India (TRAI), rather than like the Company Law Board.

On 16 December 2002, the then Minister of Finance and Company Affairs, Jaswant Singh moved a motion requesting the Lok Sabha to pass the Bill which would replace the MRTP *Act* 'because that Act is no longer an effective instrument'. However, the government did not want to have much of a discussion on the Bill. With an intervention asking for swift passage of the Bill and citing the fact that the Standing Committee had already scrutinized the Bill, the Minister for Parliament, Shri Pramod Mahajan proposed quick passage without further debate, a proposal quickly accepted by the principal opposition—the Indian National Congress—indicating that the two parties had already reached an agreement on this proposal before Mahajan put it forward.

Members from different parties made speeches favouring or opposing the Bill, in line with the stand taken by their respective parties. Opposing the law, arguing ostensibly for protection of local industry from globalization, Hooghly (West Bengal) MP Rupchand Pal (Communist Party of India) said the Bill was ill-timed, and accused the government of succumbing to pressure from international organizations like the European Commission, complaining of the lack of clarity about the judicial or corporate nature of the CCI. He proposed the matter be handled with less haste and to wait till 2005 for the WTO to take a stance on it, citing the lack of such universal competition laws even in the USA. He proposed changes in the MRTPA instead.

Other MPs opposing the Bill made similar points, but the government was able to get it passed by the Lok Sabha on the same day, the House putting its seal on the law by a voice vote.

Journey in the Rajya Sabha

The Bill was next moved for consideration and passage in the Rajya Sabha. On 20 December 2002, the then Minister of Finance and Company Affairs, Jaswant Singh moved a motion requesting the House to pass the Bill.

Like in the Lok Sabha, here too, Pranab Mukherjee, Chairman of the Standing Committee that had examined the bill, perhaps expectedly, raised concerns about the three recommendations of the committee that the government had chosen to ignore.

Speaking on the Bill, noted jurist and nominated MP Fali S. Nariman expressed disappointment at such an important Bill 'being discussed on the very last day' of the session, expressed serious concern about the lack of clarity about the judicial versus body corporate nature of the CCI, and highlighted the need for 'dynamic non-retired persons in control of the Commission'.

In his reply, the Finance Minister pointed out the reasons for not giving the body judicial status. He also assured that the government did 'not intend to treat the Competition Commission as a kind of a parking lot where we have retired personnel finding their place'.

The Bill was passed by the Rajya Sabha by a voice vote. It received Presidential assent in January 2003. The CCI was established vide notification dated 14 October 2003 and the first member, former Secretary, Ministry of Company Affairs, Vinod K. Dhall, assumed office three days later.

An era had come to a close. The iconic MRTPA was now replaced with the Competition Act.

The Immediate Challenge

The journey, however, was far from complete. Even before the sole commissioner had been appointed, the new law faced a challenge in the Madras High Court and then, in October, in the Supreme Court. In the Supreme Court hearing on 31 October 2003, the government assured the Court that the Commission would not carry out any judicial functions. Furthermore, it also promised to hold in abeyance the Selection Rule till the legal matter was settled. This effectively hamstrung the operation of the Commission till these matters were settled and the only way of that happening now appeared to be an amendment in the Act.

The controversy over the Competition Act underlines the often stressful relationship between the executive and judiciary in the country. The judiciary frequently sees executive appointments in quasi-judicial bodies as undermining its authority and is rarely tolerant of such turf invasion.

What the government had done was certainly open to such an interpretation. The selection committee created comprised the Minister of Commerce and Industry as Chairman, a reputed lawyer, and a distinguished retired civil servant. Thus, the judiciary was completely excluded from appointment in an authority that was clearly quasi-judicial in nature. The judiciary has rarely taken kindly to such omission by the executive, so the resulting furore was not that surprising at all. Further, the selection committee, armed with selection rules framed by the Ministry of Company Affairs, went ahead and appointed two serving secretaries as members of the com- mission—the Commerce Secretary and the Secretary of Company Affairs. In this, the government was fulfilling the promise the then Finance Minister, Jaswant Singh, had made to Parliament of not fill- ing the Commission with retired bureaucrats, but only technically so. The two members appointed were about to retire in a few months. The Chief Justice of India was so infuriated with the situation that he went on record saying that if the doctrine of lapse applied in India as in the US, the law would have been struck down *in limine*.[4] He observed that this way one day the executive will start appointing judges.

Soon after October 2003, the nation was gripped in the tumult of a general election and a new government came to office. The new cabinet, after an examination of the issues by a Group of Ministers, discussed the issue in its meeting of 29 September 2004 and decided to introduce changes to the Competition Act and the Selection Rules. The selection committee size was reduced from ten to six, and more importantly, it was now to be headed by the Chief Justice of India or his nominee. Thus, the primacy of the judiciary in the selection process was acceded to.

Another important modification was that the CCI would now be supplemented with an Appellate Tribunal to hear appeals against orders of the CCI, separating the expert body functions of the CCI from its adjudicatory functions. The government assured the Supreme Court that suitable legislative action would be taken. The Supreme Court closed the writ petition, leaving open all questions till after the amendment was made.

Accordingly, the Competition (Amendment) Bill, 2006 was intro- duced in Parliament on 9 March 2006 and referred to the Standing Committee on Finance on 17 April. The Standing Committee, now headed by BJP's Major General Khanduri, submitted its report to Parliament on 12 December 2006.

The Standing Committee made 18 observations. One of the major changes it proposed, which the government accepted, was making the advance notification to the Commission about potential combinations (mergers and acquisitions) mandatory from voluntary.

A fine for non-compliance was fixed at 1 per cent of the higher of turnover or assets of the combined entity. The power of the CCI to review effects on competition post-merger would continue as well.

Interestingly, the Standing Committee recommended that the Selection Committee be headed by an expert of proven track record instead of the Chief Justice of India or his nominee, as proposed in the Amendment Bill. It was a reversal of the position of the government in the critical matter and would run almost contrary to the government's submission to the Supreme Court. Naturally, the government could not accept this recommendation. However, it did accept the committee's recommendation that the selection committee be broadened by including two more experts of repute in addition to the members proposed in the Bill—the Secretary, Ministry of Corporate Affairs, and Secretary, Ministry of Law and Justice.

After these changes, the Competition (Amendment) Bill, 2006 pending in Lok Sabha was replaced with the revised Competition (Amendment) Bill, 2007, which finally became the Competition Act, 2007. The Competition Commission of India was fully constituted in 2009.

Finally, more than a decade after the first voices were raised to replace the ineffective and restrictive MRTPA with a modern Competition Act, did India get a functioning Competition Act and its associated Commission. In the next several years, the Commission has acted in several cases, the most notable ones being its action against the cement cartel DLF, and the BCCI.

Beyond the Law: Steps towards a National Competition Policy

The journey towards a more competitive India, however, was not yet complete. There was a stated need for a Competition Policy in addition to the Competition Law. The 11th Five-Year Plan made the case forcefully: 'To strengthen the forces of competition in the market, both competition law and competition policy are required. The two complement each other'.[5]

The draft Competition Policy document makes the relationship between the two even clearer:

Competition Policy means government measures, policies, statutes, and regulations including a competition law, aimed at promoting competitive market structure and behavior of entities in an economy. Competition Law is a sub-set of the Competition Policy. The Raghavan Committee had observed that 'Competition law must emerge out of a national competition policy, which must be evolved to serve the basic goals of economic reforms by building a competitive market economy.[6]

Towards this end, the Planning Commission established a Working Group on Competition Policy during the process of drafting the 11th Five-Year Plan, headed by former Member CCI, Vinod Dhall. The Working Group made a number of recommendations on contours of a National Competition Policy and coordination between the CCI and sectoral regulators. Meanwhile, the Planning Commission had set up a Task Force on National Competition Policy (NCP) under the chairmanship of Pradeep Mehta of CUTS. A draft NCP was created in 2011 but it is yet to be accepted by the government. A few of the key features of the draft NCP are shown in Box 3.1.

Box 3.1   A Few Key Features of the Draft National Competition Policy

Objectives of National Competition Policy

The National Competition Policy aims to promote economic democracy, achievement of highest sustainable levels of economic growth, entrepreneurship, employment, higher standards of living, and protect economic rights for just, equitable, inclusive, and sustainable economic and social development, and supports good governance by restricting rent-seeking practices.

In this background, the National Competition Policy will endeavour to:

a)   preserve the competition process, to protect competition, and to encourage competition in the domestic market so as to optimize efficiency and maximise consumer welfare;

b)   promote, build, and sustain a strong competition culture within the country through creating awareness, imparting training and consequently capacity building of stakeholders including public officials,

(Cont'd)

Box 3.1   *(Cont'd)*

business, trade associations, consumers associations, civil society etc.;

c) achieve harmonization in policies, laws and procedures of the central government, state government, and sub-state authorities in so far as the competition dimensions are concerned with focus on greater reliance on well-functioning markets;

d) ensure competition in regulated sectors and to ensure institutional mechanism for synergized relationship between and among the sectoral regulators and/or the CCI and prevent jurisdictional grid locks;

e) strive for single national market as fragmented markets are impediments to competition; and

f) ensure that consumers enjoy greater benefits in terms of wider choices and better quality of goods and services at competitive prices.

Competition Policy Principles

Taking into account the needs of and priorities for promoting a healthy competition culture, the principles of the National Competition Policy are:

(a) **Effective prevention of anticompetitive conduct:** The Competition Act, 2002 prohibits anti-competitive agreements and combinations which have or are likely to have appreciable adverse effect on competition. It also seeks to prohibit abuse of dominant position by an enterprise. There should be effective control of anticompetitive conduct which causes or is likely to cause appreciable adverse effect on competition in the markets within India. The Act establishes the CCI as the sole national body to enforce the provisions of the Act, as also its obligations under Section 49(3) for competition advocacy. It is envisaged that the implementation of NCP will strengthen competition culture in the market and complement the endeavours of CCI.

(b) **Fair market process:** Market regulation procedures should be rule-bound, transparent, fair, and non-discriminatory. Public interest tests are to be used to assess the desirability and proportionality of policies and regulations, and these would be subject to regular independent review.

(Cont'd)

Box 3.1   *(Cont'd)*

(c) **Institutional separation between policy making, operations, and regulation:** i.e. operations in and regulation of a sector should be independent of the government branch which deals with policy formulation in the sector and is accountable to the Legislature.

(d) **'Competitive neutrality',** such as adoption of policies which establish a 'level playing field' where government businesses compete with private sector and vice versa.

(e) **Fair pricing and inclusionary behaviour,** particularly of public utilities, which could be imbued with monopolistic characteristics and a large part of the consumers, could be excluded.

(f) **Third party access to 'essential facilities',** i.e. requiring dominant infrastructure owners to grant to third parties access (e.g., electricity, communications, gas pipe lines, railway tracks, ports etc) to their infrastructure on agreed terms and conditions and at regulated prices, aligned with competition principles.

(g) **Public Policies and programmes** to work towards promotion of competition in the market place.

(h) **National, regional, and international cooperation** in the field of competition policy enforcement and advocacy.

(i) **Where a separate regulatory arrangement** is set up in different sectors, the functioning of the concerned sectoral regulator should be consistent with the principles of competition as far as possible. Also there should be an appropriate coordination mechanism between CCI and sectoral regulators to avoid overlap in interpretation of competition related concerns.

Source: Draft National Competition Policy 2011.

Proposed Amendments to the Competition Act

In June 2011, the government established an expert committee to examine the working of the Act so far and suggest amendments. The Competition (Amendment) Bill, 2012 was tabled in the Lok Sabha on 10 December 2012 to effect changes recommended by the Committee. With the dissolution of the 15th Lok Sabha in May 2014, this Bill lapsed and will have to be reintroduced in Parliament. Major changes proposed by the Bill included:[7]

- **Applicability of the Act:** The Bill proposed to extend exemptions from the Competition Act to cover all types of IPRs, broadening the protection afforded by the original Act that covered only the Copyright Act, Patent Act, and the Designs Act.
- **Regulation of Combinations:** The Bill proposed that the threshold for determining if two enterprises are a 'group' be raised from the present 26 per cent or more voting rights to 50 per cent or more. The Bill also empowered the Government of India to specify different value of assets and turnover for any class of enterprises to further examine and regulate combinations. The time period by which the CCI has to make a ruling on a combination was proposed to be cut from 210 to 180 days of it being notified of the combination.
- **Reference to Statutory Authority:** The Bill made it mandatory for any decision of a statutory authority that could contravene any provision of the Competition Act to be referred to the CCI. It also made it mandatory for any CCI decision contravening provisions of any other act to be referred to the relevant statutory authority.
- **Inquiry and Penalties:** In case of any investigation by the Director General and imposition of a penalty on any party, the Bill makes it mandatory for that party to be heard before the CCI imposes any penalty.

The long and arduous journey towards greater competition in the country has involved several significant strides since the days of the MRTPA. However, the issue has neither been settled nor has the activism for it abated. The issue remains as current and alive today as it was almost two decades ago.

Concluding Observations

The journey of the Competition Act is a story of law-making through the incremental model where the push came mainly from the bureaucracy as India was poised on the threshold of liberalization in the early 1990s. A small group of civil society experts and activists were involved in the process but it certainly did not invoke any mass involvement.

In terms of the proposed legislative strategy framework, the methods employed for influencing the agenda were collaborative and the relation between the elected and non-elected stakeholders was cooperative, but the time taken to enact the law falls in the medium category, possibly because this law marked a very significant change in policy direction and involved a long process of deliberations within the policy circles.

Notes

1. Para 1.5.1 of the 'Report of the Expert Group', Ministry of Commerce, Government of India.
2. *Haridas Exports* v. *All India Float Glass Mfrs. Association and Others*, Supreme Court, 2002.
3. Information from the Introduction to the Report of the Standing Committee.
4. In US law, *in limine* is a motion used to request that the judge rule that certain testimony be excluded before a trial begins.
5. 'Consumer Protection and Competition Policy', Chapter 11 in the Eleventh Five Year Plan (2007–12).
6. 'Draft National Competition Policy 2011', Ministry of Corporate Affairs, Government of India.
7. PRS Legislative Research Bill Summary: The Competition (Amendment) Bill, 2012, available at http://www.prsindia.org/uploads/media/Competition%20(A)%20Bill,%202012/Bill%20Summary-%20Competition%20Amendment.pdf (last accessed on 10 December 2014).

4

Leveraging Grass-roots Activism

The Right to Information Act, 2005

The right to freedom of expression is of utmost importance as it is the foundation of the Right to Information [Act].
    — Aruna Roy, RTI pioneer and activist (Upadhyay 2015)

Democracy dies behind closed doors.
        —Judge Damon Keith, *Detroit Free Press* v *Ashcroft*,
                            303 F.3d 681 (26 August 2002)

The Context

An information revolution is sweeping India, a *New York Times* article stated somewhat dramatically in 2010 (Polgreen 2010). Improbable as it may sound, ever since India enacted the Right to Information (RTI) Act in 2005, anecdotal reports of the poor using the act to get the notoriously unresponsive public authorities to improve delivery of public services had been trickling in. A 2010 experiment on access to ration cards among Delhi's slum dwellers conducted by doctoral students of Yale University found that the RTI Act could be used effectively by some of India's most underprivileged citizens—Muslim slum dwellers of Delhi with an income of about USD 1.50 per day—to access public services such as ration cards. Another case in point was the story of Chanchala Devi of Jharkhand who wanted to build a house with the help of a government programme that gave a grant to the poor for this purpose. Although she was an ideal candidate given her economic situation, all her attempts to get the grant proved futile till she filed an RTI with the help of a local activist to find out who had gotten the grants while she waited, and why. Within days, she was given approval for the grant money (Polgreen 2010).

Although activists claimed, not without reason, that the law had not had a major effect on corruption, there were stories of scams coming to light through the act. An RTI application filed by K.S. Sagaria, a resident of Kushmal village in rural Odisha, in 2010 inquiring about the number of ponds constructed in his village under the government's national wage employment scheme revealed that the ponds had never been constructed even though money had been allocated and spent. Following complaints from villagers, the local administration was forced to take action and suspend the officials involved in the pond scam (Surie 2011). Even some of the big-ticket scams of the UPA–II regime were exposed partly through the means of RTIs, such as the 2G scam and the Adarsh Housing scam (Chandrasekhar 2014; NDTV 2011a).

India enacted the Right to Information Act in 2005 after decades of activism by grass-roots groups and civil society organizations, not only in India but all over the world. Since then, this act has proved to be a potent tool in the hands of social activists as well as ordinary citizens to tackle corruption and bring greater transparency and accountability in the government. While the act is certainly not a silver bullet for India's deep-rooted problems of government apathy and corruption, it does bring a ray of hope to the most neglected and marginalized of the population. A brief description of the act is provided in Box 4.1.

Box 4.1   Features of the RTI Act

- Every citizen of India has the right to seek information from any public authority.
- 'Public authority' includes all central and state governments; any authority, body, or institution which has been set up under the Constitution of India, by a central or state law or by any notification made by the central or state government; bodies which are owned, controlled, or substantially financed directly or indirectly

Box 4.1   *(Cont'd)*

by government funds; and NGOs which are substantially financed directly or indirectly by government funds.

- 'Information' is defined to include any material in any form, including records, memos, emails, opinions, advices, press releases, circulars, orders, logbooks, contracts, reports held in any electronic form, and information relating to any private body which can be accessed by a public authority under any other law for the time being in force.

Process of Accessing Information

- Each 'public authority' has to appoint Public Information Officers (PIOs) and First Appellate Authority (FAA), who is an officer senior in rank to the PIO.
- A request for 'information'—popularly known as an RTI application or just 'RTI'—may be filed with the PIO of a public authority.
- The PIO has to send a reply to the RTI applicant within 30 days. The applicant has to pay fees along with the application as well as for photocopying of documents as per the relevant rules.
- Information which is exempt under Section 8(1) of the Act need not be provided by the PIO.

Exemptions

- Certain information is exempted from disclosure under the act. These include information which may affect the sovereignty and integrity of the country and its security, strategic, scientific, or economic interests; information which has been expressly forbidden by a court; information that may cause breach of privilege in Parliament or state legislature; trade secrets or intellectual property whose disclosure would harm the competitive position of a third party (except in larger public interest); confidential information from foreign governments; and personal information whose disclosure has no relationship with public interest or activity.

Appellate Mechanism

- If the applicant does not receive the information within 30 days or the information received is deficient in any way, he may file an appeal

(Cont'd)

Box 4.1   *(Cont'd)*

with the First Appellate Authority (FAA) within 30 days of receiving the reply or within 60 days of filing the RTI application.

- The FAA has to issue an order in the matter within 30 days or upto 45 days citing reasons for the delay.
- If the RTI applicant is aggrieved by the order of the FAA or has not received an order within the stipulated time frame, a second appeal may be filed with the Central or State Information Commission. This appeal has to be filed within 90 days from the date of the FAA's order or from the date on which the order should have been issued.

Suo moto Disclosures

- The public authorities are required to make certain *suo moto* disclosures such as basic information about the authority (functions, duties, powers, directory, pay scale of employees), the budgetary allocation, recipients of concessions, permits and authorizations, decision-making process in the organization.

Penalty

- If the CIC finds that a PIO or a deemed PIO has, without a reasonable ground, done any of the following, it can penalize that person: refused to receive an RTI application; not furnished information within the time limit stipulated in the act; malafide refusal to the request for information; knowingly gave incorrect, incomplete, or misleading information; destroyed information which had been sought or obstructed in any manner in furnishing the information. However, the PIO has to be given a reasonable opportunity to be heard before a penalty is imposed.
- The penalty is fixed at Rs 250 per day till the application is received or the information is furnished to the applicant. This amount is subject to a maximum limit of Rs 25,000 and is paid by the person responsible individually, and not by the public authority. The burden of proof has been placed on the PIO to prove that he had acted reasonably and diligently.

Source: RTI Act, 2005.

The objective of this case study is to examine the role of civil society in promoting and securing access to information legislation and to understand the interaction between civil society and public officials, which is an important dynamic in the passage of any legislation.

The chapter has three broad sections. The first section traces the genesis and evolution of the right to information movement in India, within the global and regional context, through an analysis of the key players who spearheaded and influenced the movement, the strategies adopted for advocacy and the resultant successes and failures. The second section focuses on the interaction with public officials and the legislative history of the act. The concluding section provides an analysis of the role of civil society in influencing the passage of a landmark legislation.

Background: Worldwide Move towards Greater Transparency

Sweden was the first country to pass a right to information law in 1776, probably motivated by the Parliament's interest in access to information held by the king. Finland enacted its law in 1951, followed by the US in 1966, and Norway in 1970. The major impetus to the RTI came when the US passed a tough Freedom of Information law in 1976 after the Watergate scandal. It prompted other western democracies to frame their own laws: France and Netherlands in 1978, Australia and New Zealand in 1982, Canada in 1983, Columbia and Denmark in 1985, Greece in 1986, Austria in 1987, and Italy in 1990. By 1990, 14 countries had enacted RTI laws.

Asian countries such as Japan, South Korea, China, India, Indonesia, Bangladesh, and Pakistan adopted access to information laws between the 1990s and 2000s. In Japan, consumer and citizen groups first made the demand for an information disclosure law in the 1960s and won it after a long effort in April 2001. South Korea's law went into effect in 1998, Pakistan's in 2002. China adopted nationwide regulations (applicable to all levels of government) in 2007.[1] Australia and New Zealand passed the right to information laws in the early 1980s. Latin American countries such as Brazil, Chile, Columbia, Mexico, and El Salvador have adopted laws to allow citizens to obtain information from their governments. After a decade-long civil society campaign, 11 African countries have passed laws to allow access to information.[2]

Beginning with Hungary and Ukraine, between 1992 and 2006, 25 countries in Central and Eastern Europe and the former Soviet Union had passed Freedom of Information (FOI) laws. By September 2013, the number had reached 95. Most of these countries now had national-level right to information regulations in force—including the population giants China and India, many Latin American, African and Middle Eastern countries.[3] Since 2002, 28 September is marked as the International Right to Know Day by Freedom of Information activists.

The most basic feature for all FOI laws is the ability for individuals to ask for materials held by public authorities and other government bodies. The right to request information is generally open to citizens, permanent residents, and corporations in the country without a need to show a legal interest, with most countries now allowing anyone around the world, some even anonymous inquirers, to ask for information.

Generally, the acts apply to nearly all government bodies, including local and regional bodies where applicable. Some countries do exempt courts, legislatures, and the security and intelligence services from the purview of the law. Increasingly, countries are including non-government bodies that receive public money to do public projects under the law.

FOI laws generally allow exemptions on the ground of national security and international relations, personal privacy, commercial confidentiality, law enforcement and public order, information received in confidence, and internal discussions. Mechanisms for appeals include reviews by courts and administrative bodies. Enforcement or oversight of the law is undertaken by independent bodies but their effectiveness may vary from one country to another. Most FOI laws require government agencies to routinely release certain categories of information such as the organization structure, its primary functions, internal rules, decisions, a listing of its top employees, annual reports, and other information.

India's Journey towards Right to Information

India's ability to balance a robust, participatory democracy with a diversity of ethnicities—however imperfect—makes it the envy of the democratic world. However, it lags behind many developing economies on major socio-economic indicators—about 30 per cent of its population remains below the poverty line, about half of its children are malnourished and 37 per cent of its adults are illiterate. These are consequences of failures of public policies that were meant to eradicate poverty, address food shortage, water scarcity, universal healthcare and education, employment, and security.

This begs the question. Why are government programmes and policies woefully inadequate in addressing these problems in spite of India's democratic credentials and a steadily growing economy? Experts have identified a variety of reasons, key among those include lack of transparency in policymaking, an over-reliance on bureaucrats not only for implementing the policies but also for basic information about the sector, and very little accountability for outcomes. One of the reasons citizens are unable to hold public officials accountable is the information asymmetry between citizens and public officials.

India's journey towards a robust right-to-information regime shows that the success of civil society activism rests partly on the responsiveness of the administration and partly on the group's ability to mobilize citizens towards their cause. The movement can be broadly classified into three phases. In the first phase, from 1975 to 1996, there were sporadic demands for information from various sections of the society, culminating in a more focused demand for access to information from environmental movements in the mid 1980s, and from grass-roots movements in rural Rajasthan in the early 1990s.

Judicial Activism Paves the Way to RTI: 1975–96

The Constitution of India did not specifically mention the right to information, but the Supreme Court of India ruled in 1975 that the right to information was a fundamental right necessary for democratic functioning. Specifically, the Supreme Court recognized the right to information as an integral part of the right to freedom of speech and expression guaranteed by the Constitution (Article 19) and a necessary part of the right to life (Article 21).[4]

Despite this formal acknowledgement as a fundamental right as early as 1975, it took over 20 years for the idea of right to information to gain acceptance among the political and bureaucratic elite. The law took a few more years to be enacted.

The Indian state retained colonial era laws which made the governance system opaque. The major Acts and Rules which required certain amount of exclusion and confidentiality of information included the following: Official Secrets Act; Evidence Act, 1872; Customs Act; Post-Office Act; Commission of Inquiry Act; Reserve Bank of India Act; Conduct of Civil Servant Rules; Industrial Disputes Act; Atomic Energy Act; Medical Termination of Pregnancy Act.[5] That is not to say that there were no transparency provisions in law. Although they were violated with impunity, there were specific laws that did mandate transparency. For instance, Section 76 of the Evidence Act, 1872 required public officials to provide copies of public documents to anyone who had a right to inspect them. The Factories Act, 1948, provided for compulsory disclosure of information to factory workers 'regarding dangers including health hazards and the measures to overcome such hazards,' arising from their exposure to dangerous materials.

Thus, until the 1980s, openness in government was neither consciously promoted as a culture nor reflected in major legal changes. The impetus for change came in 1984 after the leak of the deadly gas from the Union Carbide factory in Bhopal leading to the enactment of the Environment Protection Act in 1986, which mandated public hearings and compulsory disclosures. The Bhopal gas leak suddenly made the public in India aware of how little they knew about the chemical and nuclear industry. There was, consequently, a spate of cases filed by various individuals in exercise of their right to litigate in the public interest.

In 1984, lawyer and environment campaigner, M.C. Mehta, filed one such case in the Supreme Court of India. His 'public interest' case asked the court to close down the Sriram Food and Fertilizer Industry, located in the heart of Delhi, for using and storing hazardous chemicals without maintaining the required safety measures. Unfortunately, before the Supreme Court could hear the case, an oelum gas leak occurred in the factory in 1985 causing widespread panic among residents of Delhi suffering from resulting throat, eye, and skin irritation. Consequently, the case was taken up for hearing on a priority basis. During the hearing, it emerged that although the

Delhi government had commissioned a study of the safety aspects of this industry and the findings had been submitted sometime back, they were not made public and not even shared with the industry which was the subject of the study. This and other such absurdities made the then Chief Justice of India, who was heading the bench, remark in open court that he wished someone would take up the issue of the right to information. Responding to these remarks, Kalpavriksh, one of the NGOs involved in the case, filed an intervention as a part of the ongoing case asking the court to lay down the right to information as a fundamental right. Essentially, the petition argued that the right to life implied the right to know if one's life was threatened specifically due to possible leaks of toxic chemicals or other hazardous substances. Though the Supreme Court did not pass any final orders on this petition, its contents were mentioned many times during the hearing and the court made it clear from time to time that they were not happy with the aura of secrecy that surrounded the government and industry (Florini 2007).

In 1986, the Bombay Environmental Action Group (BEAG) filed a case in the High Court of Bombay seeking specific information from the Poona Cantonment Board since they felt that some of the buildings in Poona Cantonment violated the building bylaws. While the writ petition took time to be heard which resulted in some of the buildings getting constructed, they won a larger battle in the High Court.

The Supreme Court subsequently widened this High Court judgment considerably, by entitling, with restrictions, 'any person residing within the area of a local authority or any social action group or interest group or pressure group… to take inspection of any sanction granted, or plan approved, by such local authority in construction of buildings along with the related papers and documents'.[6]

Although these progressive court orders[7] did not culminate into a movement for the RTI in the country, it did start building awareness about the need for such a law.

Government Efforts towards Transparency (1970s–1990s)

There were sporadic objections to the Official Secrets Act since 1948. For instance, in 1948 two members of the Press Laws Enquiry

Committee[8] dissented and opined that 'the application of the Act must be confined, as the recent Geneva Conference on Freedom of Information has recommended, only to matters which must remain secret in the interests of national security' (Noorani 1997).

Eighteen years after the First Press Commission's recommendation, the Second Press Commission, in 1982, opined that 'one of the chief obstacles to the free flow of legitimate information to the people is the existence of certain provisions in the Official Secrets Act, 1923'. In 1990, the Press Council of India, under Justice R.S. Sarkaria, urged the government to repeal the Act of 1923 and the enactment of a Freedom of Information Act making 'privacy' a ground for exemption (Guhan and Paul 1997).

After a spate of judicial orders requiring governments to be more transparent, for the first time in 1989, RTI was made part of the election manifesto of various political parties that represented a coalition against the Congress party. After coming to power, the then Prime Minister V.P. Singh, leading the National Front government, declared his intention of making the RTI a fundamental right. On 18 April 1990 at the 20th Conference of Ministers of Information and Cinematography, he declared:

> An open system of governance is an essential pre-requisite for the fullest flowering of democracy....The veil of secrecy was lowered many a time not in the interest of national security, but to shield the guilty, vested interests or gross errors of judgements. Therefore, the National Front Government has decided to make the Right to Information a Fundamental Right. (Sharma 2014)

In March 1990, a workshop on Freedom of Information and Official Secrecy was organized by the Centre for Policy Research in New Delhi at the request of the Ministry of Home Affairs (MHA). The workshop was attended by over 40 participants representing the academia, political parties, NGOs, armed forces, and senior government officials. The workshop, though favourable towards greater transparency, also cautioned against too much haste. It was followed by the constitution of an inter-ministerial task force by the MHA to develop a draft bill and to conduct a survey of the 'foreign experience'. The Task Force only included Joint-Secretary-level officials and its members visited a few countries. But no legislation followed due to the the tremendous resistance from the bureaucracy and the early collapse of the V.P. Singh-led coalition government (Sharma 2014: 112–13).[9]

After this attempt, there was a lull in the government on the subject of enacting an RTI law. The coalition government led by P.V. Narasimha Rao between 1991 and 1996 did not make this issue a priority although the Congress party manifesto for 1991 promised to make RTI a law (Sharma 2014).

However, during this period there was some activity on the civil society front. The Consumer Education Research Council (CERC) in 1993 drafted and circulated possibly India's first access to information draft law.[10] By far the most detailed of all the proposals, this draft, in line with international standards, gave the right to information to anyone, except 'alien enemies', irrespective of citizenship. It required public agencies to maintain their records in good order, to provide a directory of all records under their control, to promote the computerization of records in interconnected networks, and to publish all laws, regulations, guidelines, circulars related to or issued by government departments, and any information concerning welfare schemes. Requesters were liable only for the cost of supplying copies of records, with fees being waived for journalists, newspaper organizations, and public interest groups. Among other things, the CERC draft provided for an appeal against refusals to disclose information, first to a network of independent information commissioners at the national, state, and district levels, and then to an Information Tribunal. The draft was introduced as a private member's bill in 1996 in Parliament, but was never taken up for discussion.[11]

The next push came from a surprising direction. In October 1995, a workshop on the RTI was held at the Lal Bahadur Shastri National Academy of Administration (LBSNAA) in Mussourie under the aegis of N.C. Saxena (the then director of LBSNAA) and Harsh Mander. However, the participants were not confined to bureaucrats and included members of civil society organizations such as Aruna Roy, Nikhil Dey, and Kavita Srivastava (from Mazdoor Kisan Shakti Sangathan—MKSS).

Some months later, in June 1996, a new government with H.D. Deve Gowda leading the United Front coalition was formed. Rising pressure from activists against corruption led the government to initiate a National Debate on Effective and Responsive Administration and formulate specific measures for the introduction of greater transparency in the functioning of government and public bodies, regarding both their own employees, and interaction with members of the public.

The next attempt at drafting an RTI bill was undertaken by the Press Council of India who drew up a draft legislation in 1996. The drafting committee included Justice P.B. Sawant (Chairman of the Press Council), Prashant Bhushan, and Shekhar Singh. This draft was derived from an earlier one which had been prepared at the workshop convened in LBSNAA in October 1995. The draft affirmed the right of every citizen to information from any public body. Significantly, the term 'public body' included not only the State, as defined in the Constitution, but also all privately-owned undertakings, non-statutory authorities, companies, and other non-State bodies whose activities affect the public interest.[12] The National Institute of Rural Development (NIRD), Hyderabad, also prepared a bill in 1997. These two bills were merged and renamed the 'The Press Council-NIRD Freedom of Information Bill, 1997' at a workshop.[13]

On 2 January 1997, the government constituted a Working Group on 'Right to Information and Transparency' under the chairmanship of H.D. Shourie, Chairman, Common Cause, New Delhi (Shourie Committee).[14] It is, however, interesting to note that the final terms of reference of the Working Group did not mention the examination of any existing draft bill nor did it require the group to propose a draft legislation (Sharma 2014). The Committee submitted its report on 21 May 1997 after consulting Justice Sawant, and other officials and activists. It recommended that a law be enacted to ensure that there is transparency in the functioning of the government and citizens have the right to get information about any department of the government. This report was broadly endorsed by the Committee of Secretaries.

There seemed to be a broad consensus within the government about the need for an FOI bill. Both the Approach Paper to the Ninth Five Year Plan (1997–2002) and the 38th Report on Demands for Grants of the Ministry of Personnel, Public Grievances and Pensions strongly recommended the enactment of a full-fledged Right to

Information Act. An Action Plan was chalked up on 24 May 1997, which was discussed in the Conference of Chief Ministers convened by I.K. Gujral, who had taken over as the PM from Deve Gowda in April. The government stated that it would take immediate steps, in consultation with state governments, to examine the Shourie Committee Report. Prime Minister Gujral, in his Independence Day speech, promised that a Freedom of Information Bill would be introduced in the winter session of Parliament. Although the government's draft bill was still being vetted, George Fernandes introduced a Private Member's Bill[15] on the subject in September 1997.

The government's draft FOI Bill, after final touches from the Legislative Department, went to the Cabinet. The Cabinet, however, decided to refer the Bill to a Group of Ministers (GoM)[16] in October 1997.[17] The final draft approved by the GoM went to the Law Ministry in February 1998 and a Cabinet Note was sent to the Prime Minister's Office in April 1998 (Sharma 2014).

Meanwhile, political turmoil engulfed the United Front government in the coming months after the Congress withdrew support in November 1997 and President K.R. Narayanan asked Gujral to stay on as caretaker PM till fresh elections could be held in the first half of 1998. The new government of the Bharatiya Janata Party (BJP)-led National Democratic Alliance (NDA) came to power in March 1998 under the leadership of A.B. Vajpayee. On 27 April 1998, a new GoM[18] was constituted to examine the legislative proposal anew (Sharma 2014).

An interesting development occurred in October 1998 that demonstrated the government's reluctance to lift the veil of secrecy on information. Ram Jethmalani, the then Minister of Urban Development, passed an administrative order stating that any citizen would be entitled to inspect and take photocopies of any file in his ministry. Though the government had ostensibly committed itself to enacting an RTI law when this order was passed, the Cabinet Secretary, on the instructions of the Prime Minister, restrained Jethmalani from giving effect to his order (Sharma 2014).

This prompted a writ petition in the Supreme Court from the Centre for Public Interest Litigation and Common Cause seeking effectively three reliefs: (a) that the Cabinet Secretary's restraint on Jethmalani's order be declared unconstitutional and violative of the citizens' right to information; (b) that Section 5 of the Official Secrets Act, which makes it an offence for a public servant to disclose any information that has come to his knowledge in his official capacity, be declared unconstitutional; (c) that the Government of India be directed to frame and issue suitable administrative instructions on the lines of the Press Council's draft Bill, to effectuate the citizens' right to information, pending suitable legislation on the subject. The government took repeated adjournments in response to this petition, saying that it was bringing a right to information legislation.[19]

This government also fell on 17 April 1999 after AIADMK withdrew support with Vajpayee staying on as caretaker PM till fresh elections could be held. The GoM also had to be dissolved since two members (M. Thambi Durai and K.R. Janarthanan) who belonged to the AIADMK resigned from the government. On 19 July 1999, a new GoM[20] had to be constituted for the third time to scrutinize the Bill. The NDA government returned to power in October 1999 with Vajpayee once again at the helm. A new GoM was formed with the previous members adding only Arun Jaitley, Minister of Information and Broadcasting, to the mix. The GoM could finally submit its report in February 2000 and the Bill was approved by the Cabinet in May 2000 (Sharma 2014).

The Legislative Journey: First Attempt at a Law on Freedom of Information

The NDA government, under Vajpayee, introduced the FOI Bill in Parliament in July 2000. This Bill was a watered-down version of the Shourie Committee Report's Bill. With L.K. Advani at the helm of the Home Ministry, there was little done in the way of publicizing the bill, before it was referred to a Parliamentary Standing Committee on Home Affairs, headed by Pranab Mukherjee. The Committee invited feedback from a select group of people and published its report in July 2001. Some of those who deposed before the Committee included the representatives of MKSS; Maja Daruwala, Director, Commonwealth Human Rights Initiative (CHRI); Madhav Godbole, former Union Home Secretary; A.G. Noorani, Senior Advocate; Justice P.B. Sawant, Chairman, Press Council of India; B.G. Deshmukh; Manubhai Shah, Managing Trustee, Consumer

Education and Research Society (CERS); and B.G. Deshmukh, former Cabinet Secretary (gave written suggestions).[21] Despite the various suggestions made to the committee, the report did not suggest anything more than cosmetic changes to the bill.[22]

Box 4.2   Key Suggestions Made by Various Groups to the Standing Committee

The bill should be rechristened as 'Right to Information Bill' instead of 'Freedom of Information Bill' and its applicability should not be restricted only to citizens.

The bill should apply to all including organizations, parties, trusts, unions, societies, private or non-governmental, in addition to governmental bodies and agencies. It must provide for compulsory and mandatory disclosure of information that relates to health, safety, environment, and human rights.

The ultimate responsibility to ensure adherence to the provisions of the bill should be vested with the head of each public authority.

Since the intent of the bill is to put in place an effective procedure for enforcing the right to information, the procedural issues must be detailed and clearly stated.

The bill should clearly state that where information sought is regarding the life and liberty of a person, the same should be provided within 24 to 48 hours.

The bill should clearly provide that all information that cannot be denied to the Members of Parliament/Legislatures should not be denied to the public.

The working of the Government from the Cabinet Committee to the Secretaries Committee should not be exempt under the act.

The bill should provide for an independent appeals mechanism and provide for protection to 'whistleblowers'.

Section 16(1) and the Schedule should be reworded to narrow down the blanket exclusion given to entire organizations. Excluding certain organizations completely from the purview of this legislation defeats the purpose of the law. There is no rationale for exempting the administrative wings of these organizations from disclosing relevant information.

Local bodies at grass-roots level should be included and defined as competent authorities to implement the Act.

Source: 78th Report of the Standing Committee on Home Affairs, July 2001.

However, in November 2002, when no legislation was forthcoming, the Supreme Court directed that if the legislation was not passed before the next date of hearing (in January 2003) the court would consider the matter on merit and pass orders.[23] The passage of the Freedom of Information Bill by Parliament in December 2002 (it received Presidential Assent in January 2003) was perhaps in response to the prodding by the Supreme Court. However, as the act was never notified, it did not come into force.[24]

Initiatives on RTI by Some States

Pressure from activists fighting corruption led many states in India to enact RTI laws since 1997.[25] These included Goa (1997), Tamil Nadu (1997), Rajasthan (2000), Maharashtra (2000), Karnataka (2000), Delhi (2001), Assam (2002), Madhya Pradesh (2003), and Jammu and Kashmir (2009). While these laws were hardly ideal in content as well as quality of implementation, they did come through popular mobilization where activists demanded a law, drafted model laws, and put pressure on the state governments to enact them. For instance, a very weak state RTI Act in Maharashtra was repealed in favour of stronger act because of such mobilization and activism (Sabharwal and Berman 2013).

MKSS Spearheads Grass-roots Movement for RTI:[26] (1990–2000)

Sporadic civil society activism for RTI through CERC, Press Council of India, and other organizations took place through the 1990s. Various workshops, organized by Centre for Policy Research (CPR), NIRD, and LBSNAA, were attended by many activists, but the idea of RTI had not percolated to the public. Mazdoor Kisan Shakti Sangathan (MKSS), officially launched on 1 May 1990 in Rajasthan, as a solidarity group of farmers and rural workers, was the first attempt at a grass-roots movement for RTI. The seeds of the organization were sown in 1987 when the three founding activists of MKSS chose Devdungri, a small and impoverished village in Rajasthan, as their base. The three activists were Aruna Roy who had resigned from the IAS a decade earlier and worked in the development space in

Tilonia; Shekhar Singh who lived in a nearby village and worked in rural communication; and Nikhil Dey who abandoned his study in the US for more meaningful, rural social activism. Government interventions in the area were mainly in the form of famine relief work. The wages paid for the relief work were low and too erratic to provide any real social security cover (Mander and Joshi 1999).

MKSS, which sustained itself exclusively from members' and individuals' contributions, aimed to improve the living conditions of its constituents. To build awareness and get the attention of public officials, it started staging protests, public marches, rallies, sit-ins, and hunger strikes in the villages to demand fair working conditions and minimum wages for daily workers and farmers under the government-sponsored drought relief and rural development work programmes. The local administrators brushed off the demands of workers saying that their work did not appear on the muster rolls (that is, the employment and payment records). MKSS coined the slogan 'Our Money, Our Accounts', and demanded that the local administrators provide the muster rolls recording the tasks performed by each worker and the wages paid to them, as well as documentation accounting for all expenses incurred for the works carried out in the villages.

Slowly, their agitations started getting noticed in the local and even national media. Ultimately, such publicity forced the Rajasthan government authorities to consent to releasing the information requested by the villagers. Seizing this opportunity, MKSS organized a series of *jan sunwai*s (public hearings) in which the records describing the development projects, their timelines, the number of people employed, and payments made were read aloud and the villagers were called to testify whether the information reported in the books was correct. Often, someone would point out incorrect or false information. For instance, a project would be reported as completed but was never actually started, or there would be recorded payments to people who were dead in reality. Through this exercise, corrupt officials were often named and shamed, bringing to light the corruption permeating the public administration.

As media spotlighted the scandals uncovered by the jan sunwais, by the mid 1990s, the MKSS campaign started to focus on the importance of the RTI as a tool to empower poor people in the fight for their rights. On 25 September 1995, more than 2,000 villagers from all over Rajasthan rallied in Beawar (a city in Rajasthan) under the slogan 'the Right to Know, the Right to Live'. They demanded a law that would operationalize their right to information. In October 1995, a first non-official bill on access to information was drafted by the Rajasthan Academy of Administration in collaboration with MKSS and other activists. In 1996, the agitation in Beawar spread over to Jaipur. Over 70 organizations and many eminent citizens extended support and the press was also openly sympathetic. The government finally buckled and issued a press note in May 1996 stating that it would constitute a committee to work out the logistics of the assurance given by the Chief Minister about making available documents relating to local development works (Mander and Joshi 1999). However, it was not until 1998, following many public hearings and mass mobilization, that the Rajasthan government appointed a committee to draft a state right-to-information bill. The final RTI Act was approved in 2000.

Other Civil Society Groups

The RTI movement had the support and active participation of many prominent voices from civil society (in addition to MKSS). These included consumer protection groups, such as the CERC, Ahmedabad, led by Manubhai Shah; groups demanding transparency and account-ability in environmental governance, such as the CHIPKO movement and the Narmada Bachao Andolan; and those supporting the right to food campaign. The movement against widespread corruption in the bureaucracy launched by the Bhrashtachar Virodhi Andolan, led by Anna Hazare in Maharashtra, also provided the necessary breadth to this movement. Several bureaucrats who had retired from promi-nent positions, such as Madhav Godbole; prominent lawyers, such as Prashant Bhushan; retired judges from the Supreme Court, such as Justice P.B. Sawant, and from the High Courts, such as Justice H. Suresh; and senior media professionals, such as Ajit Bhattacharjea and Prabhash Joshi, voiced their support for the RTI.

The National RTI Coalition

The success of MKSS campaign in Rajasthan paved the way for the creation of the National Campaign for People's Right to Information

(NCPRI), a non-registered group whose aim is to provide support to the grass-roots movements for the RTI and lobby the government. It was established in New Delhi in 1996 following a meeting organized by the Press Council of India. The founding members of the NCPRI were journalists Ajit Bhattacharjea, Prabhash Joshi, and Bharat Dogra; advocate Prashant Bhushan; retired civil servants S.R. Sankaran and Harsh Mander; social activists Nikhil Dey, K.G. Kannabiran, Renuka Mishra, M.P. Parmeswaram, and Aruna Roy; and academic Shekhar Singh.

The coalition is unique in that it does not take institutional funding, including from international donors, on the ground that it could undermine the strictly 'grass-roots, home-grown' nature of the RTI movement across the country. It functions as a loose coalition of different movements and all policy decisions are made by an appointed Working Committee, which also raises resources and periodically reviews NCPRI's objectives, priorities, and strategies.

NCPRI's first action after its birth was to formulate a draft national RTI Bill, which was sent to the central government in 1996. The NCPRI's draft bill was taken into consideration by the government before it introduced its own much-diluted version in Parliament in 2002 (passed but never came into force).

In the meantime, NCPRI continued its campaigns across the country. In 2004, it held a national convention in Delhi, and organized more than 30 workshops across the country to discuss the need to enact and improve the existing national RTI Act.

In 2004, ahead of the parliamentary elections, the United Progressive Alliance (UPA) promised in its manifesto to re-energize the RTI law that was languishing on the statute book. Upon winning the ballot, the Congress-Party-led UPA government, published the National Common Minimum Programme (NCMP), in which it promised that 'the RTI Act will be made more progressive, participatory and meaningful'. To oversee the implementation of the CMP, the government appointed the National Advisory Council (NAC) on 31 May 2004, a body comprising development professionals who acted as an interface between the government and civil society. NAC was headed by Sonia Gandhi, the leader of the Indian National Congress Party.

The members of the NAC included many RTI activists such as Aruna Roy, N.C. Saxena, Jean Dreze, a leading figure in the campaign for the right to food and work; and Jayaprakash Narayan, a supporter of transparency and accountability in the electoral sphere. The moment could not have been more politically opportune for the RTI coalition as the NAC took up the rewriting of the RTI bill as its first task under the CMP mandate. Aruna Roy was asked to draft amendments to the FOI Act at the second meeting of the NAC. Parallel to this was the NCPRI attempt to use judicial intervention to force the government to notify the 2002 Act. This resulted in the government putting out draft rules under the Freedom of Information Act, 2002.

NCPRI and CHRI began working on a new draft law based on the experience gained from the nine states that had already implemented similar legislation and developing countries like Mexico and South Africa, which had enacted similar laws in the recent past. The NAC had multiple meetings discussing the contours of the draft act which included the exclusion of intelligence and security agencies as well as the availability of Cabinet Notes (Arora and Kailash 2014). In August 2004, CHRI and NCPRI submitted to the NAC a series of amendments to the Act of 2002. The NAC accepted most of them and forwarded them to the then Prime Minister recommending their adoption.

Legislative Journey: Second Attempt at a Law on Right to Information

Based on the suggestions made by the NAC, a new RTI bill was introduced in Parliament on 22 December 2004 which was referred to the Standing Committee on Personnel, Public Grievance, Law and Justice, headed by E.M. Sudarsana Natchiappan. The committee invited public feedback and heard a number of civil society groups in the first week of March 2005. These included Aruna Roy and other representatives of MKSS; NCPRI; Anna Hazare and Prakash Kardley, social activists; Maja Daruwala, Director, CHRI; Jean Dreze, Professor, Delhi School of Economics; Shanti Bhushan, Supreme Court Advocate and former Law Minister; Shailesh Gandhi, entrepreneur and activist; and Jayaprakash Narayan, Convener, Lok Satta. The committee also received several written suggestions from different groups, organizations, and individuals on the provisions of the bill. The committee submitted its report on 21 March 2005 with a proposed amended version of the bill.[27]

Box 4.3   Key Suggestions of Civil Society Groups

The bill should have a preamble to clearly state the scheme and scope of the law so as to be consistent with the principles of democracy and ideals of the Constitution and should apply to non-citizens as well.

The bill should not only apply to the Central Government and bodies owned or controlled by it but be extended to the states, local bodies, or authorities. Also, all political parties, MLAs/MPs/Ministers, and such other public representatives should be included in the act.

The fees charged must be reasonable, affordable, and should in no case exceed the actual cost of supplying the information. There should be a provision for waiving the fee in case the information is in the larger public interest.

The bill should make suitable provisions that information related to security, sovereignty and integrity of India, relations with foreign countries and cabinet papers etc. as exempted under sub-clauses (a) (i) of sub section (l) of clause 8 should not be an all-time exemption.

The exemptions should be qualified with a strong public interest over-riding, in the sense that the citizens should have access to information about the exempted agencies, their policies, personnel, etc., so far as the information relates to corruption and issues of public interest.

In order to ensure that the autonomy of the Commission is not impeded, the procedure for deciding an appeal by the Commission should be prescribed by the Commission itself, instead of the Central Government.

An explicit provision should be made to empower the appellate authority including the Information Commission to impose all penalties available under the law.

A penalty of Rs 250 per day's delay should be levied against the defaulting Public Information Officer beyond the stipulated deadline and disciplinary action like suspension and dismissal at the departmental level.

There should be no blanket exclusion to the intelligence and security agencies for human rights violations.

Source: Third Report on The Right to Information Bill, 2004.[28]

Considering the amendments suggested by the committee, a revised bill was placed in the Lok Sabha on 10 May 2005. The bill was approved by the Lok Sabha on 11 May and the Rajya Sabha on 12 May without much dissent. Most of the debates were focused on making the RTI Act applicable to a larger set of people and a wider ambit of information. It received Presidential assent on 15 June 2005 and the law came into force on 12 October 2005.

Developments after Enactment

The need to monitor the functioning of the RTI Act and safeguard it from any attempt to weaken its powers acquired a greater sense of urgency in 2006, when the government tried to amend the RTI Act. Among other changes, it wanted to remove 'file notings' (essentially a record of the deliberative process in the government) from its purview. There was widespread public outrage to this proposed amendment and after much deliberation, the government dropped this amendment. Even though the government was forced to refrain from amending the act, it was clear that they had not abandoned the idea. Questions about its functioning on the grounds of its usefulness and effectiveness were raised repeatedly (*Firstpost* 2016; PricewaterhouseCoopers 2009).

In 2009, fresh rumours about amendments to the RTI Act started circulating. According to activists, the real agenda remained 'file notings' though this time around they were calling it 'discussion/consultations that take place before arriving at a decision' (Singh 2011). Another issue that gained importance, mainly due to the first report of the Second Administrative Reforms Commission (ARC), was the exemption 'frivolous and vexatious' applications. The judiciary also came into the picture. In 2007, Subhash Agarwal filed an RTI application with the Supreme Court asking whether judges were submitting information about their assets to their respective chief justices. This information was denied even though the Central Information Commission (CIC) subsequently upheld the appeal. The main issue was whether the office of the Chief Justice of India was under the purview of the RTI Act. The Supreme Court challenged this order twice before the Delhi High Court even as it made some information about judges' assets public on its website, but the HC upheld the CIC's ruling.[29]

All this came together in October 2009, when just after the annual conference of CIC, the Department of Personnel and Training, Ministry of Personnel, Public Grievances and Pensions, Government of India (DoPT) organized a meeting of CICs and information commissioners from across the country to discuss the proposed amendments. RTI activists had already got wind of this meeting and had briefed many of the commissioners in advance, most of whom were sympathetic to the activists' point of view. RTI activists also wrote an open letter to the Prime Minister and the Chairperson of the ruling coalition, disputing the need and the desirability of the proposed amendments.

Subsequently, Sonia Gandhi, Chairperson of the UPA, addressed a letter to the Prime Minister on 10 November 2009, where she stated that, 'in my opinion, there is no need for changes or amendments. The only exceptions permitted, such as national security, are already well taken care of in the legislation'.[30] But the PM responded on 24 December 2009, that, 'while we are taking steps to improve dissemination of information and training of personnel, there are some issues that cannot be dealt with, except by amending the Act' (*Indian Express* 2010a). However, no further steps were taken in this matter.

On 12 August 2013, the government introduced a bill seeking to amend the RTI Act to exempt political parties from its purview. Earlier, the CIC had ruled that six national political parties—Indian National Congress (INC), BJP, Communist Party of India (Marxist) (CPI(M)), and Bahujan Samaj Party (BSP)—would fall under the ambit of the RTI Act. The bill was referred to the Standing Committee which submitted its report in December 2013 supporting the amendment.[31]

Since the Narendra Modi-led NDA government came to power in 2014, there is some fear that the RTI Act is losing its edge, visible in the increase in the pending complaints and second appeals with the CIC. Also, the post of CIC was left vacant for a long time. Venkatesh Nayak of CHRI pointed out the increased in cases pending with the CIC (39,000 in 2014 as opposed to 24,150 on 31 October 2013).[32]

It is difficult to predict the evolution of the RTI Act in the years to come. However, an even greater challenge is to continue the momentum of the movement and apply its lessons for the welfare of all citizens.

Key Observations and Concluding Remarks

The journey of the RTI Act conforms to the advocacy coalition framework of policymaking. The sustained advocacy campaigns of MKSS and later NCPRI transformed what was till then mainly an urban idea pushed by a few activists and academics, into a mass movement that quickly spread not only across Rajasthan but also to other parts of the country. Although impetus for change often comes from outside formal institutions, in this case, the state apparatus, through certain reform-oriented individuals, played a key role in bringing about the legislation.

In terms of the influence or impact on the legislative strategy, however, it can be categorized as low because it took over 20 years to become a law. While the means adopted by the activists were confrontational, it became less so after the formation of NAC when MKSS leaders such as Aruna Roy became a member of the body. The government's engagement also changed from conflictual to cooperative in 2004 with the ascendence of the UPA. Possibly, the UPA viewed its victory as a mandate for 'inclusive', 'pro-poor' policies, which prompted it to set up the NAC which played a crucial role in the legislative agenda-setting of the government. In this context, media played a positive role both during the movement as well as after the law was framed. It carried messages on how to use this law and its intended benefits.

Notes

1. Available at http://www.law.yale.edu/documents/pdf/Intellectual_Life/ CL-OGI-China_Adopts_JPH-English.pdf (last accessed on 8 March 2017).
2. See 'Access to Information Laws: Overview and Statutory Goals', available at http://right2info.org/access-to-information-laws (last accessed on 8 March 2017).

3. Available at http://right2info.org/access-to-information-laws (last accessed on 8 March 2017) and http://www.right2info.org/international-standards (last accessed on 8 March 2017).

4. *Bennett Coleman & Co.* v *Union of India*, AIR 1973 SC 783, dissenting judgment of Justice K.K. Mathews; *State of UP* v *Raj Narain*, AIR 1975 SC 865; *SP Gupta* v *Union of India*, AIR 1982 SC 149; *Indian Express Newspapers (Bombay) Pvt Ltd* v *India* (1985) 1 SCC 641; *DK Basu* v *State of West Bengal* (1997) 1 SCC 216; *Reliance Petrochemicals Ltd* v *Proprietors of Indian Express Newspapers Bombay Pvt Ltd*, AIR 1989 SC 190. Also see http://directorateheuk.org/addons/imp/guide_to_use_rti_act_2005.pdf.

5. Manual of Right to Information Act, Raj Pruthi, 2006.

6. *Bombay Environmental Action Group and Others* v *Pune Cantonment Board*.

7. For instance, *Sakal Papers (P) Ltd.* v *Union of India*, AIR 1962, SC 304; *Express Newspapers (P) Ltd.* v *Union of India*, AIR 1958, SC 578; *Brij Bhushan* v *State of Delhi*, AIR 1950, SC 129; *State of UP* v *Raj Narain* (1975); *SP Gupta & Others* v *The President of India and Others*, 1982, AIR (SC) 149; The Sriram Food and Fertiliser Industry (1984); *Bombay Environmental Action Group* v. *Pune Cantonment Board*, Bombay High Court, A.S. Writ Petition No. 2733 of 1986; *L.K. Koolwal* v *State of Rajasthan*, AIR 1988, RAJ 2; *M.C. Mehta* v *Union of India*, AIR 1992, SC 382; *Union of India* v. *Association For Democratic Reforms*, Civil Appeal No. 7178 of 2001 (Source: 'Access to the Constitution: A Neglected Right', CUTS Briefing Paper, May 1995).

8. S.A. Brelvi and Kasturi Srinivasan.

9. Manual of Right to Information Act, Raj Pruthi, 2006.

10. RTI Fellowship Report 2011, available at http://rti.gov.in/rti_fellowship_report_2011.pdf (last accessed on 8 March 2017) and CERC Bill Text, available at http://www.humanrightsinitiative.org/programs/ai/rti/india/national/cerc_rti_bill.pdf (last accessed on 8 March 2017).

11. 'Global Trends on the Right to Information: A Survey of South Asia', available at http://www.article19.org/data/files/pdfs/publications/south-asia-foi-survey.pdf (last accessed on 8 March 2017).

12. 'Global Trends on the Right to Information: A Survey of South Asia', available at http://www.article19.org/data/files/pdfs/publications/south-asia-foi-survey.pdf (last accessed on 8 March 2017).

13. 'History of Development on Right to Information in India', available at http://odishapolice.gov.in/sites/default/files/PDF/2-HISTORY.pdf (last accessed on 8 March 2017).

14. H.D. Shourie Committee Report, 1997, available at http://103.251.43.137/greenstone/collect/imgmater/index/assoc/HASH01ce.dir/doc.pdf (last accessed on 8 March 2017)

15. This Bill was drafted at a National Workshop convened by NIRD, Hyderabad on 3–4 September 1997. The NIRD draft bill was more in sync with the Press Council draft than the Shourie Committee report (see Sharma 2014).

16. The GoM included Indrajit Gupta, Minister of Home Affairs; Janeshwar Mishra, Minister of Petroleum and Natural Gas; Murasoli Maran, Minister of Industry; and Ramakant Khalap, Minister of State in the Ministry of Law and Justice (see Sharma 2014).

17. 78th Report of the Standing Committee on Home Affairs on the Freedom of Information Bill, 2000, July 2001, availbale at http://164.100.47.5/newcommittee/reports/EnglishCommittees/Committee%20on%20Home%20Affairs/78threport.htm (last accessed on 8 March 2017).

18. The GoM included L.K. Advani, Minister of Home Affairs; George Fernandes, Minister of Defence; M. Thambi Durai, Minister of Law, Justice and Company Affairs; Sushma Swaraj, Minister of Information and Broadcasting; Vasundhara Raje, Minister of State in the Ministry of External Affairs; and K.R. Janarthanan, Minister of State for Personnel, Public Grievances and Pension (see Sharma 2014).

19. Available at http://www.freedominfo.org/2002/12/freedom-of-information-law-approved-in-indi/ (last accessed on 8 March 2017).

20. The GoM included two new additions—Jaswant Singh, Minister of External Affairs; Ram Jethmalani, Minister of Law, Justice, and Company Affairs—and Pramod Mahajan, Minister of Information and Broadcasting who replaced Sushma Swaraj.

21. 38th Report of Departmentally Related Standing Committee on Home Affairs on the Demand for Grants (1997–8) of the Ministry for Personnel, Public Grievances and Pensions, 2 May 1997 (see here http://164.100.47.5/newcommittee/reports/EnglishCommittees/Committee%20on%20Home%20Affairs/38Report.PDF (last accessed on 8 March 2017).

22. 'Development on Right to Information in India from Commonwealth Human Rights Initiative', available at http://www.humanrightsinitiative.org/programs/ai/rti/india/articles/The%20movement%20for%20right%20to%20information%20in%20India.pdf.pdf (last accessed on 8 March 2017).

23. Available at http://www.freedominfo.org/2002/12/freedom-of-information-law-approved-in-indi/ (last accessed on 8 March 2017).

24. Available at http://www.freedominfo.org/2002/12/freedom-of-information-law-approved-in-indi/ (last accessed on 8 March 2017).

25. Manual of Right to Information Act, Raj Pruthi, 2006.

26. Available at http://www-wds.worldbank.org/external/default/WDS ContentServer/WDSP/IB/2009/04/03/000333038_200904030430 21/Rendered/PDF/479920WBWP0Acc10Box338877B01PUBLIC1. pdf (last accessed on 8 March 2017).

27. 3rd Report of the Standing Committee on Personnel, Public Grievances, Law and Justice, 21 March 2005 (see http://164.100.47.5/ newcommittee/reports/EnglishCommittees/Committee%20on%20 Personnel,%20PublicGrievances,%20Law%20and%20Justice/3rd% 20Report%20English.pdf (last accessed on 8 March 2017).

28. Third Report on The Right to Information Bill, 2004, Standing Committee on Personnel, Public Grievances, Law and Justice, 21 March 2005, available at http://164.100.47.5/newcommittee/ reports/EnglishCommittees/Committee%20on%20Personnel,%20 PublicGrievances,%20Law%20and%20Justice/3rd%20Report%20 English.pdf (last accessed on 8 March 2017).

29. Available at http://thewire.in/2015/09/03/the-supreme-court-still-adamantly-refuses-to-yield-to-rti-9856/ (last accessed on 8 March 2017).

30. Available at http://indiatoday.intoday.in/story/PM,+Sonia+differ+on+ RTI+Act+amendment/1/92121.html (last accessed on 8 March 2017).

31. 66th Report of the Standing Committee on Personnel, Public Grievances, Law and Justice on the RTI (Amendment) Bill, 2013.

32. Available at http://scroll.in/article/711240/right-to-information-act-is-getting-strangled-under-modi-government-activists-say (last accessed on 8 March 2017).

5

The Journey to the Right to Education Act, 2009

The 2009 Act has been enacted keeping in mind the crucial role of Universal Elementary Education for strengthening the social fabric of democracy through provision of equal opportunities to all.
—Supreme Court judgment (Chief Justice S.H. Kapadia and Justice Swatanter Kumar), 6 May 2014

The Context

After seven decades of Independence, India has achieved near universal elementary school enrolment. While social inequalities persist, the gap is becoming narrower. More children, especially girls, of marginalized groups are enroling in schools. A key driver of this change was the landmark Right of Children to Free and Compulsory Education Act, 2009 (RTE Act), which operationalized the fundamental right to education for all children between 6 and 14 years. The constitution was amended to make the right to education a fundamental right in 2002, but it took seven years to implement it on ground. The act, introduced in Rajya Sabha in December 2008, was passed in August 2009 by both Houses of Parliament. It became operational in April 2010 after the central RTE Rules were notified. Thus, India became one of the 135 countries to make education a fundamental right.

A long and sustained campaign was waged by many advocacy groups, experts, and academicians to make this happen. While there were fewer takers for the idea of universal education in the initial years after Independence, it quickly gained support among civil society and policymakers alike by the mid-1970s. However, there was considerable divergence of views on the implementation of the concept of universal education. Some believed in a common school system (with little role for the private sector) while others took the reality of the existing education sector in consideration and assigned a more prominent role to private schools.

Universal elementary education (UEE) remained on the policy agenda for successive governments since 1947. Many committees and commissions continued to recommend UEE, but governments over the years cited lack of funds and low demand as reasons for keeping the issue on a back-burner. The activism for UEE started in real earnest only after the Unnikrishnan judgment in 1993. It took almost ten years to bring about a constitutional amendment to make right to education (RTE) a fundamental right. This right could only be operationalized through an act in 2009.

Whether this fundamental right has managed to serve the purpose of its enactment is a different discussion and outside the scope of this study. This case study narrates the story of the evolution of the law, the civil society groups who were involved in the process, the tactics and methods they used to influence the lawmakers, and the role of state institutions in taking forward the agenda of UEE.

The activism for UEE has two distinct phases: 1947–2002 (till the right to education became a fundamental right) and 2002–9 (the enactment of RTE Act to operationalize the fundamental right).

Modern Education System Takes Root under British Rule

When the British left in 1947, India's literacy rate was just 12 per cent (female literacy rate in 1951 was just 9 per cent).[1] But it is wrong to assume that the British government made no efforts to educate the Indian masses. In fact, the idea of making primary education compulsory for the masses was British. Traditionally, India followed the *gurukul* system of education,[2] which was confined to boys belonging to the higher castes (with a few exceptions). This system was slowly replaced with a state education system by the British since the nineteenth century. The social, political, and constitutional developments that led to the emergence of the modern system of education in India has roots not only in India but also in the United

Table 5.1   Development of UEE in British India

Nineteenth Century	Indigenous Systems of Education Prevalent in Different Parts of India
1813	The East India Company accepts responsibility of the education of Indians through the Charter Act, 1813.
1813–53	Conflict between the Occidental and Oriental schools of thought. The Occidental school represented by Macaulay believed in the substitution of Indian culture with Western culture. Main supporters were the missionaries and younger officials of the East India Company. The Oriental school believed in the synthesis of the Eastern and Western cultures, supported by the older officials of the Company and most Indians interested in spreading education.
1854	The Woods's Despatch dispersed all controversies, stating that the main object was to spread Western knowledge and science. The Despatch stated that the central government lacked funds, so education would have to be taken up by private bodies, whether missionaries or Indians.
1854–82	The education system was westernized while the agency was Indianized. The indigenous educational system became almost extinct. By 1880, in addition to mission schools and schools run by education departments, Indians also started establishing schools and colleges.
1870–80	Compulsory education acts were passed in England.
1882–1900	The Report of the Indian Education Commission (Hunter Commission) decided that government should encourage private Indian enterprises to spread education. Between 1882 and 1900, Indians opened many schools and colleges, which became the most important agency for spreading education to the masses.

(Cont'd)

Table 5.1   *(Cont'd)*

Early Twentieth Century	Indigenous Systems of Education Prevalent in Different Parts of India
1901	Conference of Directors of Public Instruction was convened by Lord Curzon in Shimla. There was intense conflict between two groups—officials and Indians. Officials believed that the quality of education had deteriorated since 1880 and advocated government control and improvement of schools and colleges. The Indian educationists believed that while quality may have suffered, spreading Western knowledge was more important to create a renaissance in Indian life.
1906	Baroda became the first princely state to implement free and compulsory primary education. Inspired by Baroda, a movement led by Sir Ibrahim Rehmatullah and Sir Chimanlal Seatalwad was launched to introduce compulsory education in Mumbai. The government set up a committee in 1906 to examine the feasibility of the proposal, but it recommended against the move.
1910–11	Gopal Krishna Gokhale's attempt to introduce a bill to make primary education compulsory in the Imperial Legislative Council was defeated by a large majority.
1917–18	Vitalbhai Patel took up the cause and moved a bill in the Bombay Legislative Council. The Bombay Municipality Primary Education Act of 1918 was the first ever law on compulsory education.
1921	Department of Education was transferred to the control of Indian Ministers after Indian nationalists demanded the power to control the educational policy of India.

(Cont'd)

Table 5.1　*(Cont'd)*

Twentieth Century	Indigenous Systems of Education Prevalent in Different Parts of India
1921–30	Several states legislated Compulsory Education Acts and by 1930, all provinces in British India had Compulsory Education Acts on their statute books. However, actual implementation was slow due to fund crunch at the provincial government level.
1929	The Hartog Committee (an auxiliary committee of the Simon Commission 1927) observed the progress made in spreading education but criticized it for being of poor quality. For primary education, it recommended focusing on qualitative improvement rather than hasty expansion.
1930–7	The Hartog Committee report negatively impacted the growth of primary education.
1937–40	The Government of India Act, 1935 introduced Provincial Autonomy in 1937. Larger funds were made available for education and the Wardha Scheme of education was introduced. The Wardha Scheme (also known as basic education/*Nai Talim*) was developed by Mahatma Gandhi and was discussed and endorsed at the first Conference of National Education held at Wardha in October 1937. The scheme provided for free and compulsory education for seven years on a nation-wide scale, with the medium of instruction being the mother tongue. The scheme also focused on encouraging some form of manual productive work. This scheme was adopted in several provinces. The basic principles of the scheme were laid out in the Zakir Hussain Committee reports of 1937 and 1938.
1944	The Central Advisory Board of Education (CABE) submitted a comprehensive Report on Post-War Educational Development, known as the Sargent

(Cont'd)

Table 5.1   *(Cont'd)*

Twentieth Century	Indigenous Systems of Education Prevalent in Different Parts of India
	Report, which visualized a system of universal, compulsory, and free education for all boys and girls between the ages of 6 and 14 by 1984 (40 years).
1946–7	The Constituent Assembly debated this issue but decided to include it in the Directive Principles* (non-justiciable) instead of fundamental rights section. In 1947, the Committee on the Ways and Means of Financing Educational Development (Kher Committee) was set up to explore ways of achieving UEE within ten years at less cost. It estimated an annual expenditure of Rs 400 crore to operate a national system of education.

Sources: Nurullah and Naik (1951); Planning Commission (1951, 1993); Ministry of Human Resource Development.

Note: * Article 45 of the Constitution of India: 'The State shall endeavour to provide, within a period of ten years from the commencement of this Constitution, for free and compulsory education for all children until they complete 14 years of age.'

Kingdom. The drama lay in the conflict between the old and the new systems of education which the British sought to impose through missionaries, government officials, and some Indians educated under the new system. It is also noteworthy that Indian educationists and reformers played a crucial role in the development of country's education system.

Developments after Independence: Rhetoric versus Reality

Despite the efforts of the Indian education reformers, illiteracy was rampant at the time of Independence. Schools were available to only 40 per cent of the children between 6 and 11 and to 10 per cent between the ages of 11 and 17. Hugh B. Woods (1955) estimated, 'To meet the goal established by the constitution, India would need to … increase educational expenditures tenfold'.

Educating the masses looked like a daunting task. This did not deter India's policymakers from making the right noises. The First Five Year Plan (1951–6) called education an 'essential pre-requisite, next only to food' for the survival of Indian democracy. It set ambitious targets—by 1956, at least 60 per cent of children between 6 and 11 years should be provided with educational facilities and girl's enrolment should go up from 23 per cent to 40 per cent.

By the end of the first plan, about 40 per cent of children (6–14 years) were attending schools but the drop-out rate (called wastage), especially for girls, was extremely high. Reducing the allocation to education, the second plan admitted that the target of UEE within ten years of the commencement of the Constitution was not going to be met since only 49 per cent of children was likely to be enrolled by 1960–1. But it hoped that the target could be achieved in the next 10–15 years.

Despite the lack of funding, many states[3] passed legislations to make elementary education compulsory. But little was done to enforce these laws. Also, the expansion of basic education was proving to be difficult due to the lack of finances. The landmark all-India educational survey conducted between 1957 and 1959 disclosed that there were 840,033 rural habitations in India, out of which only 27 per cent had one or more schools in them. Even these could provide education to only 60 per cent of the rural population (Ministry of Education 1960).

National Policy on Education 1968

The government issued the Resolution on National Policy of Education (NPE) on 24 July 1966. The resolution had 17 principles to guide the development of education in the years ahead (Dhawan 2006). NPE 1968 was significant in many ways and became the guiding principle for educational development in the country, supplemented by the guidelines adopted in the Sixth Plan document (Dhawan 2006). It regarded human resource development as a key driver of national welfare, recommended the common 10+2+3 education structure throughout India, and provided for effective education at the primary level on a free and compulsory basis. However, again, its recommendation could not be implemented, due to inadequacy of funds and human resources.

National Policy on Education 1986

The overall elementary education system continued to suffer from major gaps in terms of availability of teachers, the number of schools, enrolment and retention of students. The need for a new policy became apparent in 1985 and the government came out with two documents in 1986—The National Policy on Education and Programme of Action. For the first time, an action plan was chalked out which included setting up of Navodaya Vidyalayas for talented children, provisioning of on-job training, and education of teachers through Administrative Staff Colleges and District Institutes of Education and Training (DIETs).

After the declaration of NPE 1986, the Ministry of Human Resource Development (MHRD) announced the Programme of Action (PoA) for its implementation. About 23 task forces were created as part of the PoA, each of which covered a specific subject in the NPE.[4]

National Education Policy 1992

The implementation of NPE 1986 was reviewed by two committees: the Ramamurti Committee (1990) and the Janardhan Reddy Committee (1992). Based on their recommendations, the NPE was modified to some extent in 1992. It focused on the continuous upgradation of skills through education, to meet the demands of the society, and a grievance redressal mechanism for education at national and state levels through Educational Tribunals.

Clearly, the biggest concern of the policymakers and educationists alike was the issue of equity in education. Thus, every committee or plan stressed on the common school system to ensure that children were not treated differentially on the basis of their parents' income. However, while the intent was good, there was serious lacuna in implementation. The efforts were mostly the 'technical fix', and not the 'adaptive solution' to the problem on ground. The country still seemed far from a policy that guaranteed free and compulsory elementary education to all. In a situation like this, it was clear that the machinery would not move until and unless the thrust was provided from some other source. This much-required thrust eventually came from the judiciary.

Judicial Order: An Impetus to Activists

In 1989, the Karnataka government issued a notification that permitted the private medical colleges in the state to charge a higher tuition fees from all students except those admitted under the 'government quota'. In 1991, Mohini Jain, a resident of Meerut, Uttar Pradesh (UP), applied for admission to an MBBS course in a private medical college in Karnataka. The college management asked her to deposit a sum of Rs 60,000 as tuition fee for the first year and to show a bank guarantee of the amount equal to the fee for the remaining years. When Jain's father intimated the management that the required amount was beyond his reach, the management refused to admit her. Jain then filed a petition in the Supreme Court challenging this notification.[5]

During the course of the case, Supreme Court of India, for the first time, raised an important question: whether right to education is guaranteed to the Indian citizen under the Constitution of India? The court observed that,

'Right to Life' is the compendious expression for all those rights which the courts must enforce because they are basic to the dignified enjoyment of life. It extends to the full range of conduct which the individual is free to pursue. The right to education flows directly from the Right to Life. The Right to Life under Article 21 and the dignity of an individual cannot be assured unless it is accompanied by the right to education. The state government is under an obligation to make endeavour to provide educational facility at all levels to its citizens.[6]

A similar issue arose in another landmark Supreme Court judgment in the case of *J.P. Unnikrishnan* v. the *State of Andhra Pradesh*. Unnikrishnan's petition asked whether as per Articles 21, 41, 45, and 46 of the constitution, the right to education could be recognized as a fundamental right. The Supreme Court noted,

The right to education which is implicit in the Right to Life and personal liberty guaranteed by Article 21 must be construed in the light of the directive principles in Part IV of the Constitution. So far as the right to education is concerned, there are several articles in Part IV which expressly speak of it—for instance Articles 41, 45, and 46.

The three Articles, 41, 45, and 46 are designed to achieve the said goal among others. It is in the light of these Articles that the content and parameters of the Right to Education have to be determined.[7]

These developments on the judicial front had far-reaching implications. It not only provided the necessary thrust to the government machinery; it also activated the civil societies throughout the country.

Campaigns for Fundamental Right to Education

The campaign for the RTE was a culmination of efforts of grassroot social-action groups, movements, and regional and national coalitions. The RTE campaign built on the campaigns against child labour that were started from the early 1990s by groups like Campaign Against Child Labour and Bachpan Bachao Andolan (BBA), learning key lessons from their successes and failures in organizing mass campaigns. There was also involvement of international networks such as Global Campaign for Education and Haki Elimu, who advocated for education for all as a human right without compromising on quality.

In India, several networks, alliances, and social action groups started a vigorous campaign for the education of all children. Grassroots mobilization, strategic use of media, and lobbying with lawmakers turned the demand for elementary education into a people's agenda. Almost all political parties had to promise to make elementary education a Fundamental Right in their election manifestos in the 1990s (National Centre for Advocacy Studies [NCAS] 2002).

Pratham was a key player among the civil society groups working towards RTE. It, along with many other groups such as MV Foundation, Child Rights and You (CRY), Eklavya, Citizens Initiative on Elementary Education, Tamil Nadu Primary School Campaign, Vidhayak Sangathan and Sramjeevi Sangathan, Campaign Against Child Labour, and BBA, saw the Supreme Court judgment as a signal to build momentum for RTE. They started with an online petition in the late 1990s. Even though the Internet was not so common then, they got over 4,500 responses from a cross-section of people. There was a four-day deadline to submit recommendations to the Standing Committee examining the constitutional amendment bill. The suggestions were collated and submitted to the Committee. However, the Committee members opined that these were made by rich people with access to the Internet. There was need to solicit opinion at the grassroots level. So began the Voice of India campaign, which was joined by many different groups such as MV Foundation, CRY, and others. The Voice of India campaign was simple enough. The idea was to get people to send a postcard to the President of India for making RTE a reality. Pratham activists travelled to many parts of the country—over fifteen to twenty cities—and met other activists, journalists, and academics. The campaign was quite successful and mounds of mails were sent to the President. A number of seminars and television programmes were organized to popularize the idea. Along with these campaigns, back-end negotiations were also happening about the provisions of the bill.

The campaign for RTE was also taken up by student organizations such as All India Students Federation (AISF), All India Students Association (AISA), Students' Federation of India (SFI), Samajvadi Jansabha, National Students' Union of India (NSUI), and others. A march was held in 1997 from Madan Mohan Malviya gate in Benaras Hindu University (BHU) with a group of 150 students on bicycles, which then went up to Doon School in Dehradun. On their way, hundreds of meetings were conducted to spread awareness of the right of citizens to education.

The Voice of India campaign catalyzed the birth of the National Alliance for the Fundamental Right to Education (NAFRE) to mobilize a wider cross-section of individuals and organizations in support of issue of Fundamental Right to education. The NAFRE was an umbrella organization and other organizations who worked under the aegis of NAFRE maintained their own identity. Sanjeev Kaura, the Chief Executive Officer (CEO) of a private company in South Africa, who came to India to fight for the cause, was the first national coordinator of NAFRE. The NAFRE had a national council with representatives from more than 200 organizations. Its secretariat was in Delhi, with the core committee having around 30 people, and the National Council having more than 100 people.

The key activities of NAFRE included organizing village, block, district, state, and national conventions to sensitize and articulate the RTE education campaign. It also invited eminent person-alities to such conventions in order to strengthen the campaign. For instance, at NAFRE's two-day National Education Convention on 10–11 April 2001 in New Delhi, His Holiness Dalai Lama released a draft of the National Status Report on elementary education. Justice Jeevan Reddy, Chairman, Law Commission of India; Indu Jain, Chairperson, Bennett Coleman & Co., Times of India Group; Justice Anil Dev Singh of the Delhi High Court (HC); and Indira Jai Singh, senior advocate of the Supreme Court pledged support to the campaign. Representatives from different political parties articulated their views on the Constitutional Amendment Bill that proposed to make education a fundamental right. There was a candle-light march to India Gate with about 5,000 first-generation learners, children, and NAFRE supporters participating in the rally, symbolically lighting up candles and taking an oath to make education a fundamental right.

Other efforts of NAFRE included a postcard campaign for the RTE where over 450,000 children sent postcards to the government demanding that RTE be made a fundamental right. These postcards were handed to the Speaker of Lok Sabha in November 2001 in New Delhi. Furthermore, it organized meetings for two months at a stretch in every state—from village level to block level—in 2001. Volunteers of NAFRE travelled across fifteen states to ensure people's participation and representation. NAFRE advocated with 1,000 panchayats to pass resolutions demanding to make RTE a fundamental right.

Foot marches in places such as Dudhi in UP, were organized in many villages with the help of partner organizations throughout 2001. Volunteers from different states participated in these foot marches and cycle rallies. Some instances of these included the mobilization of 17,000 parents from 41 districts in Lucknow by Voice of Partner, a state alliance of NAFRE's in UP; Jan Adhikar Manch (JAM), a people's organization and member of NAFRE, also mobilized people in over 30 villages of Akbarpur district in UP. They were involved in the postcard campaign, passing panchayat resolutions, wall writings, and mass meetings. On 5 July 2001, JAM, along with Jan Shikshan Kendra, organized a rally in Akbarpur to protest against reduction of budgetary allocation.

Next, NAFRE decided to start Shiksha Satyagraha at Gandhi Samadhi, Rajghat on 23 November 2001, against the 93rd Constitutional Amendment Bill. Well-known Gandhian Nirmala

Deshpande, Nafisa Ali, and cricketer Maninder Singh lighted the torch of Shiksha Satyagraha. At the Gandhi Sthal, social worker Veena Handa, along with the children from Gandhi Hindustani Sahitya Sabha, spun cotton on the spinning wheel as a symbol of qualitative education. It mobilized 40,000 people in Delhi and stated a threefold agenda, which were as follows: (a) extend the law to cover children up to 18 years of age; (b) make arrangements for necessary finances; and (c) implement a Common School System throughout the country. M.M. Joshi, the then education minister, called up some members of NAFRE and told them that he could not fulfil their demands regarding provisioning of pre-primary education free of cost due to budget constraints. He, however, assured them that he would meet the rest of the demands of NAFRE. NAFRE agreed not to protest. The bill (which stipulated provisions for the age group six to fourteen years) was introduced in the Parliament. No standing committee was constituted and the Bill was passed undebated (NCAS 2002).

After this incident, NAFRE was divided. One section, led by Anil Sadgopal, was completely against the act and wanted it to be repealed. Another section, led by Vinod Raina, wanted to go ahead and participate in drafting the law that would operationalize the right. Sadgopal continued to fight against this amendment and wanted to draft a parallel bill that would remove the 'lacunas' in the original bill.

Alternate Idea of School Voucher System

At the same time, Centre for Civil Society (CCS)—one of the leading think tanks located in Delhi—started propagating another model to promote universal education. The organization believed that a voucher system would be a better alternative, as it would enable opening up of many schools by committed individuals, and would facilitate spreading quality education to the masses by giving them an option to study in schools of their choice. They met Rahul Gandhi and proposed the same to him. He saw merit in the idea, but doubted if it would work in India. To prove its point and answer the critics, CCS decided to launch this system on a trial basis. The CCS started with 'School Choice' campaign in Delhi and implemented it further in four states—UP, Jharkhand, Orissa, and Rajasthan. In Delhi, CCS received 140,000 applications for vouchers. Fifty to sixty schools came up for class 2 to class 5. The overall results were very promising. However, the idea could not be implemented. UP, Orissa, and Rajasthan came very close to adopting this scheme, but a sudden change in political or social situation in these states prevented its adoption. With this, CCS's endeavour to promote universalization of education through its own unique ways ceased to become a reality. The idea, however, is still considered revolutionary by many.

Enactment of the Constitutional Amendment

The idea of education as a fundamental right in India seemed to start gaining significant traction. Public Interest Litigations (PILs) were filed in the HCs all over the country to enforce the Unnikrishnan Judgment. The Parliament, under pressure, introduced the 93rd Constitutional Amendment Bill in the Lok Sabha on 26 November 2001. The Bill aimed to make education a fundamental right for children in the age group of 6 to 14 years.

The day the Bill was passed in the Lok Sabha, at least 70,000 people from 16 states gathered in Delhi, demanding that education be made a fundamental right also for children up to six years of age. Many activists felt that the guarantee of education for the six-to-fourteen years category was meaningless without the state taking responsibility for Early Childhood Care and Education (ECCE). There was some support from the media. *Frontline* called the Bill 'regressive'. UK-based *BBC* wrote that 'the demonstrators wanted to create the same kind of peaceful revolution as Mahatma Gandhi achieved in his independence struggle against the British'. The agitation, however, fell on deaf ears of the legislators. The Bill was finally enacted in December 2002, and became the 86th Amendment of the Constitution of India. Consequently, the statement that 'the state shall provide free and compulsory education to all children of the age of six to fourteen years in such manner as the State may, by law, determine' was added in Part III (Fundamental Rights) of the Constitution. Part IV (Directive Principles of State Policy) replaced the existing, 'Provision for Free and Compulsory Education for Children', with 'Provision for Early Childhood care and Education to Children below the age of six Years'. This, in many ways, marked the beginning of the legislative journey to the RTE Act, 2009.

Legislative Journey to Right to Education Act, 2009[8]

In Parliament too, there were some champions of RTE, such as Ravi Prakash Verma, who was instrumental in forming the Parliamentary Forum for Children. This Forum consisted of over 150 Members of Parliament (MPs) who deliberated about the contours of the RTE.

In 2003, the NDA government came up with the Free and Compulsory Education for Children Bill. As soon as the first draft of the Bill was circulated for public review, it was heavily criticized by the civil society throughout the country. The Bill required that all private schools must reserve up to 20 per cent of seats for poor children, who would be selected by education authorities. It did not address the problems of the government schools, and to make matters worse, it proposed to make the same government officials who managed the existing (almost non-functional) schools in charge of a large portion of private schools. It was anticipated that not only would such a bill not fulfil the objective of UEE, it would also guarantee further politicization and corruption of education system.

In 2004, the second draft of the bill, with feedback incorporated in the first draft, was posted on the Education Department website. The new draft Bill on Free and Compulsory Education (2004) was a reworked version of the previous Bill based on public feedback. This Bill was criticized for empowering multiple government committees to supervise primary education (Thakore 2006).

In June 2005, a CABE committee was constituted to suggest a draft of legislation envisaged in Article 21A of the Constitution, and to examine other issues related to elementary education for achieving the objective of free and compulsory basic education. The committee drafted its own 'Right to Education Bill' within six months and submitted it to the MHRD. The MHRD sent it to the NAC where Sonia Gandhi was the Chairperson. The NAC sent the bill to the PM for his observation.

In July 2006, the Finance Committee and Planning Commission rejected the bill citing lack of funds. The states were asked to draft their own bills based on a Model Bill that was sent to them. The states promptly sent the model bill back to the Centre citing lack of funds. The bill was then virtually buried for two years.

In February 2008, the MHRD circulated another draft of the bill, which was then referred to a Group of Ministers (GoM) formed to look into the operationalization of the RTE. On 31 October 2008, the Cabinet cleared a revised draft of the bill after the GoM passed on the draft to the Cabinet earlier that month. On 15 December 2008, the Right of Children to Free and Compulsory Education Bill was introduced in the Rajya Sabha and released to the public on the Rajya Sabha website. The law was finally enacted in August 2009, to be called The Right of Children to Free and Compulsory Education Act, 2009.

Box 5.1   Key Highlights of the RTE Act,[9] 2009

- The RTE Act, 2009, which became operative on 1 April 2010, provides the fundamental right of education to children in the age group of 6 to 14 years.
- Every child has a right to free and compulsory education in a neighbourhood school, which may be government-run or privately managed (aided or unaided). It is noteworthy that in India, private schools have to be run on a non-profit basis, which means that surplus money has to be ploughed back into the institution and no dividend can be distributed to the members of the entity that owns the school.
- It is mandatory for all schools to meet certain minimum norms. Government schools have to meet the prescribed Pupil–Teacher Ratio (PTR). Other schools require a certificate of recognition from the state government, which shall be granted if the school satisfies certain norms such as PTR, infrastructure, and qualification of teachers. The act states that already established schools shall have three years to comply with this provision. If a school does not meet these norms within the prescribed timeframe, it shall be shut down. In case the school violates this provision, it shall be liable to a fine.
- Government schools have to provide free and compulsory education to all admitted children. For aided schools, the extent of free education would be proportionate to the funding received, provided that a minimum of 25 per cent seats are reserved for disadvantaged

(Cont'd)

Box 5.1 *(Cont'd)*

students. All the other schools (including unaided schools) have to reserve at least 25 per cent of seats for the students from Scheduled Castes (SCs), Scheduled Tribes (STs), low-income, and other disadvantaged or weaker groups (including children with disabilities). Unaided schools shall be reimbursed for either their tuition charge or the per-student expenditure in government schools, whichever is lower. If the per-student expenditure is higher than the government schools, the private school has to bear the cost.

- The act prohibits physical punishment or mental harassment; screening procedures for admission of children; capitation fees; private tuitions by teachers, and running schools without recognition. It also prohibits children from being held back in class, expelled, or the requirement to pass a board examination until the completion of elementary education.
- The fund sharing pattern between the centre and the states is in the ratio of 65:35 from 2010–11. The sharing pattern for Northeastern states is 90:10.

Source: The Right of Children to Free and Compulsory Education Act, 2009, available at http://ssa.nic.in/rte-docs/free%20and %20 compulsory.pdf (last accessed on 8 March 2017) and authors' summary.

Developments Post RTE Act, 2009

The RTE Act was amended in June 2012 to provide clarifications of certain clauses around minority educational institutes (like Madrasas), children with disability, and School Management Committees (SMCs).

The amendment said that nothing contained in the RTE 2009 Act shall apply to Madrasas, Vedic Pathsalas, and educational institutions primarily imparting religious instruction. It further brought children with disability (or multiple disabilities or severe disability) under the ambit of RTE. The amendment also altered the role that SMCs are supposed to play in minority schools, both aided and unaided. Their roles in these schools were restricted to be just advisory.

On 3 April 2013, a major convention in Delhi gathered India's energetic civil society, activists, and academics to mark RTE's third anniversary and assess progress. The convention presented a particularly opportune moment to see how the reality fared vis-à-vis the ambition.

It was unanimously accepted that the overall progress had not been good. Thirty thousand new schools, in addition to 1,300,000 existing schools, did little to sway the overall negative verdict. Though the enrolment rate was high (96 per cent), there was evidence that levels of learning have either stagnated, or worsened in India in recent years. It was, in fact, the case where RTE ensured right to schooling, and not right to education.

The status remains the same even today. As feared, the RTE has made more difficult for children to go to school when it should have created more opportunities for them. The Annual Status of Education Report (ASER) reports published year on year keep showing how most children in primary schools today are at least three grades behind from where they should have been. Older pupils wanting to get back into school are, in theory, eligible for catch-up lessons. But few seem to think these exist on any scale. There have been cases of increase in drop outs in some areas due to closure of private schools.

The most fundamental criticism which leads to its ineffectiveness, however, comes in its sheer nature of being based on certain input norms, and not talking much about the overall output. These input norms include prescribed PTRs, standards for buildings and infrastructure, defined school-working days, defined teacher-working hours, and the appointment of appropriately trained teachers. There is no mention at all about outputs and no requirements about improving the quality of education.

Another provision in the act which stipulated the aided schools to provide free and compulsory education, proportionate to the funding received, subject to a minimum of 25 per cent of students from SCs, STs, low-income, and other disadvantaged or weaker groups, was widely contested. The act stated that these schools shall be reimbursed for either their tuition charge or the per-student expenditure in government schools, whichever is lower. The Society for Unaided Private Schools of Rajasthan was the first to take legal action to dispute the clause by filing a writ petition which challenged the constitutional validity of this provision, on the ground that it impinged on their right to run educational institutions without government interference. To this, the judgment of the Supreme Court remained unaltered, and it upheld 25 per cent reservation in private schools, saying that the act is constitutionally valid, as it is 'child centric' and not 'institution centric'.

Key Observations and Concluding Remarks

None of the existing policy-process theories fit the complete journey of RTE. Till the 1990s, the incremental model of policymaking fit the bill. Each Five Year Plan from 1950 onwards continued with the same idea, with some tweaking. Committees and commissions were set up to recommend strategies, some of which were implemented. However, the pace and nature of the policy process changed after the Unnikrishnan judgment of 1992. From then onwards, the judicial order became the fulcrum for launching a nation-wide campaign. Thus, from 1992, the advocacy coalition framework fits the policy process. This case study is also an example of how the narrative got shaped due to the influence of many different groups, with the dominance of the groups calling for a common school system. Other experiments in providing elementary education have gained some traction in some states, but their narratives have not become a dominant voice in the sector.

The RTE movement's influence on the legislative agenda can be characterized as medium since it took about 16 years for the law to be enacted. The means adopted by the activists became increasingly confrontational as the movement gathered momentum. Although, the policymakers were willing in principal to adhere to the 1992 judicial order, they were unwilling to add to the fiscal burden since the bill's provisions entailed a large subsidy for economically and socially weaker children.

Notes

1. See http://www.census2011.co.in/literacy.php (last accessed on 8 March 2017).
2. Gurukuls were traditional Hindu residential schools of learning, typically the teacher's house or a monastery. Education was free but well-to-do students paid a *gurudakshina,* a voluntary contribution after the

completion of their studies. The teacher imparted knowledge of religion, scriptures, philosophy, literature, warfare, statecraft, medicine, and astrology. Most of students belonged to the higher castes, although there were instances where lower castes also attained education in gurukul.

3. Bihar, Maharashtra, Delhi, Kerala, Gujarat, Punjab, Rajasthan, and Andaman and Nicobar Islands.

4. Available at http://www.educationforallinindia.com/page64.html (last accessed on 8 March 2017).

5. *Miss Mohini Jain v State of Karnataka and Others* 1992 AIR 1858; see http://www.right-to-education.org/sites/right-to-education.org/files/resource-attachments/India%20Supreme%20Court,%20Jain%20v%20Karnataka,%201992.pdf (last accessed on 8 March 2017).

6. *Miss Mohini Jain v State of Karnataka and Others* 1992 AIR 1858.

7. Unnikrishnan judgment: Writ Petition (Civil) No 607 of 1992, *Unnikrishnan v State of Andhra Pradesh*; see http://judis.nic.in/supremecourt/qrydisp.asp?tfnm=12220 (last accessed on 8 March 2017).

8. 'Resources of RTE Bill', Azim Premji Foundation, available at http://www.azimpremjifoundation.org/Bills (last accessed on 8 March 2017) and Sadgopal (2003).

9. The Right of Children to Free and Compulsory Education Act, 2009; see http://ssa.nic.in/rte-docs/free%20and%20compulsory.pdf (last accessed on 8 March 2017).

6

The Struggle against Child Labour

I remember an eight-year-old girl we rescued from intergenerational forced labour from stone quarries. When she was sitting in my car right after her rescue, she asked me: 'Why did you not come earlier?'

—Nobel Peace Prize Acceptance Speech of
Shri Kailash Satyarthi, 10 December 2015[1]

India is home to the world's largest population of child labourers (UNICEF 2011). Children have been working in homes, farms, factories, and eateries ever since anyone can remember and it is simply the ubiquity of child labour that has perhaps most effectively hidden it from the eyes of the policymakers and public alike. And this, in a country whose 65-year-old constitution bans children from hazardous jobs and sets universal education as a goal for the rulers of the land.

Things have been changing, undoubtedly. The situation seems to be improving, albeit very slowly; too slowly perhaps for the comfort of anyone who cares. In 1986, almost four decades after Independence, India enacted a landmark law against child labour. It undeniably constituted a major step, but seemed to do little to change the situation on the ground. But a quarter century later, the number of child labourers is finally coming down in city tea stalls and stone quarries alike. A quarter century that has been marked by struggles of various civil society organizations in different parts of the country fighting relentlessly against the most horrendous forms of child exploitation, prodding a lethargic and indifferent state—through public campaigns, non-stop petitioning, leveraging the media, and using the relatively more responsive judiciary—to take reluctant steps in the direction of abolishing the bane of child labour from the face of the country. The list of banned industries and activities lengthened from 7 and 15 respectively in 1986 to 18 and 65 in 2009, after two amendments. In 2012, a bill was introduced in Rajya Sabha but did not get through. The new government is expected to bring a revised version of that bill soon.

Meanwhile, the movement of elimination of child labour got a shot in the arm with the passage of the Right to Education (RTE) Act in 2009. Since child labourers were almost without exception denied school education, it became easier to identify them and their employers.

Child labour is not as straightforward a matter as it may appear at first glance. As the National Commission for the Protection of Child Rights (NCPCR) points out (NCPCR 2008), child labour is a serious and enormously complex social problem in India. While a minor at work may be a shocking and outright unacceptable concept to most privileged people, virtually everything about child labour—definition, measurement, economics—is mired in multiple points of view and interpretations (as illustrated by Table 6.1). Before discussing the laws and policies to control the child labour situation in India, it is extremely important to have an understanding of the subtleties of the problem. In the sections that follow, this case study draws the distinctions between a child labourer and a working child. Thereafter, it explains the problems associated with them and analyses the dynamics of their situation in context of the policy provisions. Further, it traces the evolution of a multitude of legislations which have been enacted to tackle the child labour menace and also discusses other relevant laws, schemes, and policies. The case study concludes by discussing the advocacy strategies used by the various civil society groups in their fight against child labour, and also discusses the most recent policy efforts towards that end.

Table 6.1   Different Estimates of Child Labour in India

Sources	Definitions	Number of Working Children
National Census 2001*	Defines work as 'participation in any economically productive activity with or without compensation, wages or profit.'	12.6 million (5 per cent of child population)
Ministry of Labour and Employment*	The Child Labour Prohibition and Regulation Act, 1986 prohibits the employment of children below 14 years in hazardous occupation (listed in the schedule).	1.2 million in hazardous occupation (0.4 per cent of child population)
National Sample Survey 2009–10*	Define labour as being engaged in economic activity (include helpers in household enterprise, regular wage labour, casual wage labour).	4.9 million (1.9 per cent of child population)
UNICEF	Children aged 5 to 11 years engaged in at least one hour of economic work or 28 hours of domestic work per week. Children aged 12 to 14 years engaged in at least 14 hours of economic work or 28 hours of domestic work per week.	29 million (11.5 per cent of child population)
Non-official estimates by non-governmental organizations (NGOs)	No single definition available. Some define any child outside of school as working child.	60–115 million (23–45 per cent of child population)

Sources: Ministry of Labour, Government of India (2001, 2013); UNICEF (2013); Human Rights Watch (2003); Various NGOs: 'Small Change', Human Rights Watch, January 2003; ActionAid; Bharti Institute.
Note: *All official data is for 5–14 years age group.

Background and Status

Definitions and Standards/Conventions

In order to understand the phenomenon of child labour, it is essential to first define the term. The International Labour Organization (ILO) defines child labour as 'work that deprives children of their childhood, their potential and their dignity, and that is harmful to physical and mental development' (ILO 2004). This definition of child labour takes into account all activities whose production is intended for the market and also includes goods manufactured for personal consumption. Further, the ILO distinguishes between three categories of children—children with worker status who work full time; those who combine work and education; and those who are neither at school nor at work and are also known as 'nowhere children' (ILO 2004). It is important to note that according to ILO's definition that work must generate an income. In consequence, the 'nowhere children', which includes children engaged in domestic activity of the family and apprentices, are not taken into account in child labour statistics. This definition is problematic since the failure to regard unpaid domestic work as an economic activity in other words means ignoring the fact that such children are denied their basic right to education (Bhukuth 2008).

Another definition of child labour as given by Lieten (2002) defines it as 'any work by children that interferes with their full physical development, the opportunities for a desired minimum of education, and of their needed recreation'. This particular definition distinguishes between different types of work: those that are harmful to the physical and moral development of the child and those that are not. Similarly, the use of the terms child work and child labour allows us to distinguish between what is dangerous and intolerable and what is not. Child work refers to an activity that does not harm a child's physical and mental development, while child labour is any activity considered dangerous to a child's welfare (Bhukuth 2008). The concept of child labour is thus closely associated to exploitation. Paid work implies child exploitation, whereas unpaid work is tolerated because it is performed within the family unit. The Ministry of Labour, Government of India, also distinguishes between child labour and working children (NCPCR 2008a). Child labourers are those children who are working in factories, workshops, establishments, mines, and in the service sector, such as domestic labour. However, children who are working as part of family labour in agriculture and in home-based work are understood as working children, and are not included in the labour statistics. They are the largest category of children who are out of school and are working full-time (NCPCR 2008a).

Dynamics of Child Labour in India

There are two underlying suppositions which shape this understanding of child labour in India. The first is that, child labour is a 'harsh reality' and it is possible to mitigate only some of the harshness of its exploitative aspects (Sinha 1996). It arises out of the fact that in the present state of India being a developing country, many parents, on account of poverty, have to send their children to work in order to supplement their income and the income derived from child labour is essential for sustenance. Thus, child labour is perceived as an economic phenomenon (Bhatty 1996). This is also known as the 'poverty argument of child labour' (Sinha 1996). The second supposition is that there is a difference between child labour and exploitation of child labour. In other words, it is the same as the difference between child work and child labour, as mentioned earlier. It has been assumed that a certain amount of child labour will persist under the family environment, which is non-exploitative (Sinha 1996). At the same time, there are other forms of child labour which are exploitative in nature, such as labour in hazardous occupations, factories, and other establishments which are unacceptable and should not be allowed to continue. These principles have influenced the legislation governing child labour in India.

The Child Labour (Prohibition and Regulation) Act, 1986 (Child Labour Act) seeks to prohibit employment of children below 14 years in hazardous occupations and processes and regulates the working conditions in other employments (NCPCR 2008b). It explicitly lists these hazardous processes and occupations in various schedules. Thus, the legislation emphasizes regulation rather than prohibition of child labour. It bans the employment of children in factories and restricts employment in so-called hazardous work, but children are permitted to work in some cottage industries and service sectors where working conditions are not regulated, wages are low, and hours are long (Weiner 1996).

However, these underlying assumptions and the policies shaped as a result of them are essentially flawed in their understanding and do not help in solving the complex problem of child labour. The assumption that poverty compels parents to send their children to work is extremely convenient to those in charge of reducing, if not eliminating, child labour, because in such cases improving the economic status of the parents becomes the focal point of the situation (Sinha 1996). Also, it is a fact that 'child labour perpetuates poverty—it doesn't reduce it but condemns one generation after another to its vicious circle' (Bhatty 1996).

Another significant fallacy is the exclusion of working children from the status of child labour. These children who are engaged in agricultural work, home-based apprenticeship, rearing of cattle, and looking after younger siblings while their parents are away working, constitute almost 80 per cent of the child labour force (Bhatty 1996). Also, it is often forgotten that it does not take much for these mere working children or out-of-school children to become child labourers engaged in exploitative work. Thus, to protect children from being exploited and to effectively abolish child labour, it is imperative to treat all out-of-school children as child labourers or those who have the potential to become child labourers.

Though a blanket ban on all forms of child labour is advocated by many a people from the civil society and also supported by equal number of political activists, recent research shows that consequent to a ban, employment levels of children under the legal working age of 14 rose relative to those of legal age (Bharadwaj et al. 2013). When bans are imperfectly enforced, they raise the cost of hiring children, as employers anticipate facing stiff fines or other penalties when caught using child labour. Thus, bans may simply lower the wages that children are paid. If families send their children to work out of necessity, a drop in child wages lowers family income for those who rely on child labour to meet basic subsistence needs—compelling families to supply more child labour, rather than less (Basu 2005).

The Child Labour-related Policy Evolution in India

The fight against child labour in India has been a long and arduous one, predating even Independence. While Article 24 of the Constitution of India bans employment of children below 14 years of age in mines, factories, and other hazardous occupations, the campaign against exploitation of children has only progressed through unrelenting challenge over the years. While several acts[2] have marked the gradual progress of the process, the 1986 Child Labour Act summarized in Box 6.1 is the latest and most important legislation.

Laws aside, the policy development in the child protection sphere has also entailed several other milestones both in the judicial space, the legislative (though not directly on the child employment area), as well as on the executive side. Box 6.2 lists a few of these.

Box 6.1   The Child Labour (Prohibition and Regulation) Act, 1986—Key Features

The act defines child as a person who has not completed his/her fourteenth year of age.

It prohibits the employment of children in 18 occupations and 65 processes listed in the Schedule of the Act (including amendments made till 2006).

The act also provides for the constitution of a Technical Advisory Committee to advise for inclusion of further occupations and processes in the Schedule.

It regulates the condition of employment in all occupations and processes not prohibited under the act.

Any person who employs a child in contravention of the act is liable to punishment with imprisonment for a minimum period of three months and a maximum of one year or with a fine between Rs 10,000 and Rs 20,000 or both.

The Act also demarcates the jurisdiction of the central and state governments in terms of enforcement of the Act.

Sources: http://www.lexuniverse.com/employment-laws/india/acts/The-Children-Pledging-of-Labour-Act-1933.html (last accessed on 8 March 2017); Child Labour Act, 1986.

Box 6.2   Other Key Developments in the Area
of Protection of the Child

National Policy on Child Labour, 1987: The policy contains the action plan for tackling the problem of child labour. It envisages a legislative action plan through the Child Labour Act. It plans to converge the various welfare schemes of the government through a core group constituted in the Ministry of Labour and Employment. It also plans to launch projects for the welfare of working children in areas of high concentration of child labour.

National Child Labour Project (NCLP) Scheme, 1988: This is a major central sector scheme for the rehabilitation of child labour. The scheme seeks to adopt a sequential approach with focus on rehabilitation of children working in hazardous occupations and processes in the first instance. Children engaged in hazardous occupations are identified through a survey. These children are then withdrawn from these occupations and put into special schools to enable them to be mainstreamed into the formal schooling system. The special schools are to be opened at the district level by the project societies (registered society under chairmanship of the administrative head of the district) and would provide bridge education, skilled/vocational training, mid-day meal, stipend of Rs 150 per child per month, and healthcare facilities. The implementation of the scheme is monitored by a central monitoring committee at the Ministry of Labour and Employment.

Supreme Court judgment on child labour: In 1996, the Supreme Court directed (Writ Petition (Civil) No.465/1986 on *M.C. Mehta v State of Tamil Nadu*) the appropriate government to (a) complete survey of children in hazardous occupations; (b) ensure that employers pay Rs 20,000 as compensation to each child employed in contravention of the act; (c) give alternative employment to an adult member of the family of the child withdrawn from hazardous occupation or pay Rs 5,000 for each child employed in hazardous occupation; (d) pay interest on the corpus of Rs 25,000, created jointly by employer and appropriate government, to the family of the child withdrawn from work; (e) provide for education of the child; and (e) constitute the Child Labour Rehabilitation-cum-Welfare Fund.

Grants-in-aid scheme: The Ministry of Labour provides funds under the grants-in-aid scheme to voluntary agencies in districts that are not

(Cont'd)

Box 6.2 *(Cont'd)*

presently covered under the NCLP scheme. The agencies are chosen by the Ministry on the recommendation of the state government. The amounts extend up to 75 per cent of the project cost for rehabilitation of working children. Voluntary organizations have been receiving funds under this scheme since 1979–80. Currently, about 70 agencies are being assisted, some of which include Azad Navyuvak Mandal Santhan, Dausa, Rajasthan (Rs 5.7 lakhs), Nawada Gramudyog Vikas Samiti, Amroha, U.P. (Rs 3.4 lakhs), Centre for Development Activities, Manipur (Rs 2.3 lakhs), Rural Education Awareness Training Institute, Dausa (Rs 3.4 lakhs), and Islamic Social Educational and Cultural Development Organisation (Rs 4.6 lakhs).

The Juvenile Justice (Care and Protection of Children) Act, 2000: This act replaced the Juvenile Justice Act, 1986, retaining the same penal provision as the previous act for imposition of fine and imprisonment, but diluted it by limiting it to cases of hazardous employment.

National Commission for Protection of Child Rights (NCPCR), 2007: The NCPCR was set up in March 2007 under the Commission for Protection of Child Rights Act, 2005. The Commission's task is to ensure that all Laws, Policies, Programmes, and Administrative Mechanisms are in consonance with the Child Rights perspective as enshrined in the Constitution of India and also the UN Convention on the Rights of the Child 1989. According to NCPCR, a child is defined as a person in the 0 to 18 years age group. The Commission visualizes a rights-based perspective flowing into National Policies and Programmes, along with nuanced responses at the state, district, and block levels, taking care of specificities and strengths of each region (www.ncpcr.gov.in).

Protocol on Migration and Trafficking of Children for Labour: The government issued, in 2008, a detailed protocol for prevention, rescue reparation, rehabilitation, and re-integration of migrant and trafficked child labour to state governments.

The Right of Children to Free and Compulsory Education (RTE) Act, 2009: The 86th Constitutional Amendment Act inserted a new Article 21(8), which provides for free and compulsory education to children of the age group of 6 to 14 years under the Right to Education. The same Amendment Act provides for amendment of the Article 45 as

(Cont'd)

Box 6.2   *(Cont'd)*

Directive Principle of the State Policy to provide provision for an early childhood care and protection bill up to the age of 6 years. It is also made a Fundamental Duty of parents and guardians under New Article 51(a) to provide opportunities for education to children between the age of 6 and 14 years.

International Collaborations: A number of international agencies have funded projects in India. They include ILO's International Programme on Elimination of Child Labour (IPEC), the Indo-US Child Labour Project (INDUS), and Converging Against Child Labour, funded by the US Department of Labor (USDOL). These programmes seek to prevent and eliminate hazardous child labour and cover various districts in Andhra Pradesh, Karnataka, Bihar, Jharkhand, Gujarat, Madhya Pradesh, Maharashtra, Tamil Nadu, Uttar Pradesh, and Orissa.

Sources: Ministry of Labour, Government of India (1987, 1981, 1988, 2008); Writ Petition (Civil) No.465/1986 on *MC Mehta* v *State of Tamil Nadu*; The Juvenile Justice (Care and Protection of Children) Act, 2000; NCPCR (2007); The Right of Children to Free and Compulsory Education (RTE) Act, 2009.

The latest, though stalled, step in the legislative journey against child labour involves a Bill that was introduced in the Rajya Sabha in 2012, seeking to make progress on several fronts on the existing legislation. Box 6.3 summarizes its key features.

Box 6.3   The Child Labour (Prohibition and Regulation) Bill 2012: Key Features

- Amendment Bill, 2012 was introduced in the Rajya Sabha on 4 December 2012 by the Minister of Labour and Employment, Mallikarjun Kharge.
- The Bill seeks to amend the Child Labour (Prohibition and Regulation) Act, 1986, which prohibits the engagement of children in certain types of occupations and regulates the condition of work of children in other occupations.

(Cont'd)

Box 6.3   *(Cont'd)*

- The Act prohibits employment of children below 14 years in certain occupations such as automobile workshops, bidi-making, carpet weaving, handloom and power loom industry, mines and domestic work. In light of the Right of Children to Free and Compulsory Education Act, 2009, the Bill seeks to prohibit employment of children below 14 years in all occupations except where the child helps his family after school hours.
- The Bill adds a new category of persons called 'adolescent'. An adolescent means a person between 14 and 18 years of age. The Bill prohibits employment of adolescents in hazardous occupations as specified (mines, inflammable substance and hazardous processes).
- The central government may add or omit any hazardous occupation from the list included in the Bill.
- The Bill enhances the punishment for employing any child in an occupation. It also includes penalty for employing an adolescent in a hazardous occupation.
- The penalty for employing a child was increased to imprisonment between 6 months and two years (from three months–one year) or a fine of Rs 20,000 to Rs 50,000 (from Rs 10,000–20,000) or both.
- The penalty for employing an adolescent in hazardous occupation is imprisonment between 6 months and two years or a fine of Rs 20,000 to Rs 50,000 or both.
- The government may confer powers on a District Magistrate to ensure that the provisions of the law are properly carried out.
  The Bill empowers the government to make periodic inspection of places at which employment of children and adolescents are prohibited.

Source: Sanyal (2012).

The 2015 Effort

Although the 2012 Bill still remains pending in Rajya Sabha, the National Democratic Alliance (NDA) government, as a part of its broader agenda to initiate labour reforms and simplifying rules, also proposed an amendment to the Child Labour Act in 2015. The proposed bill, which is still in a draft stage, makes employing a child labourer below the age of 14 years a criminal offence, except for in family shops and ventures, and that too after school hours. This is in conflict with an earlier proposal which aimed for a blanket ban on any kind of work by children. The bill was introduced to harmonize the Child Labour Act with the Right to Education Act, which makes education compulsory for all children up to the age of 14. Not banning child labour brings the law in conflict with the RTE Act. The latest draft, prepared by the Union Labour Ministry, has not been approved by the Cabinet yet. As soon as it is, it might be introduced in Parliament as a new bill.

Civil Society Activism in the Child Labour Space

It is perhaps fair to say that constitutional niceties aside, it is the NGOs that have spearheaded the long and sustained efforts at rescuing and protecting individual children as well as influencing policymakers. There have been multiple movements in various parts of the country, reacting to local realities, adopting differing methods, working varying channels, even focusing on different aspects of the problem. For instance, while the most prominent movements have worked towards a goal of gradually eliminating child labour, groups like Concerned for Working Children have fought for collective bargaining rights of child workers, thereby admitting the child's right to work.

The problem is more complex than it appears at first sight. While few will probably deny that a child's place is in school, home, and playground, not in economic employment, like in many other countries, the fact remains that children have traditionally been part and parcel of the Indian workforce in the unorganized sector. It was neither seen as a crime nor exploitation. Given its ubiquitous nature, the Directive Principles of the Constitution notwithstanding, it took Indian society several decades after Independence to begin viewing child labour as a social ill to begin with.

The movement against child labour began to morph into a series of sustained civil society campaigns in the 1980s. Unsurprisingly, voices began to be raised against the most exploitative forms like bonded labour and child abuse and trafficking in the name of labour, and in the course of the next quarter century, the movement succeeded in changing the social outlook towards child labour, and in putting employers of children on the defensive. The journey has, of course, been far from smooth and activists have lost or risked lives in the protests. Underpaid and severely exploited child labour did hold the key to the fortunes of several industries, from circus to carpet weaving, and at times the opposition to the campaigns have been savage. While many groups have waged the battle against child labour in India, in the paragraphs that follow, we try to capture the journey of two most prominent ones—the MV Foundation (MVF) of Andhra Pradesh and BBA—to get a sense of the nature of the movement and its ways of influencing policy.

We begin with the journey of MVF, which is the more recent and more local in scope, and then look at the BBA story, now made famous with the award of the 2014 Nobel Peace Prize to its founder and leader Kailash Satyarthi.

MV Foundation

In 1981, Professor Shanta Sinha of Hyderabad Central University set up the MVF, named after her grandfather and eminent educationist and historian, Mamidipudi Venkatarangaiya, as a research institution on issues relating to social transformation. In 1991, after nearly a decade's work of mobilizing women for their minimum wages, MVF began working actively on the issue of child labour and rescuing bonded child labourers, and released the first 30 children from bonded labour in Ranga Reddy district.

Simultaneously, MVF also realized, by a rough estimate that about 10 per cent of out-of-school children were bonded labourers. This led to a survey being conducted to find out total number of out-of-school children in the region of Shankarpalli in Ranga Reddy district of the then undivided Andhra Pradesh. It was decided to involve the youth of the region in this survey, who could then connect with the local people. At that point of time, there was a trend of first-generation educated youths dropping out after high school or college to go back to their villages and form youth clubs. MVF tapped into this pool of youth clubs and wrote postcards to all the youth clubs in that region, inviting them to a conference to discuss issues of children of that region. Encouraged by the first of its kind invitation about 200 young people turned up for the conference. At the end of the two-day conference, 40 of those attendees were convinced to join the survey efforts of MVF and they finalized a questionnaire during the conference itself. The questionnaire sought information on the whereabouts and levels of education of children in each household and other ethnographic information. The MVF team, along with these 40 young volunteers, toured all the villages in that region, conducting the survey for about a fortnight. The survey found out that nearly 6,000 children in that region were out of school while only 4,000 went to school. It was also found that the majority of those out of school were girls. Some of these out-of-school children were found to be engaged in wage work, some in non-wage work, and some were found to be idle. Subsequently, upon further enquiry, it was found that the idle children were also engaged either in household work or sibling care at home. This effort of the survey and its findings led MVF to define child labour to further guide its own work. They decided to adopt the definition of every child out of school as either a child labour or a potential child labour.

To counter the vehement opposition to their advocacy efforts, MVF realized the need for an aggressive public campaign. The 200 youth who were a part of the first conference also joined in for this campaign. They first came out with a poster encouraging people to join the movement to release the 6,000 children, who were working, from exploitation. This caught the attention of people, especially the youth club members, who started rescuing children from workplaces and taking pride in their involvement in the movement. Subsequently, in order to improve their membership base from just youth club members, while visiting villages, MVF started identifying people who took a public stand for the issue and made them a part of their campaign. This campaign led to a large number of children going back to school. Initially, there was still an air of scepticism in the minds of the parents about the seriousness and sustainaibility of this campaign, since there had never been a public campaign of this nature ever before. Many a times, there was an adversarial response from school authorities as well, owing to the lack of infrastructure and resources to accommodate the children who were joining school after being rescued from employers.

Another major hurdle that MVF encountered during the course of its campaign was that, the schools in Andhra Pradesh at that time did not use to enrol children beyond 31st August, and hence, the children who were rescued after that point of time in the year had to wait until the next enrolment session to get into school. There was also some resistance to children from multiple age-groups going back to the same class in school. As a solution to these problems, MVF introduced the concept of 'bridge course' to cater to children who could not be enrolled into formal schools right away and needed a primer course before they could join a suitable class. The introduction of the bridge course was a major milestone in MVF's journey.

The second achievement was to bring a change in the admission policy of schools. From the very beginning, MVF has been clear about not acting on the behalf of either the community or the government. It has always played the role of a catalyst. Hence, the strategy it used to bring about this change was to meet relevant government officials like the District Magistrate, and not petition them but invite them to public functions where the local community members raised their concerns. The direct voice of the people had a much greater impact on the mind of the policymaker than the viewpoint of one NGO.

The bridge course had significant impact and got sufficient buy-in from the district administration. This led to the state government, led by N. Chandrababu Naidu, adopting their model of bridge course and running a pilot in 30,000 state schools in 1998–9. This was seen as a better alternative to night schools, the other model that was tried out. The night school seemed to give a sense of legitimacy to child labour.

Till 1996–7, although MVF was extremely local in nature and did not interact with other stakeholders or NGOs much, they were aware of the work being done elsewhere on this issue by Swami Agnivesh, Kailash Satyarthi, Nandana Reddy, and their respective organizations. The MVF started coming to limelight when they were invited to present at National Forums conducted by the Ministry of Human Resource Development (MHRD) and United Nations Development Programme (UNDP). Consequent to that, other agencies including the Government of India, impressed by their bridge course model, visited MVF and thereafter their presence and work grew beyond the state of Andhra Pradesh. In 1996, MVF also organized a National Convention with multiple partner organizations including the Centre for World Solidarity.

Drawing from its policy failure experience with the 1986 Child Labour Act, when MVF chalked down its future plan in 1999, it decided to work towards a change in policy for both child labour and compulsory education. In that stride, it drew five non-negotiable points which were to be kept in mind before arriving at any policy change. These were: a) no night schools; b) all work should be treated as hazardous and dangerous for overall growth and development for children; c) total abolition of child labour; d) any law which regulates child work instead of prohibiting it is not acceptable; and e) any child who is out of school should be seen as a child labour.

With these non-negotiable points in their agenda, they held several meetings with the Government of Andhra Pradesh to convince them to adopt these policies. As a result of MVF's advocacy efforts, in 2001, the Andhra Pradesh State Assembly passed a resolution to define all out-of-school children as child labourers. The Andhra Pradesh government also adopted the MVF bridge course model across the state and even advocated the same to the Government of India, highlighting the effectiveness of MVF's model. Further in 2003, the Andhra Pradesh government, with the help of MVF and the National Academy of Legal Studies and Research (NALSAR), also drafted a combined policy document for child labour and compulsory education. But subsequently, because of the change in power at the state and the difference in priorities, when the Telugu Desam Party (TDP) was defeated by Congress, the draft policy did not come through.

At the national level, the Union Government also adopted the bridge course model as part of the Sarva Shiksha Abhiyan (SSA). Though the government was sceptical of making MVF the implementer for the scheme, it had put in budgetary provisions in its annual growth plan for the officials to visit and learn from the MVF model. Once they were convinced of its effectiveness, MVF provided handholding support to SSA in implementing the bridge course model across different states in the country. At the same time, MVF continued its advocacy efforts as part of two nationwide campaigns, namely NAFRE and Campaign Against Child Labour (CACL). The strategy used for these campaigns was to hold rallies and organize national forums, and invite member NGOs, local MLAs, and MPs to be a part of these events. As part of CACL, they also decided to

celebrate 30 April as the Child Labour Day by organizing simultane-
ous functions across different districts to gather focus and awareness
on the issue.

Among the key people driving this agenda at the national level
were Ashok Agarwal and Shanta Sinha, owing to their acceptance
by both the government and civil society organizations. The MVF
participated in the Global March against Child Labour, organized by
the BBA, and organized the March in the entire state of undivided
Andhra Pradesh.

As the MVF relentlessly pursues the agenda of abolition of child
labour, it frequently gets stonewalled by two arguments. First, help-
lessness of individual officers or departments, since some of their
demands like the one for a blanket ban on child labour are beyond
the officials' scope of powers. Over time, MVF has developed a keen
understanding of the boundaries of influence of key departments and
officers and makes its policy pitch accordingly. The battle progresses
an inch at a time.

The economic counter-argument often thrown to MVF is the
infamous 'poverty argument'—if the children do not work, how will
the poor survive. While it does not always win the debate, MVF
itself is convinced that it is child labour that worsens poverty, not
the other way round. Child labour depresses adult wages, spreading
poverty. Poverty, therefore, cannot be a counter-argument to abolition of child labour.

However, the strength and acceptance of the poverty argument
cannot be underestimated. According to MVF, a key reason for
failure of the 2012 Bill was the popularity of the poverty argument
among policymakers. In 2014, the new government also introduced
the idea of children being allowed to work after school hours. These
arguments are constantly countered by the RTE, which makes it
compulsory for children up to the age of 14 to be in school. It also
talks about age-appropriate class in Section 4, in line with MVF's
bridge course model, and has a child-friendly admission policy
wherein enrolment is possible throughout the academic year.

While engaging with the policymakers, both in districts and the
state capital of Andhra Pradesh as well as at the Centre, MVF, in its
war against child labour, has simultaneously worked with other stakeholders as well. It has worked with the international group Stop Child

Labour Campaign's network to influence rather than sensationalize the blanket ban on all forms of child labour. It also used this forum to influence multinational corporations (MNCs) like Monsanto and Bayer to adopt a no-child-labour policy. It is of the firm belief that policy changes are better accomplished not only through pressure and petitioning but by example-setting by opinion-setters. When key MNCs change their behaviour, it sends a strong message into the entire environment and even the reluctant policymaker is likely to become more amenable to its logic than otherwise.

The work of MVF and Shantha Sinha found recognition when she was appointed the first Chairperson of the NCPCR that was set up by an Act of Parliament in 2005. She served two consecutive three-year terms there. Her winning of the Magsaysay Award also added strength to MVF's campaign.

Bachpan Bachao Andolan (BBA)

By far the most visible campaign against bonded and child labour, BBA was seeded around the same time as MVF in Andhra Pradesh. The struggle for rescuing childhood from child labour was at the genesis of this movement called Bachhpan Bachao Andolan (Save the Childhood Movement)—for it is not a single organization but a federation of hundreds of organizations working towards a common goal—in 1980–1. It started off when Kailash Satyarthi was approached by a father whose daughter, from a family of bonded labourers working in a brick kiln, was being sold off to a brothel at the age of 14 or 15. It led to the first ever legal process to a rescue operation. This, later on, transpired into a movement. The roots of the BBA, in turn, lay in the Bandhua Mukti Morcha (BMM) (Bonded Labour Liberation Front), a movement started and led in the 1980s by Swami Agnivesh. Satyarthi and Agnivesh worked together for over a decade till BBA branched out to exclusively focus on issues of child bonded labourers while the BMM continued work in the general bonded labour area, and later spread into unionization of unorganized sector workers.

The Act against child labour was a significant development in the area of child labour. But when the law came into existence in 1986, it had a number of gaps. The gaps started with the name of the law itself. On one side, India had a constitutional mandate under Article 45, which said that the state shall endeavour to provide free and compulsory primary education to all children below the age of 14 years within 10 years of the commencement of the Constitution, and on the other, there was this law which was framed as Child Labour (Prohibition and Regulation) Act. So, on one side it was prohibitive but on the other it was also regulatory in nature. The initial list of occupations has been extended to subsequently include a total of 18 occupations and 65 processes, as of now. But in all ilk of the regulatory nature of the framework and the policy itself, children continue to be employed especially in unorganized sectors like agriculture, and till a few years ago, as domestic child labour and in some other sectors. The BBA has been working on all aspects of child labour, towards prohibition of child labour. It has been tackling the problem from all angles including that of trafficking, bonded labour, education, and rehabilitation, resulting in reintegration of the children in mainstream formal society.

BBA's major campaigns formed the spine of the child rights movement in the country, though many other organizations, as part of the BBA or by themselves, continued to make significant contributions in their regions and spheres. A few milestones in the journey of BBA that capture the history of the child rights movement are as follows: a) The boycott of fireworks to protest against child labour in the fireworks industry in Sivakasi around Diwali 1991. To many urban middle-class Indians of a generation, this campaign was their first exposure to the issues and prevalence of child labour in the industry. b) First social label on child labour-free carpet, 'Rugmark' in 1994. c) The Global March Against Child Labour in 1998 across 103 countries, covering 80,000 kms, with participation from 7.2 million children, women, and men demanding international ban on child labour, leading to ILO Convention 182 against child labour. Over the years, BBA has gone global, while in India the response it managed to evoke from the public and media ranged from outright indifference to lukewarm at best, despite its methodical approach of documenting children released from bonded labour and working with media in its various raids and campaigns.

A sector where both child labour and child abuse were rampant in India was the circus industry. Research at BBA revealed that a very large number of girls from Nepal were being enticed, duped, and lied to, about jobs in circuses in India. Only a fraction of those girls were reaching the circuses and the rest were disappearing. Another equally disturbing finding was that the girls in those circuses were living a life of abject slavery, being sexually abused and harassed regularly. In January 2004, BBA worked with the Indian Circus Federation to come out with a declaration that the circuses would themselves wane out all the children that are employed; and, there was a circus training school in Kerala would be reinvigorated. The children would be trained there, and like campus placements, the circuses giving out the maximum benefits could recruit the trained artists. As a gesture of goodwill, some circuses actually released some children. This created an awareness among parents who started complaining to BBA about their children trapped in circuses.

Essentially, BBA is involved in rescue operations and has rescued over 84,000 children and people from bonded labour and trafficking, and this is the number of cases where they have successfully been able to prosecute. Cases where it is not able to prosecute are not counted as a rescued child. In a situation where it finds a child in a state of trafficking or exploitation, it believes that reparation has to be done. And when it prosecutes, it also handles reparations.

In 2004, the BBA started getting several complaints. The first one was about a circus in Palakkad, Kerala, and when the team went there for the rescue operation, it ended up rescuing 27 girls from the circus. When these girls went back home to Nepal, the news spread like wildfire and BBA started getting a large number of complaints. The next round of complaints that it received was about the Great Roman Circus in Gonda, Uttar Pradesh. When a team of about seven activists and four journalists led by Kailash Satyarthi went there to rescue the children, in the presence of the police and the Sub-Divisional Magistrate (SDM), they were assaulted badly and beaten black and blue. Satyarthi was also shot at. They were basically left alone only when the assaulters thought they were dead. This incident happened to be reported live by the television media channel *Aaj Tak*. While the team was being carried off to the hospital, all but one child from the

Circus disappeared. Amitabh Thakur, who was the Superintendent of Police (SP) of Gonda at that time, took the necessary steps and arrested the majority of the circus management. Since it became such a big issue, the government immediately set up a high-level enquiry and in three days the state labour department came out with a report saying this incident happened because Satyarthi wanted to open his own circus and hence was trying to kidnap these children. The report said this was why the circus management fought with the visiting team.

Meanwhile, the children were still missing. To protest the state inaction, Satyarthi decided to sit on a hunger strike in front of the state legislature, and he did so for a few days before he fell ill and developed a kidney infection, after which his health deteriorated fast. Hence, it was decided to call off the hunger strike and change strategies instead. In the meantime, BBA had filed a habeas corpus petition in the Lucknow bench of the Allahabad High Court (HC). The immediate response of the government was that the fundamental rights of the foreign citizens are not accrued in India and therefore the right of habeas corpus does not lie for these Nepali girls. However, the HC ruled in BBA's favour and hence the petition is maintainable. This became a well-known judgment in cases involving foreign nationals in India. Within 40 days of the incident, the HC ruled that the Director General of Police (DGP) was personally responsible for the safety and whereabouts of the girls and had to report back to the HC about what had happened to them. Consequently, all the girls were found within four hours, safe and sound, and the court was assured that they would be produced in three days, which they were.

The BBA realized that this case from Gonda was not an isolated one and that this was also not a case of mere child labour, but involved many other issues including trafficking. Trafficking is one of the two crimes, along with untouchability, which have been prohibited in India under Fundamental Rights, which prescribe punishment for these crimes under Article 23. Despite such a provision, trafficking had never been defined in India and has been practised unabated.

In 2006, BBA filed a writ petition in the Supreme Court (SC) of India on the issue of a total prohibition of child labour in Indian circuses and the larger aspects of crimes against children, like implementation of the Juvenile Justice (Care and Protection of Children)

Act, 2000 and anti-trafficking provisions. In January 2010, the SC gave a judgment ruling that the NCPCR was empowered to take action in cases of juvenile justice law, in addition to being the central authority for implementation of RTE. Eventually, the then Solicitor General of India, Gopal Subramaniam, put together a report on the Status of Child Rights in India, specifying what was required to be done on the subject. The SC gave a detailed judgment on 18 April 2011 that prohibited child labour in Indian circuses and also defined trafficking in India, for the first time, along the lines of the Optional Protocol to the UN Convention on Transnational Organized Crime. This resulted in India ratifying the said convention in May 2011. The SC also passed a series of detailed orders on how to implement the Juvenile Justice law, which became a key milestone in the history of child protection in India.

Feeling encouraged by the judgments, BBA moved four specific pleas before the SC seeking directions on a) total prohibition of child labour till the age of 14 years and prohibition in hazardous occupations till the age of 18 years; b) making child labour a cognizable and non-bailable offence; c) defining and including trafficking in the Indian Penal Code; and d) making registration of all marriages compulsory. The court took notice of the first issue of child labour and issued a notice in September 2011 to the Union Government of India on why child labour should not be prohibited in totality. The court, prima facie, also took cognizance of the fact that it appears that if a child is working, then it is in violation of the RTE, and therefore, it also violates the Constitution. Hence, there has to be a total ban on child labour till the completion of education.

Consequently, since the court had asked the Union Government about it, BBA also approached the Government of India. It started by approaching the Joint Secretary in the Ministry of Labour in charge of child labour, since he was the person who the court notice was sent to, and who in turn had to respond to it. Simultaneously, BBA ran a public awareness campaign called 'From Work to School'. This campaign included a host of celebrities to create a larger audience and thus generate a public demand for the cause. This campaign concluded with BBA organizing a national consultation in May 2012, involving a host of commissions, departments, and other organizations working in this area, none of whose response was adversarial when approached for this consultation. The then Minister of Labour and Employment, Mallikarjun Kharge attended the closing ceremony of the consultation and announced on the occasion that he was going to make all efforts for total prohibition of child labour. This campaign and consultation were very well received by the different stakeholders and the government agencies were receptive of the idea of total prohibition, because the issue of child labour had become popular in public discourse since Satyarthi had been rescuing children for the previous three decades, unlike campaigns related to issues of missing children or child sexual abuse, which had hit roadblocks.

These efforts led to the issue being tabled before the Cabinet in August 2012 and the Cabinet agreed to go ahead with a total ban on child labour. There were some amendments to the Child Labour Bill. The BBA opposed amended draft on technical grounds stating although the Bill provisioned total ban on child labour, it did not specify procedures for rescue or withdrawal of children from place of employment, procedures for rehabilitation and education after their rescue, role of police in the rescue of child labours that was already established previously through various HC and SC orders, and procedures for judicial intervention. This Bill was sent to the Standing Committee on Labour and the committee deliberated upon it in 2013. The draft Bill was made public for comments, during which time BBA also deposed before the committee with its remarks in June 2013. The Standing Committee report on the bill came out about six months later (see Box 6.4). However, since it was already close to the next general elections and there was not as much political footing for child labour as an issue, the bill was not tabled in Parliament in the next few sessions before the house was dissolved.

When the new government came in May 2014, BBA met the Minister of Labour and Employment Narendra Singh Tomar and apprised him of the previous developments in the matter of total ban on child labour. After the Standing Committee held consultations, it sent the bill back to the Cabinet with a few amendments. A newer version of the bill with additional changes was being drafted by the government and the Cabinet gave its nod to it in April 2015.

Box 6.4   Key Recommendations of the Standing Committee on Labour on the 2012 Bill

- The committee recommended that in keeping with the spirit of the Right to Education Act, 2009, this Bill should allow only those adolescents who have completed elementary education to be employed in an occupation.
- The committee observed that although the Statement of Objects and Reasons in the Bill mentioned that the bill sought 'to regulate the conditions of services of adolescents', it did not contain any provision fulfilling such an objective. Therefore, the committee suggested that regulation of working conditions of the adolescents including the criteria for their wages and settlement of disputes with regard to age of the child be included in the bill.
- The committee recommended that the definition of hazardous processes be widened to include all processes that jeopardize health, safety, and the morals of adolescents.
- The committee pointed out that the age at which a person is considered to be a 'child' varies from one act to the other and recommended that they be harmonized.
- The committee recommended that the provision allowing a child to help his family after school hours be deleted because it would be difficult to monitor whether the children are just helping their parents or are working to supplement the family income.
- The bill proposes to raise the penalty for employing a child or an adolescent in hazardous occupations and provides that parents or guardians of such a child or adolescent shall not be liable for punishment unless they allow him to work for commercial purposes. The committee observed that children are at times compelled to work with or without parental consent. Also, children may be put in a worse condition if parents are penalized. Therefore, it recommended that the government focus on providing alternative employment to adult members of the family and take a lenient view in case of poor parents and those parents who have not been able to benefit from government schemes towards reducing child labour.
- The committee advised that the fine collected from errant employers be kept in a fund named 'The Child Welfare Fund', which can be used for the rehabilitation of rescued children.

(Cont'd)

Box 6.4   *(Cont'd)*

- The bill confers the task of implementation on the District Magistrate. However, the committee pointed out that the District Magistrate is already overburdened and may not be able to devote adequate time for this. It therefore recommended that Vigilance and Monitoring Committees headed by the local MP be created to review the implementation of the Child Labour (Prohibition and Regulation) Act as well as other labour laws.
- The bill proposes to empower the appropriate government to periodically inspect places where employment of children is prohibited and hazardous processes are carried out. The Committee recommended that inspection be allowed in any place where employment of children is suspected and the employment of adolescents is prohibited.
- The committee noted that the bill contains no provision for rescue and rehabilitation of children. It recommended that instead of entrusting various ministries with this task, the government should bring a New Child Labour Policy and the machinery to implement laws, policies, and projects should be specified therein.

Sources: 'Child Labour (Prohibition and Regulation) Amendment Bill, 2012', 40th Report of the Department-related Standing Committee on Labour, 13 December 2013.

Key Observations and Concluding Remarks

Marked by ceaseless and sustained social activism and glacial legislative action, the journey of the Child Labour Bill fits in the advocacy-coalition framework since advocacy groups who believed in the eradication of child labour came together to form coalitions and pressurize the government for policy change.

As the case study shows, the activists used myriad means to push their agenda. Some like the MVF took the approach of largely working with the government and providing help in execution, through the development of the bridge course model, for instance. The MVF attained some success in seeing its model accepted first at the state level in Andhra Pradesh and then at the national level. Others, like the larger BBA, led by the nobel laureate Kailash Satyarthi, have worked hard and taken extreme risks (at his Nobel acceptance speech

Satyarthi recalled his co-workers who had laid down their lives in the struggle) to bring to light the condition of children working in abject slavery, to rescue over 84,000 children over the last three and a half decades of its existence, and be a thorn in the flesh of state and union governments to get some action out of them. They have used the judiciary to their advantage and have arm-twisted a severely status-quo-ist establishment into action.

However, the activists have not been able to push the government to enact the 2012 Bill. Studying the journey from the lens of the proposed 'legislative strategy framework', the conflictual approach of the activists have not yielded the desired result as the government also took a confrontationist stance on the issue. Given that there was no external 'triggering' event to give impetus to the movement, the impact on the legislative agenda of the government was low.

Needless to say, the job of the activists, judiciary, legislators, bureaucrats, and the police is far from done. The bane of child labour is reduced but far from conquered. Policy plays a critical role here—both in formulation as well as execution—and one is hard-pressed to think of a situation where multiple stakeholders have put their shoulders to the wheel together, even if grudgingly and reluctantly, to make creaking progress, as they have done in this area.

Postscript

While our case study narrates the journey only till the 2012 Bill, a modified version of the Bill finally got enacted in July 2016, though not to the satisfaction of most activists. The controversial parts of the new act are the reduction of the list of hazardous industries from 83 to just to mining, explosives, and occupations mentioned in the Factory Act, with powers to the government to make further exemptions; and the allowing of children to work in family or 'family enterprises'. It is unlikely that this legislation will be the last word on the issue. The struggle is certain to continue.

Notes

1. Nobel Lecture by Shri Kailash Satyarthi, 10 December 2014, Oslo, Norway, available at https://www.nobelprize.org/nobel_prizes/peace/

laureates/2014/satyarthi-lecture_en.html (last accessed on 8 March 2017).

2. The Children (Pledging of Labour) Act, 1933; Employment of Children Act, 1938; the Factories Act, 1948; the Mines Act, 1952; the Children Act, 1960; the Bonded Labour System (Abolition) Act, 1976; the Juvenile Justice Act, 1986.

7

Unfulfilled Promises

The Microfinance Bill, 2012

> *In the name of protecting India's poor, the state government of Andhra Pradesh has caused deep turmoil in microfinance. A new law clearly signals that borrowers need not repay their small-scale loans. Not surprisingly this has led to large-scale default, throwing the industry in India into a crisis it may not survive. This is having repercussions for microfinance worldwide.*
>
> —Banerjee et al. (2010)

On 22 May 2012, the Government of India introduced the Microfinance Institutions (Development and Regulation) Bill in the Lok Sabha, seeking to legislate appropriate regulatory structure for a sector that, largely overlooked by legislative and regulatory intervention, had witnessed explosive growth over a period of two decades before being brought to a grinding halt by a state regulation in Andhra Pradesh (AP). A similar bill had been introduced half a decade back but it had failed. Had it worked, the experience of the sector could very well have been very different.

In this chapter, we provide an overview of the microfinance movement in India, outlining its development to the Microfinance Bill of 2012; from its roots in the pre-1970s to its meteoric rise in the 1990s, which hit a roadblock with the crisis in AP in 2010, and the changes in the industry since the crisis.

Microfinance in India: The Emergence of an Industry and a Movement

The evolution timeline of microfinance in India consists of five major phases: the background of the financial inclusion agenda since Independence until the 1970s; the early but muted developments of microfinance from 1970 to 1990; the rapid growth phase from 1990 to 2010; the AP crisis of 2010; and the recovery.

1950–70: The Setting

Although India's relationship with microcredit began in the 1970s, the need to provide the poor with access to credit was brought home shortly after Independence in 1947, when the first survey of rural indebtedness (All India Rural Credit Survey) was prepared by the Reserve Bank of India (RBI). It documented that moneylenders and other informal lenders met more than 90 per cent of rural credit needs. The share of banks, in particular, was only about 1 per cent in total rural household debt (Basu and Srivastava 2005).

While the share of banks in total rural household debt increased only slightly to 2.4 per cent in 1971, the share of formal sources of credit in rural areas increased to 29 per cent due to the rising share of cooperatives (Basu and Srivastava 2005).

In 1969, India nationalized 14 major commercial banks in a policy known as 'social and development banking', in order to extend banking services to unbanked rural areas, and provide credit for specific activities and to certain disadvantaged groups. Targets were set for the expansion of rural branches, ceilings on interest rates were imposed, and guidelines were set for the sectoral allocation of credit. Specifically, a target of 40 per cent of advances for the priority sectors, namely agriculture and allied activities, and small scale and cottage industries, was set for commercial banks (Ramachandran and Swaminathan 2001).

1970–90: Early Years

The late 1970s to 1980s, among other measures, saw an expansion and consolidation of the institutional infrastructure for rural banking, especially through the introduction of Regional Rural Banks (RRBs) in 1972, which specialized in social and development banking in rural areas. These governmental initiatives did increase access to credit in rural areas,[1] but were biased in respect to regions, crops, and classes (Basu and Srivastava 2005).

However, rural development banks suffered massive erosion of their capital base due to subsidized lending rates and poor repayment discipline. Also, the funds did not always reach the poor and often ended up concentrated in the hands of better-off farmers (World Bank 2002). Similarly, the entire network of primary cooperatives in the country and the RRBs proved to be a colossal failure. Saddled with the burden of directed credit and a restrictive interest rate regime, the financial position of the RRBs deteriorated quickly, while the cooperatives suffered from the malaise of mismanagement, privileged leadership, and corruption born of excessive state patronage and protection (Sinha 2003).[2]

Meanwhile, beginning in the 1970s, Grameen Bank in Bangladesh and BancoSol in Bolivia, among others, led the way for microlending and group liability lending, an extension of small loans to groups of poor women to invest in microbusinesses.

Self-Employed Women's Association of India Sahakari Bank (SEWA) in Ahmedabad, Annapurna Mahila Mandal in Mumbai, and Working Women's Forum (WWF) in Chennai were early starters in India. They developed innovative strategies to tailor banking to the needs of economically weaker working women. The most well-known and successful of these initiatives was the SEWA Bank, undertaken by Elaben R. Bhatt, a lawyer and trade unionist. The SEWA was established in Ahmedabad in December 1971, and registered as a trade union in April 1972.

Around the mid-1980s, the first steps towards setting up Self-Help Group (SHGs) was taken by Mysore Resettlement and Development Agency (MYRADA), and it built upon rural chit funds and informal lending networks with the goal of evolving into a credit management group.

The government, in the meantime, decided to set up a new organization that would focus solely on the credit issue in rural areas. The National Bank for Agriculture and Rural Development (NABARD) was set up in 1982, and it took up the credit functions of RBI and the refinance function of the then Agricultural Refinance and Development Corporation (ARDC).

NABARD and MYRADA joined hands to connect the SHGs with banks. A survey of 43 non-governmental organizations (NGOs) in 11 states was conducted by NABARD between 1988 and 1989 to study the functioning of SHGs, and the possibilities of collaboration between banks and SHGs. The results were encouraging. Consequently, in 1992, MYRADA and NABARD together trained and expanded the savings groups, linking them to banks, and fostering the foundation of the SHG-Bank Linkage Program (SBLP). Other NGOs such as Professional Assistance for Development Action (PRADAN) and Development of Humane Action (DHAN), largely funded by NABARD, also pioneered the SHG model (Pulley 1989; Adams and Pischke 1992).

1990–2010: The Take-off

The liberalization of the economoy shifted the focus on financial sustainability, costing outreach dearly. The locational distribution of bank branches has also undergone a considerable shift away from the rural areas. The lending portfolio of scheduled commercial banks also reflects this shift away from rural areas (Chakrabarti and Ravi 2011).

Microfinance partly filled the resulting vacuum of credit in rural India. In 1992, NABARD sponsored the SBLP operations (Government of India 2008). Under SBLP, SHGs needed to save regularly for a minimum of six months and maintain prescribed records and accounts in order to become eligible to be linked to local banks. Currently, this programme provides credit to over 7.3 million SHGs.[3]

The liberalization of India's economy and financial sector after 1991 provided the impetus for the government to allow private players to enter the sector to provide microfinance products and services. These private microfinance service providers were called Micro Finance Institutions (MFIs) and included NGOs, cooperative societies, and Non-Banking Financial Companies (NBFCs). This diverse set of MFIs provided a range of microfinance products and services using different delivery models. Microfinance gradually evolved into an industry with diverse market players, low competition, a huge clientele, excellent long-term growth prospects, and no regulation.

The model of their operation was as follows: commercial banks or apex institutions (NABARD, Small Industries Development Bank of India [SIDBI], Rashtriya Mahila Kosh [RMK]) would lend to MFIs[4] for further lending to groups or individuals (see Figure 7.1) (Sanyal 2007).

The MFIs lent to SHGs and joint liability groups (JLGs, which are also known as Grameen groups). The number of MFIs in India involved in lending activities is estimated to be over 800. These MFIs vary significantly in size, outreach, and credit delivery methodologies. The lending activities of MFIs were not regulated except for those registered as NBFCs.

The microfinance sector in India, as in most places in the world, originated out of private initiatives of typically not-for-profits, and thrived for a long while without direct government supervision, with one exception—NABARD promoted SBLP. Until 1999, most of the MFIs were NGOs funded through grants and soft loans, and they had adopted the Grameen model of group-based lending to women in rural areas. About 800–1,000 NGOs were involved in mobilizing savings and providing microloans to the poor (Sinha 2003). Initially funded through donor support in the form of revolving funds and operating grants, these NGOs later started getting bulk loans from NABARD, SIDBI, and RMK. However, the outreach was still small as compared to the need—about 10 per cent of the 60 million poor families (Sinha 2003). This changed as some of the NGO–MFIs started growing and transforming into for-profit NBFCs, namely Spandana, SHARE Microfin, Bhartiya Samruddhi Investments and Consulting Services (BASIX) India, and Swayam Krishi Sangam (SKS) Microfinance. The sector also attracted professionals who set up for-profit NBFCs to provide financial services to people at the 'bottom of the pyramid'. In order to scale up, these NGO-MFIs needed to access capital, which was easier if they became a corporate entity regulated by the RBI. By 2010, there were five to ten large and mid-sized NBFC-MFIs, which had transformed from NGO-MFI, and 5 to 10 NBFC-MFIs

Figure 7.1 Institutional Flow of Microfinance

Table 7.1 Difference between SHGs and Grameen/JLGs

	SHGs	Grameen/JLGs
Size	Up to 20 members	5–15 members
Nature of loan	Single loan to the SHG as a whole, which decides how it should be allocated	Loan recorded in the names of Individual borrowers

Source: Ghate (2006).

promoted by professionals convinced about the opportunity at the 'bottom of the pyramid'.[5] There were also 800 NGO-MFIs operating in the sector, but their outreach and loan portfolios were much smaller (Nasir 2013).

The growth of for-profit NBFC-MFIs attracted international private equity. Three private equity deals brought in USD 52 million in 2008, followed by 11 deals the following year, which fetched USD 178 million. This was followed by the spectacular initial public offering (IPO) of SKS Microfinance, which made global headlines (Srinivasan 2010). On 28 July 2010, SKS became the first MFI in India to float its shares through an IPO. The offering was 13 times oversubscribed, and attracted leading investment groups such as Morgan Stanley, JP Morgan, and George Soros' Quantum Fund. The company valuation reached the top of the offer band price at USD 1.5 billion, and five weeks after trading began, the share price rose 42 per cent (D. Singh 2013).

This was, however, also the period in which tension started between NGO-MFIs and NBFC-MFIs, since there was a basic divergence in ideologies. The NGO-MFIs continued to be driven by social objectives of poverty alleviation, women's empowerment, and capacity building, while NBFC-MFIs became more profit oriented in order to scale-up operations. Sa-Dhan, an industry body set up in 1999, had both types of MFIs as its member. Although NBFC-MFIs had larger market share, NGO-MFIs were more numerous, which allowed them to dominate the industry body. This led the NBFC-MFIs to form their own association called the Micro Finance Institutions Network (MFIN) in 2009.[6] There are 50 such MFIs, less than one-fourth of the MFIs that exist in India, but they account for at least 90 per cent of the business. Two key initiatives of MFIN were the creation of a code of conduct for the industry and the development of a credit bureau, and both have received the status of Self Regulating Organization (SRO) (Bandyopadhyay 2014; S. Kumar 2015).

The Crisis

By June 2011, MFIs reached 31.4 million clients all over India. In terms of 'client outreach—borrowers with outstanding accounts', there was growth of 17.6 per cent MFI clients, and 4.9 per cent of SHG-Bank clients in the year 2010–11. This meant that while both SHG and MFI models coexisted, MFIs were growing at a much faster pace (Srinivasan 2011). In financial year (FY) 2011, AP had the highest concentration of microfinance operations, with 17.31 million SHG members and 6.24 million MFI clients. The total microfinance loans in the state, inclusive of both SHGs and MFIs, stood at Rs 157 billion, with the average loan outstanding per poor household at Rs 62,527, the highest among all the states in India (IFMR 2014). The implication was that MFIs had penetrated AP to almost saturation level. It also meant that there was multiple borrowing by households. A World Bank's Consultative Group to Assist the Poorest (CGAP) study indicated that the average household debt in AP was Rs 65,000, compared to a national average of Rs 7,700. This high penetration of both SHGs and MFIs also led to stiff competition for client outreach between the state government-sponsored SHG programme known as 'Indira Kranthi Patham (Velugu)'(IFMR 2014) and large, privately-owned MFIs such as SKS and Spandana, two of the fastest-growing for-profit MFIs (Chakrabarti and Ravi 2011). Thus, AP accounted for nearly 40 per cent of all microfinance activity in India. Hyderabad, the home of by far the largest number of microfinance giants, was virtually the capital of microfinance in India. Until a few months before the crisis, the state wore this distinction as a badge of honour.

The meteoric rise of the for-profit MFIs was characterized by SKS, which had made waves by attracting private equity in the microfinance sector. In August 2010, it grabbed headlines with its hugely successful IPO, oversubscribed almost 14 times. To many, it was the signal of the Indian microfinance industry coming of age. Several other capital issues were being planned. However, many engaged in social sector activism, including Muhammad Yunus himself, were less than impressed by what they perceived to be a shift of focus from social impact to investor returns.[7] The euphoria among the for-profit MFIs proved to be short-lived. Within weeks of the IPO, news broke of close to 30 farmer suicides, allegedly linked to coercive collection methods of MFIs. More than half of these were allegedly borrowers of SKS and/or Spandana (Chakrabarti and Ravi 2011).

The resulting crash in the stock of microfinance in AP has few parallels in recent times. The political establishment swung into action following the suicides, and the MFIs were demonized in the media. Vandalism of MFI offices by political goons was followed by police interrogations. Overnight, AP's lauded sector and MFIs had become pariahs (Chakrabarti and Ravi 2011). Some suggest that the AP government was not motivated by any desire to protect the poor, but to protect the uncompetitive government-backed SHG programme run by the Society for Elimination of Rural Poverty (*Legatum Ventures* 2011).

It is important to note that this was not the first time that microfinance had been at the centre of negative media glare. In 2006, a spate of suicides in the state's Krishna district had been linked to 'barbaric' practices of MFIs. The government shutdown 57 branches of the two largest MFIs (SHARE and Spandana) as well as those of few smaller MFIs, alleging unethical collection practices, illegal operational practices, poor governance, usurious interest rates, and profiteering. The impasse ended with the state setting up village and Mandal-level (second-level administrative division in the three-tier Panchayati Raj system) vigilance committees to oversee the functioning of MFIs, the industry lobby proposing a code of conduct for MFIs, and the latter voluntarily reducing interest rates (Kaur and Dey 2013).

This time the government tried to alleviate the crisis by the promulgation of the Andhra Pradesh Micro Finance Institutions (regulation of money lending) Ordinance, 2010, on 15 October, later ratified by the Andhra Pradesh Assembly with some changes on 15 December (Chakrabarti and Ravi 2011). The main features of the October ordinance included a requirement for MFIs to register themselves with government authorities, prevention of further lending in cases where loans were outstanding, and restriction on collection to once a month. The administrative bottlenecks made registration difficult and the widespread political campaign maligning the MFIs as loan sharks encouraged default. These factors brought the industry to a practical halt for several weeks in AP and scuttled the ambitious plans of MFIs hitting the capital markets (Srinivasan 2012). The reduction in collection frequency arguably affected saving discipline as well. In any case, the major players saw their recovery rates drop from above 90 per cent to below 30 per cent post-ordinance. Clearly, the activity became untenable for most players and threatened the very survival of the sector on its home turf (Chakrabarti and Ravi 2011).

Major players were beset with problems. The BASIX group had to go for restructuring. The SKS wrote off loans totalling Rs 13.62 billion and pared its staff in the state to 1,200 from around 7,000 prior to the crisis. SKS Microfinance had to scale down the number of branches in AP to 120 from 550. Its chairman Vikram Akula resigned from the board in November 2011 (*LiveMint* 2015). Spandana's daily disbursement of loans came down from Rs 250 million to Rs 70 million, employee strength to 4,000 from 14,000, and the number of borrowers to 2.8 million from 5.2 million. In 2011, with mounting

---

Box 7.1   Highlights of the Andhra Pradesh Microfinance Institutions (Regulation of Moneylenders) Act, 2010

- All MFIs should be registered with the district authority.
- No person should be a member of more than one SHG.
- All MFIs should make the rate of interest charged by them for the loans public.
- There would be a penalty on the use of coercive action by the MFIs.
- All MFIs are supposed to maintain records, registers, and a cashbook, which need to be presented when demanded.
- In case of dispute settlement between the SHGs and its members or the SHGs and the MFIs, fast track courts would be set up.
- Any person who contravenes any provision of the act shall be punishable with imprisonment for a period of 6 months or a fine up to the amount of Rs 10,000, or both.

Source: PRS Legislative Research 2010.

debt, it had to go through a debt restructuring exercise (Chakrabarti and Ravi 2011).

The repercussions of the crisis did not stay limited to AP. Banks stopped lending to MFIs all over India, for fear that a similar situation would occur elsewhere. MFIs all over faced a liquidity crunch since they were largely dependent on bank-lending as a funding source. With the sector at a standstill, MFIs, microfinance clients, banks, investors, and local governments were calling for new regulation to address the sector's issues. It compelled the RBI to step in and look into developing a policy for MFIs to end the impasse and avert such situations elsewhere (Chakrabarti and Ravi 2011).

The RBI's Board of Directors, at its meeting on 15 October 2010, formed a Sub-Committee to study the issues and concerns in the microfinance sector. The Committee, chaired by Y.H. Malegam, submitted its recommendations on 19 January 2011, which were quite far-reaching in nature and included creating a new class, NBFC-MFIs, for regulatory purposes (RBI 2011a). These NBFC-MFIs, the committee proposed, should have a net worth of at least Rs 150 million, with a minimum of 90 per cent of their assets being 'qualifying assets'. These 'qualifying assets' or microloans are non-collateralized loans to households with annual income below Rs 50,000, with loan size and/or total indebtedness not exceeding Rs 25,000. Finally, repayment should be monthly or less frequent. At least 75 per cent of the credit should be for income-generating purposes. The NBFC-MFIs would be exempt from the money lenders acts, and loans to these MFIs by banks would continue to enjoy priority-lending status. The Sub-Committee added that there needed to be a margin cap over cost of funds—12 per cent for MFIs with total loan portfolio size below Rs 1 billion and 10 per cent for others—as well as an overall interest cap of 24 per cent on individual loans. Several provisions discouraged over-borrowing, multiple-lending, and ghost-borrowing, including measures making it the responsibility of the MFIs to ensure that a borrower was not part of more than one JLG until the time a Credit Information Bureau took up the task. There are provisions for borrower protection, including those regulating recovery methods, and the suggestion to formulate a client protection code by the designated sector regulator (RBI 2011a).

Box 7.2   Malegam Committee Report: Salient Features

Terms of Reference

- To review the definition of microfinance and microfinance institutions (MFIs) for the purpose of regulating non-banking financial corporations (NBFCs) undertaking microfinance by the RBI.
- To delineate objectives and scope of regulation of NBFCs undertaking microfinance by the RBI.
- To recommend a grievance redressal system that could be put in place to ensure adherence to the regulation recommendations.
- To examine the prevalent practices of MFIs with regard to interest rates, lending and recovery in order to identify trends that impinge on borrowers' interest.
- To examine conditions under which loans to MFIs can be classified as priority sector lending and make appropriate recommendations.
- To examine the role that bodies of MFIs could play in enhancing transparency disclosure and best practices.

Key Recommendations	
Classification of NBFC-MFI	• Create separate category for NBFCs operating in the microfinance sector called the NBFC-MFI with the following features: (a) provides financial services pre-dominantly to low income borrowers; (b) with loans of small amounts; (c) for short-terms; (d) on unsecured basis; (e) mainly for income-generating activities; (f) with repayment schedules which are more frequent than those of commercial banks; and (g) which conform to the regulations specified. • An NBFC which does not qualify as an NBFC-MFI should not be permitted to give loans to the microfinance sector, which in the aggregate exceed 10 per cent of its total assets.
Interest Rate	**Pricing of Interest Rate** • A 'margin cap' of 10 per cent in respect of MFIs which have an outstanding loan portfolio at the beginning of the year of Rs 100 crore,

(Cont'd)

Box 7.2   *(Cont'd)*

	• A 'margin cap' of 12 per cent in respect of MFIs, which have an outstanding loan portfolio at the beginning of the year of an amount not exceeding Rs 100 crore, and • A cap of 24 per cent on individual loans. **Transparency in Interest Charges** • There should be three components in the pricing of the loan: (a) processing fee, not exceeding 1 per cent of the gross loan amount; (b) the interest charge; and (c) the insurance premium. • Only the actual cost of insurance should be recovered and no administrative charges should be levied. • Every MFI should provide the borrower with a loan card which shows the effective rate of interest and other terms and conditions. • There should not be any recovery of the security deposit. • There should be a standard loan agreement.
Asset Book Conditions for NBFC-MFI	At least 90 per cent of its total assets (other than cash and bank balances and money market instruments)are in the nature of 'qualifying assets'. A 'qualifying asset' shall mean a loan which satisfies the following criteria: • the loan is given to a borrower who is a member of a household whose annual income does not exceed Rs 50,000; • the amount of the loan does not exceed Rs 25,000 and the total outstanding indebtedness of the borrower including this loan also does not exceed Rs 25,000; • the tenure of the loan is not less than 12 months where the loan amount does not

(Cont'd)

Box 7.2   *(Cont'd)*

	• exceed Rs 15,000 and 24 months in other cases with a right to the borrower of prepayment without penalty in all cases; • the loan is without collateral; • the aggregate amount of loans given for income generation purposes is not less than 75 per cent of the total given by the MFIs; • the loan is repayable by weekly, fortnightly or monthly installments at the choice of the borrower • The income it derives from other services is in accordance with the regulation specified.
Capital of NBFC-MFI	**Minimum net worth**: All NBFC-MFIs are required should have a minimum net-worth of Rs 1.5 crores. **Capital adequacy ratio:** All NBFC-MFIs should be required to maintain capital adequacy ratio of 15 installment. Net owned funds should be in the form of Tier 1 capital.
Securitization and Assignment	• Disclosure is made in the financial statements of MFIs of the outstanding loan portfolio, which has been assigned or securitized and the MFI continues as an agent for collection. • Where the assignment or securitization is with recourse, the full value of the outstanding loan portfolio assigned or securitized should be considered as risk based assets for calculation of capital adequacy. • Where the assignment or securitization is without recourse but credit enhancement has been given, the value of the credit enhancement should be deducted from the Net Owned funds for the purpose of calculation of capital adequacy. • Before acquiring assigned or securitized loans, banks should ensure that the loans have been made in accordance with the terms of the specified regulations.

(Cont'd)

Box 7.2   (Cont'd)

Provisioning of Loans	• Provisioning for loans should not be maintained for individual loans but an MFI should be required to maintain at all times an aggregate provision for loan losses which shall be the higher of: (a) 1 per cent of the outstanding loan portfolio; or (b) 50 per cent of the aggregate loan instalments which are overdue for more than 90 days and less than 180days and 100 per cent of the aggregate loan instalments which are overdue for 180 days or more.
Lending Process	• MFIs should lend to an individual borrower only as a member of a JLG (Joint Liability Group) and should have the responsibility of ensuring that borrower is not a member of another JLG. • A borrower cannot be a member of more than one SHG (Self-Help Group)/JLG. • Not more than two MFIs should lend to the same borrower. • There must be a minimum period of moratorium between the grant of the loan and the commencement of its repayment. • Recovery of loan given in violation of the regulations should be deferred till all prior existing loans are fully repaid. • All sanctioning and disbursement of loans should be done only at a central location and more than one individual should be involved in this function. • There should be close supervision of the disbursement function.
Recovery Process	• MFIs should ensure that coercive methods of recovery are not used. In case of use of coercive methods, MFIs should be subject to severe penalties.

(Cont'd)

Box 7.2   *(Cont'd)*

	• MFIs should have a proper Code of Conduct and proper systems for recruitment, training, and supervision of field staff to ensure the prevention of coercive methods of recovery.
Credit Information Bureau	One or more credit information bureaus should be established and be operational as soon as possible and all MFIs should be required to become members of such bureau. In the meantime, the responsibility to obtain information from potential borrowers regarding existing borrowings should be on the MFI.
Funding of MFIs	• Bank lending to the microfinance sector both through the SHG-Bank Linkage Programme and directly should be significantly increased and this should result in a reduction in the lending interest rates. • Bank advances to the MFIs shall continue to enjoy 'priority sector lending' status. However, advances to MFIs which do not comply with the regulation should be denied such status. • The creation of one or more 'Domestic Social Capital Funds' may be examined in consultation with SEBI. • MFIs should be encouraged to issue preference capital with a ceiling on the coupon rate and this can be treated as part of Tier 2 capital subject to capital adequacy norms.
Monitoring of Compliance	• The primary responsibility for ensuring compliance with the regulations should rest with the MFI itself and it should be penalized in case of noncompliance. • Banks should also conduct surveillance of MFIs through their branches. • The RBI should have the responsibility for off-site and on-site supervision of MFIs.

(Cont'd)

	Box 7.2 *(Cont'd)*
	• The RBI should have the power to remove from office the CEO and/or a director in the event of persistent violation of the regulations.
Regulation	NBFC-MFIs should be exempted from the provisions of the Money-Lending Acts, especially since there are recommendations regarding interest margin caps and increased regulation.
	Key Features of the Proposed Micro Finance (Development and Regulation) Bill, 2010
	• Should provide for all entities covered by the Act to be registered with the Regulator. However, entities where aggregate loan portfolio does not exceed Rs 10 crore may be exempted from registration.
	• If NABARD is designated as the regulator under the proposed act, there must be close coordination between NABARD and the RBI in the formulation of the regulations.
	• The micro-finance entities governed by the proposed act should not be allowed to do the business of providing thrift services.

Sources: PRS Legislative Research (2011), and authors' own summary.

Towards a New Law

The AP crisis left MFIs such as SHARE Microfin, Asmitha Microfin, Spandana Sphoorty Financial, Trident Microfin, and Future Financial Services with negative net worth. This meant that banks would not lend to them since banking norms decreed that they could not provide fresh loans to companies with negative net worth. Lending to MFIs by banks during the year 2011–12 declined by over 38 per cent as compared to the previous year. Since banks stopped lending to MFIs, they were not able to disburse fresh loans to their clients. Banks were also hit by the crisis as 80 per cent of MFI loans were financed by the banks. Of the Rs 210 billion that banks had outstanding to

MFIs, roughly a third was borrowed from private banks. Banks and financial institutions lost their trust in MFIs' credibility to repay the loans. Loans outstanding against MFIs came down by almost 17 per cent during the year 2011–12. Gross loan portfolios also shrunk by 14 per cent in FY 2011–12, and were reduced to Rs 172 billion. The crisis hit the operational self-sufficiency (OSS)[8] of AP-based MFIs badly, which fell from 150 per cent (FY 2009–10) to 40 per cent (FY 2011–12) (Kaur and Dey 2013). The crisis affected the portfolio quality of MFIs to the extent that they became the worst performer on the global platform. As pointed out by N. Srinivasan, 'The Andhra Pradesh regulation is right on intent, but wrong in its focus, coverage, and application. Inappropriate regulation produces long-term damage that is difficult to remedy' (Kaur and Dey 2013; Srinivasan 2011).

On the regulatory side, subsequent to the Malegam Committee recommendations, the RBI came up with two significant notifications. One was to accord priority-sector status to bank lending to MFIs, and the other was the NBFC-MFIs Directions 2011. While the former covered bank lending to all kinds of MFIs, the latter covered the NBFC-MFIs, which were recognized as separate category of NBFCs. Both regulations defined qualifying assets, income criteria for borrowers, limits for indebtedness, targets for income generation loan, pricing structure including margin cap and interest rate cap, lending practices, and so on. The MFIs, by and large, were compliant with the regulatory prescriptions made by RBI (Sa-Dhan 2014).

A Credit Bureau

A key development after the issuance of the RBI notifications was the fact that all MFIs had to report to at least one of the MFI-specific credit bureaus in India (High Mark, Equifax, and more recently Experian). They also had to check every loan application with the credit bureau to establish the level of indebtedness of the applicant. The following thresholds were prescribed by the RBI (RBI 2011a):

1) Total indebtedness of the borrower should not exceed Rs 50,000.
2) The MFI should ensure that:

- Borrower does not have more than two NBFC-MFIs loans;
- Borrower cannot be a member of more than one of its SHGs/JLGs;
- It does not lend to a single person as an individual and group borrower simultaneously.

These measures ensured that there was very low likelihood of a borrower becoming over-indebted through microfinance loans as it limited both the exposure as well as the number of providers to a single borrower. However, informal borrowings from money lenders and loan sharks were not captured here.

Drafting of a New Bill

The central government also swung into action, with the Ministry of Finance constituting a committee in March 2011 to recommend a draft of a new law to regulate the sector. This committee had members from the Department of Financial Services, RBI, Indian Banks Association (IBA), NABARD, SIDBI, state governments (Bihar and Tamil Nadu), and State Level Bankers' Committee, Andhra Pradesh. The MFIs were represented by the MFIN and Sa-Dhan. The draft bill formulated by the committee was put on the website of the Ministry of Finance to invite comments from stakeholders. The Department of Financial Services organized a round table on the draft bill on 28 July 2011, where the representatives of the AP government were also invited to express their views.

After considering the comments received from various stakeholders, the government introduced the Micro Finance Institutions (Development and Regulation) Bill, 2012, which was introduced in Lok Sabha on 22 May 2012 and referred to the Departmentally Related Standing Committee on Finance on 25 May 2012.[9]

The bill sought to establish the RBI as the regulator of the sector, with powers to: (a) specify the maximum limit of the margin and annual percentage rate which can be charged by any MFI, sector-related benchmarks, performance standards pertaining to methods of operation, and set fair and reasonable methods of recovery of loans advanced by the MFIs; and (b) cause inspection of the accounts of the MFIs and take necessary action (PRS 2012).

This was, however, not the first attempt at regulating the sector. In 2007, the government had introduced the Microfinancial Sector (Development and Regulation) Bill in Parliament on 20 March 2007 and had designated NABARD as the regulator (Padmanabhan 2012). This Bill lapsed with the dissolution of the 14th Lok Sabha. We compare the provisions of the two bills in Box 7.3.

Box 7.3   Comparison of 2007 Bill and 2012 Bill

Aspects	Microfinance Bill, 2007	Microfinance Bill, 2012
Scope and application	Only NGO-MFIs registered as societies, trust, and cooperatives (that is, excluding NBFCs and Section 25 companies).	All MFIs in all forms.
Structure of the sector	One tier, MFOs only (apart from NBFCs and Section 25 companies, but no provisions applicable to them).	The sector is now covered under the provisions of the bill in its entirety.
Savings mobilization	Thrift only for MFO from members.	Thrift mobilization from public also permitted.
Supervisor	NABARD	RBI—with powers to delegate to NABARD and to other agencies as may be deemed fit.
Advisory council	Advisory, with majority consisting of officials representing specified agencies ex-officio.	In addition to a national level council, provisions have been made for state level councils as well as district level committees for monitoring of functioning of MFIs.

(Cont'd)

Box 7.3   *(Cont'd)*

Aspects	Microfinance Bill, 2007	Microfinance Bill, 2012
Grievances handling and appellate authority	MFDC may set up ombudsman.	Ombudsman provided for.
Capital norms	NOF of at least Rs 500,000 and a capital adequacy ratio of 15 per cent.	Rs 500,000 as minimum entry capital—RBI to stipulate prudential norms.
Instruments	Registration for thrift taking MFOs and information reporting for all.	Registration for all, information reporting and interest rate caps.
Customer protection	Through Ombudsman.	Norms for customer selection, size of loans, interest disclosure, process controls and interest/margin ceilings. Also through District Micro Finance Committees.
Powers of regulator	Minimal.	Power to cancel registration, order for winding up, merger and acquisition, imposition of penalties, delegation of powers, issuance of directions.

Sources: The Micro Financial Sector (Development and Regulation) Bill, 2007; The Microfinance Institutions (Development and Regulation) Bill, 2012; and authors' own summary.

Different stakeholders had diverse views on the regulations. The NBFC-MFIs, under MFIN, believed that since NBFCs were governed by the RBI, they need not be subjected to more regulation. However, the Standing Committee rejected the bill, urged the Ministry to hold wider consultations, and review its fundamental proposals. Since this bill sought to bring in unincorporated MFIs, which were few in number, under the RBI's ambit, the committee suggested instead that the states be allowed to bring unincorporated MFIs under the ambit of state money lending laws. Since the RBI also had reservation about the bill, the Committee suggested the formation of an independent regulator, which would have representatives from all concerned agencies. It also felt that the government should persist in pursuing the bank-led model for financial inclusion. Lastly, it advised that the government should consider statutory rights for bank accounts. The Standing Committee gave its report on 13 February 2014, in the last session of the 14th Lok Sabha, but the bill lapsed with the dissolution of the Lok Sabha a few months later.

Moving On

In the months since the 2014 election of the new BJP-led government of Narendra Modi, the microfinance sector has witnessed significant changes. Small banks and payments banks, major innovations in banking, are being tested out. Bandhan Bank of West Bengal became the first microfinance player to obtain a banking license. A new sector regulator, MUDRA Bank, has been introduced by the new government.

Meanwhile in AP, where all the trouble started, there are reports of a 'call money' market mushrooming, where moneylenders lend money over phone calls at rates of interest between 120 per cent and 200 per cent per annum, with collection methods that include harassment that has driven entire families to commit suicide, as well as sexual harassment and driving women borrowers, who constitute the majority, to prostitution (Sarma 2015). A study of the effects of the ruling from the Institute for Financial Management and Research (IFMR) (Sadhu et al. 2013) finds that between 2009 and 2012, MFI client households have fewer numbers of total loans outstanding, but the overall amount of indebtedness has increased over time; no increase in penetration of the banks and SHGs despite large scale withdrawal of MFI lending; clients seem to have had to substitute MFI loans with informal loans (mostly from the moneylender and landlords) for smoothing consumption and health shocks; and while 45 per cent of clients defaulted on their loans, most cited the absence of loan officers during the time of repayment and influence by political leaders and government officials as reasons for non-repayment.

Key Observations and Concluding Remarks

The story of the Microfinance Bill stands out because the need for regulation arose due to some of the excesses caused by the phenomenal growth of the sector. Till a long time, microfinance was viewed benignly by policymakers since it was an innovative tool for helping the poor to get access to credit, which was otherwise denied to them through conventional routes. Thus, it flourished without the heavy hand of government regulation. However, its success became its enemy, especially in AP, where the industry was most concentrated. The change from a mostly NGO-based non-profit model to a for-profit model to increase scale and efficiency brought with it some unintended consequences. A spate of suicides allegedly because of coercive loan recovery practices by some of large MFIs gave the state government the excuse to clamp down on their operation with a draconian law. But at the central level, there was push from some members of the industry (the non-profit group) for a law to regulate their operation, which would help them access loans and grants. The for-profit MFIs came under the RBI's regulations, which gave them the credibility they needed to raise funds. Although there were two attempts to enact a law, they could not succeed either time mostly due to the fact that the government was tied up with other matters.

The somewhat unique journey of this bill renders it difficult to place it within any of the existing policy process frameworks. In only a very broad sense, it can be placed within the advocacy-coalition framework since Sa-Dhan, an association of mostly non-profit MFIs, was involved in advocating for a law to regulate the sector.

Viewing the Bill's trajectory from the lens of the proposed framework, we find that although the method of activism was collaborative and the government was also willing to engage with the non-elected stakeholders, the bill could not be enacted. This could be because the government was preoccupied with other matters and no external incident happened to bring the matter to the immediate attention of the government. This is borne out by the fact that in AP, the government took prompt action through an Ordinance when a crisis loomed in the horizon.

Notes

1. Following bank nationalization, the share of banks in rural household debt increased to about 29 per cent in 1981, while the share of formal or institutional sources in total debt reached 61.2 per cent till 1991.
2. Since 1990, the need for cooperative reforms was articulated by many committees which were headed by Chaudhry Brahm Perkash, Jagdish Capoor, Vikhe Patil, and V.S. Vyas. The basic problem identified by these committees was that most cooperative societies lacked autonomy due to direct intrusion of the state in their governance and management. The reason was that the co-operative movement in India was initiated by the government. In 1954, the All India Rural Credit Survey Committee Report not only recommended state partnership in terms of equity, but also partnership in terms of governance and management.
3. See website of NABARD, see https://www.nabard.org/english/shgs.aspx (last accessed on 8 March 2017).
4. Private bodies based on the Grameen model of Bangladesh.
5. IFMR Capital, 'Microfinance in India', available at http://capital.ifmr.co.in/briefs/microfinance-in-india (last accessed on 8 March 2017).
6. Interviews with Matthew Titus (Sa-Dhan) and Alok Prasad (MFIN).
7. There has been a long-standing debate in the microfinance sector between those who believe that microfinance should be centred on economic and social impacts and those who advocate financial sustainability which would allow the sector to grow without subsidies or constraints of donor budgets. For a detailed discussion on the debate see Morduch (2000). Also see debate between Muhammad Yunus and Vikram Akula at http://www.muhammadyunus.org/index.php/yunus-centre/yunus-centre-highlights/656-microfinance-or-loan-sharks-grameen-bank-and-sks-fight-it-out (last accessed on 8 March 2017).
8. Operating self-sufficiency is a percentage, which indicates whether or not enough revenue has been earned to cover the MFI's total costs—operational expenses, loan loss provisions, and financial costs. See Sa-Dhan (2006).

9. 'Micro Finance Institutions (Development and Regulation) Bill, 2012',
    84th Report of the Departmentally related Standing Committee
    on Finance, 13 February 2014, available at http://www.prsindia.
    org/uploads/media/Micro%20Finance%20Institutions/SCR-%20
    Micro%20 finance %20bill.pdf (last accessed on 8 March 2017).

8

Accelerated Change

The Criminal Law (Amendment) Act, 2013

Having worked every day of my life for the last 15 years on sexual violence, I have never seen anything like that, where sexual violence broke through the consciousness and was on the front page, nine articles in every paper every day, in the center of every discourse, in the center of the college students' discussions, in the center of any restaurant you went in.

—Eve Ensler, playwright and activist on the protests in the aftermath of the Delhi gang rape in 2012

The Context

Around midnight of 16 December 2012, Safdarjung Hospital's Trauma Centre received a rape victim whose horrific story would galvanize the usually apathetic Delhi residents to take to the streets for days, force the government to set up a committee to recommend measures to address sexual violence against women, and promulgate an ordinance providing for tougher rape laws, all in the short span of about a month and a half. Quite a feat for a country not exactly known for quick and decisive policymaking!

The next day started ordinarily enough. None of the national dailies had yet picked up the story, but about 8 am onwards, television channels, such as NDTV, started broadcasting the news while social media was already buzzing with shock and outrage. One of the people responsible for spreading the news on social media was Amitabh Kumar, a young activist with the Centre for Social Research (CSR), an organization that works on women's rights and also counsels rape victims. At 3 am, he had received a phone call from the police who alerted him about the rape and the fact that his organization's intervention may be required. The first thing he did in the morning was to call up his friend and comrade-in-action Lenin Red (a nickname given for his ideological leanings), who was the leader of Jawaharlal Nehru University's (JNU) student union.

As the day wore on, the facts of the horrific incident became clearer. At around 9:30 pm on 16 December 2012, a young, 23-year-old physiotherapy student, Jyoti Singh and her friend Avnindra Pandey were waiting at the Munirka bus stop, hoping to catch a bus home. They had just watched the movie *Life of Pi* at a mall in Saket and then taken an auto to the Munirka bus stand. A private chartered bus picked them up assuring them that their destination, Palam Vihar, was on the bus route. In addition to the driver and helper, the bus had four men, who the victims thought were passengers, but they turned out to be friends of the driver and helper. These six men, one of whom only 17 years old, then proceeded to brutally beat up Pandey and rape and torture Jyoti for the next 45 minutes, all the while driving the bus around the city in a circle. They inserted a rod into the girl and pulled out her intestines after which they threw the two out on the road, naked and bleeding, near the Mahipalpur flyover. Many vehicles passed by, but no one stopped to help. Finally, at around 12:15 am, the police, on being alerted by a toll plaza patrol vehicle, picked them up and brought them to Safdarjung Hospital (*India Today* 2012).

The Snowballing of a Protest

'It could have been me'

Given the statistics[1] on rape in India, on an average 92 women are raped each day (*India Today* 2014). A question that has been asked repeatedly is why this particular case struck a chord among Delhi's urban middle class. There is no easy answer and experts and activists have posited many theories—the brutality of the rape, the centrality of the location, the identification with the victim as 'one of us'. Probably, it is a combination of all those factors.

As we spoke to a number of protestors (especially the first-timers), what stood out was the overwhelming feeling of 'it could have been me'. The victim's predicament resonated with a lot of urban women who have to use public transport to return home. For many, it was the recognition that the victim could have been them or any one of their friends, colleagues, or acquaintances that made them decide to participate in the protest.

Probably, the empathy for the victim also came from the fact that there was a heart-warmingly aspirational quality to her life story that resonated with many of the city's urban professionals. This was not just another victim, in some remote village of Uttar Pradesh or Bihar, leading a life of misery and oppression with little control over her own destiny. Despite belonging to an underprivileged family who came from a culturally conservative community, where women are not normally encouraged to study and pursue a career, Jyoti's parents made enormous financial sacrifices to fund her education (*IBN Live* 2012). They were also progressive enough to fund a daughter's education even though they had two sons, a rarity in many Indian families. Jyoti herself was an inspiration. She was a dedicated student who worked in a call centre in the evenings to partly fund her education.

By around 12:30 pm on 17 December, about 100 protestors— from JNU as well as those mobilized by Amitabh Kumar's activist network (Jagori, Youth Parliament, Youth Collective, Youth Ki Awaaz, Breakthrough, to name a few)—had gathered around the Vasant Vihar police station shouting slogans. They marched from Nelson Mandela Marg onto the Outer Ring Road, one of the most important roads in the city. By 2 pm, the Outer Ring Road was choked, bringing traffic to a standstill. The news of the protests spread like wildfire through social media like Facebook and Twitter as well as television channels who had reached the venue. Kumar, in an interview with us, said that he had posted a notice about the protest on the morning after the incident. It went 'viral', meaning it was shared over 100,000 times. He said he spread the messages through the Twitter handles of Ranjana Kumari, the head of Centre for Social Research (CSR) with a following of 54,000, and IstandforsafeDelhi. Every message, according to him, had a visibility of 20 handles. They also shot and uploaded many videos and created photo albums of the scenes of the protests.

In the evening, the police reported that they had arrested two people—Ram Singh, the driver of the bus, and his brother Mukesh. The bus was identified through CCTV footage and the police tracked the perpetrators down through the mobile phones of the victims, which had been snatched away, but one of them was not switched off.

However, the protests showed no signs of dying down. A huge crowd of over 25,000 had gathered at the capital's iconic India Gate to hold a silent candlelight march. The protestors were a mix of activists from women's organizations (Jagori, Nirantar, Saheli, All India Progressive Women's Association or AIPWA) and youth groups as well as students from different colleges and middle-class families who were not regular activists but felt strongly about the issue of women's safety and gender equality. They had found out about the candlelight vigil that the morning protestors were planning through Facebook, Twitter, and SMSs. This was a leaderless group who peacefully marched around India Gate and then sat there, without creating any chaos, to show their solidarity. The crowd dispersed after midnight as Delhi's winter chill was setting in.

But this was just the beginning of what was to be Delhi's 'Arab Spring' moment. The next two to three weeks would see protestors converging in different areas of central Delhi taking a stand against sexual assault and violence against women.

Technology—specifically the Internet and mobile devices—became important instruments for enabling protests and activism. This trend is a global phenomenon as protests throughout the world since 2010—be it the Arab Spring or the Occupy Wall Street movement—have used social media to mobilize people in large numbers. The attraction of using the Internet or mobile devices lies in the fact that these tools are less sensitive to control mechanisms traditionally employed by governments the world over.

The ease with which technology enabled the mobilization of large crowds came as a surprise both to the activists and to the state apparatus—the police and the Delhi government. Strikingly enough, the protests garnered support from beyond the well-educated activist middle class, reaching out and connecting with a diverse range of people belonging to different backgrounds. From all accounts (protestors and news reports), social media played a significant part in mobilizing people, unsurprising in a country with 65 million Facebook users and an estimated 35 million Twitter accounts. Broadband connections in India are double the size of the British general population.

Over the next three weeks, tweets with hashtags such as #IstandforsafeDelhi, #stopthisshame, #nirbhaya, #Delhigangrape, #Delhiprotests, #amanat, and #damini served as anchors to inform, educate, and galvanize mass support. And hashtags such as #theekhai sought to humiliate and punish the lack of sensitivity and inactivity of ageing politicians (in India, the average age of politicians is 65 years while two-thirds of its population is under 35 years) (Barn 2014). Many groups were formed on Facebook variously called Nirbhaya, Nirbhaya Respect Girls, Nirbhaya Damini, Protest Against Delhi Gang Rape … We Want Justice, Justice for Damini. On Google Trends' search volume index, 'Delhi gang rape,' 'Rape in Delhi', and 'gang-rape victim' were among the top search phrases in India over a week, reaching a peak on 20 December. The highest volumes were from Delhi and neighbouring states like Uttar Pradesh, Haryana, and Rajasthan (Prasad and Nandakumar 2012).

According to Pamela Philipose, Editor-in-Chief, Women's Feature Service, the mobilizations were distinct since they represented a certain concretization of a trend that had started with the anti-corruption movement in 2011 and could well entrench itself in the future. She identified three characteristics of this trend. 'First, the specific intermeshing of media institutions in the creation of news; second, the framing of the message/messages sought to be conveyed; and third, the profile of its main protagonists.' Old fashioned fact-finding and the deferring of editorial interpretation and judgment were replaced by the unmediated broadcasting of viewpoints straight from the ground in real time (Philipose 2013).

The media also accorded an unusual longevity to the gang rape incident in terms of the news cycle. It was the most extensively covered rape case in Indian media's recent history. A study of four English language publications (*Tehelka, India Today, Indian Express, Hindu*), showed that rape reporting increased by roughly 30 per cent after the Delhi rape case, with the case itself taking between 10-20 per cent of the share of rape stories across different storylines. The globalization of the Delhi bus rape intensified the press coverage, creating a large public space for debate and the venting of anger. Five narratives emerged after analysing the stories: personal, public outcry, women's safety, police handling, and legislative (Drache and Velagic 2013). The personal storyline humanized the victim, which is unusual in reporting of rape cases in India. People identified with her story, her struggles, and aspirations. In a country where women still face enormous odds—both social and economic—to achieve professional success, she was an example of courage and perseverance. The contrast between her and her rapists could not be more stark. These men, also from financially poor backgrounds, were known for indulging in drunken brawls and antisocial behaviour. Lastly, there was no real discomfort in the outrage against the rapists—they were strangers, not family members; they were poor and semi-literate, but so was Jyoti's family.

Delhi's 'Arab Spring'

The medical prognosis on the young woman was critical but stable. The doctors had put her on a ventilator after multiple surgeries and her friend received treatment for head injuries. The police had caught two more of the culprits.

As Jyoti battled for her life in the hospital, the protests gathered momentum. On 18 December, the protestors again congregated outside the Vasant Vihar police station, their numbers now swelled to 400. Chanting slogans such as 'Delhi police *murdabad*', '*Balatkariyon ko sazaa do*', and '*Nari hiton ka hanan hua to khun bahega sadkon par*', they marched from the Vasant Vihar police station at 11 am and blocked the Munirka T-point junction for nearly three hours. Among the protestors were ordinary citizens, student-activists of different ideological leanings, women's rights organizations, and youth collectives. Demanding action from the police, the agitators wanted reassurance about the safety of women in the city (Agarwal 2012).

Candlelight vigil at India Gate also continued with more and more groups and concerned citizens participating. They organized themselves through mass texting, social media, and word of mouth. The key organizers were JNUSU and women's organizations as well as religious groups such as volunteers of Sri Sri Ravi Shankar (*Times of India* 2012a; Vijetha 2012). Many of the protestors we interviewed said that this was the first time they had come out to show solidarity with the young woman and raise awareness about sexual violence against women. Predominantly middle class, there were people from less-privileged backgrounds too. An incident narrated by Shruti Kohli, who runs a magazine called *Petticoat Journal*, threw light on the matter. One of the days at the protest site, she encountered four women who arrived in an autorickshaw at about midnight at the protest venue. These women told her that they worked as domestic helps and lived in Govindpuri. They wanted to be part of the protests because they felt scared (one of them was carrying a knife). One of the women told her that these types of rapes are common in the slums where they lived but felt that such protests may have an effect on their slums too (Kohli 2012).

Since Indian law does not allow anyone to reveal the name of a rape victim in public, she was given a plethora of names by the media—Nirbhaya (fearless), Damini (lightning), Amanat (entrusted), Braveheart, India's Daughter—all signifying her courage and strength. Later, her family insisted on releasing her actual name, saying there was no reason to conceal it. Indeed, her father said he was proud of her and felt that revealing her name would give courage to other victims of rape (Tran 2013).

Relentless pressure on the police ensured that they worked over-time to nab the culprits. By 21 December, all six alleged perpetrators had been caught. They were located and nabbed in their home town. The police located Raju from his hideout near his home town in Badaun in Uttar Pradesh and brought him to the national capital. Another accused, Akshay Thakur, was nabbed from Aurangabad in Bihar.

The initial days of the protests were largely peaceful, spontaneous with no particular leader. But towards the end of the week, significant fissures had emerged. On the one hand, there were the progressive groups who were focusing on broadening the narrative to the societal causes of rape and sexual violence against women. These included various student unions, youth groups, and women's groups such as JNUSU, Youth Parliament, Youth Collective, Youth Ki Awaaz, Jagori, Saheli, Nirantar, Apne Aap, CSR, All India Democratic Women's Association (AIDWA), Revolutionary Youth Association (RYA),

AIPWA, and All India Students Association (AISA). Many of the first-time protestors also subscribed to this view. On the other hand, there were groups such as ABVP (student wing of the BJP), students from various colleges of Delhi University, and ordinary citizens who were demanding stringent punishment such as chemical castration or the death penalty for the rapists.

As the days passed, the protests grew and became more political in nature. For example, on 21 December, around 60–70 activists of the Aam Aadmi Party (AAP) held a protest in front of the residence of the Indian National Congress Party chief Sonia Gandhi. They marched to 10 Janpath—Sonia Gandhi's residence—from Jantar Mantar after a demonstration there and sat holding candles and shouting slogans against the government (*NDTV* 2012). AIDWA President Kavita Krishnan (also associated with CPI(ML)) gave a fiery 12-minute speech in front of Sheila Dixit's, then Delhi Chief Minister, residence. The speech, given in Hindi, garnered more than 50,000 views on YouTube, and focused on political responsibility, women's rights and safety, and the impact of patriarchal attitudes ingrained in Indian culture. Three Members of Parliament—Jaya Bachchan, T.N. Seema, and Jharna Das Baidya—participated in a protest outside Delhi Police headquarters demanding a public apology from the police commissioner for police inefficiency and inability to prevent crimes against women. In the memorandum submitted to the Delhi police commissioner, the protesters outside the police headquarters demanded increased patrolling and deployment of police including women police at public places, fast-track courts to deal with rape cases, increased sensitization and effective investigation, and accountability of the police in dealing with heinous crimes against women. A large number of workers of the Delhi BJP Pradesh Mahila Morcha and Yuva Morcha staged demonstration at Jantar Mantar demanding death as punishment for the culprits (Ali 2012).

The police were at a loss about how to handle these protests which had spread across Delhi—India Gate, Jantar Mantar, Rashtrapati Bhawan, North Block, Sonia Gandhi's and Sheila Dikshit's residences, and the police headquarters. Claiming that mobs of hooligans had infiltrated the protesting groups, it cracked down on the protestors. Some police vehicles were damaged, and the police eventually used tear gas, water cannons, and lathi charge to disperse the crowd. It also imposed Section 144 (power to issue prohibitory orders in urgent cases under Code of Criminal Procedure or CrPC) in and around India Gate. Officials said 35 protesters and 37 police officers had been injured, two officers seriously injured, and that six buses and several police vehicles were damaged (Gardiner and Kumar 2012). One of the police officers, Constable Subhash Tomar, lost his life battling the crowds (*Times of India* 2012b). The state crackdown on protesters was severely criticized by the protestors and the media. Prime Minister Manmohan Singh implored protesters to keep calm. He said that the anger was 'genuine and justified' and promised measures to ensure safety for women. The Home Minister, Sushil Kumar Shinde, announced several measures taken by the government on women's safety which included measures to increase number of buses at night, installation of GPS on all public transport vehicles, and proactive and enhanced patrolling by the police (Mukherjee 2012).

After sustained protests, on 24 December, the government announced the formation of a three-member committee, headed by Justice J.S. Verma, to 'look into possible amendments to the criminal law for the quicker trial and enhanced punishment of criminals, accused of committing sexual assault of an extreme nature against women'. The other two members of the committee were Gopal Subramaniam, Former Solicitor General of India and Justice (Retd) Leila Seth.[2]

Meanwhile, the victim's condition started deteriorating and in a last-ditch attempt to save her, she was airlifted to Singapore for a multi-organ transplant on 25 December. But she passed away on 29 December, provoking nationwide mourning. Every major city in India held vigils for the victim. It also gave a fresh impetus to the protestors, many of whom came in solidarity and in an attempt to reclaim public spaces. This was reflected in the new and innovative ways of protest such as flash mobs, freeze mobs, human chains, wearing black clothes, street plays, and drafting a charter of demands. Stark imageries were used by youth groups—a few participants went without any warm clothes in the cold; others stood coated in mud to symbolize shame; some youths stood still, frozen to the spot in various poses. On the day Jyoti died, there was a dummy set up in the middle of Janpath and it was covered with a cloth as if it was her body. There were also silent candlelight vigils as a mark of mourning and respect. *Kala Divas* was organized on 3 January 2013 by some of the protestors who wore black bandanas and black clothes. The crowds included lawyers, singers, NGO professionals, and many others from different parts of the country.

One of the protestors described the size of the crowd gathered in India Gate and Jantar Mantar as close to a thousand during the day, and a hundred till late hours of the night. Most protesters were between 15–35 years; largely male (but a fair number of females as well); mid-income to upper-income level. There were some working-class people too who came on non-working days. There were people from the LGBTQ community.

While India Gate, Jantar Mantar, and Vijay Chowk were the epicentres of the demonstrations and protests in Delhi, other locations included outside the Chief Minister's residence; Munirka crossing; Delhi University; Vasant Vihar police station; outside Safdarjung Hospital, where the victim was hospitalized; outside the residence of Sonia Gandhi, the Indian National Congress Party chief; shopping malls; and city squares. In Greater Noida, hundreds of residents held a condolence meet at a central crossroad at Pari Chowk. The protests were not confined to Delhi. It spilled over to Mumbai, Bengaluru, and Kolkata with groups like Majlis, Akshara, and Vimochana (Singh 2014).

As the Verma Committee started its work, soliciting feedback from the public on the matter, the protests started losing steam. By the end of January, it had mostly petered out with only stray groups remaining.

On 3 January, the five adults accused were charged with murder, rape, and kidnapping. Senior lawyer Dayan Krishnan was appointed as the special public prosecutor. The minor was to be tried separately in a juvenile court, where he could only be sentenced to a maximum of three years in a reformatory home. The question of what should be the appropriate punishment for a juvenile where he has committed a heinous crime became a contentious issue with two clear divisions—those who maintained that the law does not allow for juveniles to be tried in adult courts and those who were convinced that the perpetrator did not deserve mercy if he could commit such a heinous crime (the juvenile convict was responsible for not only luring them to the bus but also for brutalizing the victim with an iron rod, pulling out her intestines). Ram Singh, one of the adults accused, was found hanging in his jail cell on 11 March 2013. The remaining four adults were tried in a fast-track court and the case was completed on 8 July. They were found guilty of rape, murder, unnatural offences, and destruction of evidence and were given the death penalty (Barry and Sharma 2013). The verdict was appealed in the Delhi High Court but it was upheld (Ghosh 2014). All four had appealed to the Supreme Court for staying their execution but have since been executed (Talukdar 2015).

It is essential to understand that the Verma Committee's far-reaching work is part of a long journey of activism for gender justice in India. Significant changes have come about in the criminal justice system through years of work by women's rights groups. Before going into the working of the Verma Committee, we provide a brief summary of the history of women's activism against sexual violence in India.

India's Fledgling Anti-rape Movement: Historical Overview

In India, crimes related to violence against women were governed principally by the Indian Penal Code, an archaic law enacted in 1860 under the British Raj. While the code has been amended a number of times and a few stand-alone laws have been enacted to address different forms of violence against women, it was not till 2013 that the British era laws were comprehensively overhauled with regard to the provisions on sexual violence against women.

The incremental changes that were pushed through over the years have been at the behest of many dedicated women's rights activists from all over the country. Their activism was also responsible for the gradual shift in attitudes of society and courtrooms towards rape victims—from extreme hostility and distrust to a more congenial and sympathetic approach.

Rape was and remains one of the most under-reported crimes in India. For example, in 1972, only 2,562 cases of rape were reported in the country; in 1975, it had increased to 3,283, and in 1978 to 3,899. Although the issue was raised by the nationalist-feminist movement in the pre-independence era, it largely pointed to the excesses of the British state as foreigner-colonizer. Post-Independence, the Left and far Left groups focused on the excesses committed by the Indian state as well as by the ruling classes. The state repression during the Emergency came as a shock to many middle-class women and post-Emergency, civil liberties groups also highlighted cases of custodial rapes (Patel 2014).

Custodial or police rape was one of the earliest issues around which the first autonomous women's group began to get organized. In 1972, a tribal girl named Mathura was raped by two policemen, while on duty, within the vicinity of the police station. She was branded a woman of loose moral character because she had eloped with her boyfriend. The family lodged a criminal complaint against the two officers. A lady lawyer immediately took up the case, only for the Sessions Court to dismiss the case on account of the girl being of a loose moral character. The appeal in the Bombay High Court overturned the ruling on the ground that a quiet acquiescence could not be called consent. The accused were sentenced to seven and a half years of rigorous imprisonment. In 1979, the case went to the Supreme Court where the High Court ruling was set aside, and the accused were let off on the ground that the complainant was 'habituated to sex'. Moreover, the acquittal took into consideration the fact that Mathura had not 'raised any alarm for help' and the 'absence of any injuries or signs of struggle' on her body.

Meanwhile, in 1978, just as women's groups were in the process of formation, a woman called Rameeza Bee was raped by several policemen in Hyderabad, and her husband, a rickshaw puller, was murdered because he protested. Following this gruesome incident, 22,000 local citizens went to the police station, laid the rickshaw puller's dead body outside the police station, set up road blocks, cut the telephone wires, stoned the building, and set fire to some bicycles in the compound. Two platoons of armed police were called in to tackle the crowd; politicians also got into the act with Opposition members resorting to a gherao against the Chief Minister. The police fired into the crowd, which further inflamed emotions. A Hyderabad bandh was called the next day, curfew was declared in 16 areas, and nine people were killed and 80 injured by police firing. The agitation continued even after the army was called in and could only be quelled after the declaration of President's rule. Finally, a commission of enquiry under Justice Muktadar was appointed to investigate the rape and murder. Custodial rape became a 'mass' issue for the first time.

The Mathura judgment shocked four law professors—Upendra Baxi, Raghunath Kelkar, Lotika Sarkar, and Vasudha Dhagamwar—who wrote an open letter to the Chief Justice of India condemning the judgment and asking for a review in September 1979, which brought the matter to media attention. The letter (Baxi et al. 1979) emphasized the social context, 'the young victim's low socio-economic status, lack of knowledge of legal rights and lack of access to legal services, and the fear complex which haunts the poor and the exploited in Indian police stations'. It also raised fundamental questions: 'Must illiterate, labouring, politically mute Mathuras of India be condemned to their pre-constitutional Indian fate? ... Nothing short of protection of human rights and constitutionalism is at stake.' This open letter was a trigger for the anti-rape campaign which received wide media publicity and, ultimately, resulted in changes in the rape law. Prominent lawyers took up cudgels on Mathura's behalf. The national and regional language press played an important role in shaping the debates. Feminist groups were formed around this campaign including Saheli and Stree Sangharsh (Delhi), the Forum Against Rape (FAR), later renamed Forum Against Oppression of Women (FAOW) (Mumbai), Stree Shakti Sanghatana (Hyderabad), Ahmedabad Women's Action Group (AWAG) (Ahmedabad), Penna Urimai Iyyakkam (Madurai), Vimochana (Bengaluru), and Nari Mukti Sanstha (Assam). These groups used activities such as exhibitions, plays, street corner meetings, and area mobilization as tactics to raise awareness. On 8 March 1980, in response to a call by FAR, women's groups demonstrated in seven cities—Mumbai, Delhi, Nagpur, Pune, Ahmedabad, Bengaluru, and Hyderabad. They demanded a retrial of the Mathura case, the implementation of relevant sections of the Indian Penal Code, and changes in the law against rape. In both Delhi and Mumbai, joint action committees of feminist groups and socialist and communist party fronts, mainly students, were formed to coordinate the movement (Kumar 1993). The demand by these groups to reopen the case did not bear fruit since the court questioned the locus standi of these groups to represent Mathura. But it did push the envelope on the question of social justice for women and helped create awareness about the need for developing the practice of Public Interest Litigation (PIL). In 1982, the Supreme Court recognized the right of concerned citizens and NGOs to represent the oppressed or exploited people in public interest cases (Khullar 2005).

Close on the heels of the Mathura judgment came the case of Maya Tyagi. On 18 July 1980, 25-year-old Maya Tyagi, her husband Ishwar Chand, and two friends were driving to her parent's house in Faridabad, Haryana. The driver stopped the car at Baghpat Chowk to repair a flat tyre when a policeman in civilian dress tried to molest Maya and was beaten up by her husband. The police opened fire and shot him dead, then dragged Maya out of the car after which she was beaten, stripped, and paraded through the town. She was finally taken to a police station where she was raped and charged with being a dacoit. This incident aroused such furore from women's organizations and political parties that the Lok Sabha discussed this for four days (Gangoli 2007) after which the Union Home Minister, Zail Singh, went to the area with 10 women MPs and ordered an inquiry. A number of rallies and dharnas were held by about 30 women's organizations, mainly party-based but was well attended by women from different parts of Haryana. In the winter session of the Parliament, the government declared its intention of introducing a bill relating to rape and presented a draft, which was then widely debated among various stakeholders in civil society.

Another incident around this time was the alleged rape and murder of Shila Devi, the wife of an orderly serving the District Magistrate. Five thousand residents of Dahwali demonstrated against the incident but the police opened fire on the demonstrators. The BJP demanded the resignation of the Haryana government and their Delhi unit launched a one-week campaign against the increasing number of dacoities, robberies, and attacks on women in the city. Raj Narain, a politician in Janata (S) resigned from the party and threatened to go on an indefinite fast from 3 August 1980 unless the Haryana government took appropriate action against custodial rape.

These incidents, and others highlighted by feminists, local neighbourhood groups, and trade-union-based groups, intensified the demand for changes in the rape law but also put activists in a cleft stick. They wanted to rescue the issue of custodial rape from becoming a political football for fractious politicians but at the same time relied on the government to take decisive steps to deal with the problem. The debate around rape had also centred around issues of past sexual history of victims, procedures of the criminal justice system (FIR, inquest, medical examination, rights of women in custody, and burden of proof).

In November of 1980, a national conference was held in Mumbai on the 'Perspective of Women's Liberation Movement in India' where the draft anti-rape bill was widely discussed. The major contentious points were on consent and burden of proof. The legal system at that time put the onus on the victim to prove absence of consent. While the burden of proof lay with the victim in other cases, for cases of sexual violence it became almost impossible to prove the absence of consent. This, along with Mathura's case history, was one of the main reasons why the accused managed to wriggle out. The conference also heard a group of socialist feminists who had gone on a fact-finding mission to investigate an incidence of mass rape in the Santhal Parganas. They found that rape was being used in the rural areas by the police 'as a weapon of class domination'. They stated that rape was not just another atrocity but an act of political violence, thus linking women's issues to other struggles (for example, peasants, workers) (Haksar 1991).

It is interesting to note that in the 1970s, there was a rise in liberal and radical feminism in the west which focused on demands for equal opportunities as well as ending violence against women. But the Indian anti-rape campaign initially focused on the police as the visible representatives of State power and brutality against women, rather than on the interpersonal nature of sexual assault, including within family, that was the focus of the West (Gangoli 2007).

As Flavia Agnes (2009), head of Majlis and a member of FAOW recalled:

> Public campaigns initiated by women's organizations asked for legislative reforms which received a prompt reply from the state. If oppression was to be tackled by enacting laws, then the decade of the 1980s could easily be declared as the golden era for Indian women, when pro-women laws were given on a platter. During this period every single issue concerning violence against women taken up by the women's movement was transformed into legislative reform.

One Step Forward, Two Steps Back

The government drafted the Criminal Law (Amendment) Bill, 1980 on the basis of the Law Commission's recommendations[3] and the bill was referred to a Joint Committee of Parliament in December 1980. The Committee submitted its report in November 1982 after soliciting public opinion. Almost a year later, Parliament finally debated the Criminal Laws (Amendment) Bill over a four-hour period. The debates were revealing of the prevailing mindset among the policymakers, whose primary concern seemed to be to ensure the honour of a chaste woman and to protect respectable men from false accusations (Savery 2007). The bill was finally passed on 25 December 1983 and it amended the Indian Penal Code, the Code of Criminal Procedures, and the Indian Evidence Act. While the definition of rape remained more or less the same, it introduced a new category of custodial rape—such as in hospitals, remand homes, and prisons. It also made the revelation of the identity of the victim an offence. While the maximum sentence was unchanged, despite the demands of women's organizations to extend it to death penalty, the minimum sentence was changed to seven years of imprisonment. It also extended the minimum sentence to 10 years for special cases—rape by persons in a position of authority, custodial rape, rape of a pregnant woman, rape of a girl under 12 years, and gang rape. In all these cases, the burden of proof shifted to the accused and, if the victim stated that she did not consent, then the court would presume an absence of consent.

Nandita Haksar (2005: 137) narrates an incident that highlights the reaction to the changes in the rape law as well as the prevailing attitudes.

> In December 1983, a magazine called India 2000 carried an article by Salman Khurshid [then an advocate practicing in the Supreme Court] criticizing the reforms in the rape law. He called the Open Letter [written by four law professors in September 1979] 'preposterous' and stated that the letter had sparked off 'an extremely distasteful public agitation.' He also made a series of defamatory statements about Mathura calling her 'a somewhat precocious and certainly sexually forward girl' and facts of the case as being 'fishy'.

Haksar and other feminists of those times filed a case against India 2000 and Kurshid in the Press Council of India for violation of professional ethics. Although no action was taken, the editor of the magazine published the rejoinder in its January issue.

Despite its limitation, the campaign did mark a new phase in the history of the women's movement in India. Several networks of women's groups began to come together to coordinate action. However, the feeling of exhilaration regarding the success of the campaign started waning as the amended law began unfolding in trial courts. Little had changed on the ground. The procedures continued to be long and harrowing, the investigation machinery remained lackadaisical and corrupt, and the victim continued to be cross-examined on her morals and character. Marital rape also remained outside the purview. The Law Commission of India had argued that a husband has the right to sexual intercourse with his wife with or without her consent. However, the new law did include a clause, which made the forcible intercourse by a man with his judicially separated wife an offence, which was punishable with imprisonment up to two years.

The silver lining was the steady increase in reporting of rape cases. From 3,899 cases of reported rape in 1978, the number jumped to 9,518 in 1990, 13,754 in 1995, and 16,496 in 2000. As the numbers jumped, newer issues began to surface. For instance, while in criminal law, assaults with weapons were considered to be grievous since the risk of bodily injury was aggravated, the only exception was rape where penile penetration was seen as more grievous (rape was defined as penile penetration only). A series of cases where young girls had been violated and injured with insertion of objects such as iron rods, bottles, and sticks in their vaginas got swept away under the nomenclature of 'violating modesty', punishable with a maximum of two years of imprisonment (Patel 2014). Also, the judiciary continued to pass judgment on the character of a woman and based its rulings on it. The famous Suman Rani custodial rape case of 1989 was a case in point where the Supreme Court refused to apply the minimum 10-year sentence to the police officers charged because of the Dalit victim's 'questionable character' (Narula 1999). Feminists reacted with a storm of protests, held several meetings and a dharna, and burnt an effigy of the law in front of the Supreme Court. The National Front government responded with the promise of yet another amendment to the rules of evidence, but there was still no discussion around implementation and interpretation of the law.

A Shift in the Anti-rape Discourse

Around the 1990s, the discourse on rape started focusing on the definition of rape itself, which was genito-centric in nature. Also, the issue of 'freedom of choice', not only concerning husbands and lovers but also in cases of custodial rape, started coming up. The People's Union of Democratic Rights discovered several cases where the victims had run away from home because families did not approve of the men they loved and the police, using their 'runaway' status forced them away from the men and raped them (Kumar 1995).

As newer types of sexual crimes got highlighted in the media and courts, the crying need to change the definition of rape became more apparent. Cases of incest by family members, paedophilia, and the abuse of male children in children's homes started making headlines. In April 1990, there was a National Meeting of Women's Organisations Against Rape where the overwhelming concern was regarding the legal definition of rape. However, some feminists have criticized the liberal, individual-centric discourse on rape rather than linking it with other political, economic, and social struggles (Haksar 2005; Khullar 2005).

In the period between 1993 and 2012, there were several efforts to redefine sexual crime within the context of emerging concerns. The government had set up a statutory body called the National Commission for Women (NCW) in January 1992. Taking into consideration the new offences that were coming to light, the NCW drafted a Criminal Laws (Amendment) Bill in 1994 with reference to child rape.[4] It proposed the deletion of Sections 354 (violating modesty), 375 (rape), 376 (punishment for rape), and 377 (unnatural offences) of Indian Penal Code and attempted to bring them under the broad ambit of sexual assault. The bill was gender-specific for the accused, but gender-neutral for the victim. Although there was some debate on it and it was examined by the Expert Committee on Law and Judiciary (appointed by NCW), it died out due to government's apathy in taking up the issue. The issue of domestic violence was taken up by Lawyer's Collective who ran a campaign for the enactment of a new law.

Guidelines for dealing with sexual harassment at the workplace were issued by the Supreme Court in 1997 under the historic Visakha judgment. Again, the issue was brought to light by some NGOs who filed a writ petition as a reaction to the brutal gang rape of a worker (Bhanwari Devi) in a village in Rajasthan. Bhanwari Devi, a *sathin* in the Rajasthan government's Women's Development Programme, had tried to prevent a child marriage in her village. She was then gang raped by members of the upper-caste family in the presence of her husband in 1992. The trial judge acquitted the accused on the ground that rape was done by teenagers while the accused in this case were middle-aged. Also, an upper-caste man could not have defiled himself by raping a lower-caste woman. At first, the case was reported in a few local newspapers such as *Rajasthan Patrika* but the judgment led to a nationwide campaign for justice for the victim. The state government was forced to appeal the verdict in the High Court but, by 2007, the court had held only one hearing and two of the accused were dead.

The next milestone in the anti-rape movement came with the *Sakshi* v. *Union of India* case in 1999. The requirement of penile penetration for an assault to be termed as rape led to some absurd judgments.[5] Sakshi, a woman's resource centre working with victims of sexual abuse, finally filed a PIL in 1997 questioning the legal procedures during a trial. It also urged the apex court to alter the definition of 'sexual intercourse' with reference to Section 375 of the Indian Penal Code. The Supreme Court then directed the Law Commission of India to respond to the issues raised in the petition and review the rape laws.

The Law Commission, in its 172nd Report, dated 25 March 2000, recommended the amendment of the law to widen the definition of rape. It also recommended that rape be substituted by sexual assault as an offence and such assault should include the use of any object for penetration. It further recognized that there was an increase in the incidence of sexual assaults against boys and therefore recommended the widening of the definition of rape to include circumstances where both men and women could be perpetrators and victims of sexual assault.[6] The Commission had limited its consultation to four groups—Naina Kapur of Sakshi, Jasjit Purewal of Interventions for Support, Healing and Awareness (IFSHA), Kirti Singh of AIDWA, and NCW. Since 'Criminal Law' and 'Criminal Procedure' are subjects in the Concurrent List of the Constitution, the state governments were also consulted. Most of them supported the views of the Law Commission after which the Ministry of Home Affairs drafted a bill. Meanwhile, the NCW held a national consultation and drafted a separate bill on the subject in 2006, which rendered the offence of rape and sexual assault gender-neutral both for victim and accused.[7] However, the draft bill met with severe criticism from women's organizations. Also, the Home Minister, the Law Minister, and the Chairperson of NCW discussed the provisions of two draft bills and the Law Commission report. The view that emerged from the discussions was that various sexual offences specifically relating to males and females should be differentiated and the crime should remain gender-specific.[8] The Ministry again revised the bill and convened a Conference of the Home Secretaries of the State Governments and Union Territory Administrations on 7 July 2008 in Delhi to discuss the matter, but no agreement could be reached on the amendments to the laws.

Other groups working on AIDS awareness and decriminalization of Section 377 for consensual same-sex relationships also started making inroads through campaigns and court cases, the most famous being the Naz Foundation case.[9]

In January 2010, the ministry decided to form a High Powered Committee (HPC), under the chairmanship of the former Union Home Secretary, to examine the issues related to rape laws. The suggestions made by the HPC were formulated into a draft Criminal Law (Amendment) Bill, 2010 which was referred to the state governments for their comments. The provisions in the bill included the substitution of the offence of rape with 'sexual assault'. Sexual assault was defined as penetration of the vagina, the anus, or urethra or mouth of any woman, by a man, with (a) any part of his body; or (ib) any object manipulated by such man under the following circumstances: (a) against the will of the woman; (b) without her consent; (c) under duress; (d) consent obtained by fraud; (e) consent obtained by reason of unsoundness of mind or intoxication; and (f) when the woman is below the age of 18.

The draft bill was also posted on the website of the Ministry of Home Affairs for comments of the general public. The HPC, after going into the comments received from the various individuals and NGOs, the state governments and also after further consultation amongst its members finalized its report along with the draft Criminal Law (Amendment) Bill, 2011 and recommended it to the government for its enactment.

The bill was finalized after further consultations with stakeholders—both in the ministry and advocacy groups. While women's groups were largely in favour of the changes, they were against the gender-neutral character of the bill, fearing it would defeat the purpose. Thus, they submitted a list of recommendations, which the government incorporated while still keeping the gender neutrality aspect.[10] The Cabinet considered the bill in July 2012 and approved its introduction.[11] Accordingly, the bill was introduced in the Lok Sabha on 4 December 2012. In the meantime, the Protection of Children from Sexual Offences Act was passed in November 2012 to deal with sexual abuse of children. This law was gender-neutral for both victims and perpetrators.

Working of the Justice Verma Committee

Precisely a week after the Nirbhaya case, the government responded to the public outcry by setting up a three-member committee to review the laws on sexual violence on 23 December 2012. It remains a mystery why the government did not enact the pending 2012 bill on the subject but set up a committee. Justice Seth says she had expected the government to take exactly this path, thus postponing the decision for six months or more, by which time the momentum of the protest would be lost. Whatever be the reasons, it chose a panel of highly regarded legal luminaries—Justice (Retd) J.S. Verma, Justice (Retd) Leila Seth, and Gopal Subramaniam, Former Solicitor General of India—who completed its path-breaking report in a month's time, a record of sorts in India.

Justice Seth, in her book, *Talking of Justice* (2014), gives a concise insider's view to the working of the Verma Committee. Starting with the interesting anecdote of how she came to be inducted in the committee (P. Chidambaram personally persuaded her), she tells us how the committee members went beyond its limited mandate to draft a holistic report which would be 'meaningful, practical, and sound'.

The committee had solicited feedback from the public, but was unprepared to deal with the deluge of letters and memoranda it got from the public. About 80,000 suggestions had to be collated and sorted, in addition to the research that was required. That's when Gopal Subramaniam stepped in and put his entire office at the disposal of the committee. All his juniors volunteered to help. Shwetasree Majumder, a young lawyer who joined the team a bit later, was the first woman among the all-male back-office team. Later, more women were inducted, including Justice Verma's granddaughter, who was a student at Oxford and a political science major from Cambridge. The idea of having a team from diverse backgrounds was to ensure that biases could be countered with other viewpoints.

Before the actual work began, the committee decided to set the context, which was to view rape as a crime of power rather than a sexual crime. The work was divided according to areas. Shwetasree worked on the actual amendments to the laws, medical testing of rape victims, sexual harassment at the workplace, police reforms, and technology-related crimes (hacking, grooming). Bhuwan Ribhu, from Bachpan Bachao Andolan, worked on child trafficking. Mrinal Satish, a law professor, worked on sentencing since that was his PhD thesis.

The committee invited about 70 to 80 groups among those who had sent written submissions and heard their depositions over two days. The groups included women's organizations, feminists, disability rights groups, the lesbian-gay-bisexual-transgender (LGBT) community, sex workers' groups, child rights groups such as Bachpan Bachao Andolan, National Institute of Mental Health and Neurosciences (NIMHANS), and the Association of Democratic Reforms (ADR). In addition, experts and academics from India and abroad were consulted. Representatives from the administration and police such as Kiran Bedi were also encouraged to voice their opinions and experiences. These groups, given their long experience in the area, were able to give a holistic view of the problems faced by them.

Given the tight deadline, the team worked tirelessly. For those 30 days, the team's days would start at about 8:30–9 am and could go on till well after midnight. Each of the committee members believed in hearing out different opinions; therefore, the teams would discuss and debate every provision exhaustively. Some of the most controversial issues such as the definition of sexual assault, the question of consent in different circumstances, extent of punishment, the imposition of the death penalty, gender neutrality, and the penalty for juvenile offenders were discussed till a consensus was reached.

The researchers ensured that they did not just copy provisions from other countries or previous statutes. Many of the clauses that were included were original ideas based on the lived realities of groups in India.

Among the political parties, only the Indian National Congress Party sent its submission. Justice Seth, in her book, recalled an amusing anecdote on the subject. The political party sent its submission at 11:45 pm on 5 January 2013, 15 minutes before the deadline through a runner! The person woke Justice Verma up and insisted that he sign the receipt personally.

On 23 January 2013, the committee submitted a 630-page report[12] with far-reaching recommendations. It made recommendations on laws related to rape; sexual harassment; trafficking; child sexual abuse; medical examinations of victims; and police, electoral, and educational reforms. But it did not recommend the death penalty nor did it reduce the juvenile age from 18 years to 16. Some new offences were created and stiffer punishment was suggested by the panel. The new offences included disrobing a woman, voyeurism, stalking, and trafficking. The committee also touched upon marital rape and safety of women in conflict zones suggesting a review of the Armed Forces Special Protection Act (AFSPA). There was also a suggestion to bar elected representatives from holding office or to file nomination for election if a court has accepted a charge-sheet filed by an investigative agency.

The meticulously researched report was broadly welcomed by all sections of society, although there were disagreements on issues such as marital rape and gender neutrality.

Road to the Parliament

Although, the 2012 bill was being examined by the Standing Committee on Home Affairs, headed by M. Venkaiah Naidu, the government suddenly decided to promulgate an ordinance to amend the laws on 3 February 2013. In fact, the Standing Committee in its report had expressed surprise at this move. The ordinance incorporated some of the recommendations of the Verma Committee and retained a few of the provisions of the 2012 bill.

Both the ordinance and the decision to promulgate it came under heavy criticism from women activists across the country. They blamed the central government for diluting the recommendations of the Justice Verma report (Reddy 2013). Kavita Krishnan, secretary of AIPWA commented at that time, 'This ordinance is an eyewash. It is diluting the actual recommendation of the Justice Verma committee. We want a bill passed not on this ordinance but the panel's suggestions' (*Daily News and Analysis* 2013). The group organized a public protest from 21 February, gathering around Jantar Mantar to hold a people's watch over the Parliament.

The committee's recommendation relating to marital rape, police reform, and prosecution of security personnel with sexual assault had all been omitted from the ordinance (*The Hindu* 2013a).

Despite the criticisms, the government defended the move with the information and broadcasting minister, Manish Tewari, saying, 'The ordinance covers about 90 per cent of the recommendations of the Verma Committee, the rest can be added after the parliamentary debate' (Malik 2013). Manish Tewari later added that the ordinance included those issues having the broadest consensus. P. Chidambaram, the then Home Minister added that the government would wait for the recommendations of the standing committee and then would decide whether to bring this bill in the Budget session of 2013 (Makkar and Matthew 2013).

The Union Government tabled the Criminal Law Amendment Ordinance, 2013 in the Rajya Sabha on 21 February 2013, the first parliamentary seating on the Budget Session. However, the government was under tremendous pressure to pass the bill within the next four weeks, but the Opposition was pressing to take the bill to a standing committee (Joshi 2013).

The Standing Committee, already reviewing the Criminal Laws (Amendment) Bill, 2012, was now handed over the Justice Verma Report and the Criminal Laws Amendment Ordinance, 2013 to study and make recommendations for changes in the bill. It solicited public feedback and got 492 responses, which they considered along with suggestions from five state governments. The panel was expected to submit its report in the first half of the Budget Session, which they did on 1 March 2013 (*Economic Times* 2013). Two Rajya Sabha members, D. Raja and Prasanta Chatterjee gave dissent notes.

The Criminal Laws (Amendment) Bill, 2013 was approved by the Cabinet in a special meeting on 12 March 2013 (*The Hindu* 2013b) to discuss the provisions of the bill. There were a few differences within the cabinet on certain key provisions. This included lowering the consent age for sex from 18 to 16, provisions on stalking, voyeurism, and the replacement of the word 'rape' with the more gender-neutral 'sexual assault'. Based on this, an amended version was put together by a Group of Ministers (GoM), led by P. Chidambaram. The members of the GoM included Home Minister Sushil Kumar Shinde, Law Minister Ashwani Kumar, Telecom Minister Kapil Sibal, Social Justice Minister Kumari Selja, and Women and Child Development Minister Krishna Tirath (Gupta 2013a). Ashwani Kumar took the lead in putting adequate safeguards into the bill to dissuade misuse of the law. Petroleum Minister, M. Veerappa Moily, was one of the few who opposed tough punishments for malicious complaints, saying that would deter women from coming forward with instances of sexual harassment.

The GoM met again on 13 March to go over certain provisions before presenting it to the Cabinet the next day. Although the cabinet approved the bill, there was some opposition from a few including the Samajwadi Party (SP) and the Bahujan Samaj Party (BSP). The SP's spokesperson Naresh Aggarwal said they could oppose the bill in Parliament given that its provisions could be misused to harass men, and could also come in handy for employers not employing men. Individual MPs in both SP and BSP were particularly unhappy with making stalking and voyeurism non-bailable offences (Gupta 2013b). The BJP, on the other hand, objected to lowering the age of consent. The bill made rape a gender-specific crime—only a woman can be a victim, and removed the generic term 'sexual assault' which was used in the ordinance.

The bill was presented in an all-party meeting on 18 March, where it met with opposition from a number of political parties, primarily the BJP, SP, BSP, Rashtriya Janata Dal, and the Janata Dal United. As a result, the Cabinet approved a different version of the bill that increased the age of consent to 18, made the first offence of stalking bailable, and diluted the definition of voyeurism. The government was forced to take these steps as it needed a simple majority in both houses to pass the bill. While it did have the number in Lok Sabha, Rajya Sabha could have turned out to be tricky (Gupta 2013c).

The final draft was introduced in the Lok Sabha by Sushil Kumar Shinde on 19 March 2013. What followed was a lengthy debate about the causes of rape in the country which included topics like reality shows, television, movies, and what women wear. The bill was then put to vote where a few more amendments were proposed but it passed without any changes (Dasgupta 2013).

The Rajya Sabha too passed the bill on 21 March, while extracting a promise from the government that the issues will be discussed thoroughly later, the loopholes removed, and a strong and effective legislation put in place. A number of MPs had complained that they were not given sufficient time to raise their objections (Balchand 2013). Almost all the members had some reservations but succumbed to pressure since the ordinance would lapse. The bill was finally signed into law by President Pranab Mukherjee on 3 April 2013.

The act did not apply all recommendations from the Justice Verma Report, creating a storm of criticisms from various groups who suggested that this was tokenism rather than a radical change implementation tool.

Several human rights and women's rights organizations strongly criticized the act for not including recommendations related to marital rape and amending AFSPA, which is in place in disturbed areas. Also, the act was criticized for raising the age of consent from 16 to 18.

While being far from comprehensive, the amendments have substantially transformed the way legal redress for sexual offences have been framed in the law and the Verma Committee has set high standards in approaching the subject of sexual violence against women.

Key Observations and Concluding Remarks

Among the existing conceptions of policymaking, the journey of the Criminal Laws (Amendment) Act fits primarily with the punctuated equilibrium theory where an external 'trigger' event gave an impetus to the movement towards a change in the law.

From the perspective of the proposed framework, the method of activism was mostly confrontational where the government was initially unwilling to engage but came around in the face of massive protests, setting up the Verma Committee and passing a law in record time. In this case, the reason for the high impact on the legislative agenda was the external 'trigger' that set off public outrage on the streets of Delhi on an unprecedented scale.

The underlying reason for the protests was the extreme emotional reaction of the public to the brutal rape and murder of a young girl in the heart of Delhi. People connected with the victim for a variety of reasons and she provided the catalyst to the rage that was already building up in middle-class India against a corrupt, inefficient, and apathetic administration. There was also a feeling of discomfort among some of the activists because of the quick-fix solutions that were being forwarded by many of the protestors without addressing the larger socio-cultural roots of women's sexual subordination and the issue of state-sponsored violence against weaker sections of society.

However, these criticisms notwithstanding, there are many take-aways from the movement in terms of what works and what does not when campaigning for policy change. For instance, would the case have struck such a chord with the public if the rape had not taken place in a middle-class neighbourhood of Delhi? Would it have gathered as much momentum if there were no social media campaigns to inform and engage the youth? What can civil society groups and political parties learn from this experience?

We can draw a few tentative conclusions. First, it is clear that protests in Delhi get the attention of the media and, by extension, the political class, much more easily than in other parts of the country. Second, it is obviously not possible to anticipate what would trigger a mass outcry but groups need to be prepared if an opportunity presents itself for mobilization. Third, technology helps in connecting people in unprecedented scale. Therefore, groups need to be aware of the possibilities and take advantage of them when an opportunity presents itself. Fourth, in addition to traditional methods of protesting and mobilizing people, it is important to innovate with new forms of protest. This ensures interest of the public as well as the media. Fifth, groups need to have a coherent media strategy so that they are able to put their views across in a cogent manner. Sixth, it is important to ensure that protests do not get over-politicized since it can have an adverse impact on the interest of the lay public.

Since both the activists and the state apparatus were taken by surprise by the scale and intensity of the campaign, both need to learn new ways of engaging with the public who are not politically affiliated, nor connected with day-to-day activism.

Notes

1. National Crime Records Bureau data shows the number of reported rape cases in India has increased from 2,487 in 1971 to 33,707 in 2013. Today, a new incident of rape is reported every 22 minutes, a child is raped every 76 minutes, and only one in every four accused gets convicted. A lot of instances go unreported, and in some parts of the country, between one and four per cent of women have revealed that they have been raped or sexually assaulted in the past year. That implies that the actual number of victims in India is between 50 and 200 times greater than the official count.
2. Available at http://pib.nic.in/newsite/PrintRelease.aspx?relid=91155 (last accessed on 20 March 2016).
3. 84th Report of the Law Commission of India on Rape and Allied Offences, Law Commission of India, 1980.
4. Available at http://ncw.nic.in/ (last accessed on 22 March 2016).
5. Available at http://www.indlaw.com/legalfocus/focusdetails.aspx?ID=104 (last accessed on 22 March 2016).
6. Available at http://www.lawcommissionofindia.nic.in/rapelaws.htm (last accessed on 22 March 2016).
7. 'Amendments to the laws relating to rape and related provisions', available at http://ncw.nic.in/PDFFiles/Amendments%20to%20laws%20relating%20to%20women.pdf (last accessed on 22 March 2016).
8. 'One Hundred and Sixty Seventh Report on the Criminal Law (Amendment) Bill, 2012', available at http://www.prsindia.org/uploads/media/Criminal%20Law/SCR%20Criminal%20Law%20Bill.pdf (last accessed on 22 March 2016).
9. Available at http://en.wikipedia.org/wiki/Naz_Foundation_v._Govt._of_NCT_of_Delhi (last accessed on 22 March 2016).
10. 'One Hundred and Sixty Seventh Report on the Criminal Law (Amendment) Bill, 2012', available at http://www.prsindia.org/uploads/media/Criminal%20Law/SCR%20Criminal%20Law%20Bill.pdf (last accessed on 22 March 2016).
11. Available at http://www.pib.nic.in/newsite/erelease.aspx?relid=85422 (last accessed on 22 March 2016).
12. Available at http://en.wikipedia.org/wiki/J._S._Verma#Justice_Verma_Committee (last accessed on 22 March 2016).

9

Ensuring Food Security

'This cannot be. We cannot allow the state of affairs to continue.'
—Justice B.N. Kirpal, Supreme Court, on admitting
the 'Right to Food' petition, 9 June 2001.

'Campaigning activities in Rajasthan gave me plenty of opportunities to observe the deep hostility of the government bureaucracy towards the poor. There are, of course, sympathetic and dedicated individuals at all levels of the bureaucracy. But the overall mindset in these circles strikes me as extremely anti-poor.'
—Jean Dreze (2002)

What begun with a writ petition in the Supreme Court of India in 2001 culminated in the right to food (RTF) being guaranteed by the government by enacting and enforcing the National Food Security Act, 2013. This chapter in the following course traces the evolution of this piece of legislation. While doing so, it also discusses its features, the stakeholders who contributed to it, and the deliberations which went into different provisions of the act.

The Beginning

One of the most spectacular and long-drawn struggles of policy change, the battle for food security had, in the words of one of its biggest champions Colin Gonsalves (2009), 'a rather casual beginning'. Colin, an engineer turned human rights lawyer, advocate in the Supreme Court, and the founder of the Human Rights Legal Network (HRLN), had gone to Jaipur in early 2001 to attend a meeting on police reform. There, on a breakfast visit to the home of Kavita Srivastava, head of the Rajasthan unit of the People's Union for Civil Liberties (PUCL), he met the development economist and activist Jean Dreze, who was there with other friends. Rajasthan was in the throes of a three-year drought spell and the hunger situation was going from bad to worse. In 1999–2000, PUCL led by Kavita Srivastava started with a survey of the food situation in Rajasthan. About 50 grass-roots organizations had come together under the banner of the *Akal Sangarsh Samiti* to fight the drought situation in the state. That group had well-known activists like Aruna Roy, Nikhil Dey, Jean Dreze, P. Sainath, and many other participants.

Jean suggested a trip to a few nearby villages to check out the situation. While everyone who rode in the jeep was broadly aware of the situation, what they saw shocked them. Worse, this was also a time when the Food Corporation of India's (FCI) godowns, including those in Rajasthan, were spilling over with surplus grains. The total foodgrain stock in the country was 60 million tonnes, far above what was needed as per the buffer stock requirements. As Jean explained with his inimitable imagery, if the sacks of grain were laid end to end, it would cover the distance from earth to moon and back!

Colin suggested filing a public interest litigation (PIL) in the Supreme Court asking for the implementation of the British-era 'Famine Codes' in Rajasthan and the others readily agreed. Kavita and Jean prepared the data for Rajasthan and, soon enough, Colin filed the writ petition number 196 of 2001 in the Supreme Court between PUCL and the Union of India and all its states and union territories. The battle had begun.

The 'famine codes' were an elaborate set of instructions to be followed by officials in near-famine conditions (with clearly specified indicators) in preparation of famines, which included providing employment to all willing in public works for a period of six months, employing about a fifth of the population and 'gratuitous relief' to those unfit to work. It was part of the law of the land, but very few people, particularly the government officials, were even aware of it. If the Supreme Court upheld the petition, then it would compel the government to provide immediate relief to the starving populace.

The legal basis of the petition was Article 21 of the Constitution which guarantees the right to life, and imposes upon the state the duty to protect it. This is a fundamental right and the Supreme Court has held in previous cases that the right to life includes the right to live with dignity and all that goes along with it, including the right to food. The petition argued that the response to the drought situation by central and state governments, in terms of both policy and implementation, constitutes a clear violation of this right.

The petition pointed out two aspects of the state's negligence in providing food security. The first was the breakdown of the public distribution system (PDS). The failures of the PDS arose at various levels: its availability had been restricted to families living below the poverty line (BPL), yet the monthly quota per family could not meet the nutritional standards set by the Indian Council of Medical Research (ICMR). Even this was implemented erratically and the identification of BPL households was also highly unreliable. All in all, the assistance provided to BPL households through the PDS amounted to less than five rupees per person per month.

The other focus of the petition was the inadequacy of government relief works. Famine codes operational in various states govern the provision of these works, and make them mandatory when drought is declared. Despite being required to give work to 'every person who comes for relief project', the Rajasthan government has followed a policy of 'labour ceilings', which restrict employment to less than five per cent of the drought-affected population, by the government's own statistics. Actual employment has been even lower, and failure to pay the legal minimum wage had been reported at many places.

In view of the availability of resources, the petition brought to notice the State and Central governments' negligence in executing the provisions under the PDS scheme. Despite the epidemic of hunger, statistics showed that food production increased in the 1990s, while availability of food declined. In Rajasthan, for example, close to 50 million tonnes of grain were lying idle in the government's reserves while nearly half of the rural population was below the poverty line. Even worse, poor storage conditions had destroyed much of the grains. Though the amount of food being wasted far outweighed the amount needed to assure food security, the government continued to pay the expense of storage instead of distributing it to those in dire need.

But the odds were against the petitioners. Prior to this, such attempts had failed to move the Supreme Court, known for its reluctance to move in 'policy matters'. In 1996, for instance, in a similar appeal made by activist Kishen Pattanayak against the state of Odisha where people were dying of starvation in Kalahandi, the Supreme Court had reposed faith in the state's statement of steps being taken and disposed of the petition. Fearing a similar fate, Colin had advised his colleagues to keep the writ petition under wraps.

But this time proved to be different. The Supreme Court bench needed no argument to admit the plea on 9 May 2001 and asked the Attorney General to appear in the case. In the next hearing on 23 July, the Attorney General, Soli Sorabjee, pointed out that this was not an adversarial litigation and the government appreciated the concern of the petition, but indicated that fiscal constraints tied the hands of the government in the matter. But the court was in no mood to listen. The presiding judge, Justice B.N. Kirpal, who later became the Chief Justice of India in 2002, was blunt: 'either you do it or we will tell you how to do it'. That was the last time the resource argument was provided in the court. The Attorney General, in fact, stressed the seriousness of the matter to his bureaucrats and greatly assisted the movement. The court also directed the petitioner (Kavita Srivastava of PUCL) to amend the petition and make all the states and union territories parties to the petition, making it a national issue. It issued the first of its over hundred interim orders directing the states 'to see that all the PDS shops, if closed, are re-opened and start functioning within one week from today and regular supplies made'. It was the campaign's first victory, with many more to come.

If there was any remaining doubt about the Supreme Court's complete espousal of the cause, it could not have survived its next order on 20 August:

> The anxiety of the Court is to see that the poor and the destitute and the weaker sections do not suffer from hunger and starvation. The prevention of the same is one of the prime responsibilities of the Government—whether Central or the State. How this is to be ensured would be a matter of policy which is best left to the government. All that the Court has to be satisfied and which it may have to ensure is that the food grains which are overflowing in the storage receptacles, especially of FCI godowns and which are in abundance, should not be wasted by dumping into the sea or eaten by rats. Mere

schemes without any implementation are of no use. What is important is that the food must reach the hungry.[1] (De Schutter 2014)

And the court was dead serious. On 3 September, being informed by the Attorney General that 16 states and union territories had not identified their BPL families, it instructed them to do so within a fortnight, and, when that was not done, expressed its dissatisfaction. It directed 'all the state governments to forthwith lift the entire allotment of foodgrains from the central government under the various schemes and disburse the same in accordance with the scheme'. In addition, 'the food for work programme in the scarcity areas should also be implemented by the various states to the extent possible' (Gonsalves 2011). The states were given the responsibility of implementation of the following schemes: a) the Employment Assurance Scheme, which may have been replaced by Sampurna Gramin Yojana; b) Mid Day Meal (MDM) Scheme; c) Integrated Child Development Scheme; d) National Benefit Maternity Scheme for BPL pregnant women; e) National Old Age Pension Scheme for destitute persons of over 65 years; f) Annapurna Scheme; g) Antyodaya Anna Yojana; h) National Family Benefit Scheme; and i) Public Distribution Scheme for BPL and APL families.

Soon, on 28 November, came the judgment where two of the future Chief Justices of India—Kirpal and Balakrishnan—directed states to fully comply with the Targeted Public Distribution System (TPDS), issue BPL cards, and distribute 25 kg of grain per family per month. The conversation then shifted to corruption and theft of foodgrains leading to non-operating PDS shops and other implementation gaps and the Supreme Court directed the shops to stay open during fixed hours that should be clearly and publicly stipulated. Not only had the highest court completely backed the food rights groups' agenda but it was also leading the battle and continuously widening its scope. The petitioners only had to ask for it. In six months, the right-to-food agenda had moved ahead by leaps and bounds.

Getting Things in Order

This was far more than what the activists could have even dreamt of. But the expansion of the scope of the case also meant more work for them in terms of data gathering and arguing in the matter. The loose network of activists and volunteers now needed to function in a more organized manner and, more importantly, at a national scale. The volume of information to be brought to court was by no means insignificant (at times, papers were brought into courtrooms in wheelbarrows). Of course, broadly speaking, the struggle for food has been waged by many groups all over the nation separately for decades but those were a collection of unconnected local battles. The unexpected and quick judicial success of the PUCL case energized and coalesced these myriad movements and they quickly began to come together to form the loose platform called the 'right-to-food campaign'.

By this time, the activism had been taken up by the Supreme Court itself. The battle was between a judiciary committed to the cause and not at all shy about taking on grounds conventionally believed to be in the executive realm, and an executive—centre and states—increasingly on the defensive. The campaigners perhaps could not have asked for a more sympathetic court. Its job now was to progressively broaden the scope of the battle through supplementary petitions, 'interim applications', and to supply the court with systematic evidence of widespread implementation gaps. But that did not come easy.

The legal team, in the beginning of the journey was, led by Colin Gonsalves and had as its other members, Aparna Bhat of HRLN, Ramesh Kumar, and Yug Chaudhry. Later, as the members moved on, other people who joined the team included Anup Kumar Srivastava, Jai Singh, Vipin Mathew Benjamin, Puja Sharma, and Alban Toppo. A support group helping the team included Jean Dreze, Nikhil Dey, Aruna Roy, Colin Gonsalves, Harsh Mander, and Kavita Srivastava. Representatives of several Non-governmental Organization (NGO) networks including the following:

1. National Federation of Indian Women (NFIW)
2. Human Rights Law Network (HRLN)
3. People's Union for Civil Liberties (PUCL)
4. National Alliance of People's Movements (NAPM)
5. Jan Swasthya Abhiyaan (JSA)
6. National Campaign for People's Right to Information (NCPRI)

7. Bhartiya Gyan Vigyaan Samiti (BGVS)
8. National Campaign Committee for Unorganised Sector Workers (NCC-USW)
9. National Campaign for Dalit Human Rights (NCDHR)
10. National Confederation of Dalit Organisations (NACDOR)
11. New Trade Union Initiative (NTUI)
12. Breastfeeding Promotion Network of India (BPNI)

The right-to-food campaign was thus beginning to gradually shape up as a meta-network of several network organizations. It functioned on a decentralized level that was built upon local initiative and voluntary cooperation. It consisted of a range of NGOs and civil society groups and concerned individuals/activists/practitioners/professionals. The campaign had a small 'support group', a 'coordinating and facilitating' group, and a small secretariat in Delhi—the former effectively consisting of members from 11 national organizations and they convened the first 'Convention on the Right to Food and Work' in Bhopal in central India in June 2004. The Bhopal convention which became an annual event—organized at Kolkata, Bodh Gaya, and Rourkela in subsequent years—was perhaps the first major event to bring together the activists in one single venue, but by that time the struggle had covered quite a lot of ground. While a 'founding statement' was adopted and the Steering Committee was put in place, it is fair to say that in this saga, it was function that far preceded form.

This support group considered the Supreme Court hearings and played a basic facilitating role in the larger campaign in terms of organizing events and meetings. It is, therefore, effectively the steering committee which took the lead of the campaign that consisted of people from very different backgrounds like sex workers, the transgender community, disabled people's organizations, women's organizations, political parties, trade unions, and so on. In addition to this, there was a convener for the campaign to coordinate the committee and meetings. Apart from that, the campaign did not have any structure of hierarchy or leadership position. The steering committee decided the organizational strategy about the next action in the campaign and the mobilization strategy. At the state level, the structures emerged inherently and they implemented the strategy decided by the steering committee. Although, the judiciary took an active interest in the case and established the commissioner's office, the court could not have been trusted to create lasting change. This needed the support of people from the ground and this gap was filled in by the emergence of the right-to-food campaign.

All members of the support group participated in the right-to-food Campaign in their personal capacity, without remuneration. The campaign depended, in part, on formally petitioning the judiciary for the enforcement of the right of every Indian to adequate nourishment. In this, it was inspired by preceding rulings of the Supreme Court; the court has held that in cases of fundamental rights, it was willing to give little latitude to governmental pleas of financial stringency (Muralidharan 2004).

The nationwide campaign, involving many organizations and individuals (NFIW, HRLN, PUCL, NAPM, NCPRI, BGVS, and so on), realized that to make the duty-bearers accountable to deliver on their obligations and for the claimants to claim their rights, a dual-capacity development strategy is imperative. At the level of the duty-bearers, such a strategy entailed building capacities of concerned state public officials at the district and block levels through trainings, workshops, and enlisting their participation at the public hearings so that they are better able to respond to the claims made by the people. For the claimants, such a strategy involved building capacities that create sustained empowerment by raising awareness amongst the affected people through trainings, workshops, and consultations that help create consciousness about their legal rights and entitlements so that they can take recourse to legal action; participate in meetings, campaigns, and public hearings; review implementation of policy guidelines on the various food security programmes that the court had ordered the state governments to implement; and, lobby effectively and knowledgeably for policy changes.

There were different factors responsible for catalyzing the campaign in different regions. The most attractive part of the campaign to its members was the potential to create an immediate impact with the aid of orders by Supreme Court. Since the onus of implementing the Supreme Court orders lay with the states, the campaign created the public and political pressure needed for the state executive to take them up seriously. For instance, when the MDM orders were not being implemented, the campaign in 2004 held a feeding camp to feed schoolchildren in front of the houses of chief ministers and district magistrates in different states across India. Media's role has also been very critical throughout for the campaign.

Campaigns, people-centred advocacy, and lobbying were used with maximum impact to raise awareness on the right to food and in lobbying the Supreme Court and related departments of the state governments to meet their obligations in realizing this right. A multi-faceted strategy using street plays (for instance, on the MDM scheme), rallies, as well as promoting public education through the media, posters, booklets on issues like 'Know Your Rights', the Employment Guarantee Scheme (EGS), etc., was undertaken on a nationwide basis so as to have the most impact. Research and surveys also played an important role in the right-to-food campaign from inception—an informal survey of several villages in Rajasthan state was used to support the original PIL filed by the PUCL in April 2001 (Banerjee 2005).

Several new developments occurred in the months after the landmark directives of 28 November 2001. The focus had already shifted to implementation, and monitoring of existing orders assumed importance. In interim orders dated 8 May 2002 and 2 May 2003, respectively, the Supreme Court appointed former Planning Secretary N.C. Saxena and fellow former bureaucrat S.R. Sankaran as 'commissioners' for the purpose of monitoring the implementa-tion of all orders relating to the right to food. The commissioners were empowered to enquire about any violations of these orders and to demand redressal, with the full authority of the Supreme Court. They were also expected to report to the court from time to time. After Sankaran resigned in 2006, Harsh Mander was authorized to assist N.C. Saxena as 'special commissioner'.

In the course of 15 years, the case has been heard by numerous judges in the Supreme Court and the tenacity of the judges has determined the tone of orders that have been passed in this case. But broadly, the Supreme Court has widened the idea of right to life to mean the right to life and dignity. In this case, the Supreme Court passed four kinds of orders related to the eight schemes related to the right to food. These were: a) Orders which said that the eight men-tioned schemes cannot be reduced or withdrawn without the court's permission. This in effect turned these schemes into legal entitlements and the court orders became the source of law; b) Orders which expanded the entitlements of the scheme after looking at its content. For example, for the midday meal scheme, in light of the discrepancy in provisions and meals being served, the court mandated a hot, cooked, nutritious, culturally appropriate meal of 300 calories to be served; c) Orders which universalized the schemes. For example, the Supreme Court provided that every child who attends a government school across the country is entitled to one hot cooked meal every day. This meant providing food to 120 million children and thus had massive budgetary implications. Although the court usually resisted from passing judgments which had budgetary implications, they made an exception this time and gave directions since it had direct implication on the fundamental right to life; and d) Orders to create a mechanism for the enforcement of its order in form of the Office of Supreme Court Commissioners (SC Commissioner).

The strategy for the court case was jointly decided by the Case Advisory Committee consisting of the SC Commissioner's office, the legal team, and the right-to-food campaign. This case became the fulcrum for the mobilization of people for the right to food. When the court started passing orders and they were not being implemented, in every state, campaigns started coming up spontaneously to get the orders implemented, supported by an informal support group consisting of Jean Dreze, Nikhil Dey, Aruna Roy, Colin Gonsalves, Harsh Mander, and Kavita Srivastava.

The early break for the RTF brigade in the Supreme Court did not, however, continue unabated. Relative setbacks in the court case can be traced to the dates of the orders. There have been long periods of silence. To negotiate the case through the court was not an easy task. The proclivity of the judges and the public mobilization were the most important factors which decided the course of the case and the orders. Courts are also managed through perception—which, in turn, is managed through media. The opposition to the case and the campaign has always been from the governments at the centre and the states, since they did not want to spend and viewed this spending as financially imprudent. The political opposition to the government did not raise much noise either, since their economic policies were similar. They did not want to cede any fiscal space to a policy which they thought will cost lots of money and may or may not deliver the due benefits.

While the court victories for the RTF was nothing short of stunning, it did not necessarily mean the ground reality shifted as dramatically as may appear from the Supreme Court orders. The administration often reacted to the orders with partial and nominal fulfilment and the court was left with no option beyond strongly-worded observations, a weapon that was weakened with every use and which possibly undermined the authority of the apex court itself. On 2 May 2003, for instance, the court found the government approach to the case 'distressing' and noted that several states had 'not even made a beginning' in one-and-a-half years to implement the Supreme Court orders. The court was monitoring implementation by 'keeping a petition pending in the Court and requiring affidavits to be filed showing compliance' (Gonsalves 2009). The commissioners were appointed to report on implementation and, in report after report, they painted a sorry picture and pointed out the serious lacunae in the implementation. After multiple adverse comments, finally on 25 July 2007 the Supreme Court took the exceptional step of issuing notices of contempt to the chief secretaries of several states to explain the reasons for non-compliance and why 'exemplary action' should not be taken against them. This finally drove the states to actually act on the directives.

Judicial activism was reaching its limits. A new law and its proper implementation was the need of the hour. The National Food Security Act (NFSA) was perhaps the only way out. In case of NFSA, the pressure initially was from the courts and there was a small civil society movement. The court case gave rise to a very large-scale civil society mobilization. There was a lot of pressure from the states as well. The Government of India had ceded a lot of policy space to the courts which they wanted to take back. The strategy of playing states against the centre was used, where states like Chhattisgarh passed a law even before the NFSA was passed. Even if not legisla-tion, certain states like Andhra Pradesh and Odisha had a principle of giving subsidized foodgrains to a larger number of people than the official Planning Commission figures. The key in the civil soci-ety for such issues is to create a discourse or argument around it. So, one of the right-to-food campaign's major contributions is that they created a societal argument around the subject. The media also played a massive role in bringing long-lost issues to the mainstream discourse—broadly working with the NFSA. There was also parliamentary lobbying, lobbying with political parties, and lobbying with the executive which created pressure. So, there were a constellation of factors which came together to influence a legislation.

Battle on the Streets: *Parivartan*

While the courtroom successes for the right-to-food campaign were clearly the most prominent, they were neither the full story nor sufficient to push the agenda forward. A parallel and coordinated campaign was being waged in the streets. While several groups pushed the right-to-food agenda forward, the experiences of Delhi-based and Arvind Kejriwal-led *Parivartan* are probably the most widely known.

Kejriwal and Manish Sisodia, among others, had started Parivartan in India in 2001 and led a successful protest against Income Tax authorities. In February 2002, a poor widow named Triveni had approached Parivartan, complaining that PDS shops always reported 'out of stock' whenever she needed food. Obtaining her ration records and using Right to Information (RTI), Parivartan found that, on paper, she had been issued her full quota of foodgrains. Parivartan's attempts to get information on such frauds met with opposition, first from the Civil Supplies Department and then from individual PDS shop owners claiming the information to be 'private'. Subsequently, Parivartan obtained all the records for 25 ration shops in the area by mobilizing people to file their own RTI applications. It found that over 55 per cent of kerosene, 93 per cent of wheat, and 96 per cent of rice was being siphoned off by the dealers. The fact that this was happening in collusion with civic officials was clear from the fact that their repeated exposure to the evidence produced either no effect or a nominal Rs 500 fine on the shop owners. The complicity of the police was equally clear. First Information Reports (FIRs) were virtually impossible to register. In a public hearing held by Parivartan, a deputy commissioner of police asserted that, in such matters, an FIR can be registered only by the government and not organizations like Parivartan.

Parivartan's public hearings exposed the fact that several senior city officials were completely oblivious of the Supreme Court orders being passed in the RTF case that directly impinged upon their duties and activities.

The street campaigns ran from door to door mobilizing people and obviously at significant risks. Once two activists were holed up in a police station with an irate mob of 250 shop owners asking them to be handed over to be set ablaze. On another occasion, a young activist named Santosh, had her hair cut with a dagger. Emboldened by her futile complaint at the police station, the assailant's knife came at her again, missing her throat by inches and badly slitting her chin. The residents of the community protested against the attack by organizing a rally and hunger strikes. The protests gained visibility and compelled the officials to take action.

This parallel action also looped back into the courtroom. On 18 November 2004, the Supreme Court asked the Government of Delhi and the Union Government to respond to the Interim Application (IA) number 41 about the status of the vigilance commissions they had promised to set up following the actions of Parivartan. By January 2005, the authorities had to submit an affidavit stating that vigilance commissions were set up in 69 circles, raids have recovered nearly Rs 21 lakhs (a relatively paltry sum) worth of foodgrains and action had been taken against 404 PDS shop owners with 42 FIRs filed. The court was pushing a reluctant and corrupt administration into action.

Disturbingly for the nation, the Supreme Court observed on 12 July 2006, that 'there is practically no monitoring over the sums allotted for the PDS, (which) is in the neighbourhood of Rs 30,000 crore annually' (Gonsalves 2011: 16). Given the magnitude of the problem, the court constituted a central vigilance committee (CVC) headed by Justice D.P. Wadhwa to 'look into the maladies which are affecting the proper functioning of the system and also suggest remedial measures'. The Court gave this 'unusual direction in view of the almost accepted fact that large-scale corruption is involved' (Gonsalves 2011: 16).

If there was any doubt left about the scale of corruption involving PDS shops and the complicity involving people at the highest level, it must have evaporated in 2008, when the computerization of PDS records by the Food and Civil Supplies Department exposed a massive scam around duplicate ration cards. About 10 per cent of the total ration cards in Delhi were found to be bogus and, in some cases, over 100 duplicate cards were issued to individuals. In

Sundar Nagari, where Parivartan surveyed the ration-card holders, it was established that most people were not aware that duplicate cards had been issued in their names. The bogus cards, Parivartan estimated, cost the exchequer nearly Rs 260 cores over the previous four years. This, of course, was the tip of the proverbial iceberg, a mere indicator of the extent of the malaise in the system. There was widespread consensus over the notion that the PDS was not working. But opinion was rapidly getting divided among economists about what to do with the failing system—whether to fix it or to completely chuck it in favour of an alternative system of food coupons or direct cash transfer using the Aadhaar card.

Outsiders No More

As the RTF campaign was waged in courts as well as on the streets through the sporadic actions of the various NGO groups, a major ground change occurred fairly unexpectedly in 2004—the election of the Congress-Left United Progressive Alliance (UPA) combine in place of the (BJP) Bharatiya-Janta-Party-led National Democratic Alliance (NDA) government. In itself, this change of horses would have signified little break from the past at the ground level, except in rhetoric. But the new government, or more specifically, the Congress supremo Sonia Gandhi started a completely new institution—the National Advisory Council (NAC)—to advise the Prime Minister's Office (PMO) on matters of national policy. The NAC was largely filled with noted social activists and during the next eight years, several RTF activists and sympathizers, including most notably, Jean Dreze, Aruna Roy, the Supreme Court commissioner N.C. Saxena, and later Harsh Mander, all found place there. While NAC was often criticized as an extra-constitutional body, its voice mattered, perhaps no less than the Cabinet itself and it derived its authority from being chaired by none other than Sonia Gandhi herself.

Waging War from Inside—NAC I and II

The primary legislative accomplishments of the NAC I (2004–9) included the Right to Information and the National Rural Employment Guarantee Act (NREGA). The agenda for NAC I was driven completely by the Common Minimum Program (CMP), the agreement between the UPA and its Left allies. The CMP clearly stated:

> The UPA will work out, in the next three months, a comprehensive medium-term strategy for food and nutrition security. The objective will be to move towards universal food security over time, if found feasible.[2]

Such assurance notwithstanding, food security legislation was not what got pushed in the UPA I. Rather, the energy was focused on the Employment Guarantee Act (EGA). In terms of jurisprudence, the right-to-food campaign had derived its strength from the broadening of the right to life in the Constitution. Further broadening of the right to life argument also implied right to work or right to livelihood, actually a demand the RTF campaigners had thought of bringing forth before the apex court right at the beginning, but had tactically stepped back from, fearing it may be an overkill. In that sense, the NREGA did push the right-to-food agenda forward somewhat, but in a rather indirect manner and it is fair to say that, despite the presence of RTF sympathizers in the NAC, during the entire UPA regime, the battle for the right to food progressed far more in courts than on the legislative side.

The big political break, however, came in getting the right to food included in the election manifesto of the Indian National Congress Party in the 2009 elections. It is generally believed that the key reason behind the inclusion was that the NREGA improved the political chances of the Congress party significantly and the next dose of pro-poor legislation would be the Right to Food. Election promises of subsidized foodgrains is hardly a new phenomenon in India, and a cynical view of the manifesto would be that it simply pushed forth that same gesture in a big way. A more idealistic interpretation would see the inclusion as the result of a logical progression of the campaign and the atmosphere created in part by the judicial progress as well as the roll-out of the massive NREGA programme. While it may well be a bit of both, most commentators would probably lean in favour of the inclusion of the right to food in the Congress party manifesto as driven by electoral calculations rather than any ideological commitment by the party. Be it as it may, and with the efforts of non-political activists like Harsh Mander, member of NAC and also special commissioner in the right-to-food case, the Congress party agenda in the 2009 elections did read as follows:

> The Indian National Congress pledges to enact a right to food law that guarantees access to sufficient food for all people, particularly the most vulnerable sections of society. The Indian National Congress pledges that every family living below the poverty line either in rural or urban areas will be entitled, by law, to 25 kg of rice or wheat per month at Rs 3 per kg. Subsidised community kitchens will be set up in all cities for homeless people and migrants with the support of the Central government. (Congress Election Manifesto 2009)[3]

The event of the victory of Congress party now virtually made a Right to Food (or Food Security as it came to be called) Act almost an inevitability. And of course, the Congress party succeeded in getting a majority in 2009.

NAC II

Since, right to food was included in the the Congress party manifesto for the 2009 elections, it became the first agenda item for NAC II, much like NREGA was for NAC I (Khera 2013). The president in her first speech to both the Houses after the constitution of the new Lok Sabha announced that there will be a right to food. NAC II was formed in 2010 and that is when they started working on the right to food agenda.

The path, however, was still not free of hurdles. During the period of 2009–13, because of the fear of subsidy, the government was not very keen on NAC's agenda of passing a right-to-food law. Prime Minister Manmohan Singh was not very spirited about the rights-based social programmes because of the high fiscal impact. To tackle the fiscal burden, when N.C. Saxena gave a suggestion about phase-wise implementation of the right to food, it was struck down as it would not have been a wise political decision for the government. Officially, the NAC made its suggestions to the PM who would then pass it on to his ministerial colleagues. But, informally, members of the NAC did consult individual ministers on specific topics or issues. The NAC also invited people like the deputy chairperson of the Planning Commission for their remarks or suggestions on specific subjects.

Corollary to these efforts, mainly advocated by the Supreme Court and the commissioners appointed by it in regard to right to food, there were subsequent efforts made in the legislature as well. The following section documents the legislative journey of the National Food Security Act, 2013.

Legislative Journey of the National Food Security Act, 2013

On 27 October 2010, the NAC[4] submitted a draft National Food Security Bill to the Prime Minister. The Prime Minister set up an Expert Committee under C. Rangarajan to examine the bill and make recommendations. The NAC's proposed National Food Security Bill sought to address nutritional deficiencies in the population. The main features of the proposed Bill included:

- Legal entitlement to subsidized foodgrains for 75 per cent of the population (90 per cent rural and 50 per cent urban).
- Government of India to specify criteria for categorization of population into priority and general households.
- 'Priority' households (46 per cent rural and 28 per cent urban) to be entitled to 35 kg of foodgrains per month (7 kg/person) at Re 1/kg for millets, Rs 2/kg for wheat, and Rs 3/kg for rice.
- 'General' households (44 per cent rural and 22 per cent urban) to be entitled to 20 kg of foodgrains per month (4 kg/person) at a price not exceeding 50 per cent of the Minimum Support Price (MSP).
- Minimum coverage, entitlement, and price to remain unchanged until the end of the XII five-year plan.
- 72 per cent of the population to be covered in Phase I and 75 per cent in Phase II. Phase II to be completed by 31 March 2014.
- Legal entitlements for child and maternal nutrition as well as destitute and vulnerable groups.
- Reform of the PDS through computerization and smart cards.

The Rangarajan Committee made several recommendations to the draft bill in regard to foodgrain requirements and availability, subsidy implications, and implementation with focus on modernizing PDS, and identification of beneficiaries. After taking into account all the recommendations made by the Rangarajan committee, a National Food Security Bill was introduced in the Lok Sabha on 22 December 2011 by K.V. Thomas, then Minister for Consumer Affairs, Food and Public Distribution. The major highlights of this bill were as follows:

- The bill proposes foodgrain entitlements for up to 75 per cent of the rural and up to 50 per cent of the urban population. Of these, at least 46 per cent of the rural and 28 per cent of the urban population will be designated as priority households. The rest will be designated as general households.
- Priority households will be entitled to 7 kg of subsidized foodgrains per person per month. General households will be entitled to at least 3 kg.
- The central government will determine the percentage of people in each state that will belong to the priority and general groups. State governments will identify households that belong to these groups.
- The bill proposes meal entitlements to specific groups. These include: pregnant women and lactating mothers, children between the ages of six months and 14 years, malnourished children, disaster-affected persons, and destitute, homeless, and starving persons.
- Grievance redressal mechanisms will be set up at the district, state, and central levels of government.
- The bill proposes reforms to the TPDS.

Table 9.1 summarizes the differences between the bill proposed by NAC and the one that was eventually introduced in the Parliament.

Meanwhile, the Commission for Agricultural Costs and Prices (CACP) presented a paper on the National Food Security Bill, 2011 in December 2012. In its report, the CACP analysed issues in the bill, including the operational and financial implications of the TPDS. The bill makes the right to food a legal right. The CACP was of the opinion that making foodgrains available on a sustained basis may become a constraint, given current trends in foodgrain production

Table 9.1   A Comparison between the NAC Draft Bill and the Actual NFS Bill[5]

Topic	NAC Version	Bill
Preamble	To provide all citizens with adequate nutrition and an enforceable right to food	Dropped references to constitutional guarantees, judicial precedents, and international practices
Definitions	Provided clear definitions of several terms, like 'excluded households', 'food', 'malnutrition', 'starvation', and so on	Dropped at least 25 definitions, modified several others
Price fixation for priority households	Not to be revised upwards for a minimum of 10 years from date of notification	Altered to: Union government given power to modify, through notification, essential entitlements
Use of life-cycle approach	A cornerstone of the draft law, '… access to adequate and appropriate food throughout the life cycle of a human being … to ensure a healthy body and mind'	Reference to life cycle dropped
Coverage	90 per cent of rural population	Reduced to 75 per cent of rural population
Provisions for women	Entitlements for single-women priority households: 14 kg grain, general: 8 kg	both entitlements dropped
Emergency/ Disaster relief	Rations at priority-household rates for 'emergency' and 'disaster-affected' persons for one year following the disaster	Two meals free of charge for three months
People living in starvation conditions	Twice the grain specified for priority households, free for six months; 'proactive identification' of such people, investigation of starvation deaths, protocol to prevent starvation deaths	Free cooked meals twice a day; provisions for identification and investigation of deaths dropped

(Cont'd)

Table 9.1   *(Cont'd)*

Topic	NAC Version	Bill
Selection and powers of the National Food Commission	Independent public nomination process to monitor public servants and starvation conditions, will have powers of civil court to impose penalties	No public nomination, union government will make rules, no judicial powers or power to set penalties
Provisions in case of Child Malnutrition	Free, 'appropriate therapeutic foods', special care at nutrition rehabilitation centre	both provisions dropped

Source: Adapted from Sharma (2013).

and yields. Considering the government already procures one-third of the cereal production every year, it also felt that any increase in procurement could have adverse ramifications on the cereal market.

The CACP opined that operational expenditure of the TPDS would increase under the bill given the system's inefficiencies, such as leakage, diversion, pilferage, and so on. The food subsidy would also increase due to the following factors: a) a lower central issue price of grain (price at which the central government issues wheat and rice to the state governments under TPDS); b) a significant increase in the number of entitled beneficiaries; and c) the need to keep raising the MSP to cover the rising costs of production and to incentivize farmers to increase production. The CACP calculated the food subsidy to be between Rs 125,000 crore to Rs 150,000 crore as compared to the government's estimate of Rs 95,000 crore. Moreover, it estimated the total cost of implementing the bill at about Rs 7 lakh crore over a period of three years. The CACP also mentioned that cash transfers have proved to be an efficient alternative to deliver subsidies. It mentioned that, globally, countries have moved away from the physical handling of grains and such used alternatives. It recommended that the government consider programmes in other countries such as Bolsa Familia in Brazil to 'develop a more effective and appropriate policy instrument to enhance social and economic welfare'. Moreover, it suggested that the bill have in-built flexibility for states to experiment with such approaches (Gulati et al. 2012).

The bill was also referred to the Standing Committee on Food, Consumer Affairs, and Public Distribution on 5 January 2012. The Standing Committee presented its report on 17 January 2013. On 20 March 2013, official amendments to the bill were circulated in the Lok Sabha. In order to counter oppositions to various clauses of the bill, the government promulgated the National Food Security Ordinance, 2013 on 5 July 2013. Subsequently, the National Food Security Bill, 2013 drawing from the ordinance was passed by both the Houses on 2 September 2013 and came into force as the NFSA, 2013. Box 9.1 outlines the key features of the act.

Box 9.1   Key Features of the National Food Security Act, 2013

The NFSA 2013 converts the existing food security programmes of the Government of India into legal entitlements. It includes the Midday Meal Scheme, Integrated Child Development Services Scheme, and the Public Distribution System. Further, the NFSA 2013 recognizes maternity entitlements. The Midday Meal Scheme and the Integrated Child Development Services Scheme are universal in nature, whereas the PDS will reach about two-thirds of the population. The major features of the NFSA are as mentioned below:

Entitlements

- TPDS: The act specifies that up to 75 per cent of the rural population and up to 50 per cent of the urban population shall be entitled to foodgrains under the TPDS.
- Special groups: The act guarantees meal entitlements to pregnant women and lactating mothers, children, destitute, homeless, and starving persons, among others. It specifies nutritional standards for meal entitlements provided to children, pregnant women, and lactating mothers.
- Entitlements to destitute and homeless persons shall be applicable only after notification by state governments, which shall take place within one year of commencement of the act. State governments shall

(Cont'd)

Box 9.1   *(Cont'd)*

also prepare and notify guidelines for the prevention, identification, and relief to cases of starvation.

Beneficiaries

• The central government shall determine the percentage of people in each state that will be in priority and general groups. It shall also prescribe guidelines for the identification of households in each group, including criteria for exclusion.
• Every state government will be responsible for identifying persons belonging to priority and general households as well as those suffering from malnutrition, starvation, destitution, and homelessness. The list of the identified priority and general households shall be placed in the public domain.

TPDS Reforms

The central and state governments shall undertake reforms of the TPDS, including: (a) doorstep delivery of foodgrains to TPDS outlets; (b) use of information technology; (c) leveraging Aadhaar; (d) transparency of records; (e) preference to public bodies in licensing of fair price shops (FPS) and their management by women; (f) diversification of commodities offered; (g) support to local public distribution models and grain banks; and (h) schemes such as cash transfer and food coupons in lieu of foodgrains.

Grievance Redressal and Monitoring

• District Grievance Redressal Officers (DGROs) shall be appointed by state governments to enforce entitlements and investigate and redress grievances. Aggrieved persons may complain to DGROs regarding non-distribution of entitled foodgrains or meals.
• The central and state governments shall constitute National and State Food Commissions. Each commission shall consist of a chairperson, five members, and a member-secretary. At least two members shall be women and two shall belong to scheduled castes and tribes. Members may be removed on certain grounds.

(Cont'd)

Box 9.1 *(Cont'd)*

- Any person aggrieved by the orders of the DGRO may appeal to the State Commission. The next round of appeals will be heard by the National Commission. The National and State Food Commissions may either suo moto or on receipt of a complaint inquire into violations of entitlements. During inquiry, they shall have powers of civil courts. Public servants found guilty by the commissions of failing to provide relief recommended by a DGRO may be fined up to Rs 5,000. The commissions will have the power to forward any case to a magistrate having jurisdiction to try the same.
- The State and National Commissions shall advise the respective governments on implementation of the schemes under the act. The National Commission shall also advise on synergizing existing schemes and framing new schemes for entitlements.
- Every state government shall set up vigilance committees at the state, district, block, and FPS levels. These committees shall be responsible for supervising the implementation of all schemes under the act and informing the DGRO of any violation of the act or of any malpractice or misappropriation of funds.
- Every local authority, as authorized by the state government, shall conduct periodic social audits on the functioning of FPS, TPDS, and other welfare schemes, take necessary action, and publicize findings.

Responsibilities of Central and State Governments

- The central government shall allocate foodgrains to state governments with respect to entitlements for priority and general households at prices specified in schedule I of the act. It shall also: (a) procure foodgrains for the central pool; (b) provide for transportation of foodgrains to state depots; and (c) create and maintain modern and scientific storage facilities. In case of shortage of foodgrains, the central government shall provide funds to state governments.
- It shall be the responsibility of every state government to: (a) organize delivery of foodgrains from designated depots in the state to the doorstep of each FPS; (b) ensure delivery of foodgrains to the entitled persons; (c) create and maintain scientific storage sites; (d) suitably strengthen capacities of their Food and Civil Supplies Corporations; and (e) establish institutionalized licensing for FPS. State governments

(Cont'd)

Box 9.1   *(Cont'd)*

shall also pay a food security allowance to entitled persons in case of non-supply of entitlements.

Other Provisions

• The bill specifies that the central government, state governments, and local authorities shall strive to progressively realize the objectives specified in schedule III. These objectives include, among others, revitalization of agriculture; procurement-, storage- and movement-related interventions; and access to: (a) safe and adequate drinking water and sanitation; (b) healthcare; (c) nutritional, health, and educational support to adolescent girls; and (d) adequate pensions for senior citizens, persons with disability, and single women.

Source: Compiled by the authors from the National Food Security Act, 2013.[6]

Although the Food Security Act came into force on 5 July 2013, the goal of food security is a distant dream. Its 'implementation is mired in apathy and confusion' (Dreze 2015). But at the very least, the battle for policy change—waged over several decades, but most spiritedly and doggedly for over 10 years—has reached a significant milestone, creating a justiciable right for citizens.

Key Observations and Concluding Remarks

This landmark law's remarkable journey fits with a combination of punctuated equilibrium theory and the advocacy coalition theory. The impetus to the movement came after the court's landmark judgment on the writ petition filed by PUCL after which many activists came together to fight for the law in a long and sustained campaign.

From the perspective of the proposed framework, the tactics used by the activists were confrontational while the government's attitude was somewhat conflictual, especially on the issue of the financial burden the law would place on the exchequer. However, the presence of activists such as Jean Dreze, Harsh Mander, and Aruna Roy on the NAC made the government more amenable to passing the law. In addition, it was viewed as an election-winning game changer (along with some of the other rights-based laws) by the ruling dispensation, which made them amenable to take the financial risk of the law. Given that it took over 20 years for the law to be enacted, it can be said that the impact on the legislative agenda was low. The strategy used by the campaign was a multi-pronged one. Figure 9.1 taken from Banerjee (2005) summarizes the approach.

Clearly, the most effective weapon in the arsenal of the campaign was legal action with a decidedly sympathetic Supreme Court that played the key role in the epic struggle. However, the other approaches were no less important. Capacity building, both of providers (or 'duty-bearers') as well as beneficiaries ('claim-holders'), played a key role. State organizations worked with local officials, sensitizing them through training, workshops, and getting them to participate in public hearings. At the same time, the beneficiaries were trained to raise awareness of their entitlements. A sustained general awareness campaign using instruments like street plays, public education through media, rallies, posters, and so on, kept the issues in the forefront. For example, 9 April 2002 was observed as National Day of Action on Midday Meals. Soon, several states initiated cooked midday meals

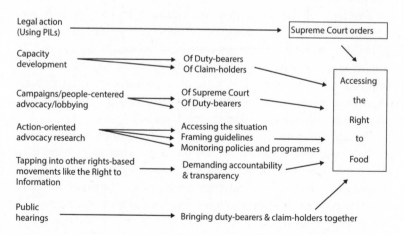

Figure 9.1 Entitlement-oriented Rights-based Strategies Used in the Right to Food Campaign
Source: Banerjee (2005).

in schools. On 13 May 2005, a countrywide *'rozgar adhikar yatra'* (March for Right to Work) brought the related right to work in the limelight.

A key part of the campaign was action-oriented advocacy research. Nothing persuaded the court or public opinion as much as methodically obtained data on state of food security in various parts of the country as well as the state of and gaps in implementation of various Supreme Court orders. The commissioners' office functioned pretty much because of sets of dedicated volunteers painstakingly documenting and collating evidence and effectively communicating them to create a compelling case for the campaign in the courts as well as in the streets.

Piggybacking on the Right to Information movement helped the cause significantly. There was, of course, a significant overlap among the champions of both movements, both starting from Rajasthan, and organizations like Parivartan (unsurprising, given that Kejriwal was at the forefront of the RTI movement) used the RTI in a major way in its move against the PDS owners. Similarly, public hearings, particularly in states with high starvation deaths—Odisha, Madhya Pradesh, Jharkhand, Maharashtra, and Rajasthan—created awareness, empowered claimants and, on occasions, even resolved problems on the spot.

The tone of the movement was clearly confrontational. It was undeniably an 'activist versus establishment' stance from the activists' point of view, while for the government functionary, the stance was one of 'agreement in principle but reservations in matters of details' approach. The activists often were of a Leftist orientation though they were quick to admit the worse-than-average indifference in implementation shown in Leftist-ruled states.

Perhaps the most amazing aspect of the movement was the level of cohesion and organization displayed by what is perhaps best described as a 'network of networks' of local organizations with no permanent organizational structure or hierarchy. The first few orders of the Supreme Court seem to have electrified activists spread around the country working disparately towards the same broad cause and they came together under a banner and organized and conducted themselves in a coordinated manner over a fairly long period of time. Their opponents were the corrupt few, the apathetic administration, and the indifferent middle class. As the movement integrated and channelized local angst and pain at deprivation, it had built the background of possibly a mass political movement, which doubtless contributed to the creation of the Aam Aadmi Party (AAP) as much as the struggle for RTI and Lokpal did, but could arguably have created a sustained national political movement. It is quite likely that it was the structured nature of the single Supreme Court PIL which provided the backbone of the movement and contributed significantly to its organization as well.

Notes

1. *People's Union for Civil Liberties and another* v *Union of India and others*, Supreme Court of India, Civil Original Jurisdiction, Writ Petition (Civil) No. 196 of 2001, 2 May 2003.
2. 'National Common Minimum Programme 2004', United Progressive Alliance Government, available at http://nceuis.nic.in/NCMP.htm (last accessed on 20 March 2017).
3. Manifesto of the Indian National Congress, Lok Sabha Election, 2009, available at http://inc.in/documents/election-doc/manifesto09-eng.pdf (last accessed on 20 March 2017).
4. The National Advisory Council (NAC) of India was an advisory body set up by the first United Progressive Alliance (UPA) government to advise the prime minister of India.
5. From the State of Livelihood Report 2012. Permission awaited.
6. Available at http://indiacode.nic.in/acts-in-pdf/202013.pdf (last accessed on 20 March 2017).

10

The Tactics of Protest

Getting to the Lokpal Act

> *Fighting corruption is not just good governance. It's self-defence. It's patriotism.*
>
> —Joe Biden, former US Vice President

Context

The war cry of 'do or die' that galvanized the Quit India movement in 1942 seemed to be back in vogue in 2011. A little-known activist from Maharashtra, Anna Hazare, went on an indefinite fast to force the government to agree to enact the *Jan Lokpal* Bill, touted as the antidote to corruption in the country. To many Indians, long habituated to public figures almost never walking the talk, Anna Hazare held the appeal of a Gandhi, especially in his simplicity and incorruptible persona and the ability to put his life at stake for a higher cause. It helped that 'corruption' had the emotive charge of 'salt' of Mahatma Gandhi's Dandi March. It touched everyone, and provided an explanation, both simple and powerful, for failures in government performance, for inefficient allocation of resources, and for disappearing public funds.

The identification of corruption as the key problem is a worldwide phenomenon. Most recent protests around the world, from Occupy Wall Street to Arab Spring, put corruption near the top of their list of grievances (Taylor 2014). In India, corruption was hardly a new problem. It has been flagged repeatedly by Transparency International (TI)

(India ranks 94th out of 176 countries in TI's Corruption Perception Index) as well as domestic surveys highlighting the presence, albeit varied in scale, of corruption in all of India's states.[1] Many experts cite India's economic policies since Independence—over-regulation, protectionism, and government ownership of industries—as the cause for corruption. Such policies led to slow economic growth, high unemployment, and widespread poverty (Goswami and Bandhopadhyay 2012).[2] The partial liberalization of the economy in 1990 and the technological revolution brought the efficiencies of a market-based system in some sectors. India was able to eliminate middlemen in certain areas such as tax filing and refunds, telephone connections, or acquiring commercial permits, hence, containing corruption to a limited extent at the lower levels. However, around 2010 India faced with a different kind of challenge. Scams to the tune of thousands of crores highlight a political-industry nexus, where the private sector appeared to be willing to pay senior public officials to get its work done. The high-profile scams that came to light in 2010 and 2011, including claims of fraud in preparations for the 2010 Commonwealth Games, a Comptroller and Auditor General (CAG) report estimating losses of Rs 1.76 lakh crore due to alleged mishandling of 2G spectrum license allocation, and questionable provision of apartment units in a major Mumbai residential development (Adarsh scam) to bureaucrats and politicians, rather than military veterans, seemed to be the tipping point for India.

The unprecedented success of the anti-corruption movement in not only getting a legislation passed but also in the birth of a new party, the Aam Aadmi Party (AAP), under the leadership of Arvind Kejriwal led the *Time* magazine to call it one of the most 'striking acts of dissent' and include it in the 'Top 10 News Stories of 2011' (Tharoor 2011).

The movement has had as many detractors as supporters who have raised interesting questions about the nature of the movement, the support it had garnered, the methods it employed, and the merits of the Jan Lokpal Bill in tackling the issue of corruption.

This case study aims to understand how laws/policies are made in India through the documentation of the journey of the law from its inception to enactment. The focus of the study would be on the evolution of the India Against Corruption movement, the key stakeholders who organized the movement, the methods they used to garner support and influence policymakers, the role of media in popularizing the movement, and the developments after the law was passed.

Pre-Lokpal Institutional Framework

India's parliament has enacted several legislations to eradicate corruption since the colonial era. A public servant[3] (such as government employees, judges, armed forces, police) in India could be prosecuted for corruption under the Indian Penal Code, 1860 and the Prevention of Corruption Act, 1988. The Benami Transactions (Prohibition) Act, 1988 sought to combat fraudulent deals. The Prevention of Money Laundering Act, 2002 penalized public servants for the offence of money laundering (PRS Legislative Research 2011b).India is also a signatory to the UN Convention against Corruption since 2005 (ratified in 2011). The convention covers a wide range of acts of corruption and proposes certain preventive policies.[4]

The three main authorities involved in inquiring, investigating, and prosecuting corruption cases were the Central Vigilance Commission (CVC), the Central Bureau of Investigation (CBI), and the state Anti-Corruption Bureau (ACB). Cases related to money laundering by public servants were investigated and prosecuted by the Directorate of Enforcement and the Financial Intelligence Unit, which are under the Ministry of Finance.The CBI and state ACBs investigated cases related to corruption under the Prevention of Corruption Act, 1988 and the Indian Penal Code, 1860. The CBI's jurisdiction was the central government and union territories while the state ACBs investigated cases within the states. States could refer cases to the CBI. The CVC was a statutory body that supervised corruption cases in government departments. The CVC could refer cases either to the Central Vigilance Officer (CVO) in each department or to the CBI. The CVC or the CVO recommended the action to be taken against a public servant but the decision to take any disciplinary action against a civil servant rested on the department authority. Though the CVC (set up in 1964) was an independent agency directly accountable to the Parliament, its role was advisory in nature. It relied on the

CBI for investigation and only oversaw the bureaucracy. Ministers and Members of Parliament (MPs) were out of its purview (PRS Legislative Research 2011b).

Prosecution could be initiated by an investigating agency only after it had the prior sanction of the central government or state government and government-appointed prosecutors undertook the prosecution proceeding in the courts. All cases under the Prevention of Corruption Act, 1988 were tried by special judges who are appointed by the central or state government.[5]

The Idea of an 'Ombudsman'

The idea of constituting an ombudsman-type institution to look into the grievances of individuals against the administration was first mooted in 1963 during a debate on 'Demands for Grants for the Law Ministry'.[6] The ombudsman is an institution, independent of the judiciary, executive, and legislature and analogous with that of a high judicial functionary. It is mostly free to choose its investigation method and agency. The expenditure of the office is under parliamentary control. In 1966, the First Administrative Reforms Commission recommended that two independent authorities at the central and state levels be established to enquire into complaints against public functionaries (including MPs) (Sanyal 2011).

The basic idea of the institution of Lokpal was borrowed from the concept of the ombudsman in countries such as Finland, Norway, Denmark, Sweden, UK, and New Zealand. In 1995, the European Union created the post of European Ombudsman. Presently, about 140 countries have the office of the ombudsman.[7] In Sweden, Denmark, and Finland, the office of the ombudsman can redress grievances of citizens by either directly receiving complaints from the public or suo moto. However, in the UK, the office of the Parliamentary Commissioner can receive complaints only through MPs (to whom the citizen can complain). Sweden and Finland also have the power to prosecute erring public servants.[8]

The Lokpal Bill was introduced for the first time in 1968 but it lapsed with the dissolution of the Lok Sabha. It was introduced seven more times in Parliament, the last time in 2001. However, the bill lapsed each time except in 1985 when it was withdrawn.[9] At the state level, 18 states had created the institution of the *Lokayukta* through the Lokayukta Acts by 2011.[10]

In 2002, the report of the National Commission to Review the Working of the Constitution urged that the Constitution should provide for the appointment of the Lokpal and Lokayuktas in the states, but suggested that the prime minister (PM) should be kept out of the purview of the authority.[11] In 2004, the United Progressive Alliance (UPA) government's National Common Minimum Programme (NCMP) promised that the Lokpal Bill would be enacted.[12] The Second Administrative Commission, formed in 2005, also recommended that the office of the Lokpal be established without delay.[13]

Genesis of 'India Against Corruption'

'Enough is Enough'

Since the issue of corruption in the body politic was hardly novel, the question that is puzzling for many analysts is why the India Against Corruption (IAC) movement attracted so much attention from the politically apathetic, urban, middle-class citizens. 'Anti-corruption' is a generic and vague issue that did not appeal to any one class. The Jan Lokpal Bill invited as many questions as it answered, besides being too technical a plank for a popular agitation. Nationalist language and symbols were out of place in an allegedly post-nationalist age and invoking Gandhi could turn out to be a political liability in the age of sectional politics (Ashutosh 2012).

Analysts have speculated about the reasons behind the success of this movement—some attributed it to the high-voltage media coverage with the emotive appeal of the issue of corruption at a time when big-ticket scams were being unearthed almost on a daily basis while others pointed to the appeal of a Gandhi-like figure in Anna Hazare in a world of venal and self-serving politicians and opportunistic activists. Perhaps, the truth, as always, lay somewhere in between.

As pointed out earlier, around 2010–11, news in the media was dominated by various scams. Images of dirty bathrooms and badly constructed facilities before the Commonwealth Games (CWG) of 2010, allegations of serious corruption by officials of the organizing committee of the games and delays in the construction of the main venue of the games remained strong in the public psyche (*India Today* 2010a). The CAG's sensational report which calculated a presumptive loss of Rs 1.76 lakh crores in the allocation of the 2G Spectrum added fuel to the fire.[14] Former Central Vigilance Commissioner P.J. Thomas was facing a legal challenge to his appointment for his alleged role in the palmolein import scam in December 2010 (*Times of India* 2010).

On 4 October 2010, Arvind Kejriwal, an IRS officer turned Magsaysay-award-winning right to information (RTI) activist who ran a Non-government institution (NGO) called *Parivartan* wrote an open letter to Sonia Gandhi severely criticizing the UPA government on its inaction against the culprits of the CWG scam. He emphasized that all the investigating agencies were under the control of the government, so expecting them to be unbiased and honest in their investigation was futile. The letter stated that on 10 August, a meeting was held to discuss and identify the critical deficiencies in India's anti-corruption systems whose minutes had already been sent to Sonia Gandhi. The participants included Karnataka Lokayukta Justice Santosh Hegde, former CVC P. Shankar, former chief election commissioner J.M. Lyngdoh, senior Supreme Court advocate Prashant Bhushan, and others. Outgoing CVC Pratyush Sinha was present as an observer. The group recommended the following:

> Create a Lokpal at the centre and Lokayuktas in states to deal with corruption. They should have jurisdiction over both bureaucrats and politicians. They should have resources and complete powers to entertain complaints, investigate them, and prosecute the guilty. These organizations should not need approvals or permissions from anyone to initiate investigations and prosecutions. At the same time, they should themselves be transparent and accountable in their functioning. Their appointment should be through a transparent and participatory process. (Kejriwal 2010)

Many other high-profile activists joined the fray, using social media as their preferred medium. Gul Panag, Dipankar Sarkar, Nabila Z. Zaidi, and Chandrashekhar Bhattacharya spearheaded a Twitter and Facebook campaign somewhat unimaginatively called 'Against CWG Corruption'. They called for a silent protest march on the lawns of India Gate on 15 October 2010 followed by a press conference that would detail the agenda of the campaigners. 'Shock and awe' through show of strength was the motto of the group. However, the police refused to give them permission to hold their march on the India Gate lawns.[15]

Meanwhile, in response to severe criticism from various quarters, the government appointed a high-level committee on 25 October 2010, which was to be headed by V.K. Shunglu to 'look into issues relating to the organizing and conduct of Commonwealth Games— Delhi 2010 and lessons to be learnt for the future'. The Shunglu Committee submitted its report on 28 March 2011.[16]

Although thwarted in their first attempt to hold a protest march, the 'Against CWG Campaign' did not die down. Teaming up with Kejriwal and Kiran Bedi, the campaign decided to keep up the pressure on the government through a press conference. On 29 October 2010, a press conference was held at the Press Club of India highlighting the fact that the Shunglu Committee had inadequate powers to investigate the CWG scam. Kejriwal contended, 'The Shunglu Committee does not have any powers to call for records from an ordinary clerk, the committee is totally powerless to enforce its directions. When agencies like the Central Vigilance Commission and the Comptroller and Auditor General find it difficult to get their orders implemented, how would the Shunglu Committee get its orders implemented?' (IANS 2010). The activists called for all concerned citizens to join them in filing an FIR at Parliament Street police station against the corruption in the CWG on 12 November at 3 pm (News One 2010). Following up on their call, on 14 November 2010, Kejriwal and other activists, such as Swami Agnivesh, Delhi Archbishop Vincent Concessao, and scientist Devendra Sharma, filed a joint 377-page complaint with 'all evidence' at Delhi's Parliament Street police station, asking it to investigate the corruption in CWG. These activists demanded that an independent commission be set up on the lines of the Election Commission to deal with corruption issues (Indian Express 2010b). According to some reports, nearly 10,000 people assembled at the Parliament Street police station (Dwivedi and Roshan 2014: 160).

However, CWG turned out to be the tip of the iceberg. Multiple corruption scandals involving politicians, bureaucrats, and the private sector grabbed eyeballs in the last three months of 2010. The Adarsh Housing Society scam—where in an alleged case of land grab in

Mumbai, top politicians, senior bureaucrats, and army officers were occupying flats on a prime property that was meant for Kargil war heroes and their widows (*India Today* 2010b)—was the first in a line of similar scams that came to light (Katakam and Bavadam 2010). Next was the expose on the Niira Radia tapes, which showed the involvement of not only senior politicians and bureaucrats but also senior journalists in the appointment of DMK's (Dravida Munnetra Kazhagam) A. Raja as the Telecom minister in 2009 (who later had to resign after pressure mounted on the government over irregularities in the allotment of the 2G spectrum) (*Open* 2010).

It was perhaps fortuitous for Kejriwal that in a brief window of a few months, a number of big-ticket scams involving politicians, bureaucrats, and journalists came to light. 'Enough is enough' seemed to be the public mood. The time seemed ripe for some serious action against VIP corruption.

Jan Lokpal to the Rescue

In 2010, Kejriwal chalked a two-pronged strategy to gain popular support—establish an institutional way (through *mohalla sabhas*) to connect with people to address their everyday grievances and find a legislative solution to corruption. The idea behind his mohalla sabhas was based on principles of direct grass-roots democracy: it allowed residents of a neighbourhood to decide how and where their quota of municipal funds should be spent. Kejriwal's organization, Parivartan, invited journalists to attend these sabhas but there were few takers (Subramaniam 2015).

On the legislative front, Kejriwal started consulting with senior Supreme Court lawyers Prashant Bhushan and Shanti Bhushan, a former Union Law Minister. Travelling to their home in Noida since autumn of 2010, he spent hours discussing the finer points of the Lokpal Bill. 'Basically, he was doing all the work,' Prashant Bhushan said in an interview with Mehboob Jelani, a journalist from *Caravan*, 'I was only being consulted, so it was an easy task, and he gets it quickly' (Jelani 2011).

By the end of October, Kejriwal had begun to circulate a draft of his bill among 'like-minded people'—and to work with those who responded positively, including Kiran Bedi, the Ramon Magsaysay award-winning police officer who turned activist, and the former Supreme Court Justice Santosh Hegde. 'I was just trying to find people who were known for fighting corruption', Kejriwal told Jelani. One such person was Anna Hazare, who had a history of fighting corruption in Maharashtra and was involved in the passing of the RTI Act in the state (Jelani 2011).

On 1 December, this group calling itself India Against Corruption sent identical letters with a draft of the Lokpal Bill to the then prime minister Manmohan Singh and the Chief Justice of India S.H. Kapadia. The letter described the existing system of investigating corruption as deeply flawed since the task was divided among multiple, ineffective agencies and demanded a 'total overhaul of the anti-corruption delivery system'.[17] Next, a press conference was organized for the release of the Jan Lokpal Bill with eminent personalities such as Kiran Bedi, Baba Ramdev, Anna Hazare, and Swami Agnivesh attending it (Sinha 2012). This was followed by a day-long seminar at Indian International Centre (IIC) on 9 December on 'How Effective are Our Anti-corruption Agencies in Tackling High Level Corruption?' On 22 December, mobilizing about 20,000 people, the Opposition led by the Bhartiya Janta Party protested against the Congress party government's handling of the 2G spectrum scam at Delhi's Ramlila ground. The rally came days after the prime minister told a Congress party conference that he had 'nothing to hide' from the 2G spectrum investigation (*BBC* 2010).

Around the end of October 2010, the government started circulating its version of the Lokpal Bill. This bill created an institutional mechanism that would investigate the political establishment for corruption-related offences, including the prime minister, all ministers in the Union Government and Members of Parliament. The bill however exempted a) any inquiry into allegations against the PM in relation to his functions concerning national security, foreign affairs, and public order; b) complaints against the president, vice president, Speaker and Deputy Speaker of Lok Sabha, deputy chairman of Rajya Sabha, sitting judges of the Supreme Court and High Courts, comptroller and auditor general of India, attorney general, chief election commissioner and other election commissioners, chairperson and members of the National Commission for Scheduled Castes and Scheduled Tribes, and chairperson and members of the Union

Public Service Commission. Also, before taking up complaints against MPs, the Lokpal would have to seek the concurrence of the presiding officers of the House to which the MP belonged (Chhibber 2010). Finally, a Group of Ministers (GoM)—chaired by Pranab Mukherjee—was formed in 2011 with the mandate to suggest measures to tackle corruption and to examine the proposal of a Lokpal Bill (*Outlook* 2011).[18]

Kejriwal's Jan Lokpal Bill was a radical departure from this model. It aimed to establish a completely independent body called the Lokpal. Agencies such as CVC and part of CBI would be merged with the Lokpal and would have jurisdiction over corruption cases against politicians, bureaucrats, and judges. It also suggested that Lokpal could initiate investigations and prosecution without needing prior sanction of any authority (*NDTV* 2011b).

The Ordinance Route for Lokpal?

Given the public mood, it was inevitable that the Opposition would hold the government's feet to the fire. The winter session of the Parliament, held between 9 November and 13 December, was a washout as Parliament continued to be stalled throughout the duration of its sitting. Both Houses saw protests over the government's reluctance to constitute a Joint Parliamentary Committee (JPC) on the issue of 2G spectrum allocation. Lok Sabha worked for 7 hours and 37 minutes, 5.5 per cent of available time and Rajya Sabha for 2 hours and 44 minutes, 2.4 per cent of available time (Kumar 2010). The stalemate in Parliament was rooted in perceived differences over the effectiveness of the Public Accounts Committee (PAC) and the JPC in investigating the issue of 2G spectrum allocation. The PAC is part of the structured committee system in Parliament and is constituted every year. Its main duty is to ascertain how the money granted (budget) by Parliament has been spent by the government. The JPC, on the other hand, is an ad-hoc body. It is set up for a specific objective and duration. The details regarding membership and subjects are also decided by Parliament. Like the PAC, JPC recommendations have persuasive value but the committee cannot force the government to take any action on the basis of its report (Rai and Burman 2010).

With the washout of the winter session, the Congress Core Group met at the PM's residence on 31 December to discuss the promulgation of an ordinance to pass the Lokpal Bill. However, at the Cabinet meeting of the UPA on 6 January 2011, several ministers questioned the logic of bringing a hurried ordinance to set up the institution of Lokpal at the central level. News reports quoted the Union Law Minister M. Veerappa Moily's statement that the Lokpal Bill might be introduced in the next Parliament session. He did not mention any plan to take the ordinance route (*Indian Express* 2011a).

Prominent Personalities Lend their Voices

Meanwhile, in January 2011, in response to a public interest litigation (PIL) filed by senior lawyer Ram Jethmalani, former Lok Sabha Secretary General Subhash Kashyap, former Punjab Police chief K.P.S. Gill, and three others, the Supreme Court rapped the government for not disclosing the names of those who had allegedly parked their black money with LGT Bank in Liechtenstein. The petitioners had alleged that most countries such as the US, France, Italy, and the UK acted against tax evaders after an employee of the Liechtenstein bank sold data on hundreds of account holders to tax authorities across the world, but India had not done anything (Singh 2011).

A number of leading industrialists, corporate bigwigs, and prominent citizens joined their voices to the chorus of action against corruption. An open letter addressed to 'our leaders' signed by Azim Premji, Jamshyd Godrej, N. Vaghul, Keshub Mahindra, Deepak Parekh, Ashok Ganguly, Anu Aga, Bimal Jalan, Nachiket Mor, Justice B.N. Srikrishna, and others raised concern over widespread 'governance deficit' almost in every sphere of national activity covering government, business, and institutions. It stated that

> ... possibly, the biggest issue corroding the fabric of our nation is 'Corruption'. This malaise needs to be tackled with a sense of urgency, determination, and on a war footing. The institution of Lok Ayuktas, vested with adequate powers, would go a long way in effecting the needed correction, as is evident from the example of Karnataka. There is a need for every State to have effective and fully empowered Lok Ayuktas and indeed for early introduction of the Lok Pal Bill at the national level, for the purpose of highlighting,

pursuing and dealing with corruption issues and corrupt individuals. (Vaghul et al. 2011)

Among regional political parties, Telugu Desam Party (TDP) president and former Andhra Pradesh Chief Minister Chandrababu Naidu came forward in support of the Lokpal Bill drafted by Kejriwal and others. Calling it an apolitical struggle, Naidu launched a 'war on corruption' through the Nandamuri Taraka Rama Rao (NTR) Memorial Trust and *Jana Chaitanya Vedika* beginning with a *padyatra* on 30 January, Mahatma Gandhi's death anniversary (*Hindu* 2011).

Delhi did not remain passive on the day of the Mahatma's death anniversary either. A protest march against corruption was organized by IAC to start from Ramlila grounds at 1 pm and conclude at Jantar Mantar. Catchy slogans like 'Gandhi *hum sharminda hain*, *bhrashtachari zinda hain*' (Gandhi, we are ashamed, the corrupt are still thriving) attracted citizens, activists, and intellectuals alike with thousands converging at the Ramlila grounds. Kejriwal was in his element, explaining patiently to the crowd the lacuna in the present laws and why they need to be replaced. The crowds responded by tearing copies of the CVC Act, the Delhi Police Special Powers Act that governs CBI, and a draft Lokpal bill proposed by the government as a symbolic act of defiance.

In order to ensure that their version of the Lokpal Bill got maximum support, a new 'Vote Bank Against Corruption' movement was launched. As Kejriwal explained, 'The idea is that one will pledge not to vote for that party that won't bring in the Lokpal Bill in both the centre and states. All such people who agree with us can SMS their names and addresses or log onto our website' (*Times of India* 2011a, 2011b). Among those who addressed the rally were Kiran Bedi, Shanti Bhushan, Prashant Bhushan, Archbishop of Delhi Rev. Vincent M. Concessao, Mehmood Madani, labour rights activist Swami Agnivesh, and senior lawyer Ram Jethmalani (*Hindustan Times* 2011). According to news reports, the protests were not confined to Delhi only. More than 52 cities, including a few in the US like New York and Washington, saw Indians come together to demand an end to corruption. In India, protests were organized at Mumbai, Kolkata, Chennai, Hyderabad, Bengaluru, Ahmedabad,

Agra, Aurangabad, Jaipur, Jhansi, Bhagalpur, Lucknow, Chandigarh, Kanpur, Gwalior, Gorakhpur, Coimbatore, Surat, Varanasi, Aligarh, Patna, Panaji, Pune, Guwahati, Pondicherry, Trichy, and Jammu (*Times of India* 2011a).

However, when the government did not pay heed to the Jan Lokpal Bill, Kejriwal and Bedi flew to Maharashtra in February 2011 to meet Hazare. 'Anna Hazare was convinced that this was a good solution to corruption', Kejriwal told Jelani. 'He had a successful history of fighting corruption, one case after another.'

During the visit, Kejriwal recalled, 'Anna called a meeting of his workers from all across Maharashtra, and he asked everyone, "Should I sit on fast?" They all agreed.' In a tiny room at the Sant Yadavbaba temple in Hazare's village, Ralegan Siddhi, he and Kejriwal sat and planned the fast-unto-death Hazare would stage in April at Jantar Mantar; they deliberately selected a date that would fall between the end of the Cricket World Cup and the start of the Indian Premier League (Jelani 2011).

Something about the 74-year-old activist Anna Hazare struck a chord, particularly among India's burgeoning middle class. Newspapers called him the twenty-first century Mahatma Gandhi (French 2011; Nelson 2011). Though an important activist in his own right, till 2011, Hazare was a relatively unknown figure outside his native state of Maharashtra. Over the course of that year, he would become a daily staple in the Indian media, his hunger strikes and imprisonment fuelling public outrage that was stoked already by ubiquitous corruption, large and small.

The Demand for Jan Lokpal

On 17 February, Anna Hazare sent a memorandum to the prime minister stating his intention to go on a fast, followed by a demand to set up a joint drafting committee for drafting the bill. The lack of interest in the Lokpal Bill was reflected in the 10th meeting of the National Advisory Council (NAC), an extra-constitutional body of civil society activists headed by UPA Chairperson Sonia Gandhi. The meeting was held on 27 February and although the Lokpal Bill was on the agenda, according to news reports, there was no deliberation on the contents of the bill. Issues such as RTI rules, food security, and Mahatma Gandhi National Rural Employment Guarantee Act (MNREGA) remained foremost.

On 27 and 28 February, Baba Ramdev organized rallies in Ramlila ground where he introduced Anna Hazare to the rest of India. On 3 March, the PM wrote to Anna Hazare inviting him for a discussion; the meeting took place on 7 March, where the PM asked him to wait till 13 May. However, Anna refused. On 8 March, the prime minister set up a subcommittee to scrutinize the Lokpal Bill, whose members included ministers A.K. Antony, M. Veerappa Moily, Kapil Sibal, and Sharad Pawar. This subgroup was part of the larger GoM formed earlier under the chairmanship of Pranab Mukherjee. However, Hazare refused to meet this group stating that a different mechanism needed to be adopted to draft the bill so that it was acceptable to all stakeholders. In a letter to Narayanasamy, Hazare said the 'subcommittee of Ministers will submit its report to the Group of Ministers, which will finally decide what kind of Lokpal Bill should be enacted. We had objected to this process in our meeting with the prime minister also …' Instead, the social activist suggested that a 'joint committee' with half of its members from the civil society should discuss clause-wise objections of the government to the Jan Lokpal Bill submitted by him to Prime Minister Manmohan Singh (*Indian Express* 2011b). The government, however, rejected the demand calling it unconstitutional and maintaining that law-making was the prerogative of the Parliament.

Around mid-March, the government led by the Indian National Congress (INC) was plunged into yet another scandal. According to a secret US state cable, leaked by Wikileaks, the Congress party offered cash for bribing Indian lawmakers to vote on the Indo-US nuclear deal back in 2008 (Foy 2011).

Anna's Indefinite Fast

By 2011, Team Anna (*Deccan Herald* 2011) were convinced that parliamentarians were not credible enough to enact a law that would demand greater accountability from them. For them, there was a clear conflict of interest. Swami Agnivesh tried to reason with the government by saying that the NAC, set up by INC president Sonia Gandhi was also a citizen's body and had drafted many laws in the UPA government's previous term.

After the prime minister rejected the demand for a joint drafting committee for the Lokpal Bill, Anna Hazare began his indefinite hunger strike at Jantar Mantar, Delhi on 5 April 2011. Media analysts allege that the strike was scheduled very wisely—just three days after the Cricket World Cup, which had kept the youth glued to the television sets. The euphoria of the World Cup, which India had won, transferred to the protest venue and within four days, amidst escalating public participation, the government had to concede and form a Joint Drafting Committee with a fifty-fifty participation of the ministers and the civil society.

The next day Anna wrote to the PM countering the allegation that he is being 'instigated by people' to go on a fast. Also, Sharad Pawar was forced to quit the GoM on corruption because of criticism from Hazare. By the third day, two rounds of talks between Anna supporters and the government had failed while Anna's fast triggered protests in his support across the country. A throng of civic activists, movie stars, and ordinary middle class citizens took his side. Strategies used to mobilize the people included 24/7 television coverage of the fast, numerous newspaper articles, updates on social media sites such as Facebook, Twitter, and YouTube, SMS campaigns, and candlelight vigils.

Box 10.1   The Campaigns in Bengaluru and Mumbai

Bengaluru

Bengaluru had a long-running history of campaigns against corruption. Since it already had the office of the Lokayukta, the focus was not the Jan Lokpal Bill but strengthening the office of the Lokayukta. Some of the campaigns that were running included Smart Vote campaign by Prithvi Reddy, later State Convenor of AAP, and *Loksatta*'s Save Lokayukta campaign. Both converged to form Corruption *Saaku*! ('Saaku' in Kannada means enough)

December 2010: The first rally was held in Bengaluru against corruption with Kejriwal, Jayaprakash Narayan, and Ashwin Mahesh at the helm. The who's who of Bengaluru were asked to come out on the street in support. There was a great response and there were 3,000 people at

(Cont'd)

Box 10.1 *(Cont'd)*

Cubbon Park. A new innovation in strategy was calling music bands (Swarathama, Thermal, Quarter) to the protest venue and having them play songs ridiculing the government (for example, *Topiwala*).

The idea for having a rally in Delhi came from the success of Bengaluru.

In Bengaluru, protests against the Chief Minister Yeddyurappa went on sporadically as part of the Save Lokayukta campaign.

Around the time of Anna's indefinite fast in April 2011, Bengaluru also saw massive protests at Freedom Park starting with around 40 supporters which swelled over the next few days to about 10,000 people.

By August, the IAC movement had morphed from a multi-state campaign to essentially a Delhi-based campaign for a particular bill. Mahesh and his team in Bengaluru were involved in mobilizing the crowd and media management. But some differences arose. JP viewed some of the demands of IAC as irrational and also felt that it would be better to have a consolidated view of civil society on the issue. Therefore, he did not organize campaigns in Hyderabad. But Mahesh remained a part of IAC since he felt that leaving it would not serve a purpose.

During Anna's fast in August, Bengaluru was able to attract the maximum number of protestors after Delhi. Thousands of people flocked to Freedom Park everyday—students, senior citizens, business leaders, celebrities, and ordinary citizens. Social media was used extensively to mobilize people along with sticker campaigns, phone calls, and human chains (Alavilli 2013; Francis 2011).

Mumbai

Mayank Gandhi was more or less running the campaigns in Mumbai. Prior to that, he was with Loksatta during the Vote Mumbai campaign, which was started when Adolf D'Souza, an activist, was first elected as a corporator. His electoral campaign was supported by Loksatta members Reuben Mascaranhas and Mayank Gandhi and other celebrities such as Shabana Azmi. Essentially, a lot of campaigns that Hazare had been involved in Maharashtra had been supported by Loksatta.

The idea of a fast in Mumbai came from Gandhi. Kejriwal and Prashant Bhushan were not major supporters of the idea because they

(Cont'd)

Box 10.1 *(Cont'd)*

felt Delhi was the power centre. But Gandhi was able to convince them on the ground that the movement was becoming too north-centric and it would be too cold in December for people to come in support if it was held in Delhi. The dates were fixed—27–29 December 2011. The fast was to be held at Azad Maidan but since the team did not get permission, it was shifted to Mumbai Metropolitan Region Development Authority (MMRDA) grounds (after a High Court intervention). However, Mumbai did not turn out the way it was expected, so much so that on the second day (28 December), Hazare refused to come out on the stage in the initial hours. He made his first appearance at 3.30 pm. Miffed at the poor show, Hazare announced the termination of the fast and left abruptly in the middle of a press conference (Tyagi 2012).

Although the majority of the supporters were in Delhi, other cities such as Bengaluru also saw significant campaigns. Finally, on 8 April, the government capitulated and accepted the demand of a Joint Drafting Committee which would consist of five nominees of the government and five nominees of Anna Hazare to prepare a draft of the Lokpal Bill. The committee would be co-chaired by Finance Minister Pranab Mukherjee and Senior Advocate Shanti Bhushan. The resolution stated that the committee would complete its work by 30 June 2011.

April to June 2011: Joint Drafting Committee Meetings and the Return of Ramdev

On 16 April 2011, the first meeting of the joint committee to draft the Lokpal Bill took place. Although the meetings began on a promising note, the two sides soon arrived at a stalemate. The government agreed to an audio recording of all meetings of the Lokpal Bill panel and to hold public consultations before a final draft was prepared, but refused to televise the proceedings live. Between April and 16 June, nine meetings were held between Team Anna and the government but they could not agree on many key points. Thus, the government decided that two versions of the bill would be submitted to the Cabinet who would then decide on the matter. However, only the government version of the bill was placed before the Cabinet. According to Team Anna, out of the 71 recommendations, only 15 of them were agreed upon. At this point, Anna threatened to fast again on 16 August.

August 2011: 13-day Hunger Strike at Ramlila Grounds, Delhi

The Cabinet finally approved the government's version of the bill and tabled it in the lower House on 8 August 2011. The bill was sent for review to the Parliamentary Standing Committee on Personnel, Public Grievances, Law and Justice headed by senior INC leader, Abhishek Manu Singhvi.

Arvind Kejriwal believed that the time was ripe to launch an indefinite hunger strike since the politicians had yet again failed to get a strong bill enacted. On 15 August, Anna Hazare visited the memorial of Mahatma Gandhi, and before he could begin his hunger strike the next day at Ramlila grounds, he was arrested along with other IAC core team leaders. The government, yet again, had to bow down to public pressure and release all the arrested members. Meanwhile, Anna Hazare had already begun his hunger strike, which he carried forward to Ramlila ground. The strike saw massive public participation and unprecedented media coverage for 13 consecutive days. Volunteers from different cities in the country either travelled to Delhi or organized protests in their own cities. The Parliament had to agree to all three major demands of IAC on the 13th day through a 'Sense of Parliament' resolution, following which a letter of acknowledgment was sent by the prime minister to Anna Hazare. The demands were: a) Citizen's charter; b) Lower bureaucracy under Lokpal; and c) Formation of state-level Lokayakutas.

On being informed about the Parliament's decision, senior IAC leader Shanti Bhushan asked Anna Hazare to call off the strike. However, supported by Arvind Kejriwal, Hazare was inclined to further prolong the strike and coax the government to agree to more demands. This led to a major war of words within the core team, but finally, Shanti Bhushan's advice was accepted and the strike was called off.

IAC's popularity reached its peak during this phase. It saw a huge outpouring of support in all the major cities of the country, especially

Delhi. However, as per media analysts, the persona of Anna Hazare had overtaken the cause. People associated more with the old khadi-clad Gandhian than with the cause of the movement. They were hardly aware of the nitty-gritty of the bill and their implications.

Alternate solutions proposed by groups like National Campaign for People's Right to Information (NCPRI) were given short shrift although Aruna Roy, a veteran social activist, as well as a member of the National Advisory Council (NAC), was a mentor to Kejriwal (NAC was set up by the ruling party to advice the central government on key policy matters). The organization had played a key role in drafting the Right to Information Bill and had plans to formulate similar solutions to a host of issues like corruption in the government and the judiciary, black money, independence of investigating agencies, and whistle-blower protection.

As the year 2011 progressed, IAC gained more clout and became uncompromising in its stance. It stopped seeking the advice of NCPRI which had been pitching for a workable solution within the existing framework, without majorly revamping the constitution.

August–November 2011: Standing Committee Meetings

The Standing Committee met various stakeholders, including Team Anna, NCPRI, National Advisory Council, the government representatives, and MPs from different political parties and included their suggestions.

The committee recommended exclusion of lower bureaucracy, judiciary, and MPs' conduct on the floor of the house from the Lokpal and the creation of separate mechanisms for citizen's charter and grievance redressal. CBI was to be independent of both the Lokpal and the government. The inclusion of the prime minister's office was left to the will of the House. These recommendations clearly contradicted IAC's demands which wanted the lower bureaucracy, the judiciary, MPs, CBI's anti-corruption wing, and the prime minister's office under the ambit of the Lokpal. In addition, the committee trumped the IAC by advocating a constitutional status to the Lokpal based on the advice of Congress Vice President Rahul Gandhi.

The core committee of IAC was unanimous in rejecting the bill. However, it was unsure of launching yet another round of protests.

The Bhushans understood that the Parliamentary procedures would take their course and that the IAC's role was limited since it had no representation in the Parliament. Kiran Bedi suggested taking the support of the opposition parties in the Parliament. Arvind Kejriwal wanted results quickly and decided to move the protests to Mumbai because of Delhi's extreme cold. He was supported by his friends in the core team—Manish Sisodia and Kumar Vishwas who, according to Kiran Bedi, had formed a 'core within the core'. Anna Hazare set yet another deadline for the Parliament. This time, he demanded that a stronger bill be passed in the ongoing winter session.

December 2011: Three Anti-Corruption Bills in Parliament

Three bills with anti-corruption provisions were tabled in the Lok Sabha in December 2011 by the INC—the Lokpal Bill, the Whistle Blowers (Protection) Bill, and the Constitution (116th Amendment) Bill to grant constitutional status to the Lokpal authority.

The Lok Sabha debated the bills for 10 hours on 27 December. The ruling coalition was able to get the Lokpal Bill and the Whistle Blowers (Protection) bill passed, but failed when it came to the Constitutional Amendment which required a two-thirds majority in the House. The entire debate was aired live on the news channels and was keenly watched by the public. It was for the first time that the people saw a detailed analysis of different aspects of the bill. Even as the MPs from ideologically opposite parties locked horns, they were unanimous in criticizing the movement for undermining the independence of the Parliament. They rooted for many wide-ranging amendments to the bill, like inclusion of the prime minister under Lokpal's ambit with safeguards, reservation in the selection panel for the backward castes, inclusion of NGOs, etc. The issue of NGOs was raised to specifically target the IAC, which was supported and funded by many NGOs. The Parliamentarians questioned why IAC did not suggest bringing them under Lokpal.

As planned, IAC claimed that the government was fooling the people by passing a weak bill and Anna Hazare subsequently launched his hunger strike in Mumbai. The poor public participation in Mumbai made the core team introspect. Arvind Kejriwal quickly realized that shifting the movement away from the heart of its struggle in Delhi was a mistake. He urged Anna Hazare to call off his strike on its second day itself and the team quickly made a move back to Delhi.

The Lokpal Bill was moved to the Rajya Sabha on 28 December 2011 after having been passed in the Lok Sabha, as required by the legislation process. The house saw another marathon debate which lasted 12 hours. In terms of number of seats, the government was in a much weaker position than in the Lok Sabha. The opposition suggested more than 150 amendments due to which the government requested for more time to modify and improve the bill. The debate continued until the chairperson of the House and India's vice president Hamid Ansari adjourned the house. This ended the winter session of the Parliament without the bill being passed and gave another opportunity to IAC leaders to unite against the government.

Continuation of the Movement: 2012

During the Budget session of the Parliament in February 2012, the bill was reintroduced. However, the session ended without the bill being passed. This galvanized Anna once again who decided to sit on a day-long fast at Jantar Mantar on 25 March 2012. Blaming the government for its insensitivity and carelessness, he also sought protection for whistle-blowers, many of whom were killed while exposing corruption cases. But this fast did not generate much traction.

Anna then decided to tour Maharashtra to create awareness for a strong Lokayukta Bill. This began on 1 May 2012 when Baba Ramdev also decided to launch an agitation from Durg in Chhattisgarh. He also announced that he would be undertaking a symbolic protest (day-long fasting) along with Anna at Jantar Mantar in New Delhi on 3 June 2012.

Both shared the stage that day and this did attract a large gathering, thereby bringing the focus back on the Jan Lokpal and the issue of black money. However, this token fast was followed by an indefinite one which began on 25 July 2012 by close associates of Anna Hazare. He himself joined the fast from 29 July onwards. Their agenda was to protest against the government's refusal to launch an inquiry against the prime minister and 14 senior Cabinet ministers, who were accused of corruption. However, the response from the public this time was far more muted as compared to Anna's fast conducted in 2011. Finally, on 3 August 2012 he broke the fast with a promise to fight for transparency in the system. Soon after, Team Anna announced that it had decided to switch tracks. Instead of trying to pressurize an unresponsive government, it would try to reform it from within by forming a political party and contesting elections. Thus, the Aam Admi Party was born.

Legislative Journey

Meanwhile, the bill was referred to a select committee of the Rajya Sabha on 21 May 2012. The committee comprised 15 members of the Rajya Sabha and was headed by Satyavrat Chaturvedi. The committee held 19 sittings in which it heard the views of a cross-section of people, both government and non-government. Among the non-government groups, it heard the views of Nripendra Mishra, the then director of Public Interest Foundation (now Principal Secretary PMO in the Modi administration); Shekhar Singh of NCPRI; Justice A.P. Shah, former Chief Justice of High Courts of Madras and Delhi; representatives of PRS Legislative Research; Jayaprakash Narayan of Loksatta; Ashok Kapur, Director General, Institute of Directors, International Academy of Law, New Delhi; V.K. Agarwal and H.C. Israni, *Bharastachar Niwaran Samiti*, Delhi; Deepak Tongli, Hyderabad; Dinesh Nath, Hansraj Jain, M.K. Rajput from Delhi; Kulamani Mishra, Odisha; K.K. Swami and Dalip Kumar Babhoota, *Akhil Bhartiya Grahak* Panchayat; J.K. Palit, Gaya; Manoj Nandkishor Agrawal, Pune; and Mahesh Pandya, Ahmedabad.[19]

The Select Committee submitted its report on 23 November 2012. It recommended that every state has to have a Lokayukta within a year from the date of notification of the act; Lokpal should have the power of superintendence over CBI on cases referred by the Lokpal and the director of CBI should be appointed by a collegium comprising the PM, leader of the Opposition of the Lok Sabha, and the Chief Justice of India (Sanyal and Kalra 2012).

The bill was finally passed in the Rajya Sabha on 17 December 2013 after making certain amendments to the earlier bill and in the Lok Sabha on 18 December 2013. The bill received the assent of President Pranab Mukherjee on 1 January 2014.

Box 10.2 Key Features of the Lokpal and Lokayuktas Act, 2013

Composition: The act creates a Lokpal at the centre which shall consist of a chairperson and up to eight members. Half of these members should have higher judicial experience and the other half should have experience in public administration, finance, insurance and banking laws, anti-corruption, and vigilance. It also provides that half the members of Lokpal shall be from amongst scheduled castes, scheduled tribes, other backward castes, minority communities, and women.

Selection Procedure: The chairperson and members of Lokpal shall be appointed by a selection committee consisting of the prime minister, the Speaker of Lok Sabha, the leader of the Opposition in Lok Sabha, the Chief Justice of India (CJI) or a sitting supreme court judge as nominated by the CJI, and an eminent jurist to be nominated by the president based on the recommendations of the other members of the selection committee.

Jurisdiction: The act specifies that the office of Lokpal shall investigate and prosecute cases of corruption. The jurisdiction of Lokpal extends to the prime minister, ministers, current and former Members of Parliament and Members of Legislative Assemblies, government employees, and employees of companies funded or controlled by the central or state government. Lokpal shall also have jurisdiction over institutions receiving foreign donations in excess of ten lakh rupees per year or such higher limit as specified. The act excludes any allegation of corruption against an MP in respect of anything said or a vote given in Parliament, from the jurisdiction of Lokpal.

Time Limit of Inquiry: It specifies a time limit of 60 days for completion of inquiry and six months for completion of investigation by the CBI. This period of six months can be extended by the Lokpal on a written request from CBI. Lokpal is also required to hear the explanation of the public servant before ordering an investigation. This, however, would not interfere with any search and seizure required to be undertaken by any agency.

Powers of Investigation and Prosecution: Any inquiry against the prime minister has to be held in camera and approved by two-thirds of

(Cont'd)

Box 10.2   *(Cont'd)*

the full bench of the Lokpal. Also, the Lokpal has the power of super-intendence over CBI with respect to cases referred by it to CBI. CBI officers investigating cases referred by the Lokpal can only be transferred with the approval of the Lokpal.

The act proposes to establish a Directorate of Prosecution within the CBI to be headed by a director who is an officer not below the rank of joint secretary to conduct prosecution of cases under the Lokpal Bill. The director of prosecution shall be appointed by the government on the recommendation of the CVC.

The CBI with the consent of Lokpal is empowered to appoint a panel of advocates, other than government advocates for conducting cases referred by Lokpal.

Funds: The central government is entrusted with the responsibility of making funds available to the CBI for conducting investigation into Lokpal-referred matters. All expenses of Lokpal shall be charged to the Consolidated Fund of India.

Penalty: The law penalizes offenders with imprisonment of up to seven years for public servants on grounds of corruption. Criminal misconduct and habitually abetting corruption has a higher penalty and would result in imprisonment up to 10 years. Making false and frivolous complaints to Lokpal would result in a fine of up to one lakh rupees and imprisonment of up to one year.

Source: The Lokpal and Lokayuktas Act, 2013.

Key Observations and Concluding Remarks

The IAC movement is a classic example of a protest geared towards a specific policy change. Its remarkable story is an almost textbook case for a combination of the punctuated equilibrium theory and the multiple streams theory of policymaking. The immediate trigger was the series of big-ticket scams that came into the media glare in 2009–10 (2G scam and the CWG scam to name a few). The IAC cashed in on the public mood of suppressed anger against the political class and used the Gandhian method of fasting to mobilize people. Here the problem was identified, the solution was proposed, and politics used to push for policy change.

It also had a high impact on the legislative agenda given the relatively short time in which it was able to get a law enacted despite using extremely confrontational tactics and a government unwilling to engage with it. Perhaps, the game changer in the process was the series of big-ticket scams that got exposed just as the movement was getting started.

It also jolted the 'business as usual' way of making policy by insisting on direct involvement of civil society activists in the drafting committee of the bill. The trajectory of the Jan Lokpal movement throws up many interesting issues to consider. First, in a democratic system, what should be the role of civil society? Second, is the use of fasting as a method of protest legitimate or a form of coercion? Third, what role do social media play in making such a movement popular? Fourth, what should the government's role be in such cases?

The unprecedented support of the urban, middle-class Indians for the movement came as a surprise. However, the legal activism of the middle class is not new, as pointed by Sitapati (2011). It first came about in the aftermath of the 1975–7 Emergency and involved middle-class judges and litigants who reinterpreted the Constitution to make courts more accessible, the grounds on which they could claim protection and a range of other remedies. Legal activists have little sympathy for elected representatives, seeing the Supreme Court as their way to pass legislation on the sly.

The strategies adopted by the IAC to mobilize support were novel in the sense that it successfully reused Gandhian motifs to popularize a campaign which forced the government to buckle. Of course, it was backed by meticulous planning and engagement with the media to garner publicity for the movement. However, the movement was severely criticized for its autocratic solution and its unrepresentative nature.

Now that the office of the Lokpal is mandated by law and Kejriwal has successfully leveraged the movement to enter politics through the Aam Admi Party, it remains to be seen whether he is able to transform the nature of Indian politics for the better.

Notes

1. See Ipaidabribe.com (last accessed on 20 March 2017); https://www. kpmg.com/IN/en/IssuesAndInsights/ThoughtLeadership/KPMG_ Bribery_Survey_Report_new.pdf (last accessed on 20 March 2017).

2. Available at http://www.cetri.be/IMG/pdf/Anti-Corruption-Movement_India.pdf.

3. The Supreme Court in the 1998 P.V. Narasimha Rao bribery case ruled that Members of Parliament (MPs) fall within the ambit of the definition of 'public servant' in the Prevention of Corruption Act, 1988. However, opinion among the judges was divided over the issue of previous sanction with one side stating that MPs could not be prosecuted since there was no authority competent to give sanction and the other suggesting that till the law is suitably amended, the Speaker of the Lok Sabha and chairman of the Rajya Sabha should give the necessary sanction.

4. UN Convention against Corruption, Signature and Ratification Status as of 12 December 2016, available at https://www.unodc.org/unodc/ en/treaties/CAC/signatories.html (last accessed on 20 March 2017).

5. Section 197 of the Code of Criminal Procedure and Section 19 of the Prevention of Corruption Act, 1988.

6. 'Problems of Redress of Citizens' Grievances', Interim Report of the First Administrative Reforms Commission, 1966.

7. The Parliamentary Ombudsman of Finland, available at http://www. oikeusasiamies.fi/Resource.phx/eoa/english/ombudsman/othercountries/index.htx (last accessed on 20 March 2017).

8. UK Parliamentary Commissioner Act, 1967, available at http://www. legislation.gov.uk/ukpga/1967/13/section/6 (last accessed on 20 March 2017).

9. Unstarred Question No. 1773, Rajya Sabha, Answered on 25 November 2010.

10. Unstarred Question No. 385, Lok Sabha, answered on 23 February 2011.

11. 'Executive and Public Administration,' Chapter 6 of the National Commission to Review the Working of the Constitution (Chairperson: M.N. Venkatachiliah), 31 March 2002.

12. National Common Minimum Programme of the Government of India, May 2004, available at http://pib.nic.in/archieve/upareport/ upa_3_year_highlights.pdf (last accessed on 20 March 2017).

13. 'Ethics in Governance,' Fourth Report of the Second Administrative Reforms Commission, January 2007.

14. Performance Audit Report on the Issue of Licences and Allocation of 2G Spectrum by the Department of Telecommunications, available at http://www.performance.gov.in/sites/default/files/departments/telecom/CAG%20Report%202009-10.pdf (last accessed on 20 March 2017).

15. https://www.facebook.com/pages/Against-CWG-Corruption/166778720003245 (last accessed on 20 March 2017).

16. Report of the High Level Committee on 'Organisation and Conduct of Commonwealth Games 2010' submitted on 28 March 2011, available at (http://www.archive.india.gov.in/high_level/sixth_report/Main_Report_HLC_28_3_11.pdf (last accessed on 20 March 2017).

17. India Against Corruption's Letter to the PM, 1 December 2010, available at http://iac.getup4change.org/doc/Letter_to_PM_dated_Dec_1.pdf (last accessed on 20 March 2017).

18. 'The Jan Lokpal Bill: Issues for Consideration and Recommendations for Improvement', available at http://www.humanrightsinitiative.org/programs/ai/rti/india/national/2009/email_alerts/JanLokpalBill-RevisedAnalyticalNote-Apr2011.pdf (last accessed on 20 March 2017).

19. Report of Select Committee of Rajya Sabha, Nov 2012, available at (http://164.100.47.5/newcommittee/reports/EnglishCommittees/Select%20Committee%20on%20the%20lokpal%20and%20Lokayuktas%20Bill,%202011/1.pdf (last accessed on 20 March 2017).

11

The Evolving Story of the Land Acquisition Act, 2013

The [2013] law was drafted with the intention to discourage land acquisition. It was drafted so that land acquisition would become a route of last resort.
— Jairam Ramesh and Muhammad Ali Khan (2015: 266)

[States] felt that if one has to benefit villages and poor farmers, to construct canals to water the fields, if we have to erect poles to bring electricity, construct roads and houses, and make available employment, we have to free this law from the clutches of bureaucracy.
— Prime Minister Narendra Modi (2015)

The Right to Fair Compensation and Transparency in Land Acquisition, Rehabilitation and Resettlement Act, 2013 has come after decades of acquisitions, deprivation, and angst in the country. In the years since Independence, as development projects and infrastructure have taken up farmlands, millions have been displaced, often with no or nominal compensation. Affecting lives and livelihoods of large numbers of people, these displacements have often led to violent protests causing death and destruction with significant political outcomes. The nature of the issue is such that ideology quickly colours positions, politicians are quick to step in, and passions run high.

Not only is public infrastructure like roads, railway tracks, and power poles essential for progress, in most parts of the country, agricultural yields are abysmally low and shifting of land use from

agriculture to industry would considerably enhance economic efficiency. From a strictly economic point of view, therefore, the problem is not one of what would increase the size of the pie but how to
ensure that the owner of the land is adequately compensated for his
contribution to development, the fruits of which society at large will
enjoy. This has proved to be an incredibly challenging problem for
the Indian polity to solve and the needle has swung from acquiring
land and displacing people at will to virtually making acquisitions
next to impossible. As Sanjoy Chakravorty (2015), author of *Price of
Land*, points out:

> It is vital to understand that farming in India simply doesn't pay. The
> average net income per acre is among the lowest in the world—well
> less than Rs. 10,000 per year. Therefore, the productivity-based price
> of farmland should be no more than Rs. 1.5 lakh per acre on average
> (for context: the average price of farmland in the U.S. is about Rs.
> 1.4 lakh per acre). In reality, almost nowhere in India is the price of
> farmland less than Rs. 5 lakh per acre now, and in much of advancing
> India (around cities and in prosperous rural regions) it is Rs. 1 crore
> and more per acre. That is, farmland prices in India are driven by
> scarcity, not productivity.

The present chapter seeks to summarize the political evolution
of the law, pointing out the roles of various stakeholder groups and
the key changes in the political environment over the years, without
attempting to judge the merits and problems with the various clauses
of the new legislation.

Evolution of the Land Acquisition Act: A Background

Landownership and the government's right to acquire land for public
purposes have remained a vexing issue for the Indian republic right
from its gestation days. In light of the highly unequal distribution
of landownership, the Constituent Assembly discussions featured
an impassioned debate on the subject of private ownership of land
at all, with a strong case made in favour of state being the owner
of all land, similar to the situation in China. However, the right to
property including landownership finally came in as a fundamental

right. However, the right of the government to appropriate privately held land for public purposes was recognized at the same time and the 1894 law that enabled land acquisition continued as the operating legislation, vide the 1948 Indian Independence (Adaptation of Central Acts and Ordinances) Order.

Challenges to Land Acquisition under the 1894 Act

The journey of the young republic in this area was difficult from the very first step. As the initial attempts at land reforms faced judicial roadblocks, it was necessary to include the landownership issue in the First Amendment to the Indian Constitution in 1951 itself, passed by the Provisional Parliament of the country. This same amendment created a new schedule—the Ninth Schedule—that put certain kinds of laws beyond judicial review.

The Land Acquisition Act (LAA), 1894 was initially intended to acquire land for public purposes. It was first amended in 1962 to allow the government to also acquire land for 'companies' in response to multiple adverse court judgments. This included both private and public firms provided it was for a public purpose. However, 'public purpose' was not defined in law; it was sufficient for the state to declare it to be so. Therefore, the end of colonial rule did not end the discord between the government and the people affected by projects in the event of land acquisition. In fact, post-1991, this discord became more pronounced as the government increasingly acquired land for the private sector (3iNetwork and Infrastructure Development Finance Company 2009).

There were several process-related deficiencies in the LAA, 1894 too, such as significant discretionary powers of the government and the collector, scope for delays in the completion of the acquisition process at various stages, and the absence of a level playing field between the government and non-government companies (the procedures prescribed for acquisition for private sector companies were far more cumbersome than those for public sector companies).

While these are some of the implicit issues that the previous legislation bore, the points of conflict in most of the cases of resistance were generic. In some cases, there might be more than one reason for resistance to land acquisition being offered by the resistors. Some of these points of conflict were as follows:

- Forcible Acquisition: When the potential land-losers have not been given much time, nor have they been consulted during the process of acquisition, it usually leads to a situation of conflict. In such situations, the state government often uses the emergency clause in the land acquisition act that allows almost no time for consultation or negotiations.
- Resistance to Compensation Level: In certain cases, potential land-losers argue that they are not being paid enough for their land. Hence, in these cases, land acquisition is possible but only at the right price. Some well-known cases of resistance to land acquisition based on price are Naya Raipur in Chhattisgarh, Machilipatnam in Tamil Nadu, and resistance to land acquisition for a power plant and an airport in Nagpur district in Maharashtra.
- Resistance to the Sale Itself: There are some situations when the land appears to be not for sale at any price. In such cases, the land seems to be priceless for the affected people. An example of such a case is related to the land acquisitions for Vedanta in Odisha where the Dongria Kondh adivasis residing in Niyamgiri hills considered the hills to be sacred and, hence, did not agree to give it up at any price (Chakravorty 2013).
- Ecological Concerns: Another common reason of resistance to the process of land acquisition could be concerns of ecological security. There are concerns about sustainable livelihood practices being disrupted, or attractive or sensitive or threatened ecological niches being spoiled.

In 1984, the definition of 'public purpose' was revised to include 'the provision of land for residential purposes … to persons displaced or affected by reason of implementation of any scheme undertaken by government, any local authority, or a corporation owned or controlled by the state'. This made displacement for a project one more reason for compulsory acquisition under the act, with no concomitant right to land on which to resettle them (Downing 2013).

In India, the power of 'eminent domain' has been interpreted as the power of the state to acquire any land within its territory. Eminent domain and the law related to compulsory acquisition of land requires that the power be invoked only for a public purpose, but what constitutes public purpose is wide open to interpretation and use. This has adversely impacted those without access to land and rights over land such as the landless and artisans, those who may have use rights but no titles, communities holding common rights, and others with inchoate interests (Downing 2013).

Rehabilitation and Resettlement (R&R)

The LAA, 1894 also made no reference to rehabilitation and resettlement (R&R). In the absence of any legally-guaranteed right to R&R, the people affected by projects, whose lives and livelihoods were disrupted, were left to fend for themselves. The compensation was computed on the basis of a set of predetermined factors which were 'to be considered in determining compensation' and, in any case, was restricted to the market value of the land. There were also 'matters to be neglected in determining compensation' which included 'any disinclination of the person interested to part with the land acquired' (Land Acquisition Act, 1894). 'In consideration of the compulsory nature of the acquisition', 30 per cent of the computed market value was to be paid as a solatium. That, in sum and substance, was the right of the person interested in the land. The act also included an 'urgency' clause which allowed the government to circumvent these procedural hurdles. It gave 'special powers to the government to take possession of the land within 15 days of the notification of intention to acquire—even before the award was decided (Land Acquisition Act, 1894).

While land reforms progressed rather haltingly over the years, the acquisition of large tracts of land for the establishment of new cities and townships throughout the country, from Chandigarh in the north to Durgapur in the east took place in the 1950s and 1960s under the 1894 law. While use of 'eminent domain' to acquire land for private industry was rare, if not unheard of, till before the end of the century, public sector undertakings (PSUs) like National Thermal Power Corporation (NTPC) and Coal India Limited (CIL) as well as government departments like the Railways and Roads and, particularly, Water Resources routinely acquired land for their operations and expansion. It is perhaps fair to say that, till the 1980s, the issue of resettlement did not feature prominently in most of these acquisitions. Compensation was paid to the landowners on record but given the abysmal yield of agriculture, most landowners were more interested in job-based compensation, rather than getting another piece of land elsewhere in lieu of their land, or cash-based compensation. Land markets were thin and transaction prices were often understated to avoid duties making them unattractive for landowners as a basis of cash compensation.

The use of jobs-for-land compensation plan, the so-called T.N. Singh Formula of 1967, formed the basis of several acquisitions by major PSUs like Coal India Limited. However, it posed problems elsewhere. So, in 1986, the Department of Public Enterprises instructed the PSUs against using this method, since these jobs had to be of the unskilled type, which were shrinking in numbers as the manufacturing sector became more skill-intensive (Mehta 2009).

The question of resettling people affected by land acquisition had not emerged as a paramount concern till at least the late 1980s and early 1990s, when the Narmada Bachao Andolan (NBA) led by Medha Patkar brought the issue to the forefront of national consciousness. Protesting against the resettlement package offered for residents of submerged villages, Patkar led a strident and sustained mass movement against the World-Bank-financed raising of height of the Sardar Sarovar dam in 1985 that resulted in them constituting the Morse Commission to look into the matter and scrap the assistance in 1992. However, the Government of India proceeded to raise the height anyway and the Supreme Court permitted it in 2000 while introducing a mechanism to monitor the resettlement process.

It is estimated that the number of people displaced by development projects in India and not rehabilitated between 1947 and 2000 exceeds 60 million (Fernandes 2008). Patterns in land acquisition reflect an aversion on the part of the government to touching politically-empowered groups. As Guha (2007) points out, adivasis who constitute only about 8 per cent of India's population, account for about 40 per cent of her project-displaced people. While there are many factors (including their presence in or near forest land) explaining this, their lack of political organization may have played a role here as well.

In parallel and at a global level, several multilateral institutions, including the World Bank, the Department for International Development (DFID), and various United Nations (UN) agencies like United Nations Industrial Development Organization (UNIDO) and United Nations Development Programme (UNDP), had taken up the agenda of resettlement and rehabilitation and were advocating it in India and elsewhere. The issue began to gather momentum in the late 1980s and early 1990s, presumably aided by the NBA movement. But work in this direction had already started at PSUs making acquisitions through the parent ministries, most notably, NTPC, a PSU that made massive land acquisitions, particularly in the Singrauli region of Madhya Pradesh. This policy later metamorphosed into its national-level R&R policy in 1993 approved by the Government of India as well as the World Bank (which was funding the project) that was generally hailed as a benchmark of R&R policies in India. It is interesting to note that this 1993 R&R policy makes explicit mention of categories of people beyond the landowners as 'project-affected persons (PAPs)' who need to be rehabilitated. There is a general perception (Dutta 2007) that the prime mover behind the much-heralded NTPC 1993 policy was the World Bank precondition to funding that the project met social and environmental conditions. The World Bank's withdrawal from the Sardar Sarovar Project in 1993 also underlined its seriousness about the resettlement and rehabilitation issue.

Land for Private Sector Industrialization and Urbanization—New Dimensions of the Issue

That land was fast becoming a key concern in industrialization in the new era is clear from the opening paragraph of the draft rehabilitation policy of 1994 of the Government of India:

> It is expected that there will be large scale investments, both on account of internal generation of capital and increased inflow of foreign investments, thereby creating an enhanced demand for land to be provided within a shorter time span in an increasingly competitive market ruled economic structure. Majority of our mineral resources …. are located in the remote and backward areas mostly inhabited by tribals. (Government of India 1994)

The NTPC R&R policy was followed by a Coal India policy the following year and soon a policy drafted by the Ministry of Rural Development which, however, was rejected by the Cabinet. At the same time, the Cabinet approved a draft land acquisition (amendment) bill in 1998 which never actually got introduced in Parliament.

Eventually, in 2003, a National R&R policy, largely a more formal version of the NTPC R&R policy, came into existence for the first time and became effective from February 2004. But, by that time, another idea was creating waves in the industry-land relationship in the country.

In February 2000, the then Minister for Industry and Commerce, Murasoli Maran visited China, primarily to aid China's joining the World Trade Organization (WTO). On his return, he started promoting the idea of Special Economic Zones (SEZs), that he was reportedly very impressed with during his visit to China. It is perhaps fair to say that this was the beginning of the great SEZ story in India, an experiment that at one point promised to be the cornerstone of India's industrial policy but largely fizzled out only a few years later. During the journey, however, the country passed the SEZ Act in 2005 which provided fiscal and labour law relief to enterprises in the SEZs. Interestingly, the question of land acquisition was not even viewed as a key problem in the initial phase of the SEZ problem. However, land proved to be the largest stumbling blocks in many cases, particularly with large SEZs (Bhattacharya and Palit 2008).

Kamal Nath, Minister of Commerce in the United Progressive Alliance (UPA) government, clarified while proposing the SEZ bill that the Indian SEZs would look quite different from Chinese SEZs that had impressed Minister Maran. For one thing, they would be more numerous and, critically, much smaller in size. Some believe that it is precisely this distinction that led to the failure of India's SEZ experiment, but Nath's observation was likely rooted more in pragmatism than in policy intent. Acquiring large tracts of land to create Chinese style SEZs would be a gargantuan challenge in India.

In any case, the SEZ Act passed in 2005 with less than two hours of somewhat confusing discussion in Parliament where members supporting the legislation mostly talked about their reservations about it. The rules came in 2006 and, over the next four years, had over 50 amendments done to them, mostly diluting whatever restrictions were initially put in them. Many of these were around the size and nature of land needed for SEZs. States were expected to make their own laws to supplement the central law.

Several states jumped at the opportunity. Somewhat surprisingly, communist-ruled West Bengal was at the forefront. Over the next few years, several SEZ and non-SEZ related land acquisitions brought the land issue to the front burner of national politics. Of these four cases—Nandigram, Niyamgiri, and Maha Mumbai SEZs, and Singur (non-SEZ) deserve longer discussion to understand their contribution in shaping the political climate on the issue and in making the acquisition of land the burning topic of the times (Bhattacharya and Palit 2008).

The Nandigram SEZ Episode

One could scarcely fault the Left Front government led by Communist Party of India (Marxist) or CPI(M) of overconfidence after their resounding victory in the 2006 Assembly elections to cap a 29-year uninterrupted rule. Its hold over the state seemed absolute. CPI(M) local committees were effectively the single points in rural West Bengal where both executive and judicial powers at that level converged. Opposition was scattered. The Indian National Congress (INC) had long become politically irrelevant and the Trinamul Congress (TMC), led by maverick Mamata Banerjee, was licking its fresh and grievous wounds in the 2006 election. The chief minister, Buddhadeb Bhattacharya, endorsed and encouraged by electoral victory, embarked on an ambitious industrialization plan to attract major investors from the rest of the country and the world. With the rising star in the CPI(M) firmament Nirupam Sen as Minister of Industry, industrialization was a key priority for the government and acquiring land was not likely to have been viewed as a huge impediment to his plans. After all, the *pattas* (land deeds) of the locality were kept in the CPI(M) office itself, such was its sway in rural Bengal.

Given this background, the ferocity of the opposition that erupted in 2006 in the Nandigram village of East Midnapore district near the Haldia port, took the administration by surprise. Protests started even before the official notification of a petrochemical SEZ the state government had planned there was actually issued. The government had just reportedly signed a Memorandum of Understanding (MoU) with the Indonesian Salim business group. Stunned by the audacity of the villagers to mount stringent opposition to the idea, the ruling party resorted to its regular tactic of settling the matter by unleashing ruthless violence through a combination of ruling party goons and the state police. But the protestors seemed prepared and determined and things went to the point of a complete polarization of the population into a pro-CPI(M) group and 'land protecting *Bhumi Uchhed Pratirodh Committee* (BUPC) (Land Eviction Prevention Committee) backed by TMC, Socialist Unity Centre of India (SUCI), and the Congress party. About 500 pro-Left families from the village were driven away. At one point, roads to the village were even dug up to isolate it from the rest of the country as a bulwark against police and party attack. The reprisal came in January and March 2007 and the two ham-handed, violent attempts by the state police-CPI(M) goon combine resulted in 14 avoidable deaths. News of the firing and deaths spread like fire, affecting the consciousness of the governor and the intelligentsia. Popular cultural figures led processions through the city of Kolkata protesting the state action. Further violence happened in November 2007 and in 2008 (Chakravorty 2013). For months and years, Nandigram became a battle zone, hundreds of families were pushed out and were living in camps, and the scattered Opposition had just been handed its key political issue. The Left front started losing political ground from under its supposedly impregnable Bengal citadel. The political leadership of the resistance was quickly captured by Mamata Banerjee, who joined hands with the Naxalites of the area and assiduously worked on the issue to eventually capture the state legislature in the elections of May 2011.

Needless to say, the Nandigram SEZ never saw the light of day and the land acquisition never happened. It is difficult to say whether that was a win or a loss for the local population. Agriculture in the area is not particularly remunerative and much of the local population do a daily 90-km bus commute to Kolkata's port area in search of livelihood (Bhattacharya and Palit 2008). But the prospect of industry and the resulting jobs and prosperity was equally unconvincing to the farmers given the government's poor past record of actually getting the industry up and running. An earlier project with land acquisition at nearby Jellingham had stalled and many landowners had never got their compensation. Villagers seriously doubted the state government's ability to get the industry up and running and, given the record, it is difficult to contradict them. In any case, the proud and confident rulers never bothered to 'sell the dream' to the local population and was forced to eat humble pie in the process. It was lose-lose for all, barring the opposition.

Maha Mumbai SEZ

It was not that only communists were having trouble getting land. Around the same time as Nandigram, similar trouble was brewing thousands of kilometres to the west, in the Raigad district of Maharashtra where Mukesh Ambani and his friend and advisor Anand Jain were contemplating a mega SEZ spanning 35,000 acres spread over 45 villages in the Uran, Pen, and Panvel talukas of the Raigad district. The Maha Mumbai SEZ was envisioned to include multiple manufacturing and service sector units and large residential areas and create 200,000 jobs. The investment planned was a whopping Rs 40,000 crore (Bhattacharya and Palit 2008).

Trouble started almost from the word 'go', in June 2006, as soon as notices were served. But, fortunately, things did not reach the gory outcome of Nandigram owing to significantly greater reasonableness and lawfulness of the acquirers. The plan was the promoters would acquire 70 per cent of the land first while the government would acquire the remaining 30 per cent. The resistance groups to this project were formed on the basis of political and ideological orientation. Twenty-two villages in the Pen and Uran talukas, supposedly irrigated from the Hetawane dam, were most strident and persistent in their refusal to part with their land. The opposition seemed to be not over the compensation amounts—the farmers were reportedly being offered Rs 10 lakhs an acre—but on the ideological issue of giving land to private developers. A group of radical activists formed the *Maha Mumbai Shetkari Sangarsh Samiti*, the communist parties formed the *Jagtikiran Virodhi Kruti Samiti* (JVKS), and social activists like N.D. Patil, together with Medha Patkar, formed the 24 *Gaon SEZ Virodhi Shetkari Sangharsh Sangathan*.

Strategies employed included marches, theatre, community meetings and organizational forums, information dissemination sessions, roadblock protests, and most effectively, hunger strikes. Protests continued through 2007 and 2008. The government was petitioned and, finally, on 24 July 2008, an hour-long meeting with the chief minister resulted in placing the issue on the table of the Legislative Assembly the following day. The opposition parties—the BJP, Shiv Sena, CPI and other—walked out of the Legislative Assembly, in support of the farmers. The promoters managed to acquire only 13 per cent of the land in the stipulated time as per the SEZ Act and the deadline was extended twice in two years.

Interestingly, the state government conducted a referendum on the issue at Pen in September 2008 where, reportedly, the SEZ proposal was soundly defeated by 91 per cent of 24,000 participating voters voting against it. However, the government has not officially declared the result. The referendum was one of its kind—the promoters had moved court against it—and the government was quick to assure that it will not be repeated for other SEZs and land acquisitions.

In January 2010, the Maha Mumbai SEZ developers suspended the land acquisition indefinitely because they had not been able to acquire the minimum 1,000 hectares of contiguous land as mandated by the SEZ Act and the courts had refused to give them further extensions of the deadline. Consequently, the government of Maharashtra formally declared the end of the Maha Mumbai SEZ and directed the farmers, whose land had been acquired, to begin using them again (Bhattacharya and Palit 2008).

Jusikhoesa Poseuko India SEZ

Yet another SEZ that landed in trouble over land acquisition (as well as environmental clearances in this case) was what promised to be India's largest ever Foreign Direct Investment (FDI) of Rs 52,000 crores to set up a 12 million tonne per annum steel plant over 4,000 acres near Paradip port in Odisha's Jagatsinghpur district. Within months of the MoU getting signed in June 2005, the Jusikhoesa Poseuko (POSCO) Pratirodh Sangram Samity (POSCO Prevention Movement Society or PPSS) was already formed to resist attempts at land acquisition by POSCO India. The issue became complicated as it involved transfer of 1,253 acres of forest land to POSCO over which a legal battle raged in the Odisha High Court, the National

Green Tribunal, and the Supreme Court for at least eight years after which approval was obtained on the state government's assurance that there were no traditional inhabitants of these forest lands.

Meanwhile, in 2012, POSCO agreed to downsize its plant to two-thirds of the capacity initially proposed (eight million per annum) owing to land unavailability and urged the government to allocate land to it so that it could start work. However, another two years passed before the 2,700 acres of land was finally acquired by the state and the final environmental clearances obtained, days before the 2014 visit of the South Korean president. That, however, was not the end of the troubles. The Modi government, with its tribal affairs minister Jual Oram being an MP from the region and a leader in anti-POSCO movements, opposed the granting of iron ore mining rights to POSCO. Finally, a decade after waiting to start operations, POSCO seems to have finally lost patience and shut down its Bhubaneswar office, ending, for all appearances, its planned entry into India (Bhattacharya and Palit 2008).

The Tata Nano Plant in Singur

If Nandigram marked the beginning of the end of Left rule in West Bengal, Singur, a fertile semi-urban area in the Hooghly district of West Bengal, close to Kolkata, was the epic battle that really caused its downfall. While not a SEZ, it was one of the first announcements of the re-elected Left front government in May 2006, at about the same time as the Nandigram SEZ was announced. Tata Motors would build its innovative Rs 1-lakh car, the Nano, in Singur and the state government would acquire 1,000 acres of land for it and lease it out to Tata Motors. Resistance developed almost immediately and spontaneously among a section of landowners, who later came to be called 'unwilling sellers' who owned between 340 and 400 acres of the 997 acres that were acquired (Ghatak and Ghosh 2011).

The state took the land, though many farmers refused to take the payment checks, and leased it to Tata Motors, which began constructing the factory amid vehement protest, almost entirely mobilized by local farmers. A few months down the road, Mamata Banerjee, in political wilderness after a poor show in the Assembly elections embraced their cause and this started a battle of several years between the government and Mamata-led agitators. The sordid drama that unfolded in Singur included the gruesome rape and murder of an 18-year-old girl, several murders, suicides, starvation deaths, all often luridly captured by 24/7 media that turned the issue into the single most important political drama for the entire term of the government.

Mamata succeeded in giving the issue state-wide importance and managed to mobilize opinion-makers from scientists, scholars, economists, writers, and film personalities alike to join her in demanding justice for the dissenting Singur farmers. In December 2006, she undertook a 25-day 'hunger strike' in Kolkata protesting against the police forcibly fencing the plant area—a fast that both brought her back and raised the Singur issue to state-level centre stage as well as national prominence. The struggle on the ground, however, still had a long way to go.

For the next three years, the Singur epic was marked by numerous fasts, highway blocks, strikes, suicides, and police action in response to the process and these were widely covered in great detail in the media. In mid-2008, the situation came to a boiling point when Mamata Banerjee demanded that 400 acres of land be returned right away, while emphasizing that she and her party were not against industry in the state. However, by then the Tatas had had enough. Tata Motors formally pulled out of Singur in October 2008 and relocated the factory to Sanand in Gujarat.

This was an anti-climactic end to the whole drama. With Tata Motors gone, the hope of industrialization in the area and its resulting prosperity disappeared. However, the land that had been given to Tata Motors, and on which structures had been built, was rendered unfit for cultivation, so it stayed that way. The limelight of political drama and the TV cameras soon shifted elsewhere and the farmers of Singur, particularly the protestors who had declined compensation for their land as a protest, were left high and dry. Tata Motors lost significant sums of money in the relocation as it had made plans and some investment in provisions for ancillary industry that was to occupy 300 of the nearly 1,000 acres in question. The only winner was Mamata Banerjee and the Opposition that had managed to completely hijack the 'pro-poor' plank from the Left front. They triumphed in the panchayat elections of 2008 and, riding largely on the Singur swing, finally dislodged the Left front from its 34-year reign in 2011.

There is, however, an even more bizarre epilogue to the story. Within hours of coming to power in 2011, Mamata Banerjee promised legislation to return the 400 acres to 'unwilling' farmers and passed such a law in about a month's time, only to be thrown out in the High Court. However, in 2016, the Supreme Court quashed the acquisition of land in Singur for the Tata Motor's project and directed that the land be returned to the farmers (Rajagopal 2016). The difficulty is where the twist comes. The law is in contravention to the 1894 law (and without Presidential assent to a state law in a concurrent subject, the central law has primacy) and 'redistribution of land' to selected farmers does not constitute 'public purpose'. It has proved to be a Pyrrhic victory for the 'unwilling farmers' and it may be a long time before they get their land back, if they ever do.

The Upshot

The four cases above, and many others like them around the country—Reliance's other mega SEZ ambitions in Haryana at Jhajjar, for instance, or the bauxite mining rights controversy of Vedanta at Niyamgiri Hills in Odisha—brought to the fore a few key conclusions and puzzles about land issues in contemporary India.

The first and the almost tautological: acquiring large tracts of contiguous land displacing a significant number of inhabitants, particularly farmers, was one of the most complex and difficult challenges of project implementation and is to be avoided as far as possible.

The irony is that in all the cases above, there is near consensus that the industrial use of the land in question is by far a more economically efficient use than the current agricultural and other uses for which the landowners fought (and won). There is almost no doubt that in pure conventional economic cost-benefit analysis, the interest of landowners would have been better served if the land acquisition had gone through. Agricultural land is highly overpriced and its yield (earnings as a fraction of the market price of the land) is abysmally poor.

The conclusions from this included the realization that pure price difference of land or income difference arising from land in its industrial versus agricultural use did not capture the utility arithmetic of landowners. Separation from land implied a certain change in 'way of life' and its concomitant riskiness which required the 'premium' for conversion to be wider than just the rupee difference in annual income brought about by the acquisition. Additionally, the stakeholder group that were not owners of land but whose livelihood depended on land—agricultural labourers, share croppers, agriculture-related suppliers and the like—were also numerous enough to be a political voice and had to be included and protected as 'project-affected people' to avert political dissent.

The political implication for state governments was no less significant. The supposedly 'pro-poor' Left government ironically collapsed over land acquisition. The Maharashtra and Odisha governments managed to keep their hold by some conscious ambivalence. For state governments now, while industrialization was an important goal, the political cost of assisting private players to acquire land was beginning to look intimidating. There was increasing need of clarity in land acquisition through a new central law.

Legislative Journey of the Land Acquisition Act, 2013

UPA-I (2004–9)

The National Policy on R&R 2004 (NPR 2004) came in for sharp criticism from the civil society almost as soon as it was announced. To many, it appeared too loose with no proper assignment of responsibilities to appropriate authorities. The newly constituted National Advisory Council (NAC-I) shared that perspective and published a 'Perspective on R&R Policy' critiquing the NPR 2004 and even produced a draft policy in 2006.

The UPA government acted on this and brought out its new R&R policy in October 2007, pretty much along the lines suggested by NAC and followed it closely with the nation's first major legislation in the area in more than a century—a package of two bills, one dealing with land acquisition and the other with R&R. NAC-I had recommended a unified bill but the bureaucracy thought it would have problems getting passed.

The 2007 bill, for the first time, introduced a mandatory Social Impact Assessment (SIA) study in case of large-scale physical displacements in the process of land acquisition. As per the bill, while acquiring land, the government had to pay for loss or damages 'caused to the land and standing crops in the process of acquisition' and, additionally, the costs of resettlement and rehabilitation of affected persons and families. This bill proposed that the compensation be determined by the 'intended use of the land' and as per prevailing market prices. It also sought to establish the Land Acquisition Compensation Disputes Settlement Authority at both the state and central levels for the purpose of providing speedy disposal of disputes relating to land acquisition compensation. The bill also proposed that land acquired as per the act which is unused for a period of five years shall be returned to the appropriate government.

The timing was interesting though. The Land Acquisition (Amendment) Bill, 2007 was introduced in the Lok Sabha on 6 December 2007. It was then referred to the Standing Committee on Rural Development, headed by Kalyan Singh. The committee submitted its report in October 2008, and official amendments to the bill were cleared by the Group of Ministers in December 2008. It was renamed the Land Acquisition (Amendment) Bill, 2009, and was passed by the Lok Sabha on the penultimate day of its tenure, 25 February 2009. The government tabled the bill in the Rajya Sabha the following day, but could not ensure its passage before the House adjourned. Consequently, the bill lapsed with the dissolution of the Lok Sabha.

UPA-II (2009–14)

In its second term, the UPA government, with the advisory support of a new NAC (NAC-II) started working on the land acquisition issue early on. The NAC weighed in on the two bills and created a group within itself to study the land issue in greater depth. The group comprised N.C. Saxena, Aruna Roy, and Harsh Mander. They issued a discussion paper about their concerns in March 2011 and on 25 May 2011 the NAC had adopted the recommendations of this working group.

Even as the new law was being discussed by NAC, fresh trouble erupted in a few villages in Uttar Pradesh (UP) including Bhatta Parsaul in May 2011, over what was generally believed to be resistance to the land acquisition attempt for the Greater Noida and Yamuna Expressway projects of the state government. Land for both projects had been acquired by the UP government under BSP leader Mayawati's regime during 2007–11 using the 'urgency' clause. Using the urgency clause to evict farmers and then transferring land to developers for residential projects after incorporating a change in land use has been a common practice in UP as in several other states, but now matters seemed to have hit a flash point.

Politics immediately gained control with Rahul Gandhi himself reaching the village and staging the dharna. Finally, the Congress party had an opportunity to lay claim to the 'pro-farmer' platform. So far, while the INC had been working towards making land acquisition more farmer-friendly, the political dividends appear to have been reaped by local parties like the Trinamul Congress. The Bhatta Parsaul incidence underlined, if any such underlines were needed, the urgent need for bringing greater clarity, fairness, and due process to the land acquisition story. Its proximity to Delhi, more than anything else, also helped the episode leap into national headlines.

On 13 July 2011, Jairam Ramesh was promoted to a full Cabinet Minister position and shifted from the Environment Ministry to the Ministry of Rural Development. His priority was clear—to get the land acquisition law drafted and passed as quickly as possible.

The relationship between the bureaucracy and the NAC was rarely comfortable in the decade of the NAC's existence. The bureaucracy always smarted at the idea of the NAC—without electoral or bureaucratic legitimacy—being able to influence the government's legislative agenda to the extent that it did. The seasoned and wily politician that he was, Ramesh knew very well that driving the bill drafting process through the ministry, particularly a law that would largely be shaped along the lines suggested by the NAC, would be a challenging task. He took to drafting the law with his own team of young and smart volunteers and kept it largely sequestered from the formal bureaucracy in the ministry. Muhammad Ali Khan, a bright young Supreme Court lawyer, led the efforts at drafting the law and the bill was introduced in Parliament on 7 September 2011, about four and half months after the NAC adoption. It was referred to the Standing Committee on 13 September.

After the Standing Committee gave its report in May 2012, there were further consultations done within the government with different ministries. A few ministries like the Railways, Highways and Industry wanted a loose law with not too many constraints and simpler procedures to land acquisition, but they all came on board in about six months' time. Once consensus was built within the government, there were consultations held with other political parties as well to convince them for passing of the bill. Two all-party meetings were held on the law and the government spent significant political capital in getting to a workable agreement and, particularly, Kamal Nath played a key role in engineering the necessary consensus.

The recommendations made by the Standing Committee were by and large accepted with two exceptions. The first one which asked to ban acquisition outright could not be accepted, as eminent domain was required to build roads, highways, and other public amenities. The second suggestion—on which there were disagreements even within the NAC—was banning acquisition for private industry. This was not accepted following consultations with industry bodies who explained how private purchase of large tracts of land tie them up in long-drawn legal battles and stall large-scale projects. The feature of acquisition of land for private industry helped protect them from such cases. This was countered in the final legislation by the inclusion of the consent clause, which took care of concerns arising out of land acquisition for private and Public Private Partnership (PPP) projects. A lesson which was learnt from the experience of the Forest Rights Act, 2006 and included in the new land acquisition legislation was the role of *Gram Sabha*s whose prior consent was required before acquiring land in tribal areas.

At different stages of the lawmaking, the state governments also made various suggestions. One of the major suggestions that was included in the final legislation was made by the Government of Madhya Pradesh about including irrigation projects under the law's ambit since acquiring land for it frequently became a daunting task. The voices of the industry in the consultations were Confederation of Indian Industry (CII), the Federation of Indian Chambers of Commerce and Industry (FICCI), and the industry-related ministries. Although, there were voices of opposition, the group which wanted a strong and progressive land acquisition law was much stronger. In fact, from among the regional parties, there was a criticism that the final proposed law was not progressive enough.

The consultations with the civil society organizations were to give them a sense of being heard. While some of their suggestions were imbibed in the law, some of it, like their demand for consent for all land acquisition projects, were not accepted. Although, the pre-legislative draft released by Ministry of Rural Development (MoRD) on 31 July 2011 mentioned requirement of consent for all projects, it was later brought down to consent being required only for private projects owing to opposition from within the government from selected lobbies. To compensate for this moderation, a clause for social impact assessment was brought in to be made mandatory for public purpose projects. The 13 legislations governing land acquisition in different sectors which were excluded from the final legislation were initially supposed to be included and was so recommended by the Standing Committee as well. Owing to opposition again from the concerned ministries, they were excluded from the land acquisition process, but still had to follow the compensation and R&R standards prescribed by the new law.

While drafting the R&R policies, the existing policies of different state governments were reviewed and the Andhra Pradesh R&R policy was used as the template since it was the most progressive one at that time. Other UPA members like the TMC also made important suggestions like the need for convergence of the land acquisition law with the Forest Rights Act, 2006, stressed on the importance of prior consent of Gram Sabha, and, drawing from their experience in Singur, also the inclusion of compensation for shared croppers. This was the first time any land acquisition law proposed compensating the livelihood losers along with the landowners.

Another clause that was introduced in the 2011 bill was to bring large-scale land purchases between two parties under the ambit of the law and provided for R&R for the project-affected people. This was done to protect the rights of the livelihood losers and protect them against exploitation in the course of private transactions. But this feature faced huge opposition majorly from the industry-representative bodies. So, as a compromise, the threshold for the amount of land in private transactions under this law was left to be decided by the state governments. Box 11.1 summarizes the key features of the act.

Box 11.1   Key Features of the Right to Fair Compensation and Transparency in Land Acquisition, Rehabilitation and Resettlement Act, 2013

The Land Acquisition Act, 2013 regulates land acquisition and lays down the procedure and rules for granting compensation, rehabilitation, and resettlement to the affected persons. The act has provisions to provide fair compensation to those whose land is taken away, brings transparency to the process of acquisition of land to set up factories or buildings, infrastructural projects, and assures rehabilitation of those affected.

The major features of this law are as follows:

(a) **Public Purpose:** The act specified that land may be required only for public purpose, which is defined to include defence and national security, roads, railways, highways, and ports built by government and public sector enterprises, land for the project-affected people, planned development, and improvement of village or urban sites and residential purposes for the poor and landless, and so on.

(b) **Consent:** In case of situations involving acquisition of land for use by the government for purposes other than those mentioned above, use by public-private partnerships, and use by private companies, the act prescribes a requirement of consent of 70 and 80 per cent of the project-affected people respectively.

(c) **Social Impact Assessment (SIA):** The act mandates the government to conduct an SIA study, in consultation with the Gram Sabha (or equivalent government body in urban areas). The SIA report is then examined by an expert group and a committee to ensure that the proposal for land acquisition meets certain specified conditions. Within 12 months from the date of evaluation of the SIA report, a preliminary notification indicating the intent to acquire land must be issued and, after satisfactory redressal of oppositions to the survey, a declaration to acquire the land is made. This is the specified procedure to be followed for carrying out transactions of land acquisition.

(d) **Emergency Clause:** The specified procedure can be waived off only in the case of an emergency for defence, national security purposes, or in cases of natural calamity. In such cases, 80 per cent of the compensation must be paid before the government takes possession of the land.

(*Cont'd*)

Box 11.1   *(Cont'd)*

(e) **Compensation:** The act designates the collector to determine the compensation for land acquisition, which he has to award within two years from the date of publication of the declaration of acquisition. First, the market value of the land to be acquired is calculated as the higher of i) the land value specified in the Indian Stamp Act, 1899 for the registration of sale deeds; or ii) the average of the top 50 per cent of all sale deeds in the previous three years for similar type of land situated in the vicinity. Once the market value is computed, it is doubled for land in rural areas. Then, the value of all assets attached to the land is also added to the value and also a 100 per cent extra compensation for forcible acquisition, before arriving at the final compensation figure.

(f) In cases when land acquisition is undertaken using the urgency provisions, the land owners are given an additional 75 per cent of the market value of the land.

(g) **Rehabilitation and Resettlement (R&R):** The act also prescribes detailed procedures for rehabilitation and resettlement in case of every acquisition. In case of acquisition of more than 100 acres, a R&R committee has to be established to monitor the implementation of the scheme at the project level and a National Monitoring Committee should be appointed to oversee the implementation of the R&R scheme for all projects at the central level.

(h) **Private Acquisition:** In case land is being privately acquired (100 acres or more in rural areas and 50 acres or more in urban), an application needs to be filed with the collector and approved by the commissioner appointed for R&R, before it is awarded. Also, the act prescribes certain infrastructural facilities like roads, drainage, provision for drinking water, banks, and so on., that every resettled area needs to be provided with.

(i) **R&R Authority:** The act mandates for a Land Acquisition and Rehabilitation and Resettlement Authority to be set up for settling any disputes relating to the acquisition, compensation, and R&R. It also restricts the change of ownership of acquired land without prior permission from the government and also regulates its use for any other purpose other than for which it is acquired.

(j) **Legislative Exceptions:** Lastly, it is important to note the act makes the exception of not bringing under its purview land acquisition

(Cont'd)

Box 11.1   *(Cont'd)*

under 16 existing laws including the SEZ Act, 2005; Atomic Energy Act, 1962; and so on.

Source: The Right to Fair Compensation and Transparency in Land Acquisition, Rehabilitation and Resettlement Act, 2013; Ministry of Law and Justice.

Developments Post-2013

With all the effort that went into crafting the 2013 law, which its primary authors, Jairam Ramesh and Muhammad Ali Khan, themselves admit was more a 'disabling' law than an 'enabling' one for land acquisition, it came in for sharp criticism almost immediately from several quarters. It did little to quell the 'development versus rights' debate and the industry as well as sections of bureaucracy thought it made infrastructure creation far more difficult.

The issues that drew maximum critique were consent, compensation, compulsory SIA, and food security (making acquisition of well-irrigated multi-crop land extremely difficult).

Indian laws are rarely known for good drafting, but a few major bloopers had crept into the hurried drafting of the law itself, posing considerable difficulties in the implementation of the act. An example was an obvious language error in Section 113 (Removing Difficulties) section of the act. This section is provided to make minor changes without changing the intent or impact of the act when faced with implementation difficulties. However, the error here made changes virtually impossible for this act. Jairam Ramesh had bypassed an elaborate process of bureaucratic discussion between various departments of the Rural Development Ministry and the Law Ministry that would have taken anywhere between 18 months and two years to complete by normal standards for a law like this. The cost of that, however, were a few key errors that had inadvertently but inevitably crept into the drafting and had survived scrutiny right till the end.

Bureaucrats started complaining that the act, while possibly motivated by noble intentions, was virtually impossible to administer given the administrative resources and personnel at the disposal of the government. However, given the fact that land was fundamentally a state subject, and there were several less than perfectly worded exemptions in the act, some of the problems could have been solved through creating clever rules for the act.

The power of the critics of the law, however, became clear with the National Democratic Alliance (NDA) government coming to power in 2014. Within six months, the new government promulgated an ordinance in December 2014 and introduced a bill in the monsoon session of the Parliament in 2015 to amend the law. The bill proposed to exempt defence, rural infrastructure, affordable housing, industrial corridors, and infrastructure projects, from the clauses of obtaining consent of 80 per cent landowners in case of a private project and 70 per cent landowners in case of PPP projects. It also exempted these sectors from conducting a social impact assessment study and from the limits on acquiring agricultural and multi-cropped land. Another important amendment that the bill proposed was to bring the compensation, and rehabilitation and resettlement (R&R) provisions of 13 other laws which govern the acquisition of land in specific sectors, in line with provisions of the Land Acquisition Act (Ghosh 2015). The Minister of Rural Development, Chaudhary Birender Singh, had reservations about the ordinance and the bill, but Finance Minister Arun Jaitley wanted to make a 'big bang' change.

The situation went out of hand for the new government, however. The Congress party mounted a spirited opposition to the bill in Parliament disrupting the monsoon session itself over the issue. The NDA government anyway did not have the numbers in Rajya Sabha to push the bill through. Consequently, the ordinance was re-promulgated twice thereafter while the bill remains pending in Lok Sabha (Chakravarti 2015). Land being a concurrent issue, however, there are ways to circumvent these clauses of the law by passing state-level laws and getting presidential assent to them. The new government will also improve its numbers in the Rajya Sabha in the near future. A lasting settlement to the issue, unfortunately, is unlikely to happen in the near future.

Key Observations and Concluding Remarks

The long-drawn-out and contentious journey of the Land Acquisition, Rehabilitation and Resettlement (LARR) Act can be understood through a mix of the advocacy coalition theory and the punctuated equilibrium theory. In this case, there was no single, long, and sustained campaign for a change in the law but protests by a multiplicity of issue-based networks such as the Narmada Bachao Andolan (initially fighting for rehabilitation of displaced people and later opposing the construction of big dams), tribal rights groups, and farmers' groups. These groups were key for agenda setting, but the trigger for policy change came from incidents like Singur, Nandigram, and Bhatta Parsaul.

The nature of activism in this case was extremely conflictual but the government was willing to engage with the grievances of the non-elected stakeholders to a large extent, especially post 2004–5. However, the time taken for the law to be enacted was very long since the attention of the government was not focused on the issue till the flare-up of violence in Nandigram and Singur. Also, the fact that Rahul Gandhi, the Congress party's 'heir to the throne' supported the agitating farmers in Bhatta Parsaul provided the impetus to get the government moving on the law.

12

In Search of a New Theory

If, in general terms, parties attempt to win power, interest groups try to influence government decision-makers, and social movements work to 'change the world' then can the three categories overlap?
—Sylvia Bashevkin (2002)

The Context

We started this book with a few questions in mind. How are laws formed in India? Who are the players influencing the law-making process? What methods do they employ to influence the process? What is the role of the government in law-making? Does India's system differ widely from other parliamentary democracies? What, if any, new lessons can be learnt from India's law-making experiences? As we have discussed earlier, most literature about the theory of law-making/policymaking process originated from the US system of law-making, which differs significantly from the parliamentary form followed in India. Therefore, we decided to study the journey of nine landmark laws in India that were passed or tabled in the last 15 years (1999–2014). In the preceding chapters, we developed nine case studies of these laws. Since the purpose of this book was to capture the policymaking process and the external influences on it, we chose a wide range of laws spanning multiple subjects— economic, social, political, and environmental.

At the end of that exercise, we compared the trajectory of these laws based on five criteria—timeline, actors, influences/triggers, geographical spread, and role of the media—then examined how well one or more of the existing policy process theories fit the narrative (the findings from that exercise are provided in Chapter 2). We found that the most common framework that seemed to fit India's policy process was a combination of punctuated equilibrium theory, multiple streams theory, and the advocacy coalition framework. Chapter 2 also provided a glimpse into emerging patterns about the changing nature of civil society organizations and their relationship with government, acceptance (or not) of new actors/influences, the variety of strategies used over the years, the impact of technological changes on strategies, and the government's responses to the stakeholders.

The findings of Chapter 2 also bear out the works of scholars who tried to answer the vexing question: Is there a non-Western policy process? According to those studies (Pye 1958; Horowitz 1989), on the one hand, there is clear variation in the institutions, participants, resources, the weight of the state relative to society, the capacity of the state to work its will, and the actual policy concerns between Western and non-Western countries in Asia, Africa, and Latin America; on the other, the constraints, the ripe moments that produce innovation, and the tendency for policy to show unintended consequences appears to display similarities that transcend these boundaries (Horowitz 1989). An explanation for some convergence of policy process perhaps lies in the fact that most of the developing countries derived their formal institutions from Western models and their informal processes mirror those of the West (Diamant 1959; Horowitz 1989). In 1957, Fred Riggs had suggested that all administrative systems could be placed on a point along a spectrum ranging from 'Industria type to the Agraria type pattern' and could then be compared with any other administrative system (Diamant 1959; Riggs 1957).

However, this is a very broad-brush understanding of the policy process given the considerable differences between developing countries (and developed countries as well)—of resources, political systems, and state capacity. Perhaps, more nuanced contrasts in the policy process would emerge if specific countries were compared, which necessitates the development of country-specific frameworks to understand the policy process. In this chapter, we embark on the journey of creating a possible framework, based on the empirical information in our case studies, to gain some insight into the nexus between the policymaking process and the complex, dynamic, and cyclical forces that influence it.

As is evident from our case studies, the policy process does not have a specific beginning or an end. Rather, it unfolds in fits and starts, with no permanent resolutions. Issues—new and old—evolve and change regularly, and, at times, lose relevance. The ever-growing tribe of activists espouses a variety of causes and develops innovative strategies to influence the policy process. New issues take centre stage while older issues evolve and change. For example, the discourse on juvenile justice changed rapidly after a juvenile was convicted of brutally gang raping a young woman in Delhi; changes to the archaic Land Acquisition Act, 1894 took over six decades and remains a contentious issue in the new government. Therefore, there is a wide variation in the timelines, the civil society groups that get involved, the level and intensity of the mobilization, the dominant narratives, and the strategies used by them. The responses from policymakers also vary depending on many factors—who is in power, strength in the Parliament, the level of interest in a subject, the complexity of the issue, to name a few.

Furthermore, the complexity of the law-making process is characterized by the wide variety in the methods adopted to influence the law-making process as well as the reactions they evoke from the lawmakers, the pace of change, and the dominant discourse pertaining to the issue. It is also mostly unpredictable. Years of negotiations may not result in any change, but a sudden external event may provide the window to force a change. In the absence of such an event, it is an uphill battle of activism, bargains, and trade-offs wherein not only the degree and time of the final swing of the needle but the entire experience and nature of the battle hinges on idiosyncratic and near-unpredictably small differences in relative strengths and alignments of political forces. Put simply, not only the duration and final outcome of the process, but even the nature of the journey—the number of players involved, the nature of negotiations, the grammar of engagement—is determined by bafflingly minute variations in a large number of 'starting conditions'. The result is something that appears to be almost a random process—somewhere a long, gruelling game of patience, somewhere a blizzard of protest in the wake of an external crisis leading to shotgun legislation. The question is to find the method in the madness.

Outlines of a Theoretical Framework for the Indian Law-making Process

The study of the political process of law-making does not have a central question that is the basis for all theories in the discipline. Thus, each of the existing theoretical frameworks of the political process studies different aspects of the process. Some may study the role decision makers (bureaucrats and legislators) play in the process, while others may study the role played by advocacy/interest groups or study the way policy changes.

Given the range of issues and the variety of context and players covered, it is not easy to even conceptualize our case studies in a common framework. In spite of the difficulties, we have made an attempt to create a framework based on the roles played by state and non-state actors in guiding the legislative agenda of the government, thus taking the policy subsystem (includes a constellation of actors such as advocates, lobbyists, legislators, bureaucrats, political parties, journalists, lawyers, watchdogs, and think tanks) as a unit of analysis. Within the subsystem, the behaviours of these actors are modulated by the rules of the game imposed by the Constitution, the parliamentary system, and the judiciary. The strategies employed by different stakeholders to further their respective interests, the bargaining and negotiations that take place among the constellation of actors and the external conditions—could be a game-changing 'trigger' event or changes wrought by forces of globalization—all come together to effect change in the legislative agendas.

Since legislative agendas of governments are set through the interaction of different stakeholders within the subsystem, we develop what we term as a 'legislative strategy framework' (Table 12.1). In this framework, we categorize the actors into two broad groups: elected (legislators and bureaucrats) and non-elected (advocacy/interest groups, media, watchdogs, think tanks) stakeholders. Laws are created through the interaction of these two broad groups. In cases where the elected representatives may be willing to engage with non-elected stakeholders, the relationship can be categorized as cooperative, if not it would be categorized as confrontational. The non-elected stakeholders try to exert influence on the elected stakeholders to enact a law. The means of influence vary widely but

Table 12.1 Proposed Legislative Strategy Framework

Laws/Bills	Means of Activism	Willingness to Engage	Time Taken to Influence Agenda*
Competition Act	Collaborative	Cooperative	Medium
Right to Information Act	Conflictual	Cooperative	Long
Right to Education Act	Conflictual	Confrontational	Medium
Child Labour Bill	Conflictual	Confrontational	Long
Microfinance Bill	Collaborative	Cooperative	Long
Criminal Laws Act	Conflictual (external trigger)	Cooperative	Short
Food Security Act	Conflictual	Confrontational	Long
Lokpal Act	Conflictual (external trigger)	Confrontational	Short
Land Acquisition Act	Conflictual	Cooperative	Long

Source: Developed by authors.
Notes: *Short: Less than 10 years; Medium: 10–20; Long: More than 20 years.

again can be categorized broadly as conflictual or collaborative. The time taken to get a law enacted can be the proxy for the impact these interactions have on the law-making process.

Within this broad framework, the degrees of conflict and collaboration (the two ends of the spectrum) can vary widely. We depict this range in Figure 12.1 using a score of one to five. Thus, means of activism ranges from conflictual to collaborative on a score of 1 to 5. Similarly, the willingness to engage ranges from confrontational to cooperative on a score of 1 to 5.

The pattern that emerges from this framework throws up a few surprises.

First, when activism is triggered by an external event, even if the government is not willing to cooperate, the time taken to influence the legislative agenda is short.

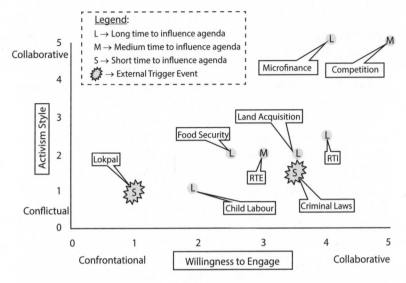

Figure 12.1 The Legislative Strategy Framework
Source: Developed by authors.

Second, it is, however, much more difficult to influence the legislative agenda without a triggering event if the means of activism is conflictual and the willingness to engage is also lacking among elected stakeholders.

Third, it is not certain that even if activists use collaborative means of activism and elected stakeholders are not confrontational, it would lead to a legislative change. This could mean that even if there is no conflict, the law denotes a significant shift in a different direction and thus requires more deliberation among stakeholders or it could mean that it is not seen as a top priority of the government.

Fourth, even if governments agree in principle about the need of a legislation, the differences about the fine print (especially if it requires significant fiscal support) could make the government hostile to the non-elected stakeholders.

Fifth, if the activists are more collaborative in their tactics, the chance are that the government will be more willing to engage with them and they may have better success in influencing the legislative agenda. As shown in Figure 12.1, there is much less chances of success without a 'trigger' event if the activists take a confrontational approach and the government also is uncooperative.

Sixth, even if the approaches of both parties (elected and non-elected) is collaborative and cooperative, without a strong champion within the government to navigate the bill, chances of it getting passed is low.

Seventh, if the activists want to take a confrontational stand with the government, they need to be able to identify and be prepared to take any 'window of opportunity' that may arise due to an unpredictable external event to push for their desired legislation.

Eighth, it is clear that influencing the legislative agenda is an uphill task and requires years of sustained effort and innovative strategies to convince the government of its demands. The elected stakeholders are mostly driven by their need to win the next election. Therefore, they are likely to take up cudgels on behalf of a particular legislation, if they see the possibility of winning the next election through. Some evidence of this is seen in the increase in the number of bills that are passed through the year before elections (see Figure 12.2).

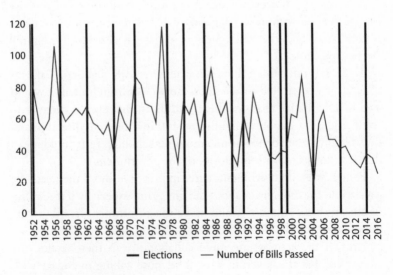

Figure 12.2　Legislative Cycle in India
Source: PRS Legislative Research.

At the risk of repetition, it is important to emphasize that the observations mentioned above are only broad initial conjectures about the nature of law-making in India. A proper theory needs to be fleshed out of these stylized observations and systematically tested using proper statistical methodology using an adequate sample. We hope the idea will receive the necessary attention from future researchers to take us to a fuller and rigorous understanding of the relationship between the nature of policy problems and the path to their resolution.

Exploring Other Theoretical Approaches

It is clear that no single conventional theory fits all the cases described in this volume nor it is easy to develop a framework that adequately captures the mind-bogglingly complex process of law-making.

In addition to the 'legislative strategy framework' we have suggested earlier, it is possible that the commonalities and patterns in the case studies can be unearthed through another, perhaps more, comprehensive lens. By applying complexity theory to the field of public policy—an approach pioneered by Paul Cairney and Robert Geyer (see Geyer and Cairney 2015; Geyer and Rihani 2010)—it may be possible to see patterns in the seemingly random nature of the law-making process. While a complete exposition of the complexity theory is beyond the scope of this book (we refer the readers to Cairney and Geyer 2015 for a comprehensive treatment), we introduce here a conceptual tool frequently used in management and now increasingly in public policy literature to suggest a structure that may be of use in thinking about the cases presented in this book and beyond.

Figure 12.3 is the conceptual tool of the Stacey diagram that analyses the nature of multi-party decision-making problem, on two dimensions: the degree of agreement of objectives among stakeholders on one hand and the extent of certainty of appropriateness of solutions on the other. The interaction between these two variable segments the space of problems into 'simple', that is, open to evidence-based policymaking, (part 1 in Figure 12.3), political (part 2), judgemental (part 3), the space of 'impossible or chaotic' problems (part 4). Between these is a space (the shaded one, part 5) that is the zone of 'complex' problems.

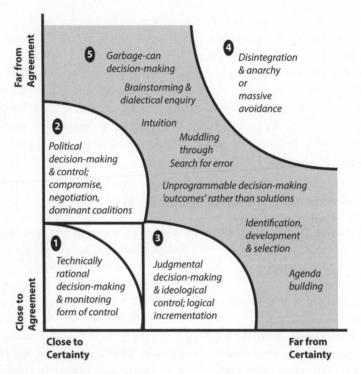

Figure 12.3   The Stacey Diagram
Source: Stacey (2002).

The central narrative of the complexity sciences involves viewing the social system as a complex, evolving system, which is beyond the control of government or any other stakeholder. It explores highly interconnected systems mathematically, and develops models that shed light on how such interconnected systems work (Colander and Kupers 2014: 320). Complexity theory aims to identify what types of systemic output occur when its members follow the same basic rules, and how sensitive the system is, or what small changes in rules will produce profound changes in systemic behaviour. In political science, the utility of complexity theory is in explaining issues that contain unpredictable political events, significant levels of uncertainty and ambiguity, or factors outside the control of policymakers (Cairney 2012; Geyer and Rihani 2010; Room 2011).

Key Features of a Complex System (Cairney 2012)

- The parts of a complex system are interdependent and the system cannot be described by breaking it down into its component parts.
- It is next to impossible to predict the behaviour of complex systems. 'They exhibit "non-linear" dynamics produced by feedback loops in which some forms of action are dampened (negative feedback) while others are amplified (positive feedback). Small actions can have large effects and large actions can have small effects.'
- Complex systems are dependent on initial conditions that produce a long-term momentum or 'path dependence'.
- The behaviour of these systems evolves from the interaction between elements at a local level rather than a central direction making it difficult to control.
- Complex systems may behave regularly for extended periods but are 'liable to change radically'. They may, therefore, exhibit periods of 'punctuated equilibria'—in which long periods of stability are interrupted by short bursts of change.
- The various problems that complexity theory seeks to address— such as predicting climate change, earthquakes, how the brain works, and the behaviour of social and political systems—can only be solved by interdisciplinary scientific groups.

Much of the complexity theory application in politics and public policy till date has focused on matters of public administration and the efficacy of laws and other policy measures. Emergence of a law has not yet been analysed using the complexity theory. However, our case studies amply demonstrate that the law-making process in India is also marked by the key elements of complexity theory: non-linear dynamics, emergent properties, path dependency, and strange attractors that make it appropriate for viewing it as a complex process and analysing it using the learnings from the burgeoning literature in that area.

Concluding Remarks

As we conclude this book, it would be fair to highlight a debate that is common in developed countries and is becoming increasingly frequent in India—the role of civil society in the policymaking process in representative democracies. The case studies in this book highlighted this fact quite prominently.

Representative democracies work on the premise that modern nations are too populous and complex to allow for direct democracy of the type prevalent in ancient Athens or Switzerland. Citizens elect people to represent them based on their political agendas, capabilities, and ethnic affiliations. Now, the question arises as to the role of citizens in such political systems. Does their involvement end with casting their ballot or is there a more active role that they can and should play in the policymaking process? Related to these is the question of the role of the representative. Does he/she only represent the interest of his/her constituents or of the nation as a whole? The Austrian political economist Joseph Schumpeter suggested that the most society could ask citizens to do is to participate in the selection of their leaders and that the complexity of public opinion and the difficulty of matching those opinions with real policy options meant that it would be futile to seek substantive connections between citizen opinion and public policy. Similar opinions were forwarded by the founders of the American nation who felt that representatives would be drawn from among the better-educated and more prominent members of society and would more readily grasp the details of the policy questions before them. Their keener sense of and stronger commitment to the public good would enable them to see beyond their own self-interest, and therefore their decisions would be more likely to advance the public interest than would be the case if the people governed directly.

We have come a long way from those times and realized that vesting the elected representative with the virtues of wisdom and the ability to rise above parochial interests was more an article of faith than reality. However, the relation between a citizen and his/her representative remains complex. A frequent criticism against politicians is that they fail to live up to the promises they make during election campaigns. But there can be instances when a candidate once in office decides not to do as he/she promised because the facts he/she discovers after the election are inconsistent with the facts as he/she understood them prior to elections. This dichotomy between acting as his/her constituents want him/her to act—as their delegate—and acting in what he/she believes to be their best interests—as their trustee—has been a recurrent theme in both theoretical and empirical studies of representation. A related and equally challenging problem is when the opinions and interests of the represented coincide, but, in the view of the representative, they are contrary to the interests of the nation. The views of Edmund Burke and James Madison—two legislators who were also political theorists—were clear on this point: in such a situation, the representative's first obligation is to the nation. The reason for somewhat digressing from the core theme of the book is because we need to keep in mind that while citizen activism is extremely important in the political system, policymakers also work under constraints and may have a better sense of the bigger picture.

In India, these debates are becoming more commonplace and critical with the legitimacy of politicians at an all-time low due to years of ineffective delivery of public services, unequal allocation of public goods, and charges of massive corruption. Civil society organizations, on the other hand, have gained legitimacy since their agendas are seen as noble, upholding the core principles of democracy, ensuring transparency and accountability, and championing the voiceless and the poor. In such a political climate, it is easy for a civil society organization to point fingers at the venality of politicians and insist on their agenda taking precedence. If all civil society groups have more or less equal access and say in the policy process, there is no issue since there would be a balance. Given the improbability of that happening, there is a real threat of the policy process being hijacked by narrow agendas rather than what serves the larger public good, a decision that is the prerogative of a legislator in a representative democracy.

This book is not a normative discussion about the legitimacy of civil society organizations versus political representatives or the efficacy and the limits of civic activism. However, as mentioned, these issues are relevant for many of the case studies we have studied in the book and have been (and in some cases, still are) hotly debated among stakeholders. Therefore, it is important to highlight these ongoing debates so that future researchers can study these cases through those lenses.

This book is a first step in understanding the puzzle of how policies are shaped through the interventions of different stakeholders as it throws light onto hitherto dark corners of the policy process. While there is somewhat more information of the legislative process through Parliamentary debates, standing committee reports, and media reports of the political wheeling dealing, the pre-legislative process remains a black box. This book attempts to lift the lid a fraction to give a glimpse of the behind-the-scene action as a law gets shaped. For those interested in activism, it strove to serve as a guide for predicting what strategies may work and at what moment in time. For policymakers, it sought to provide a glimpse of the inner workings of movements and campaigns and prepare them better for responding to such pressures. For the intelligent lay reader, it attempted to be an introduction to the complex world of policymaking with its pulls and pushes, the range of policy choices, and the perils of decision-making.

Bibliography

3iNetwork and Infrastructure Development Finance Company. 2009. *India Infrastructure Report, 2009: Land—A Critical Resource for Infrastructure*. New Delhi: Oxford University Press. Available at https://www.idfc.com/pdf/report/IIR-2009.pdf (last accessed on 20 March 2017).

Adams, Dale W. and J.D. Von Pischke. 1992. 'Microenterprise Credit Programs: Deja Vu', *World Development*, 20: 1463–70.

Agarwal, Ankit. 2012. 'Protest and Road Blockade against the Gangrape Case in Delhi', *Tehelka*, 18 December.

Agarwal, M. 2002. 'Analyses of Mergers in India', unpublished MPhil dissertation. New Delhi: University of Delhi.

Aggarwal, J.C. 2007. *Landmarks in the History of Modern Indian Education* (6th edn). New Delhi: Vikas Publishing.

Agnes, Flavia. 2009. 'Women's Rights and Legislative Reforms: An Overview', *International Journal of Legal Information*, 36(2): 263–9.

Alavilli, Srinivas. 2013. 'Karnataka's Dance of Democracy: Naavu Ready, Neevu Barteera?', *Citizen Matters*, 26 February. Available at http://bangalore.citizenmatters.in/articles/print/4964-the-need-for-effective-citizen-campaigns (last accessed on 20 March 2017).

Ali, Mohammad. 2012. 'Angry Protests across Delhi over Gang-Rape', *The Hindu*, 20 December. Available at http://www.thehindu.com/news/cities/Delhi/angry-protests-across-delhi-over-gangrape/article4220758.ece (last accessed on 20 March 2016).

Almond, G.A. and J.S. Coleman. 1960. *The Politics of the Developing Areas*. Princeton: Princeton University Press.

Anderson, A.J. 1974. *Problems in Intellectual Freedom and Censorship* (vol. 8). New York: R.R. Bowker Company.

Anderson, J.E. 1975. *Public Policy-making*. New York: Praeger.

Anderson, J.E. 1997. *Public Policymaking: An Introduction* (3rd edn). Boston: Houghton Mifflin.

Apter, David E. 1955. *The Gold Coast in Transition*. Princeton: Princeton University Press.

Arora, Balveer and Kailash, K.K. 2014. 'Strengthening Legislative Capabilities of the Indian Parliament: The National Advisory Council' in Sudha Pai and Avinash Kumar (eds), *The Indian Parliament: A Critical Appraisal*, pp. 189–230. New Delhi: Orient Blackswan.

Ashutosh. 2012. *Anna: 13 Days That Awakened India*. New Delhi: HarperCollins Publishers.

Atkinson, M.M. and W.D. Coleman. 1992. 'Policy Networks, Policy Communities and the Problems of Governance', *Governance*, 5(2): 154–80.

Ayyar, R.V. Vaidyanatha. 2009. *Public Policymaking in India*. New Delhi: Dorling Kindersley (India) Pvt. Ltd.

Bailey, S.K., Robert C. Wood, Richard T. Frost, and Paul E. Marsh. 1962. *Schoolmen and Politics: A Study of State Aid to Education in the Northeast*. New York: Syracuse University Press.

Balchand, K. 2013. 'Anti-Rape Bill passed', *The Hindu*, 21 March. Available at http://www.thehindu.com/news/national/antirape-bill-passed/article 4534056.ece (last accessed on 20 March 2016).

Bandyopadhyay, T. 2014. 'Microfinance Institutions Showing Signs of Maturity', *Live Mint*, 22 June.

Banerjee, Abhijit, Pranab Bardhan, Esther Duflo, Erica Field, Dean Karlan, Asim Khwaja, Dilip Mookherjee, Rohini Pande, and Raghuram Rajan. 2010. 'Microcredit Is Not the Enemy', *Financial Times*, 14 December. Available at https://www.ft.com/content/53e4724c-06f3-11e0-8c29-00144feabdc0 (last accessed on 8 March 2017).

Banerjee, Upala Devi (ed.). 2005. 'Lessons Learned from Rights-Based Approaches in the Asia-Pacific Region: Documentation of Case Studies', Office of the United Nations High Commissioner for Human Rights, Regional Office for Asia Pacific, Bangkok, available at http://hrbaportal.org/wp-content/files/RBA-in-AP-region3.pdf (last accessed on 20 March 2016).

Barn, Ravinder. 2014. 'Social Media and Protest: The Indian Spring', *Huffington Post*, 9 January. Available at http://www.huffingtonpost.co.uk/professor-ravinder-barn/india-social-media-and-protest_b_2430194.html (last accessed on 22 March 2016).

Barry, Ellen and Betwa Sharma. 2013. 'Many Doubt Death Sentences Will Stem India Sexual Attacks', *New York Times*, 13 September. Available at http://www.nytimes.com/2013/09/14/world/asia/4-sentenced-to-

death-in-rape-case-that-riveted-india.html?emc=edit_na_20130913&_
r=0 (last accessed on 20 March 2016).

Baru, S. 2009. 'The Influence of Business and Media on Indian Foreign Policy', *India Review*, 8(3): 266–85.

Bashevkin, Sylvia. 2002. 'Interest Groups and Social Movements', in Lawrence LeDuc, Richard G. Niemi, and Pippa Noris (eds), *Comparing Democracies 2: New Challenges in the Study of Elections and Voting*. London: SAGE Publications.

Basu, K. 2005. 'Child Labor and the Law: Notes on Possible Pathologies', *Economics Letters*, 87(2): 169–74.

Basu, P. and Pradeep Srivastava. 2005. 'Exploring Possibilities: Microfinance and Rural Credit Access for the Poor in India', *Economic and Political Weekly*, 40(17): 1747–56.

Baumgartner, F.R. and B.D. Jones. 1993. *Agendas and Instability in American Politics*. Chicago: University of Chicago Press.

Baumgartner, F.R. and B.L. Leech. 1998. *Basic interests: The Importance of Groups in Politics and in Political Science*. Princeton: Princeton University Press.

Baumgartner, F.R., C. Breunig, C. Green-Pedersen, B.D. Jones, P.B. Mortensen, M. Nuytemans, and S. Walgrave. 2009. 'Punctuated Equilibrium in Comparative Perspective', *American Journal of Political Science*, 53: 603–20.

Bayley, David H. 1962. *Preventive Detention in India: A Case Study in Democratic Social Control*. Kolkata: Eastend Printers.

———. 1963. 'Violent Public Protest in India: 1900–1960', *The Indian Journal of Political Science*, 24(4): 309–25.

———. 2015. *The Policy and Political Development in India*. Princeton: Princeton University Press.

Bayley, N. 1969. *Bayley Scales of Infant Development*. New York: Psychological Corporation.

Baxi, Upendra, Vasudha Dhagamwar, Raghunath Kelkar, and Lotika Sarkar. 1979. 'An Open Letter to the Chief Justice of India', 1979, New Delhi, (1979) 4 SCC (Jour) 17, available at http://aud.ac.in/upload/open%20 letter.pdf (last accessed on 20 March 2016).

BBC. 2010. 'Indian Opposition holds mass protest rally', 22 December. Available at http://www.bbc.co.uk/news/world-south-asia-12056911 (last accessed on 20 March 2017).

Benford, R.D. and D.A. Snow. 2000. 'Framing Processes and Social Movements: An Overview and Assessment', *Annual Review of Sociology*, 611–39.

Berry, F.S. and W.D. Berry. 1990. 'State Lottery Adoptions as Policy Innovations: An Event History Analysis', *American Political Science Review*, 84(2): 395–415.

———. 1992. 'Tax Innovation in the State: Capitalizing on Political Opportunity', *American Journal of Political Science*, 36(3): 715–42.

Berry, J.M. 1997. *The Interest Group Society*. New York and London: Longman.

Berry, J.M. 1999. *The New Liberalism: The Rising Power of Citizen Groups*. Washington, DC: Brookings Institution Press.

Bharadwaj, P., L. Lakdawala, and N. Li. 2013. 'Perverse Consequences of Well Intentioned Regulation: Evidence from India's Child Labor Ban', NBER Working Paper 19602, Cambridge: National Bureau of Economic Research.

Bhattacharya, Subhomoy and Amitendu Palit. 2008. *SEZ in India: Myths and Reality*. New Delhi: Anthem Press.

Bhatty, K. 1996. 'Child Labour: Breaking the Vicious Cycle', *Economic and Political Weekly*, 31(7): 384–86.

Bhukuth, A. 2008. 'Defining Child Labour: A Controversial Debate', *Development in Practice*, 18(3): 385–94.

Birkland, Thomas. 2001. *An Introduction to the Policy Process*. Armonk: M.E. Sharpe.

Blumer, H. 1957. *Collective Behaviour*. New York: Ardent Media.

Bose, I. 2010. 'How Did the Indian Forest Rights Act, 2006, Emerge? Improving Institutions for Pro-Poor Growth', Discussion Paper Series 39, Department for International Development, Manchester, UK. Available at http://www.ippg.org.uk/papers/dp39.pdf (last accessed on 28 March 2017).

Breunig, C. and C. Koski. 2012. 'The Tortoise or the Hare? Incrementalism, Punctuations, and Their Consequences', *Policy Studies Journal*, 40(1): 45–68.

Brewer, G.D. and P. DeLeon. 1983. The Foundations of Policy Analysis. Homewood: Dorsey Press.

Cahn, M.A. 2013. 'Institutional and Noninstitutional Actors in the Policy Process', in S.Z. Theodoulou and M.A. Cahn (eds), *Public Policy: The Essential Readings* (2nd edn). Boston: Pearson.

Caiden, N. and A.B. Wildavsky. 1980. *Planning and Budgeting in Poor Countries*. New York: Wiley.

Cairney, P. 2012. 'Public Administration in an Age of Austerity: Positive Lessons from Policy Studies', *Public Policy and Administration*, 27(3): 230–47.

Castles, F.G. 1998. *Comparative Public Policy: Patterns of Post-war Transformation*. Cheltenham and Lyme: Edward Elgar Publishing.

———. 2002. 'Developing New Measures of Welfare State Change and Reform', *European Journal of Political Research*, 41(5): 613–41.

Chakrabarti, Rajesh and Shamika Ravi. 2011. 'At the Crossroads: Microfinance in India', *Money and Finance*, ICRA Bulletin, available at http://www.icra.in/Files/MoneyFinance/atthecrossroads.pdf (last accessed on 20 March 2017).

Chakravarthy, S. 2006. 'Competition Act, 2002: The Approach', in Pradeep S. Mehta (ed.), *A Functional Competition Policy for India*, Chapter 3. New Delhi: Academic Foundation; and Jaipur: Consumer Unity and Trust Society (CUTS International).

Chakravarti, Sudeep. 2015. 'Land Ordinance: The Haunting', *Mint*, 12 February.

Chakravorty, Sanjoy. 2013. *The Price of Land: Acquisition, Conflict, Consequence*. New Delhi: Oxford University Press.

———. 2015. 'How to Design the Next Land Acquisition Law', *India in Transition*, 6 April. Available at https://casi.sas.upenn.edu/iit/sanjoychakravorty (last accessed on 20 March 2017).

Chandrasekhar, Rajeev. 2014. 'Rahul's Claim of RTI Exposing Scams Is Wrong', *Firstpost*, 3 February, available at http://www.firstpost.com/politics/rahuls-claim-of-rti-exposing-scams-is-wrong-rajeev-chandrasekhar-1371811.html (last accessed on 20 March 2017).

Chaudhuri, Anindya. 2015. 'Policy Studies, Policymaking, and Knowledge-driven Governance: A Review', *Economic and Political Weekly*, 51(23): 59–68.

Chhibber, Maneesh. 2010. 'Lokpal will be three-judge body, with PM under purview', *Indian Express*, 18 October. Available at http://indianexpress.com/article/news-archive/web/lokpal-will-be-threejudge-body-with-pm-under-purview/ (last accessed on 20 March 2017).

Chong, Dennis. 1991. *Collective Action and the Civil Rights Movement*. Chicago, IL: University of Chicago Press.

Chubb, John E. and Terry M. Moe. 1988. 'Politics, Markets, and the Organisation of Schools', *American Political Science Review*, 82(4): 1065–87.

———. 1990. *Politics, Markets, and America's Schools*. Washington, DC: Brookings Institution Press

Cobb, R., J.K. Ross, and M.H. Ross. 1976. 'Agenda Building as a Comparative Political Process', *American Political Science Review*, 70(1): 126–38.

Cobb, Roger W. and Charles D. Elder. 1977. *Participation in American Politics: The Dynamics of Agenda-Building*. Baltimore: Johns Hopkins University Press.

———. 1997. *Participation in American Politics: The Dynamics of Agenda Building*. Baltimore: Johns Hopkins University Press.

Cochran, C.L. and E.F. Malone. 2005. *Public Policy: Perspectives and Choices*. Boulder: Lynne Rienner.

Cohen, J. and A. Arato. 1992. 'Politics and the Reconstruction of the Concept of Civil Society', Cultural-political interventions in the unfinished project of enlightenment.

Cohen, Michael, James March, and Johan Olsen. 1972. 'A Garbage Can Model of Organisational Choice', *Administrative Science Quarterly*, 17: 1–25.

Cohn, Bernard S. 1957. 'India as a Racial, Linguistic, and Cultural Area', in Milton Singer (ed.), *Introducing India in Liberal Education*. Chicago: University of Chicago Press.

Cohn, C. 1993. 'War, Wimps and Women: Talking Gender and Thinking War', in M. Cooke and A. Woollacott (eds), *Gendering War Talk*. Princeton: Princeton University Press.

Colander, David and Roland Kupers. 2014. *Complexity and the Art of Public Policy: Solving Society's Problems from the Bottom Up*. Princeton: Princeton University Press.

Corkery, Joan, Anthony Land, and Jean Bossuyt. 1995. 'The Process of Policy Formulation: Institutional Path or Institutional Maze?', Study based on the introduction of Cost-sharing for Education in Three African Countries, European Centre for Development Policy Management.

Crepaz, M.M. 1996. 'Consensus versus Majoritarian Democracy: Political Institutions and Their Impact on Macroeconomic Performance and Industrial Disputes', *Comparative Political Studies*, 29(1): 4–26.

Cress, D.M. and D.A. Snow. 2000. 'The Outcomes of Homeless Mobilization: The Influence of Organization, Disruption, Political Mediation, and Framing', *American Journal of Sociology*, 105(4): 1063–104.

Consumer Unity & Trust Society (CUTS). 1995. 'Access to the Constitution: A Neglected Right', Briefing Paper, Jaipur, India.

Currie, B. 2000. *The Politics of Hunger in India: A Study of Democracy, Governance and Kalahandi's Poverty*. Basingstoke: Macmillan Press Ltd.

Daily News and Analysis. 2013. 'Women Groups Protest Anti-Rape Ordinance', 4 February. Available at http://www.dnaindia.com/india/report-women-groups-protest-anti-rape-ordinance-1796191 (last accessed on 20 March 2016).

Dalton, Russel J. 1995. 'Strategies of Partisan Influence: West European Environmental Groups', in J. Craig Jenkins and Bert Klandermans (eds), *The Politics of Social Protest: Comparative Perspectives on States and Social Movements*. Minneapolis: University of Minnesota Press.

Das, Amiya Kumar. 1982. *Assam's Agony: A Socio-Economic and Political Analysis*. New Delhi: Lancers Publication.

Dasgupta, Piyasree. 2013. 'Lok Sabha Passes Anti-Rape Bill, RS Votes Tomorrow', available at http://www.firstpost.com/india/live-lok-sabha-passes-criminal-law-amendment-bill-2013-666443.html (last accessed on 20 March 2016).

Davis, O.A., M.A.H. Dempster, and A. Wildavsky. 1966. 'A Theory of the Budgetary Process', *American Political Science Review*, 60(3): 529–47.

Deccan Herald. 2011. *Conspiracy Hatched to Stall Lokpal: Team Anna*, 30 December 2011. Available at http://www.deccanherald.com/content/215549/team-anna-blames-ansari-lokpal.html (last accessed on 15 January 2017).

De Schutter, Olivier. 2014. *International Human Rights Law: Cases, Materials, Commentary*. United Kingdom: Cambridge University Press.

De Waal, J., I. Currie, and G. Erasmus. 2000. The Bill of Rights Handbook. Cape Town: Juta & Company Limited.

DeLeon, P. 1999. 'The Stages Approach to the Policy Process: What Has It Done? Where Is It Going?', *Theories of the Policy Process*, 1(19): 19–32.

Della Porta, D. and M. Diani. 2006. *Social Movements: An Introduction*. Hoboken: Wiley-Blackwell.

Deng, F. 1997. 'Information Gaps and Unintended Outcomes of Social Movements: The 1989 Chinese Student Movement', *American Journal of Sociology*, 102(4): 1085–112.

Deo, N. and D. McDuie-Ra. 2011. *The politics of Collective Advocacy in India: Tools and Traps*. Sterling: Kumarian Press.

Desai, A. 1965. *Voices in the City*. New Delhi: Orient Paperbacks.

Dhawan, M.L. 2006. *Issues in Indian Education*. New Delhi: Isha Books.

Drache, D. and Velagic, J. 2013. A Report on Sexual Violence Journalism in Four Leading English Language Indian Publications Before and After the Delhi Rape, ICA Pre Conference Workshop on South Asian Communication Scholarship, London, 16–17 June 2013. Available at http://jmi.ac.in/upload/menuupload/Drache_Velagic_Delhi_Rape_reporting_2013June4.pdf (last accessed on January 15, 2017).

Dror, Y. 1989. *Public Policymaking Reexamined* (2nd edn). New Brunswick: Transaction Publishers.

Diamant, A. 1959. 'Is There a Non-Western Political Process?', *Journal of Politics*, 21: 123–7.

Dowding, K. 1995. 'Model or Metaphor? A Critical Review of the Policy Network Approach', *Political Studies*, 43(1): 136–58.

Downing, Casey. 2013. 'Eminent Domain in 21st Century India: What New Delhi Can Learn From New London', *Journal of International Law and Politics*, 46(1): 207–51.

Dreze, J. 2002. 'On Research and Action', *Economic and Political Weekly*, 37(9): 817–19.

———. 2015. 'Food Insecurity and Statistical Fog', *The Hindu*, 25 February.

Dua, B.D., M.P. Singh, and R. Saxena (eds). 2007. *Indian Judiciary and Politics: The Changing Landscape*. New Delhi: Manohar Publishers & Distributors.

———. 2014. *The Indian Parliament: The Changing Landscape*. New Delhi: Manohar Publishers & Distributors.

Dutta, A. 2007. *Development-Induced Displacement and Human Rights*. New Delhi: Deep and Deep Publications.

Dwivedi, Arvind Mohan and Rajneesh Roshan. 2014. *Magnetic Personality: Arvind Kejriwal*. New Delhi: Diamond Pocket Books.

Easton, D. 1953. *The Political System*. New York: Knopf.

———. 1965. *A Framework for Political Analysis*. Englewood Cliffs: Prentice-Hall.

Echeverri-Gent, J. 1993. *The State and the Poor: Public Policy and Political Development in India and the United States*. Berkeley: University of California Press.

Economic Times. 2013. 'Lower juvenile age in rape cases: BJP leader Venkaiah Naidu', *Economic Times*, 13 February. Available at http://articles. economictimes.indiatimes.com/2013-02-13/news/37079310_1_lower-juvenile-age-verma-panel-bjp-leader (last accessed on 20 March 2016).

Edelman, M. 1964. *The Symbolic Uses of Politics*. Urbana: University of Illinois Press.

Edwards, P. 1988. 'Introductory overview', in E.L. Wiener and D.C. Nagel (eds), *Human Factors in Aviation*.

Elder, C.D. and Cobb, R.W. 1984. 'Agenda-building and the Politics of Aging', *Policy Studies Journal*, 13(1).

Etzioni, A. 1965. Political Unification: A Comparative Study of Leaders and Forces. New York City: Holt, Rinehart and Winston, Inc.

Fernandes, Walter. 2008. 'India's Forced Displacement Policy and Practice: Is Compensation up to Its Functions?' in Michael M. Cernea and Hari Mohan Mathur (eds), *Can Compensation Prevent Impoverishment? Reforming Resettlement through Investments and Benefit-Sharing*, pp. 181–207. New Delhi: Oxford University Press.

Firstpost. 2016. 'Right to Information: What 11 years of the RTI Act of 2005 have done for India', 12 October, available at http://www.firstpost. com/india/right-to-information-what-11-years-of-the-rti-act-of-2005-have-done-for-india-3047286.html (last accessed on 8 March 2017).

French, Patrick. 2011. 'A new "Gandhi" shakes India', *Telegraph*, 17 August. Available at http://www.telegraph.co.uk/news/worldnews/asia/india/8706706/A-new-Gandhi-shakes-India.html (last accessed on 20 March 2017).

Fischer, Frank, Gerald J. Miller, and Mara S. Sidney (eds). 2007. *Handbook of Public Policy Analysis: Theory, Politics, and Methods*. Florida: CRC Press.

Florini, Ann (ed.). 2007. *The Right to Know: Transparency for an Open World*. New York: Columbia University Press.

Francis, Merlin. 2011. 'Hazare Agitation in Bangalore: How the Campaign was Caught in "Net"', *Daily News and Analysis*, 26 February. Available at http://www.dnaindia.com/bangalore/report-hazare-agitation-in-bangalore-how-the-campaign-was-caught-in-net-1579888 (last accessed on 20 March 2017).

Freeman, J. Leiper. 1965. *The Political Process*. New York: Random House.

Friedman, B.L. 2006. 'Policy Analysis as Organisational Analysis', in Michael Moran, Martin Rein, and Robert E. Goodin (eds), *The Oxford Handbook of Public Policy*, pp. 496–528. New York: Oxford University Press.

Foy, Henry. 2011. 'Wikileaks cash for votes allegations implicate India's Congress', *Reuters*, blog post, 17 March. Available at http://blogs.reuters.com/india/2011/03/17/wikileaks-cash-for-votes-allegations-implicateindias-congress/ (last accessed on 20 March 2017).

Gadgil, Madhav and Ramchandra Guha. 1998. 'Towards a Perspective on Environmental Movements in India', *The Indian Journal of Social Work*, 59(1): 450–72.

Gamson, William A. 1975. *The Strategy of Social Protest* (1st edn). Homewood: Dorsey Press.

———. 1990. *The Strategy of Social Protest* (2nd edn). Belmont: Wadsworth Publishing Co.

Gangoli, Geetanjali. 2007. *Indian Feminisms: Law, Patriarchies and Violence in India*. Hampshire and Burlington: Ashgate Publishing Limited.

Gardiner, Harris and Hari Kumar. 2012. 'Clashes Break Out in India at a Protest Over a Rape Case', *New York Times*, 22 December. Available at http://www.nytimes.com/2012/12/23/world/asia/in-india-demonstrators-and-police-clash-at-protest-over-rape.html?_r=0 (last accessed on 20 March 2016).

Gerston, L.N. 2010. *Public Policy Making: Process and Principles*. Armonk: M.E. Sharpe, Inc.

Geyer, R. and P. Cairney (eds). 2015. *Handbook on Complexity and Public Policy*. Cheltenham: Edward Elgar Publishing.

Geyer, R. and S. Rihani. 2010. *Complexity and Public Policy*. London: Routledge

Ghatak, Maitreesh and Parikshit Ghosh. 2011. 'The Land Acquisition Bill: A Critique and a Proposal', *Economic and Political Weekly*, 46(41): 65–72.

Ghate, Prabhu. 2006. *Microfinance in India: A State of the Sector Report, 2006*. Delhi: Microfinance India, CARE, Swiss Agency for Development and Cooperation, Ford Foundation. Available at http://www.accessdev.

org/downloads/state_of_the_sector_06.pdf (last accessed on 22 March 2017).

Ghosh, Deepshikha (ed.). 2014. 'Delhi Gang-Rape Case: High Court Confirms Death Sentence for Four Convicts', available at http://www.ndtv.com/india-news/delhi-gang-rape-case-high-court-confirms-death-sentence-for-four-convicts-553796 (last accessed on 20 March 2016).

Ghosh, Joyita. 2015. PRS Bill Summary, The Right to Fair Compensation and Transparency in Land Acquisition, Rehabilitation and Resettlement (Second Amendment) Bill, 2015. Available at http://www.prsindia.org/uploads/media/Land%20and%20R%20and%20R/Bill%20Summary-LARR%202nd%20Amendment.pdf (last accessed on 22 March 2017).

Giugni, M., D. McAdam, and C. Tilly (eds). 1999. *How Social Movements Matter*, vol. 10. Minneapolis: University of Minnesota Press.

Godwin, K., S. Ainsworth, and E.K. Godwin. 2012. *Lobbying and Policymaking*. Washington, DC: CQ Press.

Goldstone, Jack A. 1980. 'The Weakness of Organisation: A New Look at Gamson's *The Strategy of Social Protest*', *American Journal of Sociology*, 85(5): 1017–42.

Gonsalves, Colin. 2009. 'Introduction to Fourth Edition: The Indian Right to Food Case', in Anup Kumar Srivastava and Manisha Tiwary (eds), *Right to Food*. New Delhi: Human Rights Law Network.

———. 2011. *Kaliyug: The Decline of Human Rights Law in the Period of Globalisation*. New Delhi: Human Rights Law Network.

Goswami, Devika and Kaustuv K. Bandhopadhyay. 2012. 'The Anti-Corruption Movement in India', available at http://www.cetri.be/IMG/pdf/Anti-Corruption-Movement_India.pdf (last accessed on 20 March 2017).

Government of India. 1994. *Draft National Policy for Rehabilitation of Persons Displaced as a Consequence of Acquisition of Land*. New Delhi: Ministry of Rural Development.

———. 2008. 'Report of the Committee on Financial Inclusion', Committee on Financial Inclusion.

Grant, Laura. 2010. '"The Second Freedom Struggle" Transnational Advocacy for EFA Case Study: National Coalition for Education in India', Master of Science, International Development Studies Thesis, Universiteit van Amsterdam. Available at https://educationanddevelopment.files.wordpress.com/2008/04/2010-grant.pdf (last accessed on 20 March 2017).

Greenberg, D. 1977. 'The Dynamics of Oscillatory Punishment Processes', *The Journal of Criminal Law and Criminlogy*, 68(4): 643–51.

Greenberg, George, Jeffrey Miller, Lawrence Mohr, and Bruce Vladeck. 1977. 'Developing Public Policy Theory: Perspectives from Empirical Research', *American Political Science Review*, 71(4): 1532–43.

Grover, V. 1997. *Political Process, Government Structure and Administration*. New Delhi: Deep and Deep Publications.

Gudavarthy, A. 2013. *Politics of Post-civil Society: Contemporary History of Political Movements in India*. New Delhi: SAGE Publications.

Guha, R. 2007. *India after Gandhi: The History of the World's Largest Democracy*. Basingstoke: Pan Books.

Gulati, Ashok, Jyoti Gujral, and T. Nandakumar. 2012. 'National Food Security Bill: Challenges and Options', Commission for Agricultural Costs and Prices, Department of Agriculture and Cooperation, Ministry of Agriculture, Government of India, available at http://cacp.dacnet.nic.in/ViewQuestionare.aspx?Input=2&DocId=1&PageId=42&KeyId=470 (last accessed on 20 March 2017).

Gupta, Dipankar. 1982. *Nativism in a Metropolis: The Shiv Sena in Bombay*. New Delhi: Manohar Publishers.

Gupta, Smita. 2013a. 'Cabinet Divided on Anti-Rape Draft Law', *The Hindu*, 12 March. Available at http://www.thehindu.com/news/national/cabinet-divided-on-antirape-draft-law/article4500256.ece?ref=related News (last accessed on 22 March 2017).

———. 2013b. 'Roadblocks Ahead for Anti-Rape Bill', *The Hindu*, 14 March. Available at http://www.thehindu.com/news/national/roadblocks-ahead-for-antirape-bill/article4508975.ece?ref=relatedNews (last accessed on 22 March 2017).

———. 2013c. 'Anti-Rape Bill Diluted, Union Cabinet Approves New Version', *The Hindu*, 18 March. Available at http://www.thehindu.com/news/national/antirape-bill-diluted-union-cabinet-approves-new-version/article4521675.ece?ref=relatedNews (last accessed on 22 March 2017).

Gusfield, Joseph. 1981. *The Culture of Public Problems: Drinking-Driving and the Symbolic Order*. Chicago: University of Chicago Press.

Hai Do. 2010. *The Policy Process in Vietnam: Critical Roles of Different Actors*. Vietnam: Social Publishing House of Vietnam.

Haksar, Nandita. 1991. 'Violation of Democratic Rights of Women', in A.R. Desai (ed.), *Expanding Governmental Lawlessness and Organized Struggles*, pp. 262–7. Bombay: Popular Prakashan.

———. 2005. 'Human Rights Lawyering: A Feminist Perspective', in Mala Khullar (ed.), *Writing the Women's Movement: A Reader*. New Delhi: Zubaan.

Hamm, Keith. 1983. 'Patterns of Influence among Committees, Agencies, and Interest Groups', *Legislative Studies Quarterly*, 8: 379–426.

Hansen, Philip. 1993. *Hannah Arendt: Politics, History and Citizenship.* Cambridge: Polity Press.

Hargrove, E.C. and M. Nelson. 1984. *Presidents, Politics, and Policy.* New York: McGraw-Hill College.

Harris, P.W. 1988. 'The Interpersonal Maturity Level Classification System: I-Level', *Criminal Justice and Behavior*, 15(1): 58–77.

Heclo, Hugh. 1977. *A Government of Strangers: Executive Politics in Washington.* Washington, DC: The Brookings Institution Press.

———. 1978. 'Issue Networks and the Executive Establishment: Government Growth in an Age of Improvement', in A. King (ed.), *The New American Political System*, pp. 87–124. Washington, DC: American Enterprise Institute.

Herberle, R. 1951. *Social Movements: An Introduction to Political Sociology.* New York: Appleton-Century-Crofts.

Hindu. 2011. 'TDP to Launch Anti-Corruption Agitation Tomorrow', 29 January. Available at http://www.thehindu.com/news/national/andhra-pradesh/tdp-to-launch-anticorruption-agitation-tomorrow/article1137504.ece (last accessed on 20 March 2017).

Hindu. 2013a. 'Wanted: A Verma Ordinance', 4 February. Available at http://www.thehindu.com/opinion/editorial/wanted-a-verma-ordinance/article4375579.ece?ref=relatedNews (last accessed on 20 March 2016).

———. 2013b. 'Cabinet to Take Criminal Law (Amendment) Bill on Tuesday', 11 March. Available at http://www.thehindu.com/news/national/cabinet-to-take-criminal-law-amendment-bill-on-tuesday/article4497422.ece?ref=relatedNews (last accessed on 20 March 2016).

Hindustan Times. 2011. 'Forward March against Corruption', 31 January. Available at http://www.hindustantimes.com/newdelhi/forward-march-against-corruption/article1-656622.aspx (last accessed on 20 March 2017).

Hobsbawm, Eric. 1959. *Primitive Rebels: Studies in Archaic Forms of Social Movement in the 19th and 20th Centuries.* Manchester: Manchester University Press.

Hogwood, B.W. and L.A. Gunn. 1984. *Policy Analysis for the Real World.* London: Oxford University Press.

Hogwood, Brian W. and B. Guy Peters. 1982. 'The Dynamics of Policy Change: Policy Succession', *Policy Sciences*, 14(3): 225–45.

———. 1983. *Policy Dynamics.* Brighton, Sussex: Wheatsheaf Books.

Hood, Christopher C. 1983. *The Tools of Government.* London: Macmillan.

Hopmann, D.N., C. Elmelund-Præstekær, E. Albæk, R. Vliegenthart, and C.H. De Vreese. 2012. 'Party Media Agenda-Setting: How Parties Influence Election News Coverage', *Party Politics*, 18(2): 173–91.

Horowitz, D.L. 1989. 'Is There a Third-World Policy Process?', *Policy Sciences*, 22(3–4): 197–212.

Howlett, M. and M. Ramesh. 1998. 'Policy Subsystem Configurations and Policy Change: Operationalizing the Postpositivist Analysis of the Politics of the Policy Process', *Policy Studies Journal*, 26(3): 466–81.

Howlett, Michael, M. Ramesh, and Anthony Perl. 2003. *Studying Public Policy: Policy Cycles and Policy Subsystems*. Canada: Oxford University Press.

Huber, Evelyn, Charles Ragin, and John D. Stephens. 1993. 'Social Democracy, Christian Democracy, Constitutional Structure, and the Welfare State: Towards a Resolution of Quantitative Studies', *American Journal of Sociology*, 99: 711–49.

Human Rights Watch. 2003. 'Small Change: Bonded Child Labour in India's Silk Industry', available at https://www.hrw.org/report/2003/01/22/small-change/bonded-child-labor-indias-silk-industry (last accessed on 8 March 2017).

Huntington, Samuel. 1996. *The Clash of Civilizations and the Remaking of World Order*. New York: Simon and Schuster.

IBN Live. 2012. 'Gangrape Victim's Family Sold Land for Her Education', *IBN Live*, 21 December. Available at http://www.ibnlive.com/news/india/gangrape-victims-family-sold-land-for-her-education-527785.html (last accessed on 22 March 2016).

IFMR. 2014. 'Microfinance in India: Sector Overview—FY Ended March 2014', IFMR Investments Document, available at http://investments.ifmr.co.in/wp-content/uploads/2014/11/201403-Microfinance-Sector-Overview-March-14.pdf (last accessed on 8 March 2017).

India Today. 2010a. 'CWG: How Showpiece Turned Shocker', *India Today*, 25 September. Available at http://indiatoday.intoday.in/story/cwg-how-show-piece-turned-shocker/1/113979.html (last accessed on 20 March 2017).

————. 2010b. 'Top Armymen, Netas Grab Plot for War Widows', 25 October. Available at http://indiatoday.intoday.in/story/top-armymen-netas-grab-plot-for-war-widows/1/117730.html (last accessed on 20 March 2017).

————. 2012. 'Medical Student Gang-Raped in Delhi Battles for Life, Her Friend Discharged', *India Today*, 17 December. Available at http://indiatoday.intoday.in/story/medical-student-gangraped-in-delhi-battles-for-life/1/238200.html (last accessed on 22 March 2016).

————. 2014. 'Statistics: 92 Women Raped in India Every Day, 4 in Delhi', *India Today*, 4 September. Available at http://indiatoday.intoday.in/story/india-rape-92-women-every-day-4-delhi-statistics/1/380956.html (last accessed on 22 March 2016).

Indian Express. 2010a. 'Sonia Okay with RTI Act, PM for Some Changes', 10 April, available at http://indianexpress.com/article/news-archive/web/sonia-okay-with-rti-act-pm-for-some-changes/ (last accessed on 8 March 2017).

———. 2010b. 'Ramdev, Bedi, Kejriwal File Joint Police Complaint over CWG', 14 November. Available at http://archive.indianexpress.com/news/ramdev-bedi-kejriwal-file-joint-police-complaint-over-cwg/711071/ (last accessed on 20 March 2017).

———. 2011a. 'UPA Divided, Lokpal off Cabinet Agenda Today', 6 January. Available at http://indianexpress.com/article/news-archive/web/upa-divided-lokpal-off-cabinet-agenda-today/ (last accessed on 20 March 2017).

———. 2011b. 'Hazare Not to Meet Ministers over Lokpal Bill', 27 March. Available at http://indianexpress.com/article/india/latest-news/hazare-not-to-meet-ministers-over-lokpal-bill/ (last accessed on 20 March 2017).

Indian National Congress. 2009. 'Manifesto of the Indian National Congress', Lok Sabha Elections. Available at http://www.congress.org.in (last accessed on 22 March 2017).

Indo Asian News Service (IANS). 2010. 'Shunglu Committee Only a Cover-up, Allege Social Activists', 29 October. Available at https://www.yahoo.com/news/shunglu-committee-only-cover-allege-social-activists.html (last accessed on 20 March 2017).

International Labour Organization (ILO). 2004. 'Investing in Every Child: An Economic Study of the Costs and Benefits of Eliminating Child Labour', International Programme on the Elimination of Child Labour (IPEC), Geneva.

Ingram, H. and S.R. Smith (eds). 1993. *Public Policy for Democracy*. Washington, DC: Brookings Institution.

Jasper, J.M. 1997. *The Art of Moral Protest: Culture. Biography, and Creativity in Social Movements*. Chicago: University of Chicago Press.

Jelani, Mehboob. 2011. 'The Insurgent', *Caravan*, 1 September. Available at http://www.caravanmagazine.in/reportage/insurgent (last accessed on 20 March 2017).

Jenkins, W.I. 1978. *Policy Analysis: A Political and Organisational Perspective*. London: Martin Robertson.

Jha, A.K. 2004. *Women in Panchayati Raj Institutions*. New Delhi: Anmol Publications.

John, P. and S. Bevan. 2012. 'What Are Policy Punctuations? Large Changes in the Legislative Agenda of the UK Government 1911–2008', *Policy Studies Journal*, 40: 89–108.

Jones, Bryan D., Frank R. Baumgartner, and James L. True. 1998. 'Policy Punctuations: U.S. Budget Authority, 1947–1995', *Journal of Politics*, 60: 1–33.

Jones, Charles O. 1970. *An Introduction to the Study of Public Policy*. Belmont: Wadsworth.

Joshi, Anuradha. 1999. 'Progressive Bureaucracy: An Oxymoron? The Case of Joint Forest Management in India', Network Paper 29a, London: Rural Development Forestry Network, Overseas Development Institute.

Joshi, Sandeep. 2013. 'Ordinance on Crimes against Women Tabled', *Hindu*, 22 February. Available at http://www.thehindu.com/news/national/ordinance-on-crimes-against-women-tabled/article4439945.ece?ref=relatedNews (last accessed on 20 March 2016).

Kapur, D. and P.B. Mehta. 2007. *Indian Higher Education Reform: From Half-Baked Socialism to Half-Baked Capitalism*. Centre for International Development Working Paper No. 108, Harvard University, available at https://casi.sas.upenn.edu/sites/casi.sas.upenn.edu/files/uploads/half%20baked.pdf (last accessed on 20 March 2017).

Kashyap, S. 2011. *Our Constitution*. New Delhi: National Book Trust.

Katakam, Anupama and Lyla Bavadam. 2010. 'Now, Loan Scam', *Frontline*, 27(25). Available at http://www.frontline.in/static/html/fl2725/stories/20101217272512900.htm (last accessed on 20 March 2017).

Kaur, P. and S. Dey. 2013. 'Andhra Pradesh Microfinance Crisis and Its Repercussions on Microfinancing', *Global Journal of Management and Business Studies*, 3(7): 695–702.

Kejriwal, Arvind. 2010. 'Open Letter to Sonia Gandhi', *Outlook*, 4 December. Available at http://www.outlookindia.com/article/open-letter-to-sonia-gandhi/267215 (last accessed on 20 March 2017).

Kellow, Aynsley. 1988. 'Promoting Elegance in Policy Theory: Simplifying Lowi's Arenas of Power', *Policy Studies Journal*, 16(4): 713–24.

Kesselman, M., J. Krieger, and W.A. Joseph. 2012. *Introduction to Comparative Politics*. Boston: Wadsworth.

Key, V.O. Jr. 1965 [1961]. *Public Opinion and American Democracy*. New York: Knopf.

Khan, Azeez Mehdi. 1997. *Shaping Policy: Do NGOs Matter? Lessons from India*. New Delhi: Society for Participatory Research in Asia.

Khera, Reetika. 2013. 'Democratic Politics and Legal Rights: Employment Guarantee and Food Security in India', Institute of Economic Growth Working Paper No. 327, University of Delhi, available at http://web.iitd.ac.in/~reetika/WP326democraticpolitics.pdf (last accessed on 20 March 2017).

Khullar, Mala (ed.). 2005. *Writing the Women's Movement: A Reader*. New Delhi: Zubaan.

Kingdon, J.W. 1984. *Agendas, Alternatives and Public Policies* (1st edn). Boston: Little, Brown & Co.

———. 1995. *Agendas, Alternatives, and Public Policies* (2nd edn). Boston: Little, Brown & Co.

———. 2003. *Agendas, Alternatives, and Public Policies* (3rd edn). New York: Longman Publishing Group.

Kitschelt, H. 1986. 'Political Opportunity Structures and Political Protest: Anti Nuclear Moments in Four Democracies', *British Journal of Political Science*, 16(1): 57–85.

Kjellberg, Francesco. 1977. 'Do Policies (Really) Determine Politics? And Eventually How?' *Policy Studies Journal* (Special Issue), 5: 554–70.

Knoke, D., Franz Urban Pappi, Jeffrey Broadbent, and Yutaka Tsujinaka. 1996. *Comparing Policy Networks: Labor Politics in the US, Germany, and Japan*. New York: Cambridge University Press.

Knoke, D. and E.O. Laumann. 1987. *The Organizational State: Social Choice in National Policy Domains*. Madison: University of Wisconsin Press.

Knoke, D. and F.U. Pappi. 1991. 'Organizational Action Sets in the US and German Labor Policy Domains', *American Sociological Review*, 56: 509–23.

Knoke, D., F.U. Pappi, J. Broadbent, and Y. Tsujinaka. 1996. *Comparing Policy Networks. Labor Politics in the U.S., Germany and Japan*. New York: Cambridge University Press.

Kochanek, S.A. 1974. *Business and Politics in India*. Berkeley: University of California Press.

———. 1996. 'Liberalisation and Business Lobbying in India', *Journal of Commonwealth and Comparative Politics*, 34(3): 155–73.

Kohli, A. 1987. *The State and Poverty in India: The Politics of Reform*. New York: Cambridge University Press.

———. 2001. *The Success of India's Democracy* (vol. 6). New York: Cambridge University Press.

Kohli, Shruti. 2012. 'Protest of the People, for the People, by the People', *The Petticoat Journal*, 30 December, available at http://petticoatjournal. com/sto-ries/protest-of-the-people-by-the-people-for-the-people/ (last accessed on 22 March 2017).

Kothari, R. 1960. 'Direct Action: A Pattern of Political Behaviour', *Quest*, 24: 1–24.

Kumar, Radha. 1993. *The History of Doing: An Illustrated Account of Movements for Women's Rights and Feminism in India, 1800–1990*. New Delhi: Zubaan.

———. 1995. 'From Chipko to Sati: The Contemporary Indian Women's Movement', in Amrita Basu (ed.), *The Challenge of Local Feminisms*, pp. 58–86. Boulder: Westview Press.

Kumar, Rohit. 2010. 'Vital Stats: Parliament in Winter Session', PRS Legislative Research, available at http://www.prsindia.org/

parliamenttrack/vital-stats/parliament-in-winter-session-2010-1426/ (last accessed on 20 March 2017).

Kumar, S. 2015. 'Sa-Dhan Gets Self-regulatory Organization Status after MFIN', *Live Mint*, 12 March.

Kumar, Ravi and Savyasaachi (eds). 2013. *Social Movements: Transformative Shifts and Turning Points*. New Delhi: Routledge.

Lang, Kurt and Gladys Lang. 1961. 'Liberalization and Business Lobbying in India', in Lang, Kurt and Gladys Lang (eds), *Collective Dynamics*. New York: Thomas Y. Crowell Company.

Lasswell, H.D. 1956a. 'The Political Science of Science: An Inquiry into the Possible Reconciliation of Mastery and Freedom', *American Political Science Review*, 50(4): 961–79.

———. 1956b. *The Decision Process: Seven Categories of Functional Analysis*. College Park, Maryland: University of Maryland Press.

Lasswell, H.D. 1958. *Politics: Who Gets What, When, and How*. New York: Meridian Books.

Legatum Ventures. 2011. 'Microfinance in India: A Crisis at the Bottom of the Pyramid,' *Legatum Ventures*. Available at http://www.legatum.org/attachments/MicrofinanceCrisis.pdf (last accessed on 20 March 2017).

Lieten, G.K. 2002. 'Child Labour in India: Disentangling Essence and Solutions', *Economic and Political Weekly*, 37(52): 5190–5.

Lindblom, C.E. 1959. 'The Science of "Muddling Through"', *Public Administration Review*, 19(2): 79–88.

Lippmann, W. 1946. *Public Opinion*. New Brunswick: Transaction Publishers.

Lipsky, M. 1970. *Protest in City Politics*. Chicago: Rand McNally.

Liu, S.Y. 2010. 'Accountability in China: Primitive attempts', in Bjorn Stensaker and Lee Harvey (eds), *Accountability in Higher Education: Global Perspectives on Trust and Power*. New York: Routledge.

Liu, X., E. Lindquist, A. Vedlitz, and K. Vincent. 2010. 'Understanding Local Policymaking: Policy Elites' Perceptions of Local Agenda Setting and Alternative Policy Selection', *Policy Studies Journal*, 38: 69–91.

LiveMint. 2015. 'SKS Microfinance to raise Rs 400 crore in FY15,' *LiveMint*, 4 February. Available at http://www.livemint.com/Companies/VrH5K5J3NEKbO1zVEeb7EL/SKS-Microfinance-to-raise-400-crore-in-FY15.html (last accessed on 20 March 2017).

Lowi, T. and M. Olson. 1970. 'Decision Making vs. Policy Making: Toward an Antidote for Technocracy', *Public Administration Review*, 30(3): 314–25, doi:10.2307/974053.

Lyons, W.E., D. Lowery, and R.H. DeHoog. 1992. *The Politics of Dissatisfaction: Citizens, Services, and Urban Institutions*. Armonk: ME Sharpe.

Mack, L.E. 1971. 'Ground Water Management in Development of a National Policy on Water', Report NWC-EES-71-004, National Water Commission, Washington, DC.

Madan, D.B. 2009. 'Capital Requirements, Acceptable Risks and Profits', *Quantitative Finance*, 9(7): 767–73.

Makkar, Sahil and Liz Matthew. 2013. 'Govt Defends Ordinance on Sexual Crimes', *Livemint*, 4 February. Available at http://www.livemint. com/Politics/5PIVOz9oohL1Gy1DwFELIL/None-of-Verma-panel-recommendations-rejected-Chidambaram.html (last accessed on 20 March 2016).

Malik, Surabhi (ed.). 2013. 'We Have Accepted 90% of Justice Verma Panel's Recommendations: Law Minister to NDTV', available at http://www.ndtv.com/india-news/we-have-accepted-90-of-justice-verma-panels-recommendations-law-minister-to-ndtv-512210 (last accessed on 20 March 2016).

Mander, Harsh and Abha Joshi. 1999. 'The Movement for Right to Information in India: People's Power for the Control of Corruption', Paper presented at the conference on Pan Commonwealth Advocacy, Harare, Zimbabwe, 21–4 January, available at http://www.humanrightsinitiative.org/programs/ai/rti/india/articles/The%20Movement%20for%20RTI%20in%20India.pdf (last accessed on 8 March 2017).

Manor, J. 1993. *Power, Poverty and Poison: Disaster and Response in an Indian City*. New Delhi: SAGE Publications.

Mathur, H.M. 2013. *Displacement and Resettlement in India: The Human Cost of Development*. Oxford: Routledge.

Mathur, K. 1994. *Top Policy Makers in India: Cabinet Ministers and Their Civil Service Advisors*. New Delhi: Concept Publishing Company.

———. 2013. *Public Policy and Politics in India: How Institutions Matter*. New Delhi: Oxford University Press.

Mathur, K. and J.W. Bjorkman. 1994. *Top Policymakers in India: Cabinet Ministers and Their Civil Service Advisors*. New Delhi: Concept Publishers.

———. 2009. *Policy-making in India: Who Speaks? Who Listens?* New Delhi: Har Anand Publications.

Mathur, K. and N.G. Jayal. 1992. *Drought Policy and Politics in India: The Need for a Long-Term Perspective*. New Delhi: SAGE Publications.

Mathur, Velath P. 2009. 'Development and Displacement: Rights-Based Theoretical Analysis', in R. Modi (ed.), *Beyond Relocation: The Imperative of Sustainable Resettlement*. London and New York: SAGE Publications.

McAdam, D. and A. Snow David (eds). 2009. *Readings on Social Movements: Origins, Dynamics, and Outcomes*. UK: Oxford University Press.

McAdam, D., J.D. McCarthy, and M.N. Zald. 1996. *Comparative Perspectives on Social Movements: Political Opportunities, Mobilizing Structures, and Cultural Framings*. Cambridge: Cambridge University Press.

McAdam, Doug. 1996. 'Conceptual Origins, Current Problems, Future Directions', in Doug McAdam, John D. McCarthy, and Mayer N. Zaid (eds), *Comparative Perspectives on Social Movements: Political Opportunities, Mobilizing Structures and Cultural Framing*. New York: Cambridge University Press.

McCarthy, J.D. and M.N. Zald. 1977. 'Resource Mobilization and Social Movements: A Partial Theory', *American Journal of Sociology*, 82(6): 1212–41.

———. 2001. 'The Enduring Vitality of the Resource Mobilization Theory of Social Movements', in Jonathan H. Turner (ed.), *Handbook of Sociological Theory*, pp. 533–65. New York: Springer.

McCombs, M.E. and D.L. Shaw. 1972. 'The Agenda-setting Function of Mass Media', *Public Opinion Quarterly*, 36(2): 176–87.

Meenakshi, J.V. and R. Ray. 1999. 'Regional Differences in India's Food Expenditure Pattern: A Complete Demand Systems Approach', *Journal of International Development*, 11(1): 47–74.

Mehta, Lyla (ed.). 2009. *Displaced by Development: Confronting Marginalisation and Gender Injustice*. New Delhi: SAGE Publications.

Mehta, P.B. 2003. *The Burden of Democracy*. New Delhi: Penguin India.

Meyer, D.S., V. Jenness, and H.M. Ingram (eds). 2005. *Routing the Opposition: Social Movements, Public Policy, and Democracy*, vol. 23. Minneapolis: University of Minnesota Press.

Meyer, T. 2014. 'From Contract to Legislation: The Logic of Modern International Lawmaking', *Chicago Journal of International Law*, 14(2): 559–623.

Mezey, M.L. 2008. *Representative Democracy: Legislators and Their Constituents*. Lanham: Rowman & Littlefield Publishers.

Ministry of Education, Government of India. 1960. *Report of the All India Education Survey (1960)*, available at http://aises.nic.in/1stsurveyreports (last accessed on 20 March 2017).

Ministry of Human Resource Development, Government of India, *Elementary and Adult Education in India: Historical Perspective*, available at http://www.teindia.nic.in/mhrd/50yrsedu/y/3P/45/3P450401.htm (last accessed on).

Ministry of Labour, Government of India. 1981. 'Grants-in-aid on Child Labour'.

———. 1987. 'The National Policy on Child Labour, 1987', available at http://www.labour.nic.in/childlabour/child-labour-policies (last accessed on 21 March 2017).

————. 1988. 'National Child Labour Project (NCLP) Scheme, 1988'.

————. 2001. 'State-wise Distribution of Working Children According to 1971, 1981, 1991 and 2001 Census in the Age Group 5–14 Years', Census Data on Child Labour, available at http://labour.nic.in/sites/default/files/Census1971to2001.pdf (last accessed on 8 March 2017).

————. 2008. 'Protocol on Prevention, Rescue, Repatriation, and Rehabilitation of Trafficked and Migrant Child Labour'.

————. 2013. 'Child Labour', Press Information Bureau, available at http://pib.nic.in/newsite/erelease.aspx?relid=97646 (last accessed on 8 March 2017).

Mintrom, M. and S. Vergari. 1998. 'Policy Networks and Innovation Diffusion: The Case of State Education Reforms', *The Journal of Politics*, 60(1): 126–48.

Mitra, N. 1992. 'Energy Policy Planning in India: Case of Petroleum and Natural Gas', *Economic and Political Weekly*, 27(35): M109–M115.

Moe, T.M. 1984. 'The New Economics of Organization', *American Journal of Political Science*, 28(4): 739–77.

————. 1990. 'Political Institutions: The Neglected Side of the Story', *Journal of Law, Economics, and Organization*, 6: 213–53.

Mooij, J.E. 1999. *Food Policy and the Indian State*. New Delhi: Oxford University Press.

Mooij, J.E. and V. de Vos. 2003. 'Policy Processes: An Annotated Bibliography on Policy Processes, with Particular Emphasis on India', Working Paper. London: Overseas Development Institute.

Moran, Micheal, Martin Rein, and Robert Goodin. 2008. *The Oxford Handbook of Public Policy*. Oxford: Oxford University Press.

Morduch, Jonathan. 2000. 'The Microfinance Schism', *World Development*, 28(4): 617–29.

Mukherjee, Ashish. (ed.). 2012. 'Home Minister Sushil Kumar Shinde's Statement on Delhi Gang-Rape', available at http://www.ndtv.com/india-news/home-minister-sushil-kumar-shindes-statement-on-delhi-gang-rape-508303 (last accessed on 20 March 2016).

Muralidharan, R. 2004. 'A Framework for Designing Strategy Content Controls', *International Journal of Productivity and Performance Management*, 53(7): 590–601.

Nakamura, R.T. 1987. 'The Textbook Policy Process and Implementation Research', *Review of Policy Research*, 7(1): 142–54.

Nanda, Prashant K. 2015. 'Govt to Modify Child Labour Law', *Livemint*, 27 April. Available at www.livemint.com/Politics/Psp775wW1VA4TqFHeqxRJI/Govt-to-modify-child-labour-law.html (last accessed on 20 March 2017).

Narula, Smita. 1999. *Broken People: Caste Violence against India's Untouchables*. USA: Human Rights Watch. Available at https://www.hrw.org/reports/1999/india/India994.htm (last accessed on 20 March 2016).

Nasir, S. 2013. 'Microfinance in India: Contemporary Issues and Challenges', *Middle-East Journal of Scientific Research*, 15(2): 191–9.

National Centre for Advocacy Studies. 2002 (July–September). 'Advocacy Update', Pune, India.

National Commission for the Protection of Child Rights (NCPCR). 2008a. 'Magnitude of Child Labour in India: An Analysis of Official Sources of Data (Draft)', available at http://ncpcr.gov.in/showfile.php?lid=131 (last accessed on 8 March 2017).

———. 2008b. 'Abolition of Child Labour in India: Strategies for the Eleventh Five Year Plan', available at http://ncpcr.gov.in/showfile. php?lid=69 (last accessed on 8 March 2017).

National Commission to Review the Working of the Constitution. 2001. 'A Consultation Paper on *Review of the Working of Political Parties Specially in Relation to Elections and Reform Options*', National Commission to Review the Working of the Constitution, 8 January. Available at http://lawmin.nic.in/ncrwc/finalreport/v2b1-8.htm (last accessed on 20 March 2017).

NDTV. 2011a. '2G Scam: RTI Activist Vivek Garg Feels Lucky to Get Pranab Note', 23 September, available at http://www.ndtv.com/india-news/2g-scam-rti-activist-vivek-garg-feels-lucky-to-get-pranab-note-468430 (last accessed on 20 March 2017).

———. 2011b. 'What Is Jan Lokpal Bill, Why It's Important', available at http://www.ndtv.com/india-news/what-is-the-jan-lokpal-bill-why-its-important-452223 (last accessed on 20 March 2017).

———. 2012. 'Arvind Kejriwal's Group Protests against Delhi Gang-Rape outside Sonia Gandhi's Residence', available at http://www.ndtv.com/delhi-news/arvind-kejriwals-group-protests-against-delhi-gang-rape-outside-sonia-gandhis-residence-508235 (last accessed on 20 March 2016).

Nelson, Dean. 2011. 'Anna Hazare's Anti-Corruption Campaign Sparks Gandhi Cap Revival', *Telegraph*, 21 August. Available at http://www.telegraph.co.uk/news/worldnews/asia/india/8714098/Anna-Hazares-anti-corruption-campaign-sparks-Gandhi-cap-revival.html (last accessed on 20 March 2017).

Neustadt, R.E. 1960. *Presidential Power*. New York: New American Library.

News One. 2010. 'Shunglu Committee Only a Cover Up, Allege Social Activists', 29 October. Available at http://www.inewsone.

com/2010/11/01/shunglu-committee-only-a-cover-up-allege-social-activists/2509 (last accessed on 20 March 2017).

Noorani, A.G. 1997. 'The Right to Information', in Guhan S. and S. Paul (eds), *Corruption in India: An Agenda for Change*, pp. 114–43. New Delhi: Vision Books.

Nurullah, Syed and J.P. Naik. 1951. *History of Education in India during the British Period*. University of Michigan: Macmillan.

Oliver, H. 1989. 'The Labour Caucus and Economic Policy Formation, 1981–1984', in Brian Easton (ed.), *The Making of Rogernomics*, pp. 11–52. Auckland: Auckland University Press.

Open. 2010. 'Some Telephone Conversations', 20 November. Available at http://www.openthemagazine.com/article/nation/some-telephone-conversations (last accessed on 20 March 2017).

Osman, F.A. 2002. 'Public Policy Making: Theories and Their Implications in Developing Countries', *Asian Affairs*, 24(3): 37–52.

Ostrom, E. 1986. 'An Agenda for the Study of Institutions', *Public Choice*, 48(1): 3–25.

———. 1990. *Governing the Commons: The Evolution of Institutions for Collective Action*. Cambridge: Cambridge University Press.

———. 1998. 'A Behavioral Approach to the Rational Choice Theory of Collective Action: Presidential address, American Political Science Association, 1997', *American Political Science Review*, 92(1): 1–22.

———. 2007. 'Institutional Rational Choice: An Assessment of the Institutional Analysis and Development Framework', in P.A. Sabatier (ed.), *Theories of the Policy Process* (2nd edn). Cambridge: Westview Press.

———. 2011. 'Background on the Institutional Analysis and Development Framework', *Policy Studies Journal*, 39(1): 7–27.

Ostrom, E., L. Schroeder, and S. Wynne. 1993. *Institutional Incentives and Sustainable Development: Infrastructure Policies in Perspective*. Boulder: Westview Press.

Outlook. 2011. 'GoM on Corruption to Firm Up Lok Pal Bill at the Earliest', 21 January.

Padmanabhan, Vishnu. 2012. 'Legislative Brief: Microfinance Institutions (Development and Regulation) Bill, 2012', PRS Legislative Research, 28 December. Available at http://www.prsindia.org/uploads/media/Micro%20Finance%20Institutions/MFI%20Brief.pdf (last accessed on 20 March 2017).

Pai, S. (2013). 'New Patterns of Mobilization in the 1990s and Beyond', in Atul Kohli and Prerna Singh (eds), *Routledge Handbook of Indian Politics*, pp. 261–9. New Delhi: Routledge.

Pai, Sudha and Avinash Kumar. 2014. *The Indian Parliament: A Critical Appraisal.* New Delhi: Orient Blackswan Pvt. Ltd.

Patel, Vibhuti. 2014. 'Campaign against Rape by Women's Movement in India', *Deportate, esuli, profughe: Università Ca' Foscari di Venezia: Venezia,* 24: 36–47, available at http://www.unive.it/media/allegato/dep/n24-2014/Ricerche/03_Patel.pdf (last accessed on 20 March 2017).

Peng, Yin (ed.). 1992. *Political Advertising and Elections.* Taipei: Cheng Chong.

Peters, B. Guy. 1999. *American Public Policy: Promise and Performance.* Chappaqua: Chatham House/Seven Rivers.

Peters, B. and Wessler, H. 2008. *Public Deliberation and Public Culture: The writings of Bernhard Peters, 1993–2005.* Basingstoke and New York: Palgrave Macmillan.

Philipose, P. 2013. 'Anxieties in the Republic: Media Metamorphosis and Popular Protest', *Economic and Political Weekly,* XLVIII(6).

Piven, Frances Fox and Richard A. Cloward. 1977. *Poor People's Movements: Why They Succeed, How They Fail.* New York: Pantheon Books.

———. 1971. *Regulating the Poor: The Functions of Public Welfare.* New York: Vintage.

Planning Commission, Government of India. 1951. 'Education', Chapter 33 of the First Five Year Plan (1951–6), available at http://planningcommission.gov.in/plans/planrel/fiveyr/index1.html (last accessed on 20 March 2017).

———. 1993. 'Elementary and Adult Education in India: Historical Perspective', Report of National Development Council Committee on Literacy, Planning Commission, available at http://www.teindia.nic.in/mhrd/50yrsedu/y/3P/45/3P450401.htm (last accessed on 20 March 2017).

Planning Commission, Government of India, 'Education', Chapter 33 of the *First Five Year Plan (1951–56),* available at http://planningcommission.gov.in/plans/planrel/fiveyr/index1.html.

Polgreen, Lydia. 2010. 'Right-to-Know Law Gives India's Poor a Lever', *The New York Times,* 28 June. Available at http://www.nytimes.com/2010/06/29/world/asia/29india.html?pagewanted=1&hpw&_r=0 (last accessed on 8 March 2017).

Polletta, F. 2002. 'Plotting Protest: Mobilizing Stories in the 1960 Student Sit-Ins', in J.E. Davis (ed.), *Stories of Change: Narrative and Social Movements.* New York: State University of New York Press.

Prasad, Akanksha and Indu Nandakumar. 2012. 'Delhi Gang Rape Case: Social Media Fuels Rally at India Gate', *Economic Times,* 24 December. Available at http://articles.economictimes.indiatimes.com/2012-12-24/

news/35991878_1_delhi-gang-adhvith-dhuddu-social-media (last accessed on 22 March 2016).

PricewaterhouseCoopers. 2009. 'Understanding the "Key Issues and Constraints" in implementing the RTI Act', available at http://rti.gov.in/rticorner/studybypwc/index-study.htm (last accessed on 8 March 2017).

PRS Legislative Research. 2010. 'Andhra Pradesh Micro Finance Institutions (Regulation of Moneylending) Act, 2010', 16 December. Available at http://www.prsindia.org/theprsblog/?p=547.

———. 2011a. 'Report Summary: Malegam Committee on Microfinance, January 2011', Sana Gangwani, 15 March.

———. 2011b. 'Corruption Laws in India', available at http://www.prsindia.org/administrator/uploads/general/1302844978_PRS%20Note%20on%20corruption%20laws.pdf (last accessed on 20 March 2017).

———. 2013. 'Bill Summary: The Competition (Amendment) Bill, 2012', 21 January. Available at http://www.prsindia.org/uploads/media/Competition%20(A)%20Bill,%202012/Bill%20Summary-%20Competition%20Amendment.pdf (last accessed on 10 December 2014).

———. 2012. 'The Micro Finance Institutions (Development and Regulation) Bill, 2012 (Bill No. 62 of 2012)', Available at http://www.prsindia.org/uploads/media/Micro%20Finance%20Institutions/Micro%20Finance%20Institutions%20%28Development%20and%20Regulation%29%20Bill%202012.pdf (last accessed on 20 March 2017).

Pruthi, Raj Kumar. 2006. *Manual of Right to Information Act, 2006.* New Delhi: Pentagon Press.

Pulley, Robert V. 1989. 'Making the Poor Creditworthy: A Case Study of the Integrated Rural Development Program in India', World Bank Discussion Papers 58, Washington, DC: The World Bank.

Pye, L.W. 1958. 'The Non-Western Political Process', *The Journal of Politics*, 20(3): 468–86.

Rai, Chakshu and Anirudh Burman. 2010. 'JPC vs PAC', Blogpost. Available at http://www.prsindia.org/theprsblog/?p=473 (last accessed on 20 March 2017).

Rai, S. and R. Johnson (eds). 2014. *Democracy in Practice: Ceremony and Ritual in Parliament.* London: Palgrave Macmillan.

Rajagopal, Krishnadas. 2016. 'Return Singur Land to Farmers, SC orders West Bengal govt.,' *The Hindu*, 31 August 2016. Available at http://www.thehindu.com/news/national/Return-Singur-land-to-farmers-SC-orders-West-Bengal-govt./article14600055.ece (last accessed on 2 February 2017).

Ramachandran, V.K. and M. Swaminathan. 2001. '*Does Informal Credit Provide Security? Rural Banking Policy in India*, vol. 12. Geneva: International Labour Office.

Ramesh, J. 2015. *Green Signals. Ecology, Growth, and Democracy in India.* New Delhi: Oxford University Press.

Ramesh, Jairam and Muhammad Ali Khan. 2015. *Legislating for Justice: The Making of the 2013 Land Acquisition Law.* New Delhi: Oxford University Press.

Rao, M.S.A. (ed.). 1978. *Social Movements in India,* vols 1 and 2. New Delhi: Manohar Publications.

Rao, M.S. 2000. *Social Movements in India: Studies in Peasant, Backward Classes, Sectarian, Tribal and Women's Movements.* New Delhi: Manohar Publishers.

Ray, Raka. 1999. *Fields of Protest: Women's Movements in India.* Minneapolis and London: University of Minnesota Press.

Reddy, B. Muralidhar. 2013. 'Despite Protest, Ordinance on Sexual Offences Promulgated', *The Hindu,* 3 February. Available at http://www.thehindu.com/news/national/despite-protest-ordinance-on-sexual-offences-promulgated/article4375214.ece (last accessed on 20 March 2016).

Reddy, Gaddam Ram and B.A.V. Sharma. 1979. *Regionalism in India: A Study of Telangana.* New Delhi: Concept Publishing Company.

Reserve Bank of India (RBI). January 2011a. Report of the Sub-Committee of the Central Board of Directors of Reserve Bank of India to Study Issues and Concerns in the MFI Sector. Available at https://rbidocs.rbi.org.in/rdocs/PublicationReport/Pdfs/YHMR190111.pdf (last accessed on 20 March 2017).

————. December 2011b. *Introduction of New Category of NBFCs—Non-Banking Financial Company-Micro Finance Institutions (NBFC-MFIs)—Directions.* Reserve Bank of India. Available at https://rbi.org.in/scripts/NotificationUser.aspx?Id=6857&Mode=0#234 (last accessed on 20 March 2017).

Richardson, I.F. and A.G. Jordan. 1979. *Governing under Pressure: The Policy Process in a Post Parliamentary Democracy.* Oxford: Martin Robertson.

Richardson, J., G. Gustafsson, and G. Jordan. 1982. 'The Concept of Policy Style', in J.J. Richardson (ed.), *Policy Styles in Western Europe,* pp. 1–16. London: Allen & Unwin.

Riggs, F.W. 1957. 'Agraria and Industria: Toward a Typology of Comparative Administration', in William J. Siffin (ed.), *Towards a Comparative Study of Public Administration,* pp. 23–116. Bloomington: Indiana University Press.

Ripley, Randall B. 1985. *Policy Analysis in Political Science.* Chicago: Nelson Hall Publishers.

Robinson, S.E. and W.S. Eller. 2010. 'Participation in Policy Streams: Testing the Separation of Problems and Solutions in Subnational Policy Systems', *Policy Studies Journal,* 38(2), 199–216.

Rochon, Thomas R. 1998. *Culture Moves: Ideas, Activism, and Changing Values*. Princeton: Princeton University Press.

Rogow, A.A. and H.D. Lasswell. 1963. *Power, Corruption, and Rectitude*, pp. 132–3. Englewood Cliffs: Prentice Hall.

Room, G. 2011. *Complexity, Institutions and Public Policy: Agile Decision-making in a Turbulent World*. Cheltenham: Edward Elgar Publishing.

Rose, R. 1973. 'Comparing Public Policy: An Overview', *European Journal of Political Research*, 1(1): 67–94.

Rosenstone, Steven J. and John Mark Hansen. 1993. *Mobilization, Participation, and Democracy in America*. New York: Macmillan.

Sabatier, P.A. 1988. 'An Advocacy Coalition Framework of Policy Change and the Role of Policy-Oriented Learning Therein', *Policy Sciences*, 21(2–3): 129–68.

———. 1991. 'Toward Better Theories of the Policy Process', *PS: Political Science & Politics*, 24(2): 147–56.

———. 2007. *Theories of the Policy Process*. Boulder: Westview Press.

Sabatier, P.A. and H.C. Jenkins-Smith. 1988. 'Symposium Editors' Introduction', *Policy Sciences*, 21(2): 123–7.

Sabatier, P.A. and H.C. Jenkins-Smith. 1993. *Policy Change and Learning: An Advocacy Coalition Approach*. Boulder: Westview Press.

———. 1999. 'The Advocacy Coalition Framework: An Assessment', in P.A. Sabatier (ed.), *Theories of the Policy Process*, pp. 117–68. Boulder: Westview Press.

Sabatier, P.A. 1999. 'The Need for Better Theories', in P.A. Sabatier (ed.), *Theories of the Policy Process*. Boulder: Westview Press

Sabatier, Paul A. and Christopher Weible (eds). 2014. *Theories of the Policy Process*. Boulder: Westview Press.

Sabharwal, Meghna and Evan M. Berman (eds). 2013. *Public Administration in South Asia: India, Bangladesh, and Pakistan*. Florida: CRC Press.

Sadgopal, Anil. 2003. 'Education for Too Few', *Frontline*, 20(24), available at http://www.frontline.in/static/html/fl2024/stories/20031205002809700.htm (last accessed on 8 March 2017).

Sa-Dhan. 2014. *The Bharat Microfinance Report 2014*. Available at http://www.sa-dhan.net/Resources/Finale%20Report.pdf (last accessed on 20 March 2017).

Sa-Dhan. 2006. 'What Is Operating Self-Sufficiency? How to Use It in Microfinance?' *Microfinance Manager Series: Technical Note #13*, available at http://www.sa-dhan.net/Adls/Technicalnotes/Technical_Notes_13.pdf (last accessed on 20 March 2017).

Sadhu, S., V. Prathap, and M. Tiwari. 2013. 'Assessing the Effect of Andhra Pradesh Microfinance Crisis on the Access to Finance of the MFI Clients', Working Paper, Chennai: IFMR-Centre for Micro Finance.

Saha, J. 2015. 'Among the Beasts of Burma: Animals and the Politics of Colonial Sensibilities, c. 1840–1940', *Journal of Social History*, 48(4): 910–32.

Sanyal, K. 2007. 'Legislative Brief on the Micro Finance Sector (Development and Regulation) Bill', PRS Legislative Research, 21 June.

———. 2011. Background Note on 'Issues Related to the Lokpal Bill', PRS Legislative Research.

———. 2012. 'Bill Summary: The Child Labour (Prohibition and Regulation) Bill, 2012', PRS Legislative Research, 26 December.

Sanyal, Kaushiki and Harsimran Kalra. 2012. 'Select Committee of the Rajya Sabha on the Lok Pal and Lokayuktas Bill, 2011', PRS Legislative Research, 23 November. Available at http://www.prsindia.org/uploads/media/Lok%20Pal%20Bill%202011/Select%20Committee%20and%202011%20Bill%20comparison.pdf (last accessed on 20 March 2017).

Sapru, R.K. 2011. *Public Policy: Art and Craft of Policy Analysis*. New Delhi: PHI Learning Pvt. Ltd.

Sapru, R.K. 2012. *Public Policy: Formulation, Implementation and Evaluation*. New Delhi: Sterling Publishers.

Sarma, Shruti. 2015. 'The Story behind Andhra's Call Money Racket', *Business Standard*, 21 December.

Sartori, G. 1976. *Parties and Party Systems: A Framework for Analysis*. New York: Cambridge University Press.

Savery, Lynn. 2007. *Engendering the State: The International Diffusion of Women's Human Rights*. UK: Routledge.

Savyasaachi and R. Kumar. (eds). 2015. *Social Movements: Transformative Shifts and Turning Points*. New Delhi: Routledge.

Scharpf, F.W. 1997. *Games Real Actors Play: Actor-Centered Institutionalism in Policy Research*. Boulder: Westview Press.

Schattschneider, E.E. 1960. *The Semi-Sovereign People*. New York: Holt, Rhinehart and Winston.

Schmidt, V.A. 1997. 'European Integration and Democracy: The Differences among Member States', *Journal of European Public Policy*, 4(1): 128–45.

Schneider, A.L. and H.M. Ingram. 1997. *Policy Design for Democracy*. Lawrence: University of Kansas Press.

Schneider, M. and P. Teske. 1993. 'The Antigrowth Entrepreneur: Challenging the "Equilibrium" of the Growth Machine', *The Journal of Politics*, 55(3): 720–36.

Scruggs, L.A. 2003. *Sustaining Abundance: Environmental Performance in Industrial Democracies*. Cambridge: Cambridge University Press.

———. 1999. 'Institutions and Environmental Performance in Seventeen Western Democracies', *British Journal of Political Science*, 29(1): 1–31.

Sellon Jr., G.H. and S.E. Weiner. 1996. 'Monetary Policy without Reserve Requirements: Analytical Issues', *Economic Review-Federal Reserve Bank of Kansas City*, 81(4): 5.

Sen, A. 1999. *On Ethics and Economics*. Oxford and New York: Basil Blackwell.

Seth, Leila. 2014. *Talking of Justice: People's Rights in Modern India*. New Delhi: Aleph Book Company.

Shah, A. 2004. 'Fiscal Decentralization in Developing and Transition Economies: Progress, Problems, and the Promise', World Bank Policy Research Working Paper No. 3282, Washington, DC: World Bank.

Shah, T. 2001. *Wells and Welfare in the Ganga Basin: Public Policy and Private Initiative in Eastern Uttar Pradesh, India*, vol. 54. Colombo: International Water Management Institute.

Sharma, Prashant. 2014. *Democracy and Transparency in the Indian State: The Making of the Right to Information Act*, pp. 112–13. Edinburgh South Asian Studies Series. Oxon, New York: Routledge.

Sharma, Vipin (ed.). 2013. *State of India's Livelihoods Report 2012*. New Delhi: SAGE Publications. Available at http://www.accessdev.org/downloads/soil_report_2012.pdf (last accessed on 20 March 2016).

Shepsle, K.A. 1989. 'Studying Institutions: Some Lessons from the Rational Choice Approach', *Journal of Theoretical Politics*, 1(2): 131–47.

Sheth, D.L. 1984. 'Grassroots Initiatives in India', *Economic and Political Weekly*, 19(6): 259–62.

———. 1983. 'Grass-Roots Stirrings and the Future of Politics', *Alternatives*, 9(1): 1–24.

———. 1987. 'Reservations Policy Revisited', *Economic and Political Weekly*, 22(46): 1957–87.

Shonfield, A. and S. Shaw. 1972. *Social Indicators and Social Policy*. London: Heinemann Educational for the Social Science Research Council.

Shroff, Z.C., M.J. Roberts, and M.R. Reich. 2015. 'Agenda Setting and Policy Adoption of India's National Health Insurance Scheme: Rashtriya Swasthya Bima Yojana', *Health Systems & Reform*, 1(2): 107–118.

Simon, Herbert A. 1947. *Administrative Behaviour: A Study of Decision-Making Processes in Administrative Organisation*. New York: Macmillan.

———. 1955. 'A Behavioral Model of Rational Choice', *The Quarterly Journal of Economics*, 69(1): 99–118.

Singh, D. 2013. 'A Study of Success of First IPO of SKS Microfinance', *Global Journal of Management and Business Studies*, 3(2): 163–70.

Singh, Gyanant. 2011. 'SC Puts Govt on Mat over Black Money Secrecy', *India Today*, 15 January. Available at http://indiatoday.intoday.in/story/govt-may-disclose-the-black-money-list/1/126675.html (last accessed on 20 March 2017).

Singh, M.M. 2013. 'Collateral and Monetary Policy', Working Paper 13-186. Washington, DC: International Monetary Fund.

Singh, Richa. 2014. 'New Citizen's Activism in India: Moments, Movements and Mobilisation', Centre for Democracy and Social Action, New Delhi, available at http://southasia.oneworld.net/Files/new-citizens2019-activism-in-india (last accessed on 20 March 2016).

Singh, Shekhar. 2011. 'The Genesis and Evolution of the Right to Information Regime in India', in *Transparent Governance in South Asia*, pp. 43–78. Delhi: The Indian Institute of Public Administration. Available at http://www.iipa.org.in/www/iipalibrary/RTI-PDF/Chap-4.pdf (last accessed on 22 March 2017).

Sinha, Aseema. 2005. *The Regional Roots of Development Politics in India: A Divided Leviathan*. Bloomington: Indiana University Press.

Sinha, N. 1996. 'The Political Economy of India's Telecommunication Reforms', *Telecommunications Policy*, 20(1): 23–38.

Sinha, S. 1996. 'Child Labour and Education Policy in India', *The Administrator*, 41(3–4).

———. 2003. 'Financial Services for Low Income Families: An Appraisal', *IIM Bangalore Management Review*, 15(2): 54–65.

Sinha, Subrata. 2012. *Anna Hazare and Second Freedom Fight of India*. New Delhi: Subrata Sinha.

Sitapati, V. 2011. 'What Anna Hazare's Movement and India's New Middle Classes Say about Each Other', *Economic and Political Weekly*, 46(30): 39.

Smelser, N.J. 1962. *Theory of Collective Behaviour*. New York: Free Press.

Smith, K.B. 2010. *The Public Policy Theory Primer*. Boulder: Westview Press.

Smith, K.B. and Christopher W. Larimer. 2013. *The Public Policy Theory Primer* (2nd edn). Boulder: Westview Press.

Smithey, L.A. 2009a. 'Conflict Transformation, Cultural Innovation, and Loyalist Identity in Northern Ireland', in M. Ross (ed.), *Culture and Belonging in Divided Societies: Contestation and Symbolic Landscapes*. Philadelphia: University of Pennsylvania Press

———. 2009b. 'Social Movement Strategy, Tactics, and Collective Identity', *Sociology Compass*, 3(4): 658–71.

Snow, D.A. and D. McAdam. 2010. *Readings on Social Movements: Origins, Dynamics and Outcomes*. New York: Oxford University Press.

Spitzer, R.J. 1987. 'Promoting Policy Theory: Revising the Arenas of Power', *Policy Studies Journal*, 15(4): 675–89.

Srinivasan, N. 2010. *Microfinance India: State of the Sector Reports*. New Delhi: SAGE Publications.

————. 2011. *Microfinance India: State of the Sector Report 2010*. New Delhi: SAGE Publications.

————. 2012. *Microfinance India: State of the Sector Report 2011*. New Delhi: SAGE Publications.

Stacey, R.D. 2002. *Strategic Management and Organisational Dynamics: The Challenge of Complexity* (3rd edn). Harlow: Prentice Hall. Available at http://www.gp-training.net/ training/communication_ skills/consultation/equipoise/complexity/stacey.htm (last accessed on 20 March 2017).

Steinberger, P.J. 1980. 'Typologies of Public Policy: Meaning Construction and the Policy Process, *Social Science Quarterly*, 61(2): 185–97.

Stolle, D. and T.R. Rochon. 1998. 'Are All Associations Alike? Member Diversity, Associational Type, and the Creation of Social Capital', *American Behavioral Scientist*, 42(1): 47–65.

Stone, Deborah. 1997. *Policy Paradox: The Art of Political Decision Making*. New York: W.W. Norton.

Stone, Deborah. 2002. *Policy Paradox: The Art of Political Decision Making* (2nd edn). New York: W.W. Norton.

Strauss, L. 1947. 'On the Intention of Rousseau', *Social Research*, 14(4): 455–87.

Subramaniam, Vidya. 2015. 'Reaching for the Stars: The Incredible Rise of Arvind Kejriwal', The Hindu Centre for Politics and Public Policy, 25 February. Available at http://www.thehinducentre.com/the-arena/article6929534.ece#Three (last accessed on 20 March 2017).

Sunderasan, S. 2011. 'Epilogue: Rational Exuberance for Renewable Energy', in *In Rational Exuberance for Renewable Energy*, pp. 107–13. London: Springer.

Surie, M.D. 2011. 'Right to Information in India: An Effective Tool to Tackle Corruption', the Asia Foundation. Available at http://asiafoundation.org/in-asia/2011/09/28/right-to-information-in-india-an-effective-tool-to-tackle-corruption/ (last accessed on 20 March 2017).

Sutherland, Edwin H. 1950. 'The Diffusion of Sexual Psychopath Laws', *American Journal of Sociology*, 56(2): 142–8.

Talukdar, Sreemoy. 2015. 'Delhi Gangrape: Juvenile to Walk Free on Sunday as HC Refuses Stay; Time Rajya Sabha Passed New Bill', available at http://www.firstpost.com/india/nirbhaya-case-the-juvenile-should-remain-in-jail-if-released-he-could-prove-to-be-a-threat-to-society-2548344.html (last accessed on 20 March 2016).

Talwar, R. 2013. *Courting Injustice: The Nirbhaya Case and Its Aftermath*. New Delhi: Hay House, Inc.

Tandon, R. and R. Mohanty (eds). 2003. *Does Civil Society Matter? Governance in Contemporary India*. New Delhi: SAGE Publications.

Tarrow, S. 1996. 'Making Social Science Work across Space and Time: A Critical Reflection on Robert Putnam's Making Democracy Work', *American Political Science Review*, 90(2): 389–97.

Taylor, Alison. 2014. 'From the Arab Spring to Occupy, Corruption 2.0 Rallies the Masses', available at http://www.forbes.com/sites/riskmap/2014/06/16/from-the-arab-spring-to-occupy-corruption-2-0-rallies-the-masses/ (last accessed on 20 March 2017).

Thakore, Dilip. 2006. 'Rising Criticism of Right to Education Bill, 2005', Education World.

Tharoor, Ishaan. 2011. 'Anna Hazare's Hunger Fasts Rock India', *Time*, 7 December. Available at http://content.time.com/time/specials/packages/article/0,28804,2101344_2101368_2101650,00.html (last accessed on 20 March 2017).

Thomas, J.W. and M.S. Grindle. 1990. 'After the Decision: Implementing Policy Reforms in Developing Countries', *World Development*, 18(8): 1163–81.

Tiebout, C.M. 1956. 'A Pure Theory of Local Expenditures', *The Journal of Political Economy*, 64(5): 416–24.

Tilly, C. 1999. *Durable inequality*. Berkeley: University of California Press.

Times of India. 2010. 'CVC Launches Portal against Corruption', 10 December. Available at http://timesofindia.indiatimes.com/india/CVC-launches-portal-against-corruption/articleshow/7073913.cms (last accessed on 20 March 2017).

———. 2011a. 'Country Stands Up against Corruption Today', 30 January. Available at http://timesofindia.indiatimes.com/city/delhi/Country-stands-up-against-corruption-today/articleshow/7386802.cms (last accessed on 20 March 2017).

———. 2011b. 'Delhi Acts against Corruption', 31 January. Available at http://timesofindia.indiatimes.com/city/delhi/Delhi-acts-against-corruption/articleshow/7393612.cms (last accessed on 20 March 2017).

———. 2012a. 'Candlelight Vigil at India Gate', 19 December. Available at http://timesofindia.indiatimes.com/city/delhi/Candlelight-vigil-at-India-Gate/articleshow/17670897.cms (last accessed on 22 March 2016).

———. 2012b. 'Delhi Gang Rape Case: Constable Dies on Duty, Many Questions Remain', 26 December. Available at http://timesofindia.indiatimes.com/city/delhi/Delhi-gang-rape-case-Constable-dies-on-duty-many-questions-remain/articleshow/17761284.cms (last accessed on 20 March 2016).

Tran, Can. 2013. 'Nirbhaya's Father: I Want the World to Know My Daughter's Name', *Digital Journal*, 6 January. Available at http://www.digitaljournal.com/article/340628 (last accessed on 22 March 2016).

Truman, D.B. 1951. *The Governmental Process: Political Interests and Public Opinion*. New York: Alfred A. Knopf.

Turner, R.H. and L.M. Killian. 1964. *Collective Behavior*. Englewood Cliffs: Prentice Hall.

Tyagi, Ankit. 2012. 'Cracks Appear between Team Anna's Delhi and Mumbai Groups after MMRDA Fiasco', *India Today*, 5 January. Available at http://indiatoday.intoday.in/story/cracks-appear-between-team-annas-delhi-and-mumbai-groups-after-mmrda-fiasco/1/167296. html (last accessed on 20 March 2017).

UNICEF. 2011. 'The State of the World's Children 2011', available at http://www.unicef.org/sowc2011/pdfs/SOWC-2011-Main-Report_EN_02092011.pdf (last accessed on 21 March 2017).

UNICEF. 2013. 'The State of the World's Children 2013: Children with Disabilities', available at https://www.unicef.org/sowc2013/ (last accessed on 8 March 2017).

Upadhyay, Kavita. 2015. 'Freedom of Expression Basis of RTI, says Aruna Roy', *The Hindu*, 17 October 2015, available at http://www.thehindu. com/news/national/other-states/freedom-of-expression-basis-of-rti-says-aruna-roy/article7771947.ece (last accessed on 8 March 2017).

Urbinati, N. 2006. *Representative Democracy: Principles and Genealogy*. Chicago: University of Chicago Press.

Vaghul, N., Deepak Parekh, Ashok Ganguly, Jamshyd Godrej, Sam Variava, M. Narasimham, Yezdi Malegam, Anu Aga, A. Vaidyanathan, Bimal Jalan, Keshub Mahindra, Azim Premji, Nachiket Mor, and B.N. Srikrishna. 2011. 'An Open Letter to Our Leaders', *Hindustan Times*, 17 January. Available at http://www.hindustantimes.com/newdelhi/an-open-letter-to-our-leaders/article1-651546.aspx (last accessed on 20 March 2017).

Valocchi, S. 1990. 'The Unemployed Workers Movement of the 1930s: A Reexamination of the Piven and Cloward Thesis', *Social Problems*, 37(2): 191–205.

Varshney, Ashutosh. 1995. 'Democracy, Development, and the Countryside: Urban-Rural Struggles in India', Cambridge Studies in Comparative Politics. Cambridge: Cambridge University Press.

Varshney, A. 2014. *Battles Half Won: India's Improbable Democracy*. London: Penguin.

Vijetha S.N. 2012. 'JNU Students Take to Streets against Capital's Shame', *The Hindu*, 19 December. Available at http://www.thehindu.com/news/cities/Delhi/jnu-students-take-to-streets-against-capitals-shame/article4216577.ece (last accessed on 22 March 2016).

Vyasulu, P. and V. Vyasulu. 2000. 'Women in the Panchayati Raj: Grassroots Democracy in India', in *Women's Political Participation and*

Good Governance: 21st Century Challenges, pp. 41–7. New Delhi: United Nations Development Programme.

Wanat, J. 1974. 'Bases of Budgetary Incrementalism', *American Political Science Review*, 68(3): 1221–8.

Weible, C.M., P.A. Sabatier, and K. McQueen. 2009. 'Themes and Variations: Taking Stock of the Advocacy Coalition Framework', *Policy Studies Journal*, 37(1): 121–40.

Weible, C.M., P.A. Sabatier, H.C. Jenkins-Smith, D. Nohrstedt, A.D. Henry, and P. DeLeon. 2011. 'A Quarter Century of the Advocacy Coalition Framework: An Introduction to the Special Issue', *Policy Studies Journal*, 39(3): 349–60.

Weiner, Myron. 1996. 'Child Labour in India: Putting Compulsory Primary Education on the Political Agenda', *Economic and Political Weekly*, 31(45–46): 3007–9, 3011–14.

Wiener, A. and A. Wolman. 1962. 'Formulation of National Water Resources Policy in Israel', *Journal American Water Works Association*, 54(3): 257–263.

Wildavsky, A. 1980. *Speaking the Truth to Power: The Art and Craft of Policy Analysis*. Boston: Little, Brown.

Wilson, Woodrow. 1908. *Constitutional Government in the United States*. New Brunswick: Transaction Publishers.

Wood, Hugh B. 1955. 'Education in India under the Five-Year Plan', *The Elementary School Journal*, 55(9): 522–4.

Woods, H.D. 1955. 'Canadian Collective Bargaining and Dispute Settlement Policy: An Appraisal', *Canadian Journal of Economics and Political Science/Revue canadienne de economiques et science politique*, 21(04): 447–65.

World Bank. 2002. *Annual Report 2002: Consultative Group to Assist the Poorest (CGAP)*. Washington, DC: World Bank.

Yadav, Y. 2008. 'Whither Survey Research? Reflections on the State of Survey Research on Politics in Most of the World', Malcolm Adiseshiah Memorial Lecture, Chennai.

Zahariadis, N. 1992. 'To Sell or Not to Sell? Telecommunications Policy in Britain and France', *Journal of Public Policy*, 12(4): 355.

———. 1995. *Markets, States, and Public Policy: Privatization in Britain and France*. Ann Arbor: University of Michigan Press.

———. 2003. *Ambiguity and Choice in Public Policy: Political Decision Making in Modern Democracies*. Washington, DC: Georgetown University Press.

———. 2007. 'The Multiple Streams Framework: Structure, Limitations, Prospects', in Paul A. Sabatier (ed.), *Theories of the Policy Process* (2nd edn), pp. 65–92. Boulder: Westview.

Zakaria, F. 2008. *The Post-American world*. New York: W.W. Norton.

Index

About the Authors

Rajesh Chakrabarti is professor and executive vice dean at the Jindal Global Business School, O.P. Jindal Global University, Sonipat, India, and co-founder at Sunay Policy Advisory Pvt. Ltd. He has taught finance for over a decade and a half—at the University of Alberta, Canada, Georgia Tech, USA, and the Indian School of Business (ISB), Hyderabad, India. As the founding executive director of the Bharti Institute of Public Policy at ISB's Mohali campus, he helped design and launch one of India's leading public policy programmes. He has also been executive vice president, Research and Policy at the Wadhwani Foundation, New Delhi, India. Rajesh has held visiting positions at various places including IIM Calcutta, ISI Delhi, IDF Gurgaon, ICN Nancy, France, and the Federal Reserve Bank of Atlanta. He has authored and edited many books, and has written several book chapters and articles on finance, economics, and management in leading international scholarly journals. He has been a columnist with the *Financial Express* and is frequently quoted in the media. His current research interests are in the areas of management and public policy. Rajesh is an alumnus of Presidency University, Kolkata, and IIM Ahmedabad, and earned his PhD from the University of California, Los Angeles.

Kaushiki Sanyal is the CEO and co-founder of Sunay Policy Advisory Pvt. Ltd, a public policy research and consulting firm based in Gurgaon, India. She has over a decade of experience in public policy research and outreach including advising members of parliament with the PRS Legislative Research, leading research projects at the Bharti Institute of Public Policy, ISB, and consulting for the Vidhi Centre for Legal Policy, the World Bank, and Rajiv Gandhi Foundation. She is an alumna of the US Department of State's prestigious International Visitor's Leadership Program. She has published several articles in journals, edited volumes, and leading newspapers, and her recently authored book, with Rajesh Chakrabarti, *Public Policy in India* (2016) is a leading introductory volume for public policy in India. She has an MA in political science and a PhD in international relations from the Jawaharlal Nehru University, New Delhi, India.